# Epic Heroes on Screen

**Screening Antiquity**
**Series Editors: Monica S. Cyrino and Lloyd Llewellyn-Jones**
Screening Antiquity is a cutting-edge and provocative series of academic monographs and edited volumes focusing on new research on the reception of the ancient world in film and television. Screening Antiquity showcases the work of the best-established and up-and-coming specialists in the field. It provides an important synergy of the latest international scholarly ideas about the conception of antiquity in popular culture and is the only series that focuses exclusively on screened representations of the ancient world.

**Editorial Advisory Board**
Antony Augoustakis, Alastair Blanshard, Robert Burgoyne, Lisa Maurice, Gideon Nisbet, Joanna Paul, Jon Solomon

**Titles available in the series**
Rome *Season Two: Trial and Triumph*
Edited by Monica S. Cyrino

Ben-Hur: *The Original Blockbuster*
By Jon Solomon

*Cowboy Classics: The Roots of the American Western in the Epic Tradition*
By Kirsten Day

STARZ Spartacus: *Reimagining an Icon on Screen*
Edited by Antony Augoustakis and Monica S. Cyrino

*Ancient Greece on British Television*
Edited by Fiona Hobden and Amanda Wrigley

*Epic Heroes on Screen*
Edited by Antony Augoustakis and Stacie Raucci


**Forthcoming Titles**

*Designs on the Past: How Hollywood Created the Ancient World*
By Lloyd Llewellyn-Jones

*Screening the Golden Ages*
Edited by Meredith Safran

*Pontius Pilate on Screen: Soldier, Sinner, Superstar*
By Christopher McDonough

*Screening Divinity*
By Lisa Maurice

*Screening Antiquity in the War on Terror*
By Alex McAuley

# Epic Heroes on Screen

Edited by Antony Augoustakis and Stacie Raucci

EDINBURGH
University Press

Edinburgh University Press is one of the leading university presses in the UK. We publish academic books and journals in our selected subject areas across the humanities and social sciences, combining cutting-edge scholarship with high editorial and production values to produce academic works of lasting importance. For more information visit our website: edinburghuniversitypress.com

© editorial matter and organization Antony Augoustakis and Stacie Raucci, 2018
© the chapters their several authors, 2018

Edinburgh University Press Ltd
The Tun – Holyrood Road, 12(2f) Jackson's Entry, Edinburgh EH8 8PJ

Typeset in 11/13 Sabon by
Servis Filmsetting Ltd, Stockport, Cheshire

A CIP record for this book is available from the British Library

ISBN 978 1 4744 2451 6 (hardback)
ISBN 978 1 4744 2452 3 (webready PDF)
ISBN 978 1 4744 2453 0 (epub)

The right of Antony Augoustakis and Stacie Raucci to be identified as the editors of this work has been asserted in accordance with the Copyright, Designs and Patents Act 1988, and the Copyright and Related Rights Regulations 2003 (SI No. 2498).

# Contents

Series Editors' Preface  vii
Editors' Acknowledgments  ix
Contributors  x
List of Illustrations  xiv

Introduction: The Reinvention of the Ancient Hero  1
Antony Augoustakis and Stacie Raucci

### PART I HERCULES

1. Hercules and the Millennial Generation  13
   Jon Solomon

2. Hercules: The Mythopoetics of New Heroism  28
   Alastair J. L. Blanshard

3. Hercules, Putin, and the Heroic Body on Screen in 2014  43
   Emma Stafford

4. Heroes and Companions in *Hercules* (2014)  60
   Angeline Chiu

5. Sacrifice and Salvific Heroism in *Supernatural* (2005–)  74
   Meredith E. Safran

### PART II EPIC HEROES

6. Russell Crowe and Maximal Projections in *Noah* (2014)  93
   Monica S. Cyrino

7. The Immortality of Theseus and His Myth  111
   Margaret M. Toscano

| 8 | The Changing Faces of Heroism in *Atlantis* (2013–15)<br>Amanda Potter | 125 |
| --- | --- | --- |
| 9 | Xena: Warrior, Heroine, Tramp<br>Anise K. Strong | 141 |
| 10 | Divergent Heroism in *Centurion* (2010)<br>Hunter H. Gardner | 156 |

PART III ANTIHEROES

| 11 | The Hero in a Thousand Pieces: Antiheroes in Recent Epic Cinema<br>Dan Curley | 173 |
| --- | --- | --- |
| 12 | Trouble in the Tehran Multiplex: Xerxes, *300*, and *300: Rise of an Empire* in Iran<br>Lloyd Llewellyn-Jones | 191 |
| 13 | Ancient (Anti)Heroes on Screen and Ancient Greece Post-9/11<br>Vincent Tomasso | 206 |
| 14 | Making Modern (Anti)Heroes, the Ancient Way<br>Alex McAuley | 222 |

| Filmography | 238 |
| --- | --- |
| Bibliography | 244 |
| Index | 264 |

# Series Editors' Preface

Screening Antiquity is a new series of cutting-edge academic monographs and edited volumes that present exciting and original research on the reception of the ancient world in film and television. It provides an important synergy of the latest international scholarly ideas about the onscreen conception of antiquity in popular culture and is the only book series to focus exclusively on screened representations of the ancient world.

The interactions between cinema, television, and historical representation is a growing field of scholarship and student engagement; many Classics and Ancient History departments in universities worldwide teach cinematic representations of the past as part of their programs in Reception Studies. Scholars are now questioning how historical films and television series reflect the societies in which they were made, and speculate on how attitudes toward the past have been molded in the popular imagination by their depiction in the movies. Screening Antiquity explores how these constructions came about and offers scope to analyze how and why the ancient past is filtered through onscreen representations in specific ways. The series highlights exciting and original publications that explore the representation of antiquity onscreen, and that employ modern theoretical and cultural perspectives to examine screened antiquity, including stars and star text, directors and *auteurs*, cinematography, design and art direction, marketing, fans, and the online presence of the ancient world.

The series aims to present original research focused exclusively on the reception of the ancient world in film and television. In itself this is an exciting and original approach. There is no other book series that engages head-on with both big screen and small screen recreations of the past, yet their integral interactivity is clear to see: film popularity has a major impact on television productions and, for its part, television regularly influences cinema (including film spin-offs of popular television series). This is the first academic series to identify and encourage the holistic interactivity of these two major media institutions, and the first to promote interdisciplinary research in all the fields of Cinema Studies, Media Studies, Classics, and Ancient History.

Screening Antiquity explores the various facets of onscreen creations of the past, exploring the theme from multiple angles. Some volumes will foreground a Classics "reading" of the subject, analyzing the nuances of film and television productions against a background of ancient literature, art, history, or culture; others will focus more on Media "readings," by privileging the onscreen creation of the past or positioning the film or television representation within the context of modern popular culture. A third "reading" will allow for a more fluid interaction between both the Classics and Media approaches. All three methods are valuable, since Reception Studies demands a flexible approach whereby individual scholars, or groups of researchers, foster a reading of an onscreen "text" particular to their angle of viewing.

Screening Antiquity represents a major turning point in that it signals a better appreciation and understanding of the rich and complex interaction between the past and contemporary culture, and also of the lasting significance of antiquity in today's world.

Monica S. Cyrino and Lloyd Llewellyn-Jones
Series Editors

# Editors' Acknowledgments

We would like to thank the European Cultural Centre at Delphi, where the international conference "New Heroes on Screen" took place from June 29 to July 2, 2015. Delphi, the center of the ancient known world, the site associated with so many ancient heroes and heroines, was a wonderful venue for an inspiring and stimulating conference. In particular, we would like to express our gratitude to the staff of the Centre for their hospitality and efficiency. We would also like to thank the authors for their enthusiasm in embracing this project and for their inspiring contributions to this volume. Special thanks are owed to Carol Macdonald at Edinburgh University Press for her support of this volume from the very beginning, and to her editorial staff for their assistance in the production process. We have greatly benefitted from the feedback provided by the two anonymous reviewers: their comments and suggestions made this into a stronger and much improved volume. We owe thanks to Mitchell Toolan, a wonderful undergraduate research assistant, for his help in the final proofing of this volume. We are also indebted to Monica S. Cyrino and Lloyd Llewellyn-Jones, the series co-editors, for their support. Finally, we would like to thank our families and colleagues for their encouragement. This volume is dedicated to them.

# Contributors

**Antony Augoustakis** is Professor of Classics at the University of Illinois, Urbana-Champaign, USA. His research interests include Roman comedy and historiography, Latin imperial epic, women in antiquity, classical reception, and gender theory. He is the author of *Motherhood and the Other: Fashioning Female Power in Flavian Epic* (Oxford University Press 2010) and *Statius, Thebaid 8* (Oxford University Press 2016). He is the editor of the *Brill Companion to Silius Italicus* (Brill 2010), *Ritual and Religion in Flavian Epic* (Oxford University Press 2013), *Flavian Poetry and its Greek Past* (Brill 2014), and *Oxford Readings in Flavian Epic* (Oxford University Press 2016), and co-editor of *A Companion to Terence* (Wiley-Blackwell 2013). He has published numerous articles and book chapters on various topics of the literature and culture of Greco-Roman antiquity. He is the editor of the journal *Classical Journal*.

**Stacie Raucci** is Associate Professor of Classics at Union College in Schenectady, New York, USA, where she teaches a course on the ancient world in the cinema. Her academic research focuses primarily on the reception of the ancient world in popular culture and Roman love elegy. She is the author of *Elegiac Eyes: Vision in Roman Love Elegy* (Peter Lang 2011) and co-author of *Rome: A Sourcebook on the Ancient City* (Bloomsbury 2018). She has published articles and delivered papers on the popularization of antiquity, Medusa Barbie, Roman orgies in film, and the HBO series *Rome*.

\* \* \* \* \* \* \* \* \*

**Alastair J. L. Blanshard** is the Paul Eliadis Professor of Classics and Ancient History at the University of Queensland, Australia. He is the author of *Hercules: A Heroic life* (Granta 2005), which examined Western culture's fascination with this hero. Together with Kim Shahabudin, he wrote *Classics on Screen: Ancient Greece and Rome* *on film* (Bristol Classical Press 2011). He is one of the series editors for Cambridge University Press's Classics After Antiquity series, and he is an associate editor for the *Classical Receptions Journal*. He is the subject-area editor in classical reception for the *Oxford Classical Dictionary*.

**Angeline Chiu** is Associate Professor of Classics at the University of Vermont, USA. She was educated at Baylor University, the University of Vermont, and Princeton University, and her research interests include ancient drama, Roman epic, mythology, and classical reception. She is the author of *Ovid's Women of the Year: Narratives of Roman Identity in Ovid's Fasti* (University of Michigan Press 2016).

**Dan Curley** is Associate Professor of Classics at Skidmore College, Saratoga Springs, USA. His teaching and research interests include ancient tragedy, Latin poetry, and the classical world on film. Common to all of these is the creation and transformation of mythical characters for reading and viewing communities. Recent work includes *Tragedy in Ovid: Theater, Metatheater, and the Transformation of a Genre* (Cambridge University Press 2013).

**Monica S. Cyrino** is Professor of Classics at the University of New Mexico, USA. Her academic research centers on the reception of the ancient world on screen, and the erotic in ancient Greek poetry. She is the author of *Aphrodite* (Routledge 2010), *A Journey through Greek Mythology* (Kendall-Hunt 2008), *Big Screen Rome* (Blackwell 2005), and *In Pandora's Jar: Lovesickness in Early Greek Poetry* (Rowman & Littlefield 1995). She is the editor of *Rome, Season Two: Trial and Triumph* (Edinburgh University Press 2015), *Screening Love and Sex in the Ancient World* (Palgrave Macmillan 2013), and *Rome, Season One: History Makes Television* (Wiley-Blackwell 2008), and co-editor of *Classical Myth on Screen* (Palgrave Macmillan 2015) and *STARZ Spartacus: Reimagining an Icon on Screen* (Edinburgh University Press 2016). She has published numerous articles and book chapters and often gives lectures around the world on the representation of classical antiquity on film and television. She has served as an academic consultant on several recent film and television productions.

**Hunter H. Gardner** is Associate Professor of Classics at the University of South Carolina, USA. She is the author of *Gendering Time in Augustan Love Elegy* (Oxford University Press 2013) and co-editor of *Odyssean Identities in Modern Cultures: The Journey Home* (Ohio State University 2014). She is currently working on a monograph on plague narratives in Latin literature and their impact on representations of contagion in Western literature, film, and visual arts.

**Lloyd Llewelyn-Jones** is Professor of Ancient History at Cardiff University in Wales, UK. His research focuses on ancient Persia, Greek culture, and Hellenistic history as well as the reception of antiquity in film. His publications include *King and Court in Ancient Persia* (Edinburgh University Press 2013), *The Culture of Animals in Antiquity* (Routledge 2017), and *Designs on the Past: How Hollywood Created the Ancient World* (Edinburgh University Press 2018). He is the series editor of Edinburgh Studies in Ancient Persia and co-editor of Screening Antiquity.

**Alex McAuley** is Lecturer in Hellenistic History at Cardiff University in Wales, UK. He has published widely on the reception of the ancient world in film and television, particularly on how depictions of antiquity have been impacted by the "war on terror." In addition, he also works extensively on the Hellenistic dynasties, the local history of the Greek mainland, and Greek government and federalism.

**Amanda Potter** is a Research Fellow at the Open University, UK, where she was awarded a PhD in 2014 for her thesis on viewer reception of Greek myth in *Xena: Warrior Princess* and *Charmed*. Her research interests are Greek mythology and ancient history on television, particularly viewer engagement with the ancient world via this medium. She has published on a variety of topics in classical reception and Greek mythology-based fan fiction.

**Meredith E. Safran** is Assistant Professor of Classics at Trinity College in Hartford, CT, USA. She is the co-editor, with Monica S. Cyrino, of *Classical Myth on Screen* (Palgrave Macmillan 2015). She is currently editing a volume of papers on cinematic and televisual representations of classical "golden ages" for Edinburgh University Press and writing a monograph analyzing the television series *Battlestar Galactica* as a twenty-first-century American *Aeneid*.

**Jon Solomon** is Robert D. Novak Professor of Western Civilization and Culture at the University of Illinois at Urbana-Champaign, USA. He is the author of *Giovanni Boccaccio: The Genealogy of the Pagan Gods* (Harvard University Press 2011), *The Ancient World* in the Cinema (Yale University Press 2001), *Ptolemy's Harmonics: Translation and Commentary* (Brill 1999), *Ancient Roman Feasts and Recipes* (E. A. Seemann 1977), and *The Complete Three Stooges* (C3 Entertainment 2001). He is the editor of *Accessing Antiquity: The Computerization of Classical Studies* (University of Arizona Press 1993), *Apollo: Origins and Influences* (University of Arizona Press 1994) and *Ancient Worlds in Film and Television: Gender and Politics* (Brill 2013).

**Emma Stafford** is Senior Lecturer in Classics at the University of Leeds, UK. She is the author of numerous works on Greek myth, religion, and iconography, and their post-classical reception, including *Worshipping Virtues: Personification and the Divine in Ancient Greece* (Duckworth 2000) and *Herakles* (Routledge 2012). She is also coordinator of the Leeds-based project Hercules: A Hero for All Ages, which explores receptions of Heracles from the end of antiquity to the present day.

**Anise K. Strong** is Associate Professor of History at Western Michigan University, Kalamazoo, MI, USA. She is the author of *Prostitutes and Matrons in the Roman World* (Cambridge University Press 2016). She has published extensively on classical reception, gender and sexuality, and the history of non-elites, and is currently working on a book on women's desire in films and television about the ancient world. Her favorite ancient historical heroine is Artemisia.

**Vincent Tomasso** is Assistant Professor of Classics at Trinity College, Hartford, CT, USA. He researches, writes, teaches, and presents about Homeric poetry and its reception by Greeks of the imperial period, as well as the reception of ancient Greece and Rome in modern popular culture. He has published many articles and chapters in both areas.

**Margaret M. Toscano** is Associate Professor of Classics and Comparative Studies at the University of Utah, USA. She has published articles on the series *Rome* and *O Brother, Where Art Thou?* Her interest in gender and myth has led to articles on female desire on Attic Greek vases and the Cupid and Psyche myth. She is the co-editor of *Hell and its Afterlife: Historical and Contemporary Perspectives* (Routledge 2016). She has published extensively on Mormon feminism.

# List of Illustrations

Figure I.1 The three Herculeses of 2014: Dwayne Johnson in *Hercules* (Paramount Pictures), Kellan Lutz in *The Legend of Hercules* (Summit Entertainment), and John Hennigan in *Hercules Reborn* (Asylum).   5

Figure 1.1 Kellan Lutz as Hercules whips one of his father, Zeus', thunderbolts à la Steve Reeves in *The Legend of Hercules* (2014). Summit Entertainment.   25

Figure 2.1 Confounding expectations as the Centaurs prove just to be an optical illusion in *Hercules* (2014). Paramount Pictures.   39

Figure 3.1 Arius (Christian Oliver), Horace (James Duval), and Hercules (John Hennigan) contemplate how to breach the defenses of Enos in *Hercules Reborn* (2014). Asylum.   48

Figure 3.2 Dwayne Johnson in *Hercules* (2014), wielding the club and wearing the lionskin. Paramount Pictures.   52

Figure 4.1 Hercules (Dwayne Johnson) and his companions in *Hercules* (2014). Paramount Pictures.   64

Figure 5.1 Zachariah (Kurt Fuller) illustrates the angels' plan for Dean (Jensen Ackles) in *Supernatural* Episode 4.22: "Lucifer Rising." Warner Brothers.   81

Figure 6.1 Russell Crowe as the Roman general Maximus in *Gladiator* (2000). DreamWorks.   94

Figure 6.2 Russell Crowe as the titular biblical patriarch in *Noah* (2014). Paramount Pictures.   95

Figure 7.1 With the dramatic sky as backdrop, Theseus' son Acamas (Gage Munroe) gazes at the statue of his father killing the Minotaur at the end of *Immortals* (2011), visually representing various concepts of immortality. Relativity Media.   120

Figure 8.1 Jason (Jack Donnelly), Pythagoras (Robert Emms), and Hercules (Mark Addy) at the market in *Atlantis* Episode 1.3: "A Boy of No Consequence" (2013).   131

## List of Illustrations

Figure 9.1  Meg (Lucy Lawless), pretending to be Xena, eagerly kisses a confused Joxer (Ted Raimi) in *Xena: Warrior Princess* Episode 2.6: "Warrior ... Princess .... Tramp" (1996). MCA Television.   146

Figure 10.1  Quintus Dias (Michael Fassbender) as a fugitive in Caledonia after escaping from a Pictish camp, at the opening of *Centurion* (2010). Pathé Productions.   158

Figure 11.1  Alexander (Colin Farrell) weeps antiheroically after his victory at Gaugamela in *Alexander* (2004). Warner Bros.   179

Figure 12.1  Xerxes the god-king (Rodrigo Santoro); publicity images from *300* (2007) and *300: Rise of an Empire* (2014). Warner Bros.   193

Figure 12.2  The Great King Xerxes looks at his Hollywood image through a distorting mirror. Iranian cartoon, March 2007. Author's copy.   203

Figure 13.1  In Oliver Stone's *Alexander* (2004), Alexander, dressed as Heracles, prepares to drink from the cup that will kill him. Warner Bros.   213

Figure 13.2  Sheikh Suleiman's magic saves Perseus and his companions from certain death in *Clash of the Titans* (2010). Warner Bros.   218

Figure 14.1  Reading his own *laudatio*? Ashton Kutcher as Steve Jobs in *Jobs* (2013) recording the famous "Here's to the crazy ones" Apple commercial. Open Road Films.   232

# Introduction: The Reinvention of the Ancient Hero

Antony Augoustakis and Stacie Raucci

The movie *Troy* (2004) opens with a voiceover by the wily warrior Odysseus in which he asks if the names and deeds of Homeric heroes will endure for centuries to come: "Will our actions echo across the centuries? Will strangers hear our names long after we're gone and wonder who we were?"[1] Likewise the film ends with another voiceover, again by Odysseus, in which he states that "If they ever tell my story, let them say that I walked with giants. Men rise and fall like the winter wheat, but these names will never die. Let them say I lived in the time of Hector, tamer of horses, let them say I lived in the time of Achilles." This metatheatrical moment, thousands of years after the supposed occurrence of the action of the film, connects the modern viewers quite clearly to the stories of these ancient epic heroes. The voiceover brings the film full circle, from the questioning of the immortality of the heroes to the solidification of their names in our current memory.[2] But Odysseus' statement can be applied to far more than the Homeric heroes of *Troy*. Before there was Odysseus and Achilles in *Troy*, there was Maximus in *Gladiator* (2000), whose success ushered in an active age of the ancients on screen. While the cinematic tradition has included heroic figures from the ancient world since the early days of cinema, the beginning of the twenty-first century until very recently has proved to be prime time for recreating the heroes of the ancient world and immortalizing them on screen. Even if we are unable to determine the precise reason for the rapid release of so many onscreen ancient heroes in a short time (as it is a complicated dance of filmmakers, audience, marketing, and money), we can note that there has been a clear uptick in their sheer numbers in recent years. Sometimes the characters have been reinvented versions of earlier ones, remade in new costumes for new audiences with new values and taste. In other cases, they have been characters newly invented but with the veneer of antiquity lending a setting or backstory to a greater effect.

These onscreen characters range from the mythical to the historical to the purely fictional. They span from soldiers and gladiators (e.g. Maximus in *Gladiator*, General Quintus Dias in *Centurion*, 2010, and Milo in *Pompeii*, 2014) to mythological legends (e.g. Hercules or Perseus in *Clash of the Titans*, 2010, and *Wrath of the Titans*, 2012, and Theseus in *Immortals*, 2011, and *Atlantis*, 2013–15) to biblical figures (Jesus or Noah). Sometimes the same character, such as Hercules, is recreated repeatedly in the same year, allowing us to draw close comparisons among different versions of the Hercules saga.[3] The heroes from the ancient world appear in many large Hollywood productions, following in the paths of the heroes of earlier cinematic eras, while at the same time we see them on the small screen, whether in docudramas (*Roman Empire: Reign of Blood*, 2016) or in a limited run series (Arte's *Odysseus*, 2013) or in series that last for multiple seasons (*Rome*, 2005–7). With rapidly changing ways of viewing TV and film, it has become easier than ever to domesticate the ancients and bring them into the living rooms of the viewing audience, especially since technological advances have turned rooms into small cinematic spaces. Furthermore, the facility of watching films and TV shows on mobile devices, including phones and tablets, has even made the ancient heroes portable and able to seep into the daily lives of viewers. The changes in the viewing experience can alter how characters are received by audiences, making audience identification with ancient heroes an easy and everyday occurrence, rather than the extraordinary experience possible to be had only in a movie theater.

All of the characterizations, whether they are somewhat based in history or mostly fictional or with a foundation in mythology, require some degree of imagination, with their purpose being not to convey directly a true-to-life ancient world. Rather, filmmakers continue to use the ancient world as a means to explore issues relevant to modern society, issues that speak to a twenty-first-century viewer. The connections between the ancient world on screen and the wider world have been explored for many years by scholars of Classical reception studies.[4] Why then this volume at this time?

This volume written by scholars in the flourishing field of reception studies, enters the conversation at an active point in the history of the ancients on screen, when new ancients commonly arrive multiple times per year. It investigates how ancient heroes and antiheroes are being created in the twenty-first century and for what purpose. The chapters in this volume also look back to earlier manifestations of the ancient hero on screen to find the place of recent representations within the tradition of the cinematic hero. They question to what extent these new heroes are conforming to old traditions or breaking with them. They explore what aspect of the most recent time period is ever so fruitful for the production and consumption of ancient heroes. Using diverse critical practices, the authors question what it means to be an ancient hero on the screens of the twenty-first century. The answer of course is not a constant one, nor can it ever be.

The volume as a whole works from the problematic concept of a "hero." The word itself, both in academic discourse and in the wider world, has been used very broadly. Do we limit its use to those with superhuman abilities? Or to those who have taken a specific kind of journey? As Joanna Paul notes, the term "hero" is not easily defined, with meanings ranging "from the agent of the most outstanding and courageous deeds, to simply the (overwhelmingly male) protagonist of a narrative."[5] The issue is further problematized by the presence of heroes outside of the ancient world, since these depictions of the ancient hero have not existed in a vacuum, but are rather part of a wider cultural trend in Hollywood and the United States. In 2006–10, NBC aired a series called *Heroes* (and in 2015–16, its sequel *Heroes Reborn*) about seemingly ordinary people with extraordinary gifts. The series, with its tagline "Save the cheerleader, save the world," brought the idea of an everyday "hero" into the living rooms of viewers each week. The "heroes" consisted of a high school student, a nurse, a police officer, and an office worker, among others, but all with supernatural gifts. They often did not understand their own gifts, and struggled with living with them, as well as with the seemingly everyday demands of life, such as difficulties with family relationships and jobs. With their hidden gifts but ordinary lives, the heroes could be just like the viewers watching the show. Series creators and filmmakers fashion such connections to the audience and promote identification with their onscreen heroes, ancient or modern.

At the same time that ancient heroes have been on the rise, superheroes have also surged, including new and sometimes intertwining versions of Superman, Batman, Thor, and Wonder Woman. Of course, just as with the ancient heroes on screen, other heroes do not necessarily need superpowers to be part of this phenomenon. The ensemble cast of *Scorpion* (2014–) contributes to society with their exceptional intelligence, while in real life CNN runs a segment called *CNN Heroes: Everyday People Changing the World* (2007–). The CNN heroes are honored for helping and inspiring others around the world. Celebrities gather to honor these heroes, who are recognized with monetary awards for their causes. At the 2017 ceremony, Olympic medal winner Laurie Hernandez said that the CNN honorees "show … that you can inspire other people and I feel like that should be the goal for everyone."[6] Are the ancient heroes meant to inspire the audience? Maybe. Even if they are not, they are clearly part of a cultural trend that places heroes at the forefront. Although distanced from viewers by time, the ancient heroes provide a tool with which viewers can experience alternative realities while working through issues of the present. As a concept, "hero" has an inherent instability and malleability, which create the conditions of possibility for all of these different kinds of heroes on our screens.

Even in antiquity, heroic figures were not constructed in a static way. They were never one-dimensional, simplistic creations. Rather, they were already manipulated by authors at different time periods and in varying texts to create appropriate figures for particular audiences. Ancient writers continually recreated heroes and their corresponding values, and so do filmmakers today: one may think of the various versions of the adventures of Hercules in antiquity, often different from Greek to Latin authors, where not one single version is sanctioned as the most reliable. Ancient heroes continue to be constructed with particular goals in mind, whether they are the expressions of cultural values, the societal norms of a particular region, or the continuation of a cinematic tradition.

The chapters in this volume explore the complicated nature of the ancient hero (and the antihero) and the ways these figures are (re) invented on screen in recent works. We have accordingly organized the fourteen chapters that follow into three parts.

The first part focuses on the recent reinventions of Hercules in several post-millennial productions (Figure I.1). The most recent years have brought renewed and significant interest in Hercules with several movies focused on this one figure (in particular *Hercules* and *The Legend of Hercules* in 2014). Looking back to earlier images of the hero, this section shows the trajectory of this ancient hero on screen.

Jon Solomon provides the foundation for this first section, with a detailed examination of the history of Hercules on screen. He assembles the Hercules corpus of the past sixty years, separating the works into three clusters: European ancients from 1958 to 1965; the 1990s, which included the *Hercules* TV series and the Disney film; and finally the most recent productions of 2014. Such a detailed walk through the corpus allows one to place the most recent productions in the

Figure I.1 The three Herculeses of 2014: Dwayne Johnson in *Hercules* (Paramount Pictures), Kellan Lutz in *The Legend of Hercules* (Summit Entertainment), and John Hennigan in *Hercules Reborn* (Asylum).

tradition of the onscreen Hercules and find points of inspiration from one cluster to the next. Solomon's study effectively demonstrates the extensive scope of the Hercules corpus and the inherent difficulties in determining what is part of the mythic tradition and what is not.

Continuing to think about the point of inspiration between Hercules narratives, Alastair Blanshard approaches the most recent Hercules films and examines in what ways they are innovative when compared to their predecessors. He shows a turn, starting from Disney's *Hercules* (1997), in which the hero became a more flexible figure. Blanshard further attributes the new flexibility of the Hercules character to audience reception of cinematic texts. He describes a new type of audience familiar with the "mega-text," texts with storylines across genres. Audiences familiar with comics, fan fiction, and other artistic genres are capable of thinking about the hero in terms of tradition and adaptation. Blanshard's analysis reveals a new type of Hercules, who is less a slayer of monsters and more in tune with his internal struggles.

Emma Stafford places the two recent Hercules films, including the lesser known "mockbuster" *Hercules Reborn* (2014), in dialogue with the Hercules display of Russian president Vladimir Putin. She focuses on the aesthetic elements of the films, including the body of the ancient hero, his dress, and the setting.

Angeline Chiu in turn shows how Brett Ratner, working from Steve Moore's 2009 graphic novel as a foundation for the 2014 film *Hercules*, utilized the role of companions in this innovative framing of the Hercules myth. She focuses on an overlooked aspect of the narrative. Instead of Hercules performing his labors alone, Ratner's version of the myth uses an ensemble cast to support the legendary warrior, creating a group identity rather than just an individual heroic identity. The companions all come from mythological bases of their own, but contribute here to a composite identity of heroism. The result is a more effective hero, as well as a resulting focus on storytelling.

Meredith Safran approaches the mythological figure of Hercules through an indirect representation of the ancient hero, allowing us to think about issues of adaptation of ancient heroes. Rather than Hercules appearing directly on screen, the audience finds him in the long-running apocalyptic sci-fi series CW's *Supernatural*. Despite an overt Christian narrative context in which the plot brings the audience to expect a Jesus figure, the character of Dean Winchester follows the path of Hercules.

While Hercules has been the most consistently depicted ancient figure in the past few years, other heroes of the ancient world appear prominently in numerous productions. In the second part of the volume, we turn to these other epic heroes, from the biblical Noah to the mythological heroes Theseus and Jason, to the fictional female warrior Xena, and finally to soldiers in Roman Britain. The contributions in this part, while not at all exhaustive, provide a sense of the range of recent ancient heroes, both male and female and both TV and film.

First, Monica Cyrino examines the biblical patriarch Noah as played by Russell Crowe in Darren Aronofsky's *Noah* (2014). Starting from the foundation of Richard Dyer's idea of a "star text" in which actors bring echoes of their old roles to new performances and thereby engage viewers on multiple levels, Cyrino frames Crowe's performance in *Noah* as what she terms a "maximal projection." Crowe brings his role as Maximus Decimus Meridius, the soldier who becomes a gladiator during the reigns of Marcus Aurelius and Commodus, to his later role as Noah. Through the repetition of things such as physical gestures, bodily movements, interactions with characters, and even sometimes dialogue, Crowe performs what Cyrino terms "star-peats." These "star-peats" compel the audience to engage with Noah through the earlier hero figure of Maximus, resulting in a reading of the complex character as both righteous and flawed.

Margaret Toscano tackles the reinvention of another mythological figure, Theseus. She analyzes two films from different genres: one is the popular action film, *Immortals*, and the other is a philosophical art film *Ship of Theseus* (2013). She shows how neither work provides a retelling of the Theseus myths. Rather, they use the figure of Theseus to ask questions about the desire for immortality and the complexities of personal identity. While one film, *Immortals*, is set in the ancient world, *Ship of Theseus* is set in modern India, allowing viewers to ask what of the myth is recognizable once recreated in a new form.

Amanda Potter examines the BBC series *Atlantis*, a fantasy-adventure series set in ancient Greece. In addition to the male heroes Jason, Hercules, and Pythagoras, the series creates female models of heroism in its presentation of the mythological figures Medea, Ariadne, and Medusa. The series shows the complexities of heroism by letting its heroes change and grow over time. Through such a non-static depiction of heroism, viewers are able to relate to the characters in the series, something they have grown accustomed to do with other television stories. Since this is an instance of ancient heroes in a TV series, we can see what happens to heroes with a sustained narrative.

Anise Strong then examines the oldest of the ancient heroes in this section of the book, the mythical warrior woman Xena in the eponymous *Xena: Warrior Princess*. The show first aired at the end of the twentieth century (1995) and continued through the early twenty-first century (2001). The depiction of Xena is significant not only because of her gender, but also because of the onscreen precedents she set for future characters. Strong shows that Xena set the trend for women on screen who could be sexually active and polyamorous and not be coded as immoral or deviant. By following a model that more typically applied to male characters of the ancient world, Xena represented a more complicated image of heroism for female characters. Such a representation laid the foundations for a number of later characters, such as Saxa in STARZ *Spartacus* (2010–13) and Starbuck in *Battlestar Gallactica* (2005–9).

Hunter Gardner offers an analysis of heroic identity in the movie *Centurion*, focusing on the heroism of the Roman soldiers Virilus and Quintus Dias of the legendary Ninth Legion, traditionally considered to have disappeared in Roman Britain. Through an examination of their differing models of heroism, the film questions the epic tropes of heroic identity. Gardner shows how Quintus' character diverges from traditional representations of military virtue. The depiction of Rome's imperialism allows viewers a commentary on modern imperialist undertakings.

The third part of the book moves on to investigating the construction of antiheroes. Just as it is difficult to define a hero because the definition is dependent upon cultural circumstances, so it is difficult to define an antihero. In some instances, one character may seem to be both hero and antihero at the same time and it is not always clear where the line between the two should be drawn. In other cases, heroes are purposely morphed into antiheroes to create a new (misguided) representation.

Dan Curley determines how onscreen antiheroes are the product of the fragmentation of traditional heroic storytelling. Using Alexander the Great, Perseus, and Hercules as case studies, Curley shows how these new antiheroes are symptomatic of a new time of non-conformity, with heroes who do not conform to social mores, religious authority, or outdated cinematic modes of conveying values. The heroes that came before can be seen as conforming to traditional systems. Curley demonstrates how antiheroic films work to disrupt the systems of the classicizing, traditional heroic journeys.

It is only recently that reception studies in Classics has started to consider seriously the issue of audience reception and fan reaction.[7] While we sometimes are left only with imagining the audience, Lloyd Llewellyn-Jones undertakes a concrete study of how audiences in a particular location received the movie *300* (2007). He examines how antiheroic constructions of the Persian King Xerxes in *300* and its sequel *300: Rise of an Empire* (2014) elicited strong negative reactions in Iran. Hollywood reinvented Xerxes as a force of evil, creating a corrupt representation of an Iranian national hero. Llewellyn-Jones shows how Iranian audiences received this plundered and corrupted version of their ancestral past.

Vincent Tomasso looks at how 9/11 has altered our engagement with classical antiquity. He examines how the heroes of ancient Greece became antiheroes on screen in a post 9/11 world. He shows how at this time period engagement with figures such as Alexander, Leonidas, and Perseus moved away from the behaviors seen in their earlier onscreen counterparts and how films such as *300*, *Clash of the Titans*, and *Alexander* (2004), while set in antiquity, provide the distance for audiences to explore issues raised by 9/11. At the same time, the depiction of these new antiheroes reflects a revised approach on screen to the representation of mythical thinking (elements of magic, religion, myth – aspects of ancient Greece that were central to pop culture depictions) that came into question along with the destabilization of American identity.

In the final chapter, Alex McAuley makes a connection between the *laudatio funebris*, the funeral oration of ancient Rome, and the modern biopic. He shows how biopics have the ability, like these ancient funeral speeches, to communicate the values of a society. However, in this process, they have the capability to create not only heroes, but also antiheroes. He shows how modern biopics use the Roman funeral speech to create new onscreen antiheroes that are of more appeal to audiences than their heroic counterparts. The chapters that came before this one encourage us to consider the ways heroes on screen are a conscious creation of the filmmakers, with each new hero a reflection of many factors, including ones from both ancient and modern societies. In this final chapter, McAuley invites us to make an even more direct connection to the ancient world, seeing a similarity in the death practices of an ancient society and the way celebrities are currently memorialized in the public eye.

At their base, the chapters as a whole remind us of the enduring nature of the ancient hero on screen. While the heroes of the twenty-first century are not and should not be the heroes of earlier generations, they continue to challenge audiences to question their own times and the representations made in them.

## NOTES

1 On this voiceover as the "film's self-conscious remembrance and re-creation of the glorious deeds of ancient heroes," see Cyrino (2007: 131).
2 The "neverendedness" of ancient Greek or Latin epic poetry endows it with rich modes of cinematic visuality: the last moment of the *Iliad* looks back to its very beginning, by way of juxtaposing Hector's pyre to Achilles' *menis*; the film's last scene effectively alludes to the Homeric formula "Hector tamer of horses" and by extension to the last line of the *Iliad*, thus combining the visual with the aural, as we see the flames of the pyre and hear the voice of the narrator concluding the work, epic or film.
3 This volume refers to both Heracles, the Greek version of the name, and Hercules, the Roman version. Some films clearly dealing with Greek myth use the Romanized version of the name.
4 See for instance the groundbreaking works by Solomon (2001), Winkler (2001), and Cyrino (2005). The list of useful scholarship on the cinematic reception of the ancient world is now quite long, including monographs (such as Paul 2013) and edited volumes (such as Cyrino and Safran 2015).
5 Paul (2013: 176).
6 Kann (2017).
7 See Potter (2015, 2016) on fan reception of HBO-BBC *Rome* (2005–7) and STARZ *Spartacus*.

# PART I
# *Hercules*

# 1 Hercules and the Millennial Generation

Jon Solomon

Hercules films and television programs have proliferated in three clusters of concentrated production and wide popularity.[1] The first consists primarily of the European "ancients" produced between 1958 and 1965; the second of the 1990s television series *Hercules: The Legendary Journeys*, its spinoffs, and the Disney film (1997); and the third of the recent 2014 Hercules products that have been offered in the new millennium. Classical reception studies focusing on the modern era often require the preliminary steps of identifying, collecting, and surveying the corpus to be investigated. This is certainly true for the filmed Hercules corpus studied here, so the relatively limited critical and scholarly analysis that has already been published will be relegated to the scholarly citations, while the purpose here is to survey the corpus, the origins of each cluster, their chronological span, media types, and plot range. In this instance, in assembling the Hercules corpus of the past sixty years, we will see the various characterizations of the ancient hero. Also a significant by-product will be the observation that the mythological figure Hercules has generated an extraordinarily large and varied number of filmed products that differentiates him from other successfully dramatized legendary figures.

## CLUSTER ONE

The first cluster begins with Italian producer Federico Teti, who in 1957 invited a 1950s Mr. Universe, Steve Reeves, to play the role in Galatea Film's *Le fatiche di Ercole*, directed by Pietro Francisci, a film that claimed to have adapted Apollonius' *Argonautica* but focused more on physical, political, and romantic labors for Hercules.[2] The film might have languished in Italy, but Joseph E. Levine, as he told

*Variety*, refurbished it for American audiences and spent enormous sums of money on promotion.[3]

> When I was told about "Hercules," I flew over to Italy to look at it. The picture broke down when we were showing it, the titles were bad, it was in Italian and I couldn't understand it, but there was something in it that made me realize there was a potential fortune tied up in it. I took it apart, dubbed it in English, and spent $120,000 for sound effects [i.e. dubbing] and titles. The new main title alone cost me $15,000. I saw in Steve Reeves, who plays Hercules, a man whose physical attributes, ability and enormous strength appealed to the women.[4]

For its American release in May 1959, Levine renamed the film, simply, *Hercules*. Advertising slogans ("Mighty Saga of the Mightiest Man") and promotional materials focused on the mythological Hercules and suggested to potential audiences that the bodybuilding champion Reeves was Hercules *redivivus*.[5] A July 1959 half-page display ad in the *New York Times* depicts Reeves' V-shaped torso and bearded square jaw on the left side, while on the right the copy tells us:

> The story of Hercules is over 3000 years old ... and just as it made a fast-paced, fast-moving tale for the ancient Greeks who told it and retold it at campfires, in market-places, in theatres ... it makes a fast-paced, fast-moving modern movie. (Hercules, if you've forgotten your mythology, was the mighty hero who performed acts of incredible strength and heroism.) Steve Reeves, "Mr. Universe," plays Hercules. He's so superbly muscled and thewed that you can well believe he killed a lion and conquered a bull bare-handed.[6]

Across the top of the page in large font is "HERCULES," balanced by "HERCULEAN" across the middle of the page, the latter describing the efforts Macy's department store makes for their customers ("The job is Herculean ... yes, for everything Macy's does is on an epic and heroic scale").

By the time Warner Brothers released the film in 600 theaters, a record number at the time, Levine had incurred nearly $1.2 million in promotional costs.[7] While critics recognized the sketchy narrative flow, the inconsistency of the dubbing synchronization, and the potential attraction to only unsophisticated audiences,[8] the film played in thousands of theaters, was seen by over 20 million people, and grossed some $18 million.[9]

Although it is not a rule of popular culture and commerce, the first successful product often establishes an icon, style, or brand that provides an exemplar for copies, imitations, or sequels. The enormous success of *Hercules* encouraged Levine to provide the same kind of lavish exploitation for its sequel, *Ercole e la regina di Lidia*, also starring Reeves and directed by Francisci, and released in the United States as *Hercules Unchained* in July 1960.[10] The latter so saturated the market that 1,000 prints were in distribution simultaneously in the United States and 500 in the United Kingdom. The impact of *Hercules* was felt immediately by a number of Italian production companies and American distributors, and it was not lost on Richard Nason of the *New York Times*:

> "Hercules" has set a new high-water mark in mass response for a comparatively cheap film of its kind. It has forced American and Italian companies to launch crash programs for the production of legendary and Biblical spectacles and it has sent American distributors scurrying to Italy to buy up gimmick films that can be adapted to the hard sell that Mr. Levine has revived with a vengeance.[11]

The number of predominantly Italian, mytho-historical Hercules films – often referred to as *pepla* in Europe – that followed, all of them starring a bodybuilder, is difficult to calculate with precision, but it certainly numbered in the dozens.[12] The Hercules films, such as *Le fatiche di Ercole* and *Ercole e la regina di Lidia*, were distributed internationally and exhibited under different titles, at least translated into the local language and frequently changed entirely. The films that include the name Ercole in the original Italian title are, in chronological order (with the U.S. release title(s) in parentheses): *Gli amori di Ercole* (*The Loves of Hercules*, *Hercules and the Hydra*, 1960), *La vendetta di Ercole* (*Vengeance of Hercules* [a.k.a. *Goliath and the Dragon*], 1960), *Ercole al centro della terra* (*Hercules in the Haunted World*, 1961), *Ercole alla conquista di Atlantide* (*Hercules and the Captive Women*, 1961), *Maciste contro Ercole nella valle dei guai* (*Hercules in the Valley of Woe*, 1961), *Ulisse contro Ercole* (*Ulysses Against Hercules*, 1962), *La furia di Ercole* (*The Fury of Hercules*, 1962), *Ercole contro Moloch* (*Conquest of Mycenae/ Hercules Against Moloch*, 1963), *Ercole sfida Sansone* (*Hercules, Samson & Ulysses*, 1963), *Ercole, Sansone, Maciste e Ursus gli invincibili* (*Samson and the Mighty Challenge*, 1964), *Ercole contro i figli del sole* (*Hercules Against the Sons of the Sun*, 1964), *Ercole contro i tiranni di Babilonia* (*Hercules and the Tyrants of Babylon*, 1964), *Ercole l'invincibile* (*Hercules the Invincible*, 1964), and *Ercole contro Roma* (*Hercules Against Rome*, 1964). Many of these films were released under multiple titles. *Gli amori di Ercole*, for instance, was released for American television as *Hercules and the Hydra*. A few Italian Hercules films, e.g. *Maciste il vendicatore dei Maya* [a.k.a. *Ercole contro il gigante Golia*] (1965), were apparently not released in the United States.

The Italian titles of some films, e.g. *Maciste contro Ercole nella valle dei guai*, featured the name of one of the other muscular heroes that were less familiar to non-Italian audiences. In the United States the titular name was sometimes translated to Hercules, in this instance with the release title *Hercules in the Valley of Woe*. Others include *Maciste contro i Mongoli* (*Hercules Against the Mongols*, 1963), *Golia e il cavaliere mascherato* (*Hercules and the Masked Rider*, 1963), *Sansone contro il corsaro nero* (*Hercules and the Black Pirate*, 1963), *Maciste nell'inferno di Gengis Khan* (*Hercules Against the Barbarians*, 1964), *Maciste e la regina di Samar* (*Hercules Against the Moon Men*, 1964), *Sansone e il tesoro degli Incas* (*Hercules and the Treasure of the Incas*, 1964), and *Ursus, il terrore dei kirghisi* (*Hercules, Prisoner of Evil*, 1964).

Some did not specify another hero, e.g. *La valle dell'eco tonante* (*Hercules of the Desert*, 1964) and *La sfida dei giganti* (*Hercules the Avenger*, 1965). *Il magnifico gladiatore* (1964) places Hercules (a.k.a. Attalus) in the reign of the Roman Emperor Galenus, but his name appears in the title in only the Serbian release *Herkul gladijator*. *Maciste il vendicatore dei Maya* (1965) and *Il conquistatore di Atlantide* (*The Conqueror of Atlantis*, 1965) did not include Hercules in the title in any language, but in both films the protagonist is Hercules (Kirk Morris).

In addition, there were films that did not at all contain the name Ercole in the original Italian title or Hercules in the U.S. title but translated the name of one of the other muscular heroes. In (West) Germany, for instance, *Il terrore dei barbari* (1959) was released as *Herkules, der Schrecken der Hunnen*, *Sansone* (1961) as *Herkules im Netz der Cleopatra*, *Goliath contro i giganti* (1961) as *Die Irrfahrten des Herkules*, and *La vendetta di Ursus* (1961) as *Herkules, der Held von Karthago*. Illustrating the confusion that interferes with assembling this part of the corpus, *Maciste nella terra dei ciclopi* (1961) was released in the U.S. as *Atlas Against the Cyclops* and in Germany as *Maciste, der Sohn des Herkules*. French releases included *La fureur d'Hercule* (*Ursus*, 1961) and *Goliath et l'Hercule noir* (*Goliath e la schiava ribelle*, 1963). Years later *Maciste, l'eroe più grande del mondo* (1963), released in the United States as *Goliath and the Sins of Babylon*, was released on video in France as *Hercule et les Titans*.

Beginning in 1964, Levine repackaged a number of Italian Maciste, Goliath, and Ursus films specifically for a "Sons of Hercules" American television series: *Ursus* in 1961 (*Ursus, Son of Hercules*), *Maciste, l'uomo più forte del mondo* in 1961 (*Mole Men Against the*

*Son of Hercules*), *Il trionfo di Maciste* in 1961 (*Triumph of the Son of Hercules*), *Marte, dio della Guerra* in 1962 (*Venus Against the Son of Hercules*), *Maciste contro i mostri* in 1962 (*Fire Monsters Against the Son of Hercules*), *Ursus nella terra di fuoco* in 1963 (*Son of Hercules in the Land of Fire*), *Perseo l'invincibile* in 1963 (*Medusa Against the Son of Hercules*), *Goliath e la schiava ribelle* in 1963 (*Tyrant of Lydia Against the Son of Hercules*), *Maciste, gladiatore di Sparta* in 1964 (*The Terror of Rome Against the Son of Hercules*), and *Anthar l'invincibile* in 1964 (*Devil of the Desert Against the Son of Hercules*). A few others were repackaged versions of films already cited here in other contexts, e.g. *Ercole l'invincibile* (*Hercules the Invincible*) as *Son of Hercules in the Land of Darkness*. *L'eroe di Babilonia* (1963) was changed to *Hercule, héros de Babylone* in France and then later released in the United States as *The Beast of Babylon Against the Son of Hercules*. Similar was *L'ultimo gladiatore* (1964), repackaged as *Messalina vs. the Son of Hercules*.

In a category of its own was the big-screen parody *The Three Stooges Meet Hercules* (1962), produced by Norman Maurer, released by Columbia, and featuring another bodybuilder, Samson Burke.[13] Meanwhile, expediting the transfer to television was the ever-expansive Levine. He announced in March 1962 that Embassy Pictures would form a syndication unit and that CBS was already an eager buyer for his portfolio, which included the two Hercules films as well as *Attila the Hun*.[14] Sales amounted to $1 million in the first week alone.[15] When *Hercules* premiered on WOR-TV in New York in January 1963, it earned not only the largest audience the station had ever attracted but more than the other local network stations combined.[16] In June 1962, Trans-Lux Television began to advertise *The Mighty Hercules*, a cartoon series designed originally to consist of 130 5½-minute episodes in color or black and white, for broadcast in 1963.[17] By the fall of 1963 the cartoon series was playing in major American urban markets.[18] Adding to what was said above, it was in the fall of 1963 that Levine arranged the "Sons of Hercules" series with thirteen titles, not only prepared with a Western-sounding, guitar-accompanied intro, but edited as either full-length features during primetime, or as one hour "cliffhangers" complete with "See Part Two" end-titles, recaps, and narration-over-flashback sequences for matinees.[19] Levine had already announced that he was considering a Hercules television series in 1959, but it was not until January 1964 that Levine confirmed his plans to budget $4 million to produce 32 one-hour color episodes in Italy for an American – and then internationally syndicated – television program named *Hercules*.[20]

Levine produced the pilot, *Hercules and the Princess of Troy*, aired in September 1965, but the popularity of Hercules-inspired films was waning and production was slowing in Italy, so the pilot was never sold. Nonetheless, it aired on television in the 1980s and was repackaged for sale in home-entertainment formats.

Although only twenty-five episodes were produced, in 1966 WSB-TV in Atlanta reported that *The Mighty Hercules*, having garnered some of the highest ratings of any children's show in the market, would be renewed for three more years, and that WITI-TV in Milwaukee had just purchased the color episodes.[21] Liberty Films of Japan renewed the series through 1970.[22] The series even engendered a commercial spinoff. Frank H. Fleer Corporation, the bubblegum maker, used *The Mighty Hercules* cartoon characters on its wrapper tattoo-transfers, surpassing sales of every cartoon image the company had previously used. Their public announcement gives us a colorful, contemporary description of the scope of the success:

> All the Hercules gum sold in the last seven months, Trans-Lux has figured using an average blown-bubble as base, would make a bubble circling 6,782 miles – the size of the moon.[23]

The 1958–65 cluster also inspired Arnold Schwarzenegger's first major film, *Hercules in New York* (1970), which in turn seems to have been the inspiration for *Hercules* (1983) and *The Adventures of Hercules II* (1985), the two Italian productions featuring Lou Ferrigno, another championship bodybuilder who had just finished his successful television run in *The Incredible Hulk* (1977–82). There was even spillover into the karate craze of the 1970s in *Mr. Hercules Against Karate* (1973). But by then the Hollywood film studios and consortia in Europe had generally ceased production of "ancients" altogether, leaving the Hercules legacy primarily to television and video formats in the 1970s and 1980s.

## CLUSTER TWO

The origins of the second cluster can be pinpointed to 1992, when MCA TV and Universal Television reacted proactively to congressional committees, government agencies, and activist groups attempting to curb television violence.[24] Their solution, as expressed by MCA-TV president Shelly Schwab, was to create the MCA/Universal Action Pack, which would "avoid gratuitous violence" and promote "wholesome action entertainment."[25] Interestingly, according to a survey of station managers at Universal Television, MCA learned that they lamented the dearth of new "two-hour action movies," many dozens of which the first Hercules cluster supplied for years. MCA consequently allotted $100 million for the production of twenty-four first-run telefilms directed by six different established directors, the most successful of which turned out to be Sam Raimi's *Hercules: The Legendary Journeys* (1995–9).[26] As in many instances, Hercules, the ancient mythological hero, was selected over a competing literary property, in this instance Robert E. Howard's Conan the Barbarian, because of the latter's potential copyright entanglements.[27] Still, Universal felt insecure that the five pilot Hercules films would succeed because they uniquely combined action, romance, and camp humor, but as it turned out this multi-genre formula played particularly well in the expanding international market. Ned Nahl, executive vice-president of Universal Television, commented that the foreign distributors "have been saying the American cerebral shows don't play for our audiences. 'Hercules' does. It's language-proof and it's fun."

In developing a new formula for a dramatized Hercules film project, co-producer Robert Tapert made it clear at the time that they consciously avoided the bodybuilder type by casting Kevin Sorbo:

> We knew we couldn't go with a traditional muscle man. Our model for the character was always a Joe Montana type, a star quarterback who wasn't off-putting because of his size or good looks, just a decent good guy you'd want to sit at a bar with or invite into your living room. Kevin is just that type.[28]

Similarly, there was no interest in shooting the episodes in Italy or an authentic Mediterranean setting. For the background scenery they chose instead New Zealand to portray "a beautiful but dangerous fantasy world before the rise of Greece and Rome." In the foreground they placed an array of computer-generated and composited mythological creatures that relied upon the recently developed cinematic technologies showcased in such films as *Terminator 2: Judgment Day* (1991) and *Jurassic Park* (1993) and now available for television productions. In addition to the digital innovations, Raimi employed the unique style of camera work – e.g. with slow-motion close-ups of arrows flying through the air toward their target – that he had recently showcased in his films *Darkman* (1990) and *Army of Darkness* (1992). And to attract additional demographics, *Hercules: The Legendary Journeys* cast a large number of young women and costumed them scantily, much as did *Baywatch*, the international television ratings leader at the time. *Hercules: The Legendary Journeys* consequently reached a broad range of demographics, and after five 1994–5 pilots and 111 episodes in six seasons, by 1996 it surpassed even *Baywatch* and *Star Trek: Deep Space Nine* as the most popular syndicated television show in the world.[29]

Echoing the geographical dissemination of Heracles/Hercules as the hypostasis of the pre-Hellenic earth goddess, many of the episodes incorporated ancient mythological narratives and characters found in the ancient corpus of Herculean mythology. The initial 91-minute pilot, *Hercules and the Amazon Women*, featured Hippolyta as well as Alcmene and Zeus.[30] Episode 2 ("Eye of the Beholder") featured the fifty daughters of Thespius. Hera, the ancient Greek namesake of Heracles, appropriately served frequently as a divine antagonist.[31] Iolaus (Michael Hurst) usually played the role of his sidekick, and in Episode 29 ("Let the Games Begin"), Hercules establishes the first Olympic Games. Many episodes include appropriate female characters named Deianeira and Omphale, male friends and foes named Iphicles, Antaeus, Eryx, and Charon, and hybrid mythological animals such as Cerberus and the Minotaur. Several episodes feature centaurs, whether named Nessus and Chiron or Deric and Ceridian. There were equally appropriate Hercules-specific expeditions to the Underworld, Troy, and the frozen north to meet with Prometheus. Others took him further afield in encounters with Jason, Aphrodite, Cupid and Psyche, and the prophetess Cassandra, who forecasts the doom of Atlantis. The "Mythic Connections" entries in Robert Weisbrot's *Official Companion* suggest that these were intentional.

On the other hand, none of these characters or expeditions faithfully replicate ancient myths. Like the films of the 1960s (and ancient-setting operas of the seventeenth and eighteenth centuries), the stories invariably incorporate innovative characterizations, subplots, and, dialogue, and inevitably result in happy endings. Even episodes associated with such canonical Herculean labors as the stables of Augeus and the Golden Hind, like the aforementioned episode with the daughters of Thespius, include numerous innovations. To expand further the character base, divine representatives such as Ares, Nemesis, and Echidna often amplify Hera's protagonist role, and continuing characters named Salmoneus and Autolycus periodically accompany Hercules instead of Iolaus. In several episodes the latter plays the protagonist: in Episode 28 ("Heedless Hearts") he acquires visionary power, and in two episodes (32 and 48) his cousin Orestes is a doppelganger played by Hurst. Other familiar names usually cut loose from their mythological roots include Oedipus, Callisto, Medea, and Arachne, along with Hellenic-like neologisms such as

Parnassa and Darphus. Beginning near the end of the third season, several episodes were set in such post-ancient, pseudo-historical lands as eighteenth-century France (Episode 54) and modern Los Angeles (Episode 74) when Kevin Sorbo disappears during a New Zealand shoot. The fourth season began with Hercules and Autolycus climbing a beanstalk (Episode 60). Later there were encounters in Sumeria (Episodes 82, 83, and 89), Norway (Episode 87), medieval Britain (Episode 100), and Egypt (Episode 109), bringing in such characters as Arthur, Merlin, and Nefertiti.

While the original cluster of Hercules films usually cast sexy femmes fatales to tempt the bodybuilder star, in the 1990s film and television guidelines were significantly updated, so the series supplied not only bountiful cleavage and athletic bodies but a generous supply of cerebral gender equality. Most notable of these female characters was the one given the name Xena (Lucy Lawless), who was written into three different episodes in the first season and transformed from a villain contemplating world domination to a beneficent heroine. It did not take long before Raimi and Tapert were greenlighted to produce *Xena: Warrior Princess*. This spinoff was as successful as *Hercules: The Legendary Journeys*, running from 1995 to 2001 in 134 episodes, in which Hercules played a role in two episodes (Episode 8: "Prometheus"; Episode 102: "God Fearing Child") that appropriately involved Prometheus and Zeus. Following the formula used in *Hercules: The Legendary Journeys*, Raimi and Tapert provided Xena with a sidekick, named Gabrielle (Renee O'Connor). At the time, the rarity of a television adventure series starring two women inspired a diverse following, not to mention a number of academic studies.[32]

In addition, after Raimi and Tapert executive-produced a pilot starring Ian Bohen, they featured the young Ryan Gosling in a spinoff aimed at the teen demographic, *Young Hercules*, which ran on the Fox Kid Network for fifty episodes during the 1998–9 season. The premise of the early episodes is that Alcmene sends teenage Hercules to Chiron's Academy, where he befriends classmates Jason and a young woman named Kora. Zeus has a frequent presence, and a number of episodes include roles for other Olympian gods whether as adolescents or as adults. A mature Ares frequently serves as the villain, as does his companion Strife. Some of the plots were based on ancient myths but with significant innovations. A series of four connected episodes (20–3), for instance, incorporate a young musician Orpheus and his girlfriend Eurydice, who perform for Bacchus and his vampire-like followers, and conclude with a journey to the Underworld to visit Jason's father Aeson. Two episodes (37 and 41) feature the Golden Hind, but in the second Artemis transforms Iolaus into a deer.

After the hiatus from the mid-1960s to mid-1990s, Hercules was now back in full force a full generation after the end of the first cluster. Raimi and Tapert also executive-produced the 1998 animated film *Hercules and Xena – The Animated Movie: The Battle for Mount Olympus*. Voiced by Sorbo, Lawless, Hurst, O'Connor, and others, the film intertwines the two familiar heroic duos with a major war, instigated by Hera, between the Olympian gods and the Titans. Other productions included the American–Japanese Jetlag *Hercules* (1995), the Italian Orlando Corradi's 90-minute animated biography that aimed to include most of the twelve labors, and the independent spoof *Hercules Returns* (1993), in which inept theater owners ad lib the soundtrack of *Samson and the Mighty Challenge* (*Ercole, Sansone, Maciste e Ursus gli invincibili*, 1964), much like the contemporaneous Hercules spoofs on *Mystery Science Theater 3000*. In addition, two video games were licensed in 1999, when Saffire and Titus produced *Xena: Warrior Princess: The Talisman of Fate* for Nintendo, and VU Games and Electronic Arts produced *Xena: Warrior Princess* for PlayStation.

A struggle between the Olympian gods and the Titans was also developed as a plot element for Disney's animated feature *Hercules*, released some six months earlier in 1997, although the Disney staff decided to make Hades, not Hera, the villainous antagonist. Their conception of Hercules, reconfigured as the young hero of a romantic musical, differed as well. Co-directors Ron Clements and John Musker had begun considering a mythological subject in 1992, ultimately preferring Hercules to Odysseus because the *Odyssey* seemed "more sacred" and would prevent them from taking "quite a few liberties."[33] Identifying Hercules as "the first superhero," they highlighted his demigod status so they could illustrate both Olympian and earthly settings, contrasting them with the darker Underworld as well, and they fused "the impulsive, headstrong, resolute" part of Hercules with "the innocent hero, the idealist." They introduced a new ensemble formula by creating a comically gruff satyr named Philoctetes as Hercules' trainer and a love interest, Meg[ara], who was designed to be more intelligent than the hero.[34]

*Hercules* earned over $250 million worldwide, was accompanied by a spectrum of commercial merchandising, and warranted a direct-to-video release, *Hercules: Zero to Hero* (1998). The video employed the same concept as *Young Hercules* in that it focused on Hercules' youthful adventures, in this instance at the Prometheus Academy, and it, too, served as the first episode of a syndicated television series, *Hercules: The Animated Series*. This series consisted of sixty-five episodes in 1998–9 and included dramatized realizations of Icarus, Adonis, Pandora, Pygmalion, Circe, Morpheus, Medusa, Galatea, and the three Fates, among others. The modernizations that characterized so many of the *Hercules: The Legendary Journeys* and *Xena* episodes were represented in Episode 9 ("Hercules and the Pool Party"), in which the evil Hades sneakily gives all the Olympians a drink from the River Lethe, and Episode 63 ("Hercules and the Kids"), where the kindergartners at the Prometheus Academy include Alexander the Great and Brutus.

The simultaneous distribution of all these Hercules projects in the mid-to-late-1990s is a particularly extraordinary demonstration of the extreme popularity of Hercules. Combined, they amount to well over 300 hours of original programming, not to mention many hundreds of additional hours of rebroadcasts, which averages out to approximately five Hercules or Herculean hours per week for six years. This total certainly compares favorably with some of the most successful fantasy and sci-fi media icons of the era, such as the *Star Trek* franchise and *Doctor Who*. Again, the Hercules-specific reason for this is the hero's origin as an opposite-gender hypostasis of the Great Goddess worshipped throughout the entire Mediterranean basin for several millennia and incorporated into a broad range of myths, making the Herculean corpus unique among the mythological heroes. Moving forward, it is important for us to mark this cluster of Hercules television programs as the inspiration for the renascence of "ancient" films in the next millennium. The millennial and post-millennial generation of "ancient" films begins with Hercules.[35]

## CLUSTER THREE

At first there were made-for-television films such as the Zoetrope/Hallmark *The Odyssey* (1997) and *Cleopatra* (1999), and these were followed by the hugely popular and critically acclaimed *Gladiator* (2000), which set such projects as *Troy* (2004), *Alexander* (2004), and *300* (2007) as well as the popular STARZ *Spartacus* premium-television series (2010–13) into motion. The first subsequent Hercules project was Hallmark's two-part miniseries *Hercules* (2005), the first non-animated film to attempt a chronological biography. The first episode moves chronologically from the miscegenated inception of Hercules and Iphicles and establishes Hercules' associations with Linus, Megara, and Deianeira and his subservience to King

Eurystheus. In part two Hercules performs six of his twelve labors, ultimately marrying Deianeira. As with all its predecessors, innovations vary the canonical myths and characters considerably, but some are uncommonly "mature" for Hallmark productions. Alcmene, a priestess of Hera, is raped and later commits suicide by leaping off a cliff. When Megara is drunk or drugged, Hercules has sex with her and later murders his three sons, perhaps a distant homage to Euripides. Even Iphicles and Eurystheus have a sexual encounter. The scenes with the earthbound Antaeus are particularly innovative while remaining myth-specific. After Hercules weakens him by tossing him in a river and imprisoning him in a tower, Megara revives his strength with a handful of dirt, and then, fully strengthened when he is underground, he is killed as the cave ironically collapses on him. This is after Hercules learns that Antaeus was his biological father. The Hallmark *Hercules* was followed by *Hercules in Hollywood*, a low-budget parody of the Schwarzenegger film.

The post-*Gladiator* momentum created the impetus for a new slate of specifically mythological films such as *Minotaur* (2006), *Clash of the Titans* (2010), *Percy Jackson & the Olympians: The Lightning Thief* (2010), *Immortals* (2011), *Wrath of the Titans* (2012), and *Percy Jackson & the Olympians: Sea of Monsters* (2013), and by 2014 a new generation of the child and adolescent demographics was introduced to the third cluster of Hercules projects. In 2014 alone there were four different issues – *Hercules*, *The Legend of Hercules*, *Hercules Reborn*, and *Hercules: Hero, God, Warrior* – as well as an American reissue of *Hercules: An Animated Classic*, and even an Indian *Hercules* about a contemporary man whom people ironically called "Hercules." In addition, an alcoholic, financially overextended, and physically overweight Hercules was one of the companion characters in the British television series *Atlantis* (2013–15).[36]

Both *The Legend of Hercules* and *Hercules* were produced by Hollywood studios and issued in 3-D.[37] The former, advertised with such slogans as "Before the Myth, There was the Man," and "Witness the Rise of a God," was released in January and starred Kellan Lutz, a former model. The plot develops romantic and political intrigues among the immediate Herculean mythological family members. Alcmene despises and fears Amphitryon, and Hercules (a.k.a. Alcides) and Iphicles form a love triangle with Hebe, all enhanced by CGI (computer-generated imagery) longshots, gladiatorial spectacles, slow- and stop-action editing, and a Reeves-like unchaining leading to the climax of wielding a whip made of Zeus' lightning (Figure 1.1). *Hercules*, starring the ex-wrestler Dwayne Johnson, who combined a

Figure 1.1 Kellan Lutz as Hercules whips one of his father, Zeus', thunderbolts à la Steve Reeves in *The Legend of Hercules* (2014). Summit Entertainment.

large, muscular body and camera-friendly screen persona, was based on Steve Moore's graphic novel *Hercules: The Thracian Wars*.[38] In a 2008 *Comic News* interview, Moore and Radical Comics president Barry Levine said that they specifically designed a "grittier" Hercules instead of a "prettified fantasy movie" for an audience accustomed to a darker genre.[39] Aware of the Bronze Age period in Greek history, Moore also describes his personal library as including Hesiod and Apollodorus and says he used the *Oxford Classical Dictionary* for "quick references" while writing. Nonetheless, the film is inexplicably set in 358 BC and the plot depends on a traditional Hollywood formula by setting Hercules as the leader of a group of companions (Amphiaraus, Autolycus, Tydeus, Atalanta, and Iolaus) who are convinced or forced to undergo difficult tasks, one of which is to defend Thrace from the evil warlord Rhesus.[40] After its July release, it earned nearly $250 million at the box office, making this film far more successful than its 2014 Hercules contemporaries. August brought the release of *Hercules Reborn*, set in 13 BC, a relatively gruesome vehicle for another former wrestler, John Hennigan. The plot refurbished the generic hero-plus-companion (Hercules and Arius Dudunakis) versus villainous royal pretender (Nikos, King of Enos) to-save-the-princess (Theodora) formula, authenticated somewhat by reference to the earlier murder of Megara, because of which the guilt-ridden Hercules has become an alcoholic. *Hercules: Hero, God, Warrior* was an edutainment compilation DVD from The History Channel and Lionsgate that included three previously produced television documentaries: *Hercules: Power of the Gods* (1998), *Clash of the Gods: Hercules* (2009), and *In Search of History: The Greek Gods* (2004).

Unfortunately, not enough time has passed for there to have been a body of published scholarly analysis about this recent spate of Hercules films, and their impact in popular culture has been minimal compared to that of the first two clusters. So we will end our survey here.[41]

## CONCLUSION

The classicist may not find here a single film or television series that effectively narrates the collected myths of the ancient Greek Hercules, even if a number of films and episodes include segments or plot elements that echo ancient sources and a few of the writers acknowledged their influence. Nonetheless, the extraordinary size and scope of the Herculean corpus in film and television reflect the essence of the ancient Herculean mythological corpus in that there is no unified characterization of Hercules, no biographical consensus, and no general agreement on where the mythological tradition ends and literary innovation begins. It would seem that the simple conclusion to be reached at this point is that the concept of a semi-divine, monster-slaying strongman who is susceptible to suffering but ultimately triumphs and re-emerges to fight another battle has thrived for several millennia, prospering as a religious and artistic figure in antiquity, and making many others prosper today as a superior icon of the commercialized film and television industry.

## NOTES

1. Because this chapter lists so many titles, many of them having alternative titles and release dates, and because the television series include so many episodes, I have not included them all in the filmography.
2. Blanshard and Shahabudin (2011: 58–76); Fourcart (2012: 21–45); Della Casa and Giusti (2013: 21–46); Solomon (2014: 163–71).
3. McKenna (2008: 87–116).
4. Parsons (1959).
5. Wyke (1997b: 63–8).
6. *New York Times*, July 22, 1959, 7.
7. D'Amelio (2014: 164–5).
8. *Variety*, May 13, 1959, 6.
9. Lucanio (1994: 12–13).
10. Éloy (1998: 32–3); Clauss (2008).
11. Nason (1959).
12. Lucanio (1994: 1–56); D'Amelio (2011); Rushing (2016: 65–99).
13. O'Brien (2011).

14 *Variety*, March 21, 1962, 5, and January 23, 1963, 3.
15 *Broadcasting*, February 18, 1963, 64.
16 *Variety*, January 16, 1963, 28; *New York Amsterdam News*, January 5, 1963, 15.
17 *Broadcasting*, June 4, 1962, 33.
18 *Broadcasting*, July 1, 1963, 43.
19 *Variety*, October 9, 1963, 27.
20 *Variety*, July 1, 1959, 18, and January 15, 1964, 27.
21 *Back Stage*, November 18, 1966, 2.
22 *Variety*, August 3, 1966, 35; *Back Stage*, October 30, 1970, 3; *Broadcast*, April 11, 1997, 7.
23 *Variety*, August 3, 1966, 34.
24 Weisbrot (1998: 3–6); *Broadcasting & Cable*, August 2, 1993, 12–13.
25 *Broadcasting & Cable*, October 4, 1993, 25; *Variety*, January 15–21, 1996, N16.
26 *Broadcasting & Cable*, June 20, 1994, 18.
27 Weisbrot (1998: 4–6).
28 Weisbrot (1998: 4–6); cf. Sorbo (2011: 28–31).
29 E.g. *Variety*, February 12, 1996, 29.
30 Blondell (2007).
31 E.g. Episodes 1, 3, 6, 7, 22, 26, 34, 42, 45, 49, 55, and 111.
32 E.g. Tolley (1999); Kennedy (2003); Lodge (2009); Steimer (2009); see further Strong in this volume.
33 Rebello and Healey (1997: 52); Thomas (1997: 165–6).
34 Pallant (2011).
35 E.g. *Variety*, April 24, 2000, 27.
36 See Potter in this volume.
37 Rushing (2016: 26–8).
38 Moore and Wijaya (2008).
39 Vamvounis (2008).
40 Cf. the blog post of July 29, 2014, at https://aelarsen.wordpress.com.
41 The following chapters by Blanshard, Stafford, Chiu, and Curley explore the new Hercules films in greater detail.

# 2 Hercules: The Mythopoetics of New Heroism

Alastair J. L. Blanshard

## INTRODUCTION

It was the mythological figure of Hercules that provided the inspiration for, and helped fuel the success of, comics' greatest hero, Superman.[1] It is therefore only appropriate that the world of comics should in turn be one of the revitalizing forces that has brought Hercules back to the cinematic screen. One of the most recent and potent examples of the cinematic appropriation of the Herculean myth cycle is *Hercules* (2014), a film that adapts for the screen Radical Comics' graphic novel *Hercules: The Thracian Wars* by Steve Moore (art by Admira Wijaya). Together with *The Legend of Hercules* (2014), *Hercules* (2014) provides a useful opportunity to revisit the status and critical responses to the Hercules myth in the first decades of the twenty-first century.[2]

This chapter attempts to place these films within the broader history of cinematic imaginings about Hercules as well as articulate their novel contribution to this tradition. In contrast to earlier versions, in these more recent films we see a cinematic hero more attuned to the problematic nature of heroic mythology and more aware of the narrative problems that such mythology presents to filmmakers. In my analysis, I trace the origins of this new, textually flexible, less canonical hero-type to a recalibration of the status of myth that emerged in the late 1990s where critical modes such as pastiche, irony, and intertextuality encouraged a more playful and less reverent approach to mythical adaptions. Disney's *Hercules* (1997) is emblematic of this turn. This capacity to reimagine the character of Hercules has been further facilitated by the recent emergence of an audience now trained through the rise of the "mega-text" – texts whose storylines inhabit and cross multiple genres (comics, film, television shows, books, fan writing) – to think newly about topics such as canonicity, tradition, and adaptation. Myth and comic-book storylines have increasingly started to overlap in recent years.[3] Indeed, we can trace the influence of comics not only in providing subject matter, but also in the provision of new reading practices for approaching mythological storylines. In doing so, these films are able to rise to the challenge of how to represent Hercules in the post-Romantic age.

## MORE THAN PEPLUM REHEATED?

At first glance, it is tempting to see 2014's *Hercules* and *The Legend of Hercules* as direct descendants of the peplum tradition of Hercules films of the early 1960s. These genre films, produced primarily in Italy although occasionally also in France, proved extremely popular in the United States and the United Kingdom, providing fodder for numerous drive-ins and budget cinemas. These highly formulaic films, which combined action and feats of heroic strength with demure maidens and scantily clad seductresses, all set within a mythological or antique landscape, propelled their bodybuilder lead actors to international stardom. By the end of the run of peplum film in the mid-to-late 1960s, over 170 such films had been produced, and at its height over 10 percent of the Italian film industry was involved in the making of peplum films.[4]

Certainly the casting of the professional-wrestler-turned-actor Dwayne "The Rock" Johnson in *Hercules* (2014) was designed to evoke the bodybuilder tradition of former Herculeses such as Steve Reeves, Mark Forest, and Reg Park. Indeed, Johnson was not the first "Rock" to play Hercules; that title goes to the bodybuilder Peter Lupus, who played Hercules under the pseudonym "Rock Stevens" in the peplum *Hercules and the Tyrants of Babylon* (1964). A similar desire informed the casting of the muscular actor and underwear model Kellan Lutz as Hercules in *The Legend of Hercules*. Like peplum films of the 1960s, both the 2014 *Hercules* and *The Legend of Hercules* enjoy staging scenes that show off the bodies of their lead actors. For example, both films feature scenes where Lutz and Johnson reprise the famous "lateral spread" struck by Reeves in *Hercules* (1958), a pose in which the hero is chained with his arms outstretched in such a way as to emphasize his lateral, pectoral, and deltoid muscles.[5]

It is not just in bodily aesthetics that Johnson and Lutz evoked the peplum heroes of the past. They are similarly outsider figures to the profession of acting, having made their reputations in fields apart from cinema. Johnson held the record of world champion ten times for the World Wrestling Entertainment (WWE) franchise. Lutz has interspersed his acting career with an arguably more successful career in modeling and advertising. He was the face of Calvin Klein's X underwear campaign as well as the love interest in the TV advertisement for Hilary Duff's "With Love" perfume line. Like the peplum bodybuilders, both Johnson and Lutz have displayed only a limited acting range. They have been primarily cast in mainstream action films (Johnson: *The Scorpion King* (2002), the *Fast and the Furious* franchise (2001–17); Lutz: the *Twilight* franchise (2008–12), *Immortals* (2011)), where their roles have demanded little emotional breadth or nuanced acting.

The affinity between peplum and these modern Hercules films was stressed in the marketing of the films. Comparisons between Johnson and Steve Reeves abounded. Johnson repeatedly raised the figure of Reeves as his inspiration in his press interviews for the film. Even in markets where the peplum tradition had not been particularly strong such as Hong Kong, Johnson was still keen to express his infatuation with Reeves. Johnson gushed to the *South China Morning Post*:

> I grew up loving and admiring Hercules [played by Reeves]. There's that iconic moment where Hercules breaks his chains from the pillars and screams "I am Hercules!" For me, as a kid, that was a mesmerising moment. I remember having a poster of Steve Reeves, in the old days, where those posters look painted, so I was always inspired by it.[6]

The director, Brett Ratner, was also keen to place the film within the peplum cinematic genealogy. In the same interview, he drew direct comparisons between Johnson and the bodybuilder Herculeses of the past: "We all loved Steve Reeves, we all loved Arnold [Schwarzenegger]. But for this generation, Dwayne is the ultimate Hercules."

Superficially in terms of narrative structure, there is some similarity between the films of 2014 and the 1960s. Reflecting their post-war political context, peplum films were often based on a story of a fight against oppression. The overthrow of tyranny and the freeing of an enslaved population was one of Hercules' standard tasks in these films.[7] The enemy might change its appearance – sometimes it was a vampy queen, sometimes a wicked bearded king, sometimes a hairy Mongol chieftain – but its core ideology remained the same: totalitarian despotism. Fifty or so years later, both Lutz and Johnson also found themselves pitted against the forces of tyranny. Lutz leads a rebellion against King Amphitryon of Tiryns (Scott Adkins), who desires to bring all of Greece under his control, while Johnson battles King Cotys of Thrace (John Hurt), who conspires with King Eurystheus (Joseph Fiennes) to achieve the same end. The climactic sequence of the 2014 *Hercules*, where Johnson topples the colossal statue of Hera, mimics the equivalent scene in the most famous of the pepla, the 1958 *Hercules*, where Reeves pulls down the portico of the palace of Pelias. Like Reeves, Johnson turns the chains that bind him into deadly weapons, flailing all who come before him.

Yet while the plotlines and the athletic bodies that inhabit them remain the same, the frame in which these adventures occur, and the critical purpose for which they are enacted, have shifted dramatically. Peplum cinema was largely focused on perpetuating mainstream values.[8] In contrast, the "new Hercules" is much more open to interrogating such values. These films may end up reaffirming conventional morality, but this is not before it is given a critical review. The Hercules of peplum cinema was a wholesome, virtuous figure who knew his place in the world and whose moral compass never wavered. The modern Hercules is a more damaged individual who is plagued by doubt and uncertainties. In an interview, Steve Moore commented on the distance between peplum and his comic *Hercules: The Thracian Wars*,

> I saw the Italian Steve Reeves Hercules movies when I was a kid, which look great when you're 10 and have the advantage that, no matter how hammy they are, they do play the story straight. But they have a completely different feel to the sort of grim fatalism I'm bringing to the story.[9]

Moore describes the peplum films as playing the story "straight" and this highlights another difference between these films and peplum. These new Hercules figures stand in a different relationship with the canons of Greek mythology. The two most important examples of the genre, the 1958 *Hercules* and *Hercules Unchained* (1959), positioned themselves as firmly within the realm of authoritative myth. They took their storyline from established mythic exemplar. This *Hercules* reworks the story of Jason and his pursuit of the Golden Fleece, while *Hercules Unchained* places its plot within the narrative of the *Seven Against Thebes*. This continuity with the myth was signaled by the title sequences in these films, in which the *Argonautica* of Apollonius of Rhodes, the *Aedipus* [sic] *at Colonus* by Sophocles, and *The Seven Against Thebes* by Aeschylus are cited as sources, even if the titles do admit that the cinematic versions are "freely adapted" from this material. The implicit claim of these films is that their action takes place clearly within the world of traditional myth. The filmmaker merely replaces the poet in chronicling the adventures of the hero. The conceit of these films is that we are being presented with the versions that would have come down to us if Apollonius or Sophocles had been given access to a camera. In contrast, the new Hercules films stand critically detached from the myths that inspired the films. They circle around these myths, critiquing and deconstructing them.

## THE RISE OF THE IRONIC AND METATEXTUAL HERO-NARRATIVE: DISNEY'S *HERCULES* (1997)

In looking for the origins of this new critical sensibility, it is worthwhile considering intervening cinematic texts between the peplum films of the 1960s and the Hercules films of 2014. We need to consider precursor films that facilitated, or at least signaled the possibility of, the type of thinking found in the 2014 *Hercules*. Just as it is impossible to tell the story of *Gladiator* (2000) and the revival of the Roman epic without thinking through films such as *Amistad* (1997) that helped established both DreamWorks and David Franzoni as the studio and the writer respectively for historical epics, so too we should consider the films that help to create the conditions of possibility for the creation of the new Hercules films. A candidate that deserves consideration in such a context is Disney's *Hercules* (1997).

From its opening scene, Disney's *Hercules* signaled its distance from the preceding cinematic tradition surrounding this Greek hero. The film opens seemingly conventionally with a panning shot through a museum collection of classical sculpture while Charlton Heston, a voice synonymous with epic cine-antiquity, intones about an age of gods and heroes. At this point, the film seems set to replicate the standard heroic narratives stylized in peplum cinema. However, suddenly the new, lively voice of a black female cuts across Heston's monologue. The voice comes from one of the Muses portrayed on one of the vases in the museum. She berates the narrator for his portentous, solemn tone and promises to tell the story of Hercules in a more fitting manner. Together with her sister Muses, she highjacks the narrative, redirecting the film away from its peplum predecessors and toward a much more ironic and self-reflexive outcome. In a knowing wink to the flavor of the film, the opening number is ironically called "The Gospel Truth," but everything about the song from its populist vocabulary and anachronistic lyrics to its jazzy, flippant style calls into question its status as an account of myth. This sets the tone for the rest of the film. The film revels in anachronism and incongruity.

The references to contemporary popular culture are legion. It plays fast and loose with its mythic source material.

The irreverence toward mythic and cinematic precedent was a deliberate move on the part of the film's directors, John Musker and Ron Clements. "Hercules appealed to us because it didn't seem as sacred a thing as something like the *Odyssey*. We had to feel that whatever we chose, we would be able to take quite a few liberties."[10] The effect of this move on the part of Disney was to frame the Hercules hero-narrative as one where a wide variety of possibilities existed. It challenged the idea that there was an authentic Herculean narrative and altered the task of the filmmaker. Previously the task of the filmmaker working with the Herculean material had been to attempt to graft new limbs on to the main trunk of tradition; filmmaking that privileged consistency with cinematic precedent rather than radical divergence. Disney's *Hercules* raised the potential that Hercules could be remade anew. It made the narrative extremely porous to contemporary concerns about the rise of celebrity culture, the disintegration of the nuclear family, and negotiating the passage from adolescence to manhood.

As well as introducing a new sensibility toward myth and preceding traditions of representation, Disney's *Hercules* also displays a number of other features that proved important in subsequent depictions of Hercules in cinema. The film created a mythic space in which other cinematic narratives and intertexts could permeate. It is full of allusions to other popular films. Additionally, one of the freedoms that Disney's *Hercules* establishes for itself is the freedom to insert celebrity into antiquity. The film does not try to hide the star power of its voice-actors. Using a technique employed in *Aladdin* (1992) for the representation of Robin Williams' Genie, Hercules' satyr trainer is a barely transformed Danny DeVito. Philoctetes (Phil) has the same small stature, portly physique, and facial features as the star actor. When Steve Reeves became Hercules, he did so as a relatively unknown figure, famous only within the selective and marginal world of professional bodybuilding. He could become Hercules – and in an important sense only Hercules – because there was no cinematic trace of him prior to the film. He was anonymous in the way that Dwayne Johnson can never be. In significant ways, in the 2014 *Hercules*, you can never see Hercules and not see "the Rock," and creating a space for this to happen is important. Finally, Disney's *Hercules* reorders narrative priorities away from labors and adventures toward the goal of personal development. For example, the labors of Hercules are dispensed with via a breezy montage in a musical number ("Zero to Hero"). As a diagnostic tool, the film helps identify the capacity that emerged toward the end of the twentieth century for rewriting the Hercules myth.

## NEW HEROISM IN THE AGE OF THE MEGA-TEXT

The irreverence toward mythic traditions displayed by Disney's *Hercules* opened up new ways of telling the Hercules story on film. The most recent Hercules films benefit tremendously from the latitude created by this. In addition, they have been assisted by the rise of a new sensibility toward ideas of the canon and continuity. The "turn to irony" of mid-to-late 1990s popular culture helped complicate the relationship between source text and adaptation. This relationship has only been further complicated by the rise of the genre-crossing "mega-text."

The term "mega-text" was developed by Daniel Bernardi in his attempt to analyze the socio-cultural effects of the *Star Trek* franchise. For Bernardi, it was important to recognize that *Star Trek* existed not just in one medium, but rather as

> a relatively coherent and seemingly unending enterprise of televisual, filmic, auditory, and written texts. In addition to the four prime-time series, the cartoon series, and the eight films, there is a gushing current of comic books, magazines, novels, compendia, biographies, and autobiographies ... scholars contribute ... probably the largest group of producers of Trek texts are the fans, who write and distribute thousands of original stories ... and disperse hundreds of thousands of comments and criticisms about the mega-text in cyberspace.[11]

Bernardi subtitled his discussion of the *Star Trek* mega-text "Where no text has gone before," and while it may be true that *Star Trek* was the first mega-text, it certainly was not the last. Facilitated by the amalgamation of media companies, the rise of cross-media ownership, and the general trend for media convergence, mega-texts have proliferated. The *Star Wars* franchise is just as prevalent and polyvalent as *Star Trek*. Marvel and DC Comics now have large film presences in addition to their proliferation in television shows, video games, books, and fan fiction. Indeed, at times the model of the mega-text seems to be the only viable model for mainstream popular imaginative works. As a stand-alone producer of comics, Marvel filed for bankruptcy in December 1996. However, reinvented as the license holder for multiple products in film comics and video games series, Marvel is a powerhouse, arguably one of the most significant forces in contemporary culture.[12] Chuck Tyron has done much to show how traditional ways of consuming cinematic products have been revolutionized by the new environment of media convergence to such an extent that it is no longer possible to think of popular cinema as a stand-alone product.[13] Whereas films would once have been conceived as individual products that were then "spun off" into other modes of representation, they now originate as multi-platform entities with gaming, DVD, and fiction markets built in from the very beginning. We live in the age of the entertainment franchise.[14]

In attempting to understand the narrative complexities and dynamics of the mega-text, scholars have regularly compared it to a form of mythology. The value of this insight is not just that it recognizes that the relationship between myth and the mega-text lies in thematic content, so that, for example *Star Trek II: The Wrath of Khan* (1982) perpetuates an archetypical mythic death/rebirth cycle, or that both *Star Wars* and *Star Trek* perpetuate the "American monomyth" of the redeemed hero.[15] Rather it is valuable because it includes a recognition that in its sprawling complexities, numerous potential inconsistencies, and multi-vocal nature, the contemporary mega-text shares many features with mythological systems.

Making sense of the mega-text has produced a new type of consumer of popular culture, one much more adept at dealing with multiple narratives and their inevitable inconsistencies and incongruities. This new way of reading was recognized by the narratologist Karin Kukkonen in her 2010 essay "Navigating Infinite Earths."[16] In contrast to previous models of readership, which resisted the idea of multiple contradictory narratives and attempted to assimilate discordant narratives into "subworlds" where they could be explained away as "allegories" or "dreams" (*Alice in Wonderland* is paradigmatic here), contemporary readers, especially those familiar with comic-book storylines,

> take a multiworld model of reality – the multiverse – largely as an ontological given. The storyworlds of the superhero multiverse involve not just plural ... "subworlds," that is the imaginings, hopes, and beliefs of characters ... but rather fully parallel, equally actualized realities.[17]

Such reading practices are necessitated by commercial practices where the complexities of licenses mean that different creative companies can own the license to produce narratives for characters that theoretically share the same fictional universe. The most notable of these complex rights agreements involves the Marvel franchise, where rights to individual characters are divided between Marvel, Sony, and

Twentieth Century Fox. This has resulted in a number of parallel and contradictory storylines and different silos of continuity where narratives might be consistent within one studio's output (e.g. the Marvel Cinematic Universe), but irreconcilable with the output of another. Consumers have become adept at dealing with the idea that origin stories can be written and rewritten for the purposes of continuity ("ret-con-ed") or that narratives can be either "canon" or "non-canon." The "reboot experience" is now a commonplace feature of contemporary science-fiction and fantasy franchises.[18] Importantly, many fans have now come to expect these reworkings of familiar storylines to provide something different, with stories that are too faithful to original source material being dismissed as "retreads."[19]

The effect of these new consumption practices is that when filmmakers and viewers approach the Hercules story, they do through the frame of the mega-text. Such a move is understandable. Were it not for the absence of a primary rights-holder, the Hercules storyline has all the attributes of a popular franchise. It crosses genres into film, TV, cartoons, comics, and video games. Collectively, it is a rambling, expansive set of narratives as diverse and incongruous as any contemporary mega-text. Parallels can be drawn with the Tarzan franchise, which display a similar diversity of trans-media representations.[20]

The freedom offered by the mega-text's practice of ret-con-ed origin stories and multiple narratives means that not only are filmmakers freer to reinvent the Hercules myth, but they can play with audience expectations about such reinvention. Fans who have grown up on the mega-text, especially in its comic-book instantiations, know that much latitude is possible. For example, *Fantastic Four* (2005) has the group gaining their powers while visiting a space station and being affected by cosmic rays, while in *Fantastic Four* (2015), their powers are caused by a teleportation accident on a trip to a mysterious planet "Zero." In *Spider-Man* (2002, dir. Sam Raimi), Peter Parker becomes Spider-Man through being bitten by a genetically enhanced superspider while on a school trip and can produce webs from his wrists. In *Amazing Spider-Man* (2012), Parker's powers are partly due to work done on cross-species genetics by his father and they don't include the ability to produce webs. In *Spider-Man: Homecoming* (2017) he is given a new family backstory. The cumulative effects of these constant rewritings of popular narratives is that audiences know that while certain key features of any popular narrative will remain in a cinematic reworking, they do not know exactly which ones will be kept and which will be rejected.

*The Legend of Hercules* plays with these new narrative possibilities. Midway through the film, while on campaign in Egypt, the commander of the Greek troops gestures toward an eagle hovering protectively over the men, "Some say the golden eagle's a sign from Zeus." It is an idea quickly dismissed by Hercules, "Yes, and some believe it's just a bird." This is a paradigmatic moment in the film. Our uncertainty about whether the bird is a divine omen or just an opportunistic scavenger reflects the central conceit of this film, namely that it is not clear until the final scene whether Hercules is actually a demigod, the son of Zeus, or not. Confirmation of this fact is constantly deferred throughout the film. His divine status is eventually confirmed at the end of the film when he harnesses a bolt of lightning to slay his enemies – oddly, a revelation that comes through a power not attested in myth – but until this point Hercules' status has remained ambiguous.

In this film, Hercules is pitted against his father Amphitryon, a bloodthirsty tyrant who desires to conquer all of Greece and hates his son, who he believes is the illegitimate offspring of his wife's infidelity. The lover who cuckolded Amphitryon is never shown. While the conception scene at the start of the film seems to support Hercules' claims to divinity, it is not complete proof. Zeus is pointedly not shown, and while the raging lightning and thunder that accompany Alcmene's orgasms support the idea of the father being Zeus, Amphitryon's actions raise a specter of doubt. When he enters, he has no doubt that he has caught his wife with a mortal lover. The scene leaves it open as to precisely what has happened. Is Alcmene a religious fanatic who has deluded herself into believing she is sleeping with a god? The mad priestess she met prior to this promised her a visit by the god, but can we trust her? The possibility that Hercules (given the name Alcides by his father) is not the son of Zeus (and what this might mean in any case) is maintained for the majority of the film. Throughout most of the movie Hercules does nothing so heroic that it would call into question his mortality. After his birth, twenty years supposedly pass without any incident of note and when we return to the action, Hercules seems to be nothing but a well-meaning young man with a buff body and a nice smile.

In keeping with the suppression of the supernatural in this film, the monsters that Hercules faces in this film are prosaic rather than fantastic. When the Nemean lion appears it is unclear whether it is lack of skill that makes the spears useless against it or an impenetrable hide. No Hydra, Stymphalian bird, or other unnatural creature make an appearance. Instead, the greatest danger is presented by an ambush of Egyptian soldiers. Indeed, in the ambush scene the film plays with its denial of the fantastic. On first sighting, the shadows of the Egyptian soldiers make them resemble either a multi-bodied giant or the heads of the Hydra before resolving into the shadows of a pack of men, confounding the expectations of those familiar with Herculean mythology.

The narrative capaciousness afforded by the "reboot" genre allows *The Legend of Hercules* to play with its subject matter and take a few storyline-hopping detours along the way. The scenes where Hercules is condemned to row in the galleys, for example, owe much to the galley sequences from *Ben-Hur* (1959), while Hercules' time fighting in the arena is derivative of *Gladiator*. Yet despite these pastiche elements and the central is-he-isn't-he plot tease, the film ultimately ends up conforming to the standard Herculean narrative. Hercules arrives back in Greece in time to rescue the girl and overthrow his father.

While *The Legend of Hercules* offers a substantial "reboot" to the Hercules storyline, it fails to harness the radical potential that the turn toward self-reflection and metatheatricality allows. In contrast, the 2014 *Hercules* takes up this challenge. This film is a story in love with storytelling. The opening scene of the film initiates its thematic concerns with truth and fiction. The opening words are "You think you know the truth about him. You know nothing." The audience is then treated to a highlights package of Hercules' greatest hits. In less than four minutes we see the infant Hercules strangle the snakes sent to kill him while the adult Hercules is shown dispatching the Hydra, the Erymanthian boar, and the Nemean lion. Although not quite as efficient as Disney's "Zero to Hero" sequence (which only requires two minutes and twenty seconds), the sequence does effectively remove the mainstays of Herculean myth from the narrative and allows space for a new story to emerge. More importantly, this sequence also serves to problematize the status of these stories, as it quickly emerges that these myths are just stories that Iolaus has invented to distract his captors until Hercules can arrive to save him. "What a load of crap.... You know what I think? This friend of yours doesn't even exist," declares Gryza, the leader of the pirates that have captured Iolaus. And he's right. This Hercules is just a mortal around whom fabulous stories have grown up.

In making Hercules resolutely mortal, the film presents a significant challenge to traditional mythic narratives. This was not the first time that Hercules had been made mortal in the twenty-first century. The made-for-television *Hercules* (2005) is based on a similar premise.[21]

Figure 2.1 Confounding expectations as the Centaurs prove just to be an optical illusion in *Hercules* (2014). Paramount Pictures.

However, for the 2014 *Hercules*, the mortal origins of Hercules are just the start of a major act of reinvention. Scriptwriter Evan Spiliotopoulos has described the film as a "complete deconstruction of the myth."[22] In franchise terms, it is a complete reboot. Throughout the film the traditional features of the Hercules myths are undercut and rationalized at every point. Centaurs prove to be just a trick of the light, nothing more than men mounted on horseback. Monstrous opponents turn out to be nothing but men in costume (Figure 2.1). Cerberus turns out to be just the product of drug-induced delirium. In a key scene midway through the film, the royal princess Ergenia (Rebecca Ferguson) discusses the myths about Hercules with his companions. Again concerns with truth – its dynamics, where to locate it, and how to determine it – predominate:

> "Is it true? Did Hercules slaughter his own family?".... "No myths, I want the truth".... "No one knows the truth. Not for sure.".... "You know how a rumor spreads. How a legend grows".... "And that, my Lady, is the truth".... "The truth (scoffs), whatever the truth, the death of his loved one haunts Hercules. Only the gods can help him, if he listens."

Here we learn that the stories about Hercules – namely everything the audience knows about the hero – are just fictions promulgated by his crew to scare their enemies.

In so deliberately undercutting the mythical Hercules, the film makes a significant departure from the spirit and conception of the comics on which the film was based. In an interview with Mike Conroy appended to the hardcover complete edition of *Hercules: The Thracian Wars*, Steve Moore self-identified as a pagan and explained the implications for his treatment of Hercules:

> I've done my best to treat Hercules and the other characters with respect ... to me, Hercules is a god who deserves to be treated in the same ways as Christ, Odin, Krishna or any other deity that the human race has taken to its heart in its long and turbulent history.[23]

Moore's treatment of the Hercules myth was reverential. In a manner similar to the early peplum films, the aim of his stories was to supplement the Hercules canon, not revise it: "I've tried to do nothing that would violate the original cycle of myths ... as far as we are concerned the Twelve Labors probably did take place much as described."[24]

The rationalization of myth, such as practiced in the 2014 *Hercules*, has a long history going all the way back to antiquity itself.[25] Yet what distinguishes this example is the way that it is used to create space for the vulnerable, haunted hero. The death of his wife and children, for which Hercules holds himself responsible – incorrectly as it turns out – plagues him. He experiences night sweats and distressing dreams, and exhibits all the features of a trauma victim. His pain makes him fearful of engaging with people. "He made me vow to keep the world away from him. To make sure that he would never harm innocents again," declares Atalanta. The exterior may be strong, but inside Hercules is crippled. "He is a broken man."[26]

The all-too-mortal Herculeses of *The Legend of Hercules* and the 2014 *Hercules* help resolve one of the problems of adapting the hero for a modern audience, namely his seeming invulnerability. As Karl Galinsky has pointed out, one of the greatest obstacles to Hercules' adaption after the Renaissance has been his godhead.[27] This was a problem not only for Christians who worried about his pagan status, but for Romantics who demanded heroes who shared human frailty and susceptibility to the cruelty of fate and nature. It is for this reason that it is the suffering Hercules of Greek tragedy that predominates in the nineteenth century.[28]

## CONCLUSION

The legacy of this Romantic sensibility is still felt within contemporary popular cinema. Since the 1990s, there has been a trend for

> Hollywood male star/heroes ... [to be] constructed as more internalized versions of their historical counterparts. More film time is devoted to explorations of their ethical dilemmas, emotional traumas, and psychological goals, and less to their skill with weapons, their athletic ability, or their gutsy showdowns of opponents.[29]

Hercules is catching up to this trend. In his two most recent outings, he has shown himself as anything other than the triumphant, all-conquering monster-slayer. The monsters have disappeared and it is now his inner demons that he faces. Of course, this piteous, tragic Hercules has always been present within Greek myth, but we need to acknowledge the amount of intellectual and critical work that needs to be done to bring it to the fore and make opaque sizable components of the Hercules myth. This is the result of decades of training audiences to become more flexible in their expectations about myths and to expect and appreciate narratives that draw upon multiple sources and origin points. This creates a moment when it is possible to confound expectations and rewrite myth for one's own convenience without seeming to violate any sense of authenticity. The degree of latitude is worth noting. After all, the most famous and popular thing known about Hercules is his labors. The remarkable feat of the 2014 *Hercules* and *The Legend of Hercules* is that they erase the labors and still leave a recognizable hero standing at the end.

## NOTES

1. Dethloff (2011: 103).
2. For the larger history of representations of Hercules in cinema and television, see Solomon in this volume.
3. Raucci (2015: 168).
4. Wagstaff (1998); Blanshard and Shahabudin (2011: 61).
5. Wyke (1997b: 66).
6. Mottram (2014: 6).
7. Blanshard (2017: 434, 446).
8. Lagny (1992: 170); Dyer (1996: 94–5, 1997: 169); Günsberg (2005: 97).
9. Vamvounis (2008).
10. Thomas (1997: 166).
11. Bernardi (1998: 7).
12. Johnson (2007, 2012: 1–3).
13. Tyron (2009).
14. Thompson (2007: 3–6).
15. Death/rebirth: Roth (1987). Monomyth: Jewett and Lawrence (1977: 1–23); Geraghty (2005); Curley in this volume.
16. The essay was reprinted as Kukkonen (2013).
17. Kukkonen (2013: 156).
18. Urbanski (2013).
19. Urbanski (2013: 8).
20. Morton (1993).
21. Safran (2015).
22. Sunshine and Ratner (2014: 17).
23. Conroy (2008: 125); cf. Sunshine and Rattner (2014: 173–4).

24 Conroy (2008: 126).
25 Hawes (2014).
26 Sunshine and Ratner (2014: 25).
27 Galinksy (1972: 187).
28 Galinsky (1972: 236–49).
29 Jeffords (1993: 245); cf. Spicer (2001: 195–8).

# 3 Hercules, Putin, and the Heroic Body on Screen in 2014

Emma Stafford

## INTRODUCTION: THE LABORS OF PUTIN

As noted in the two preceding chapters, 2014 saw several new instantiations of Hercules on screen. In the same year, on October 6, an extraordinary exhibition was unveiled in Moscow to celebrate the Russian president's sixty-second birthday: *The Twelve Labors of Putin* consisted of a series of paintings by anonymous artists depicting a Herculean Putin:[1]

1. wrestling the Nemean lion of terrorism;
2. fighting the many-headed Lernaean hydra of Western sanctions;
3. shooting down the Stymphalian birds/warplanes of Western intervention in Syria;
4. capturing the Ceryneian hind of the Sochi Olympics;
5. restraining an oligarchic Erymanthian boar;
6. clearing the Augean stables (here imagined as those of horses rather than the traditional cattle) of corruption;
7. taming the Cretan bull of Crimea;
8. leading home the Diomedean horses of the Mistral warship contract with France;
9. holding the Amazonian belt of the South Stream gas pipeline;
10. bringing back the Geryon's cattle of a trade deal with China;
11. holding up the world on his shoulders, Atlas-style, as champion of peace in Ukraine;
12. holding the leash of a straining Cerberus/United States.

Stylistically, they fell into four groups of three: two groups were in a modern realist style; the other two emphasized continuity with ancient Greek mythology by adopting the style of an Attic red-figure vase, the figures in red against a black background, with a border of meander patterns. In most cases Putin was depicted in classical dress, wearing a short tunic that sometimes covered just one shoulder, leaving half his chest bare; this was sometimes complemented by leather armbands, and often revealed bare thighs; in three cases (labors 4–6) the upper part of the tunic was replaced by a golden corselet, above knee-high greaves. The exhibition was organized by Mikhail Antonov, leader of a Putin supporters group on Facebook, so this was a popular expression of enthusiasm rather than state propaganda. However, it was quite in keeping with the steady stream of official news-reports and photos promoting an image of Putin as a macho, hunting and fishing, outdoors hero – as I write the Kremlin has released a 46-minute video of the bare-chested president swimming, diving, and spear-fishing on his annual August holiday in the Siberian lakes.[2] While perhaps a source of wry amusement for external observers, within Russia this Herculean imagery seems to work – as one reporter commented on the 2014 exhibition: "despite the pressure that Russia is under from Western sanctions, Vladimir Putin has been enjoying the kind of approval ratings of late domestically that Western politicians, and even Hercules himself, could only dream of."[3]

Such an appropriation of Hercules in political imagery has a very long history. In antiquity, leaders from Alexander the Great to Nero, Domitian, and Commodus were identified with the hero via portraiture depicting them with his trademark lionskin and club, especially in the ubiquitous medium of coinage, and similar usage surfaces at regular intervals across Europe from the Renaissance onward.[4] In the twentieth century, the identification of the political leader with a strongman figure can be seen most strikingly in the case of Mussolini, who promoted athletics as conducive to a fascist ideal of masculinity, and had himself photographed in such macho guises as that of a skier stripped to the waist.[5] Jacqueline Reich has recently argued persuasively for a link between this ideology and the films featuring the hero Maciste (played by former dock-worker Bartolomeo Pagano), often identified with Hercules, who enjoyed enormous popularity from his debut as a black African slave in *Cabiria* (1914), via an extraordinary transformation into the immaculately dressed white hero of *Maciste* (1915), through a spinoff series that ran until 1926.[6] A more recent example is Arnold Schwarzenegger, who actually played the part of Hercules in his debut film *Hercules in New York* (1970) and later embodied the strongman hero of *Conan the Barbarian* (1982), before graduating to political prominence as governor of California

(2003–11), parallels with his film characters being exploited in his campaigning and throughout his two terms in office. Robert Rushing has explored this and other examples of the "biopolitics of the muscled male body on screen," surveying the peplum genre – broadly defined as encompassing a wide variety of strongman films and TV series from Maciste to the present day – and demonstrating multiple ways in which it has mediated a popular ideal of "the muscular hero as a protector of the state."[7] Rushing builds on earlier scholarship on the cultural significance of the mid-twentieth-century peplum, and especially its mediation of contemporary notions of masculinity.[8] Scholarship by classicists has also made an important contribution in this area.[9]

My aim here is to review the Herculean displays of 2014 in light of this scholarship on earlier material, comparing the Putin exhibition to three films that preceded it earlier in the year. The films in question are Renny Harlin's *The Legend of Hercules* (released January 2014), Brett Ratner's *Hercules* (released in July 2014), and Nick Lyon's low-budget, direct-to-video "mockbuster" *Hercules Reborn* (also released in July 2014). I shall focus particularly on aesthetic elements: the visual presentation of their central figure – his costume, his accoutrements, and the type of action shots that showcase the heroic body – and the settings against which the heroic action occurs.

Harlin's and Ratner's works have already been well introduced in the chapters by Jon Solomon and Alastair Blanshard in this volume, the latter having demonstrated that there are many respects in which these two films transcend the mid-twentieth-century peplum genre. A few introductory words are needed, however, for *Hercules Reborn*, which provides some instructive comparisons to the two Hollywood films, its lower production values meaning that the hero's presentation is reduced to essentials. One important narrative difference is its demotion of Hercules to a secondary role, the protagonist and romantic lead being Arius Dudunakis (Christian Oliver), constantly accompanied by his friend Horace (James Duval). The significance of Hercules to the story, however, is flagged not only by the film's title, but by the sequence which accompanies the opening titles: inside a shadowy palace, a woman's screams are heard before she comes into view, desperately trying to escape with three children, only to be overtaken by a raging Hercules, who rips the statue of a falcon from its setting and hurls it down on top of them; afterward, we see an armed male figure stealthily recorking a bottle. This suitably horrifying rendition of Hercules' madness apes that in Ratner's *Hercules*, and performs a similar role in providing an explanation for the hero's initially less-than-heroic state and motivation for his eventual overthrow of the villain, who (it transpires) was actually responsible for Megara and the children's death. The film's action begins "10 years later" in the city of Enos, where the evil general Nikos (Dylan Vox) overthrows the king and queen before forcing himself on Arius' fiancée, princess Theodora (Christina Ulfsparre), brutally killing the wife and child of Arius' cousin Tymek (Jeremy Inman) and generally terrorizing the *populus*; Arius and Horace must find Hercules and return to save the city. In the United Kingdom, *Hercules Reborn* has a British Board of Film Classification 15 certificate, as compared to the other two films' 12 rating, reflecting "strong" rather than "moderate" violence. It shares the other films' affectation of BBC English accents for the main characters, despite the fact that not one of the actors concerned is from the United Kingdom.

## COSTUMING THE HERCULEAN BODY OF 2014

As noted already in this volume, the casting of Dwayne "The Rock" Johnson in Ratner's *Hercules* calls on a tradition stretching back to the 1950s and 1960s and the bodybuilder stars of the peplum genre proper. Born in 1972, at 42 Dwayne Johnson was a little older than most of his predecessors in the role – Steve Reeves was 32 in *Hercules* (1958), Reg Park about the same age in *Hercules Conquers Atlantis* (1961), Arnold Schwarzenegger a mere 23 in *Hercules in New York* – a maturity in keeping with the narrative inspired by the graphic novel on which the film is based. In the interview by Mike Conroy, Steve Moore himself comments that his protagonist is:

> still a ferocious warrior, but rather older than he's usually portrayed and with more in the way of character flaws and human relationships... we've taken a slight liberty in making Hercules and his companions about 40 years old.[10]

Nonetheless, Johnson's vital statistics are more impressive than that of his fellow 2014 Herculeses: he is the tallest at 6 foot 5 inches (1.96 meters), the heaviest at 262 pounds (18¾ stone), and has seventeen championship reigns in World Wrestling Entertainment (WWE) to his name, including ten as world champion, as well as a substantial filmography. Attention was drawn to his physique in pre-film publicity such as interviews in *Train* magazine and *Muscle and Fitness* concerning a punishing regime that even had its own Twitter hashtag, #HerculesWorkout; this was accompanied by #12LaborsDiet ("What kind of meal plan did The Rock follow to get his immortal physique for Hercules?"), followed for twenty-two weeks and consisting of seven meals a day packed with protein, carbs, and fat – including the tongue-in-cheek item "1 cup Nemean Lion blood upon rising (served fresh and warm)."[11] Johnson's sheer size allows him to tower over other actors, even without the exploitation of clever camera angles, and his size is the butt of the occasional humorous remark. Another WWE star was cast in *Hercules Reborn*, John Hennigan – also known as John Morrison, Johnny Nitro, or Johnny Mundo. Born in 1979, so 35 in 2014, he is of more modest proportions than Johnson, but still matches Steve Reeves' height of 6 foot 1 inch (1.85 meters), and weighs in at a solid 224 pounds (16 stone). His wrestling titles include three WWE Intercontinental Championships and one Extreme Championship Wrestling (ECW) World Heavyweight Championship. By contrast, *Legend of Hercules* star Kellan Lutz's background in male modeling and acting suggests a softer image, more in the mold of Kevin Sorbo in *Hercules: The Legendary Journeys* (1995–9).[12] He is again 6 foot 1 inch (1.85 meters) tall, but a mere 176 pounds (12½ stone), and born in 1985, so 29 in 2014.

The difference in the three actors' ages is underlined by the designers' decisions about hair. Lutz's Hercules has the same short cut the actor sports when modeling for Calvin Klein and is more or less clean-shaven; Hennigan's has unruly long hair contrasting with fairly short facial hair – again not far from the actor's regular off-set look; Johnson's meanwhile, in complete contrast to the bald, clean-shaven look espoused by the actor for some years, has long hair accompanied by a luxuriant beard. This yak's-fur beard was one of the reasons it reportedly took three hours every day to get Johnson into his costume, and is much mentioned in interviews.[13] The beard is amongst a number of elements that Ratner's film does *not* take from the graphic novel.[14] It is, however, a fairly regular feature in the mid-twentieth-century peplum – sported e.g. by Steve Reeves, Reg Park, and Alan Steele – as it is of ancient Greek and Roman representations of the hero, although instances of a beardless Heracles/Hercules can be found from the fifth century BC onward, especially in contexts where there is some narrative justification for a younger look.

The physique of all three 2014 heroes is displayed to the best possible effect by their costumes. Our first sight of Lutz in *The Legend* as Hercules has him decorously clothed in a white tunic, astride a white horse, alongside the similarly accoutred Hebe (Gaia Weiss): both are thus immediately coded as good, in contrast to the dark-haired, blue-clad Iphicles, who conspires against the innocent couple throughout the film.[15] Hercules' white tunic is back in place in the last two scenes of the film, in the very domestic tableau where he reclines on a four-poster bed with Hebe and their new baby, and again as he walks the battlements, white cloak billowing in the moonlight. In between, however, he is more often than not bare-chested. The romantic nature of his relationship with Hebe, and of the plot as a whole, is established early on in the scene where he climbs the cliff beside a waterfall before taking a death-defying plunge into the pool below. The narrative justifies his having stripped to a tasteful white loincloth, and the camera can linger on his sexily wet torso when he emerges to embrace the anxious Hebe – herself now sporting the wet-tunic look. Once Hercules has been effectively banished, and fallen into the hands of the fight-promoter Lucius, Lutz is seen stripped to the waist in action, his taut torso displayed against leather armbands, shorts, and footwear. Water is again used to enhance the bare flesh on display in his first fight-scene in Sicily,[16] and even the armor he wears in the arena back in Tiryns leaves his chest and thighs open to view.

Hennigan's character likewise spends much of *Hercules Reborn* topless, his bare chest set off by leather armbands and a sword-belt across one shoulder; a short leather skirt leaving his legs bare from mid-thigh to mid-calf, above cloth- and leather-bound footwear. The bare flesh is frequently spattered with blood, reflecting the film's relatively violent tenor overall; the relative nudity is emphasized by

Figure 3.1 Arius (Christian Oliver), Horace (James Duval), and Hercules (John Hennigan) contemplate how to breach the defenses of Enos in *Hercules Reborn* (2014). Asylum.

the fact that his companions Arius and Horace remain permanently clothed (Figure 3.1). The aesthetic here might be compared to Zack Snyder's *300* (2007), infamous for its costumes showcasing the nude male torso framed by leather shorts and shoulder straps, or the STARZ *Spartacus* series (2010–13), though of course frequent baring of the male chest has always been a feature of the peplum genre. Significantly, the only occasions on which Hennigan's Hercules is covered up, in a hooded cloak, is when he is not himself – when in disguise in order to enter Enos by stealth, and previously when drunk in a tavern in Sagev, "city of the lost souls," before being recruited to Arius' cause. The character's dereliction at this point is justified, of course, by the premise of his post-madness remorse, but it brings to mind the Hercules of Greek Old Comedy – especially Aristophanes' *Frogs* – drunk and belching, thrown out of the tavern for not having paid his bar bill. There is comedy, too, in the chorus of tavern regulars declaring "I am Hercules!" in a parody of the famous scene in *Spartacus* (1960), when they hear that a reward is being offered. When the drunken, vomiting Hercules himself makes the same claim, Arius and Horace do not believe him: the identification can only properly be made the next day, when a sobered-up Hercules springs to their defense, cloak thrown aside, bare chest and shoulders soon streaked with the blood of Nikos' men; this time, his quiet "I am Hercules" is accepted. At the very end of the film, Hercules makes a brief appearance "scrubbed up," wearing body armor and with hair tidied into a ponytail – but as soon as he has politely declined the generalship of the newly crowned Arius and Theodora's army, he reverts to body-revealing type, his bare flesh shown off to advantage as he rides away from Enos astride a white horse.

By contrast to this emphasis on the bared chest, in the 2014 *Hercules*, Johnson's impressive upper body is more often than not clad in a leather corselet. This is, however, molded to mimic the muscles beneath, drawing the viewer's attention all the more to his powerful biceps, while a short leather skirt again reveals his legs from mid-thigh to mid-calf, above substantial leather sandals. We only see him topless twice, the first time being when Ergenia is treating his shoulder-wound after the battle in the Bessi heartland, the occasion providing motivation for the removal of his armor. The second is the much lengthier sequence that starts when Hercules comes round from a blow to the head to find himself chained in a cave, his companions imprisoned around him. His relative nudity here initially signifies his weak position – a prisoner stripped of his armor and weapons – but as he strains against the chains in his desperation to save Ergenia from execution, egged on by Amphiaraus, lingering shots of his glistening chest, back, and shoulders articulate the transformation from helplessness to strength, leading up to the climactic moment where he rips the chains from their setting and quite literally leaps into action. As Blanshard notes in this volume, the accompanying battle-cry "I am Hercules!" is an homage to Steve Reeves in the 1958 *Hercules*, but it is striking that the statement of identity should once again coincide with the revelation of the bared torso. Hercules continues bare-chested for the remaining twelve minutes of the film, semi-nudity now signifying his revived strongman status, throughout the companions' escape and final triumph over Cotys.

The potential sex appeal of the scantily clad muscleman for different demographics was noted as long ago as 1974 by Joseph Levine in an interview about the 1958 *Hercules*: "And the picture had Steve Reeves. He appealed to women, and some men."[17] Scholars have discussed the peplum's tendency to set "aberrant" desire within a conservative framework, and the methods employed in the peplum for the repression of homoeroticism, along with their (arguable) lack of success.[18] It is perhaps surprising that any such need for repression should be felt in 2014, but it is certainly the case that all three of our films keep within the safe confines of heteronormativity by a variety of tactics.[19] In *The Legend*, for example, the potential eroticism of Lutz's bare torso can be allowed free rein in the securely heterosexual context of scenes with Hebe; in the almost exclusively masculine contexts of battle and gladiatorial competition, however, this potential is kept in check by presentation of the bare flesh as dirty, blood-streaked, or wounded – as well as by the heroic body's constant employment in violent action. Altogether, *The Legend* is quite conservative in its focus on a traditional girl–boy relationship, uncomplicated by any hint of alternative love-interests, let alone any alternative sexualities. The post-madness setting of the plots of both *Hercules* and *Hercules Reborn* makes any romance for the hero problematic – assumed guilt for the murder of first wife Megara drives both heroes until the revelation of another's perfidy toward the end of the film. *Hercules Reborn* neatly sidesteps the issue by displacing the only romantic relationship onto Arius, not providing any potential love-interest at all for Hercules himself; the potential appeal of the hero's body to the viewer is again limited by its embroilment in bloody action. A more subtle approach is taken by *Hercules*, in which the widowed Thracian princess Ergenia is a strong contender for his interest, but reminders of Megara repeatedly intrude when the possibility of romance seems to be in the air. The wound-tending scene mentioned above, for example, is followed by a shot of the topless Hercules lying on his back to sleep, with firelight playing on the bare flesh of his arms, chest, and thighs – but any eroticism is quickly extinguished by the nightmare flashback to Megara's death, and by the time Hercules emerges from the shelter he is wearing a leather undershirt. At the start of the later sequence, there is certainly potential for an erotic viewing of the chained Hercules, but once again visions of Megara intervene, and soon we are swept away by the frenetic pace of the action.

The most distinctive element of Johnson's costume in *Hercules* is the very realistic lionskin that complements the corselet. It is worn in the fashion of the Heracles depicted on archaic Greek vases, that is with the upper jaw drawn up over the hero's head like a hood, the rest hanging down over his shoulders – the canonical style for all later imitators, including Steve Moore's Hercules. In the opening scene, it is the lion's head we see first, momentarily looking straight at us, until Hercules raises his lowered head to show his own face. Not only does the lionskin serve as an immediate identifier, being Hercules' most recognizable attribute across the ages, but it is also a reminder of the killing of the Nemean lion. Traditionally the first labor, and the single most frequently depicted of the hero's exploits in antiquity – in surviving Attic vase-painting alone, there are more than 800 examples of the scene – the story is being told just before Hercules' entrance, accompanied by magnificent CGI. Iolaus' narration of the labors is of course problematized, the strong suggestion being that these adventures never really happened, but Johnson's leonine costume seems to provide evidence to the contrary – a contradiction only finally resolved in the end credits sequence.[20] The Nemean lion encounter is also narrated in *The Legend*, in the more straightforward style and with the lack of conviction typical of its appearances in the mid-twentieth-century peplum, from the 1958 *Hercules* onward. However, Hercules inexplicably allows Iphicles not only to take the credit for his own bare-handed victory but also to wear the lion's pelt on their return to the palace. Once Hercules has begun to establish a following toward the end of the film, he appears on horseback wearing a lionskin over his armor, but its identity as that of the Nemean lion is uncertain – the head is not visible, no explanation is offered for its acquisition – and, as O'Brien comments, it "receives little emphasis given its narrative and thematic significance"[21] (Figure 3.2). The lion motif is completely absent from *Hercules Reborn*.

Figure 3.2 Dwayne Johnson in *Hercules* (2014), wielding the club and wearing the lionskin. Paramount Pictures.

## THE HERCULEAN BODY IN ACTION

Wrestling the Nemean lion provides Lutz and Johnson with an opportunity for muscular display, in a tradition that goes right back to depictions of the Nemean lion encounter in Greek art. The narrative excuse for bare-handed engagement with the beast is, of course, the lionskin's invulnerability, a motif first spelt out in literature in a victory ode by Bacchylides (13.46–54), appropriately celebrating the success of Pytheas of Aigina, winner of the all-out wrestling at Nemea in the 480s BC: "with all kinds of skill Perseus' descendant [i.e. Heracles] lays neck-breaking hand on the flesh-eating lion, for glittering, man-taming bronze refuses to pierce its unapproachable body, and his sword was bent back."[22]

This provided ideal subject matter for contemporary Greek art, which was especially interested in the nude, athletic male body, using the late archaic/early classical period's new techniques in both sculpture and painting to depict it from a variety of angles. Likewise the peplum has traditionally included a lion-wrestling scene, or invoked the classical tradition of Hercules' encounter with Antaeus, the giant who can only be beaten if lifted up, away from the strength-restoring power of his mother earth – as memorably depicted in *Hercules Unchained* (1959), where the giant is played by former Italian heavyweight boxing champion Primo Carnera. Wrestling sits alongside other vehicles for bodily display, such as the static, bodybuilder poses discussed by O'Brien and others.[23] As noted by Blanshard in this volume, such tactics are duly invoked in the two 2014 Hollywood films, and *Hercules Reborn* makes particular use of its star's WWE-champion credentials: Hennigan at least twice lifts a man several feet off the ground, and in the final showdown in the courtyard at Enos, while under the influence of Nikos' madness-inducing potion, he hefts a huge boulder above his head. When restored to sanity, he subdues Nikos' champion Cyrus (Marcus Shirrock) – actually a little taller than Hennigan, his own strongman status indicated by bared chest – with a classic wrestling hold, seated on Cyrus' prostrate form, arms round his neck and under one armpit, although he resorts to a sword for the gory, throat-slashing *coup de grace*. Bare-handed killing is reserved for the archenemy, Nikos, whose head Hercules seems about to crush before breaking his neck. The slaying of Cyrus, incidentally, is accompanied by the cry "I am no god!" giving Hercules himself the last word in a debate that has run throughout the film amongst the other characters as to his (semi-) divine or human status – a problematizing we have already seen in the case of the other 2014 Herculeses.[24]

The ancient hero Hercules does not always fight bare-handed, however, being traditionally equipped with a club. Of his 2014 descendants, only Johnson's Hercules can claim such a weapon, but it is a particularly fearsome one of enormous size: as long as the hero's leg, its thick end almost as big as his head in diameter, set with huge animal teeth, echoing the teeth of the lionskin. He is carrying it on his first appearance as he emerges from the smoke, and he wields it to deadly effect in the battles against Rhesus' men in the Bessi heartland and beneath Mount Asticus. It is confiscated when Hercules is imprisoned by Cotys, but restored to its rightful owner after general Sitacles' unsuccessful attempt to wield it against him. The hero has it as he emerges from his imprisonment to fight Cotys' men outside, and is still holding it in the final scene as the Thracian army lay down their weapons before him and take up the chant "Hercules!" Both Lutz's and Hennigan's characters are more conventionally equipped with swords, although Lutz does briefly acquire a metal mace from the last of the six Greek champions he overcomes in the arena at Tiryns, which he holds aloft in victory as the audience obligingly chant "Hercules!" Lutz's more usual sword temporarily becomes a supernatural weapon in the final battle at Tiryns, emanating a stream of lightning lit by the storm with which

Zeus is showing support for his son, but it has reverted to normal as Hercules pursues Amphitryon into the palace, and a dagger is used for the final fatal blow against the king. Most of Hennigan's fighting is done with two swords, facilitating maximum bloodshed, often in slow- and stop-action editing, in the gory style of *300* and the STARZ *Spartacus* series.[25]

## SETTING THE SCENE FOR THE HERCULEAN BODY

The three films adopt different approaches to creating a suitable ancient world for their heroes to inhabit. *The Legend of Hercules* was filmed in Bulgaria, and uses both sets and CGI to create locations that draw on elements from a variety of periods: the palace at Tiryns incorporates both a version of Mycenae's Lion Gate (with griffins rather than lions) and elements of the reconstructed Minoan palace of Cnossus; the arena in which Hercules fights in Sicily looks like a Roman amphitheater, though with a strangely pitted floor, while a classical Greek-style theater is the setting for the fight at Tiryns. The whole concept of gladiatorial display is of course Roman, rather than Greek, and such details as the *retiarius* fighting with a net at Tiryns perhaps take their inspiration from *Gladiator*. As has been pointed out, gladiatorial combat is in fact a regular feature of ancient-world-themed films in general, and not restricted to those set in Rome[26] – there are e.g. particularly fine arena scenes in *Hercules Unchained*, where the hero is pitted against tigers. Other Roman elements include *bulla*-charms hang around the bedroom of Hercules and Hebe's baby.

The occasional Roman motif intrudes in *Hercules*, too – the hero's childhood home has a mosaic of Zeus – but for the most part the look is Greek. The actual locations in Croatia and Hungary are completely disguised by monumental sets, with extensive use of CGI for exterior backdrops. As Solomon comments in this volume, the film's notional setting in 358 BC is inexplicable – both because of its odd specificity, and because of Steve Moore's insistence on a much earlier setting for the graphic novel on which the film is based, in the Mycenaean period c. 1200 BC.[27] Even in the graphic novel, however, the few panels with architectural elements are more or less classical Greek in style. In the film, Cotys' Thracian court is replete with Doric columns, dwarfing the odd anachronistic, Roman-style aqueduct supported on arches, and most impressively classical Greek of all is the imaginative reconstruction of the Athenian Acropolis that features in flashbacks to Hercules' earlier life. While not following the actual ground plan of the Acropolis, it is based on a study of the terrain, and gives a magnificent general impression of the monumentalized hilltop, with views across the lower town and out to sea. There are numerous Ionic temples and colonnades, a colossal Athena Parthenos statue, and a huge theater, on the lines of that at Epidaurus. Interiors are very brightly lit, in marked contrast to the dark, fire-lit interiors of Thrace, signaling the "paradise lost" quality of Athens, at least in Hercules' memory.[28]

Just as arbitrary as the fourth-century BC setting of the 2014 *Hercules* is *Hercules Reborn*'s declaration of 13 BC as the date for Hercules' madness, this putting the main action of the film c. 3 BC. Though probably not deliberate, the relatively late date provides some historical excuse for the inclusion of Roman elements here, such as the name of the character "Horace" and Arius' Roman-soldier-style costume, with leather corselet, skirt, and greaves, under a red cloak (see Figure 3.1 above). However, much of the background gives only a very general impression of antiquity: both Enos and Sagev are walled cities surrounded by North African desert – the film was entirely shot in Morocco – the walls of the first topped with square crenellations, the second with Moorish triangular ones. Interiors feature the occasional simple column and drapes, of no particular period. The only properly classical elements to be seen are in external shots of the palace at Enos, which is approached via a courtyard surrounded by Corinthian columns, from which steps lead up to a monumental doorway flanked by Doric columns.

The two Hollywood films both feature statues of Hera, the hero's archenemy from ancient Greek literature onward. Near the beginning of *The Legend*, Alcmene visits a temple of Hera to pray for an end to Amphitryon's brutality: the goddess' statue is twice life-size, in the style of an archaic Greek *kore*,[29] broken off at the knees. At the film's halfway point, Alcmene invites her husband to pray with her, ostensibly for Hera's blessing on Iphicles' marriage to Hebe, in front of a *different* statue, this time an exact replica of one of the surviving archaic *korai* from the Athenian Acropolis; angered by her revelation of Zeus' fathering of Hercules, Amphitryon stabs her to death before it. A further statue group appears as witness to Hercules' final duel with Amphitryon, an adult male figure flanked by two children, with no obvious classical precedent. In *Hercules*, the hero's childhood home – as narrated by Iphitus – is adorned with a classical-style statue of Hera, from the eyes of which emerge the two snakes that attack the infant Hercules in a particularly chilling CG effect. Later, a colossal statue of Hera is the most striking element of Cotys' CG-created city: it is of very similar design to the small-scale domestic one, and our attention is drawn to it both by its prominence as Hercules and his companions arrive at the court, and by Ergenia's comments – "it took five years and a thousand men" to build the temple of Hera. The toppling of this statue by Hercules provides the climax of the final battle, its falling head carrying Cotys along as it smashes through the city walls and plunges into the abyss beyond. One might think not just of the palace-toppling of the 1958 *Hercules*, but also of the archaic *kore*-type statue in *Hercules Unchained* that stands at the entrance to Thebes and watches over the final battle between Eteocles and Polyneices. As in the earlier films, the 2014 statues function at a variety of levels: they enhance the general impression of the ancient-world setting; they are a tangible incarnation of the deity concerned (in *The Legend*, Hera actually speaks via possession of her priestess); and they provide a static counterpoint to the violent action of the heroic body and others.[30] The one statue to appear in *Hercules Reborn* is the falcon wielded by Hercules against his family. Hera is, however, briefly invoked later in the film, when Nikos reveals that it was he who administered the potion that sent Hercules mad – a potion made up by "a shaman of the goddess Hera."

## CONCLUSION: HERCULEAN POLITICS IN THE TWENTY-FIRST CENTURY

To return, then to the Putin exhibition. The artists/organizers concerned may or may not actually have seen any of the 2014 Hercules films – Ratner's *Hercules* certainly did well in Russia, grossing over $1 million in its opening week in late July,[31] and Johnson's leather corselet could be the inspiration for the gold garment worn by Putin in three of the paintings. The image of Putin the exhibition portrays will, in any case, inevitably have been influenced by broader popular perceptions of the ancient hero, perceptions that in turn are reflected and refracted in the films. There is a relatively straightforward correlation between the different media in their portrayal of the heroic body: both Putin and Hercules are presented in the strongman's costume of bared arms and thighs, and partially/intermittently bared chest or muscle-mimicking corselet; the still medium of painting captures Putin mid-heroic-action, just as the moving picture dwells on moments within action sequences that display Hercules' strength;

both media make some attempt to set the heroic body in a visual context that appeals to popular perceptions of the classical past. Where the two differ significantly is in their approach to the narrative context in which their hero performs. The Russian exhibition's direct engagement with Hercules' labors is in striking contrast to the downplaying and/or problematizing of the labors in all three films. At one level this simply reflects the exhibition's lack of sophistication in comparison to the more complex narratives of the films. At another, the contrast may draw the critical viewer's attention to an irony beyond the cosmetic mismatch between the aging president's body and that of the idealized hero. As has been noted, "While the Herculean strongman's goal is to rid society of the evil ruler, the hero refuses the political power for himself; he'd rather leave the power in the hands of the legitimate heir to the throne."[32]

The 2014 *Hercules* conforms to this pattern (see Blanshard in this volume), while *Hercules Reborn* foregrounds the theme by making its totalitarian villain so brutal, and by its final shot of Hercules' lone departure from a city now ruled by the legitimate heir to the throne and her virtuous man. Such a selfless rejection of power is hardly an apt narrative for Putin. A better analogy is provided by *The Legend*, at the end of which Hercules uncharacteristically settles down in royal domesticity as the benevolent new ruler of Tiryns. The exhibition's insistence on the labors, however, keeps the viewer's attention firmly focused on the simple message that Putin is the strongman savior, the invincible slayer of Russia's monstrous opponents.

There is further work to be done on the place of Hercules, and classical mythology more broadly, in modern political discourse, and on the relationship between such discourse and popular culture.[33] The material may often seem unworthy of study because of its ephemeral nature or lack of high art status, but I hope here to have offered an example of why such study is important for the understanding of contemporary society.

## NOTES

I would like to thank the original audience at the Delphi conference for many useful comments, and the editors for their patience. Since 2015 my acquaintance with post-classical receptions of the Greek Heracles has been deepened and broadened by interaction with the many contributors to my project Hercules: A Hero for All Ages. I should also thank my Italian film studies colleague Alan O'Leary for introducing me to both Jacqueline Reich and Rob Rushing.

1. Luhn (2014); Rosenburg (2014a). The exhibition's organizer was again involved in celebrating Putin's status as cultural icon for his sixty-fourth birthday two years later: Luhn (2016).
2. Cole (2017).
3. Rosenburg (2014b).
4. For an overview of Hercules as political role-model in antiquity and beyond, see Stafford (2012: 137–70, 218–24).
5. Dyer (1997: 170–6; photo pl. 4.19).
6. Reich (2015: see esp. 187–237); see also Reich (2011). Reich (2013: 36) notes that early versions of the *Cabiria* script called the character "Ercole," renamed Maciste by the writer Gabriele d'Annunzio, who apparently thought it derived from an ancient Greek title for Hercules (*makistos*).
7. Rushing (2016: 4). The term "peplum" was adopted in the 1960s by French critics, referring (inaccurately) to the short tunics worn by both male and female characters in contemporary sword-and-sandal films: see Aziza (1998: 7–11, 2009: 13–19). O'Brien (2014: 3–4) notes the term's relative neutrality, in contrast to the more derogatory "sword-and-sandal" label, and its confinement to scholarly discourse; cf. Cornelius (2011: 1–3) on both terms.
8. See, for instance, the volumes by O'Brien (2014) and Cornelius (2011), but also Lagny (1992); Dyer (1997: 145–83); Günsberg (2005: 97–132); Burke (2011); D'Amelio (2011). O'Brien (2014: 2–9) provides an overview of scholarship on the peplum proper, noting its place in broader discussions of European film vs. Hollywood, and art vs. popular cinema. On peplum and Italian cinema, see also Lucanio (1994: 12–56); Giordano (1998); Bondanella (2009: 159–79); Brunetta (2009: 161–4).
9. Notably Wyke (1997a, 2002), as well as more recently Nisbet (2008: 45–55); Blanshard and Shahabudin (2011: 58–76); Pomeroy (2013). See also Solomon (2001: 117–23, 306–23); Blanshard (2005: 157–66); Winkler (2007); Pomeroy (2008: 29–59); Shahabudin (2009). My own contributions to the field are Stafford (2012: 232–6, 2017).
10. Conroy (2008).
11. See www.bodybuilding.com ("Dwayne Johnson's Rock-Hard Hercules Workout and Diet Plan," July 16, 2014); O'Kelly (2014).
12. On Sorbo, see Solomon in this volume; Blondell (2005) discusses the cross-gender appeal of *Hercules: The Legendary Journeys*, of which Sorbo's casting is an element.
13. See *Toronto Sun*, July 22, 2014 ("Hair from The Rock's 'Hercules' Beard Came from Yak's Testicles").
14. The uneasy relationship between the two is noted by Chiu in this volume.
15. O'Brien (2014: 98–9). Cf. D'Amelio (2011: 18, "colors in the peplum genre are crucial semiotic signs that help indicate the characters' moral

identity") and Günsberg (2005: 102), both citing screenwriter/director Duccio Tessari's rules for peplum production no. 3. The association of white clothing with virtue goes back to Prodicus' "Choice of Heracles" and beyond; see Stafford (2017).

16　Cf. O'Brien (2014: 42) on the use of water to enhance the appeal of Steve Reeve's torso in *Hercules* (1958).

17　Pat O'Haire cited in McKenna (2008: 108); Levine is here repeating a comment from a 1961 interview (with Guy Talese, "Joe Levine Unchained: A Candid Portrait of a Spectacular Showman," *Esquire*, January 1, 68), but significantly the earlier interview omitted the final three words.

18　Günsberg (2005: 104–9); Rushing (2008, 2016: 65–99); O'Brien (2014: 39–41).

19　See Pierce (2011) on the preservation of heteronormativity in *Gladiator* (2000), *Troy* (2004), and *300*.

20　See Chiu in this volume.

21　O'Brien (2014: 98). For a selection of lion-tamers acting as unconvincing stunt doubles for peplum stars, see e.g. http://www.peplumtv.com/2013/01/spot-lion-tamer.html.

22　My translation.

23　See O'Brien (2014: 36–7, 41); also e.g. Wyke (1997a) and Günsberg (2005: 110–11).

24　See Blanshard in this volume.

25　See Rushing (2016: 33–62) on "time in the peplum."

26　Blanshard and Shahabudin (2011: 221–2, 224).

27　Moore and Wijaya (2008: end pages).

28　On the CGI work on the film by Method Studios and Milk VFX, see Wilson (2014) and Hogg (2014), with related links; also the DVD extra "The Effects of Hercules." Cf. Garcia (2008) on the creation of "Greece" in earlier films.

29　Statue of a young woman.

30　See Rushing (2016: 45–54, 81 fig. 2.2) on the peplum hero's relationship with statuary. Cf. Williams (2009) on the interplay between classical sculpture and display of the heroic body in *Ben-Hur: A Tale of the Christ* (1925).

31　Tartaglione (2014).

32　D'Amelio (2011: 15–16); see also Dyer (1997: 174).

33　A number of papers in the volumes to be produced by the Hercules: A Hero for All Ages project (http://herculesproject.leeds.ac.uk/) will address the use and abuse of Hercules in political discourse from the Renaissance to the present day.

# 4 Heroes and Companions in Hercules (2014)

Angeline Chiu

## INTRODUCTION

With the exception of his nephew Iolaus' help against the Hydra in the second canonical labor, the Hercules of classical myth largely works alone in his heroic adventures.[1] Cinematic depictions of Hercules during the 1950s and 1960s peplum or sword-and-sandal era largely follow suit,[2] and more recent film and television reimaginings of the quintessential Greek mythological hero present him working with single sidekicks or very small groups at most.[3] The 2014 Brett Ratner film *Hercules* takes another tack entirely.[4] Based on the late Steve Moore's 2008 graphic novel *Hercules: The Thracian Wars*, the screenplay by Ryan Condal and Evan Spiliotopoulos features a large ensemble cast. While Dwayne Johnson plays the titular hero with charismatic star power and commensurate top billing, this Hercules works extensively with five companions. Each one has a complex relationship with mythological precedent and modern adaptation, and together these six form a tightly knit band of adventurers verging on adoptive family. The heroic name and reputation of "Hercules" soon reveals itself as the composite, corporate identity of Hercules the individual and his comrades seamlessly cooperating as a unit. This new company both draws from heroic fellowships of classical myth and reconfigures them for an innovative original narrative.

## STEVE MOORE'S GRAPHIC NOVEL AS ADAPTATION AND SOURCE

Complex layers of reception are at work in the finished film. Brett Ratner directed from the script by Condal and Spiliotopoulos, who in turn adapted Steve Moore's graphic novel.[5] In an interview in 2008,

Moore spoke at length about the inception and execution of *Hercules: The Thracian Wars* for Radical Comics, giving valuable insight into his artistic vision and creative choices.[6] Imagining "a grittier, more human Hercules, which played down the more mythological aspects and emphasized that of the warrior," Moore framed group dynamics as the fundamental starting point of his adaptation: "Obviously a warrior doesn't fight alone, so my first job was to give him some companions."[7] In choosing Amphiaraus, Atalanta, Autolycus, Iolaus, Meleager, and Tydeus, Moore took care to ascertain that

> apart from Meneus, who was invented for the series, all the other characters in Hercules's band are actual legendary characters who would have been alive at the same time [i.e., the generation before the Trojan War], and whose personalities are largely based on what we know of them from their original stories.

Moore specifically avoided modern retellings and instead explicitly drew from English translations of those "original stories" of ancient authors such as Homer, Hesiod, and Apollodorus, among others.[8]

The subsequent transition from Moore's graphic novel to Ratner's film was not an amicable one. Despite Moore's initial confidence that his artistic vision would be respected ("I'm assured, though, that everyone wants the movie to be a pretty close adaptation of the comic book, which suits me"),[9] he was ultimately neither consulted nor compensated for his work, and he did not want his name attached to the project, which he declared "sounds like it's going to be idiotic."[10] Nevertheless, the end result is the film as it exists, and though it may not adhere closely enough to Moore's original graphic novel for his taste, it still draws from his work; it is the screen adaptation that global audiences saw and therefore is the subject of this chapter. Above all, though particular details about Hercules and his band have changed – notably the deletion of Moore's mythologically based Meleager and wholly invented Meneus – the fundamental narrative principle of the Herculean legend as group effort carries through.

## HERCULES AND COMPANIONS IN ANCIENT HEROIC MYTHOLOGICAL GROUPINGS

The Ratner film's depiction of Hercules and his companions resonates with other heroic groupings in Greek mythology.[11] Of these, three are significant as sources and literary *comparanda* for the relationships on screen: the Seven Against Thebes, the Calydonian Boar Hunt, and the quest of Jason and the Argonauts for the Golden Fleece. A brief overview of representative sources reveals the raw narrative material from which Moore and then the filmmakers drew. In terms of Hercules' companions specifically, these ancient groupings provide a basic precedent and framework for their ties with each other.

The myth of the Seven Against Thebes presents Tydeus and Amphiaraus as two of the eponymous warrior allies.[12] This establishes them unassailably in the same universe and time frame, along with characterizing Tydeus as a brutal fighter and Amphiaraus as a seer as well as warrior. Apollodorus' account (*Library* 3.6.8) also elaborates Amphiaraus' ill will toward Tydeus that led the seer to sabotage in gruesome fashion Tydeus' chance to gain immortality:

> And Melanippus, the remaining one of the sons of Astacus, wounded Tydeus in the belly. As he lay half dead, Athena brought a medicine that she had begged of Zeus, and by which she intended to make him immortal. But Amphiaraus hated Tydeus for thwarting him by persuading the Argives to march to Thebes; so when he perceived the intention of the goddess he cut off the head of Melanippus and gave it to Tydeus, who, wounded though he was, had killed him. And Tydeus split open the head and gulped up the brains. But when Athena saw that, in disgust she grudged and withheld the intended benefit. (trans. Frazer)[13]

Atalanta also appears in the Seven Against Thebes narrative, but she does not participate in hostilities herself. Neither does she interact with Tydeus or Amphiaraus; instead she has a tangential role as mother of the youngest of the Seven, Parthenopaeus.[14]

The Calydonian Boar Hunt encompasses more of the characters who become the Ratner Hercules' companions. Different mythographers offer varied assortments of participants, but the lists are each a "who-is-who" of notables gathered to hunt the monstrous beast. All include Meleager, whom Moore made and the filmmakers then unmade a companion to Hercules. Apollodorus states that the chase took place during Hercules' servitude to Omphale, queen of Lydia[15] – thus explaining his absence – and in his list of hunters includes Amphiaraus and Atalanta.[16] Pausanias in his *ekphrasis* of Athena's temple at Tegea states its depiction of the boar hunt included Atalanta, Iolaus, and Amphiaraus.[17] Ovid's account includes the same three.[18] Meanwhile, the catalogue in Hyginus contains Iolaus and Atalanta, but not Amphiaraus.[19] In sum, Iolaus, Amphiaraus, and Atalanta all appear as colleagues with a common purpose in the ancient literary evidence. Hercules, however, is not a significant presence in any configuration.

Jason's Quest for the Golden Fleece is the mythological precedent that places Hercules in the same narrative with various of the companions. Among the Argonauts Apollonius of Rhodes lists Hercules with Hylas; Atalanta in this version wished to join the quest, but Jason, fearing that his shipmates would fight for her love, prevented her from going.[20] Hercules leaves the quest by the end of the first book.[21] Valerius Flaccus has Jason travel with Hercules and Tydeus.[22] Apollodorus' account is the most extensive, including Hercules, Amphiaraus, Autolycus the "son of Hermes," and Atalanta.[23] In short, Hercules occasionally appears among the Argonauts, but he soon drops out of view and the expedition, ostensibly in search of lost Hylas and/or to perform his canonical Twelve Labors but effectively to yield the story to Jason.

So far, this overview has established that the companions moved in generally the same mythological narrative circles by the Hellenistic era of mythographers. In terms of the comrades' specific personal relationships with each other and with Hercules, however, these attested heroic groupings provide rather less scope for imagination. Aside from Amphiaraus hating Tydeus, the figures who will be Hercules' comrades in the film do not much interact particularly with each other.[24] Neither, with two notable exceptions, do they have significant personal contact with Hercules. The first exception is a note in Apollodorus stating that Autolycus taught young Hercules how to wrestle.[25] The second, far more famous exception is Iolaus, usually identified as Hercules' nephew, who helps him defeat the Hydra.[26] Pausanias also calls Iolaus a participant in most of the labors of Hercules, as does Diodorus Siculus.[27] Other sources note that Iolaus' loyalty to Hercules extended to the hero's children; Iolaus as an old man miraculously recovers his youth in order to defend them and defeat their persecutor Eurystheus.[28]

## ADAPTATION AND CAMARADERIE IN *HERCULES* (2014)

Steve Moore's innovation lay in taking these pre-existing mythological figures (Amphiaraus, Atalanta, Autolycus, Iolaus, Meleager, Tydeus) and creating a new heroic grouping to tell a fresh adventure (Figure 4.1).[29] The focal point is Hercules, but the others come in already carrying backstories, personalities, and narrative expectations of their own. Ratner's movie takes from and builds on Moore's creative vision, and in so doing it makes its own choices in how to tell the story, notably eliminating Meleager and Meneus. The resulting movie is a separate work and artifact, one in a long line of cinematic treatments of Hercules as muscular action hero.[30] Let us now turn to the film itself.

Figure 4.1 Hercules (Dwayne Johnson) and his companions in *Hercules* (2014). Paramount Pictures.

The social dynamics of Hercules and his companions depend first on how that movie presents, identifies, and characterizes these figures. For the most part, they arise recognizably from their ancient mythological precedents. Tydeus (Aksel Hennie) is a brutal fighter incapable of speech and prone to violent nightmares; he is almost a type of savage berserker. In an understated allusion to his act of cannibalism that revolted Athena, at one point Tydeus in a tavern eats so grotesquely that a female patron looks on with mingled horror and disgust. Autolycus (Rufus Sewell) is a strategist, clever, practical, and sardonic in keeping with his mythological life as thief and wily rogue. Amphiaraus (Ian McShane), the warrior-prophet of myth, is nearly unchanged; indeed he repeatedly speaks of foreseeing his own death – the reason for his reluctance to join the Seven Against Thebes – as he wields a spear in battle.[31] Atalanta (Ingrid Bolsø Berdal) remains the formidable fighter, deadly with her bow and arrow.[32] Her characterization has undergone an assimilation with the Amazon myth; the movie version of Atalanta hails from Scythia, not Arcadia, and she identifies herself as an Amazon.[33] The one glaring exception to the companions' general mythological adherence is Iolaus (Reece Ritchie). In a twist of irony, the figure known in myth for being Hercules' helpmate in dangerous labors and an adventurer in his own right is here the one companion who does very little physical fighting. Instead Iolaus is a slick, fast-talking youth, focused on building the reputation of Hercules and acting as the *de facto* public relations arm of the group. He does, however, repeatedly call Hercules "uncle."

As for Hercules himself (Dwayne Johnson), he makes his first appearance only after a voiceover narration by Iolaus tells his backstory and sets up audience expectations of an impressive entrance.

This introduction includes what are the most familiar aspects of the Hercules story: his demigod descent from Zeus and the beautiful mortal Alcmene, the hatred of Hera, his defeat of two serpents while yet a baby, and his performance of the Twelve Labors. Iolaus' story specifically refers to the Lernaean Hydra, the Erymanthian boar, and the Nemean lion, in that order. When Hercules finally appears on screen, he emerges dramatically from a billow of smoke while wearing a lionskin and carrying a massive club: the quintessential iconography of the hero in art both ancient and post-classical. This instantly recognizable image, however, is at odds with the response of Iolaus' intended audience that quickly reveals itself to be not the general viewer but a gang of skeptical pirates. "What a load of crap!" the brigands' leader snorts dismissively. When Iolaus insists, "Every word is true!" and resumes his heroizing tale of the Nemean lion, Hercules appears and personally concludes: "I did it with my bare hands." He adds with some subversive humor, "Or so they say." From the film's beginning Hercules – lionskin, club, mountainous physique, and all – comes enmeshed within ideas of storytelling, reputation, glory (*kleos*), and public image: Hercules the man as opposed to Hercules the figure of epic narrative or even Hercules the brand. Furthermore, this Hercules indicates that he well understands the complication.

## SHARED HEROISM IN *HERCULES* (2014)

Group dynamics among these six disparate figures reveal a complex network of interdependent relationships. While Hercules is the public face of the fellowship, the others are clearly colleagues, not underlings, minions, or sidekicks. The film offers three separate scenes, all dissimilar in tone and detail, that illuminate different aspects of this group vis-à-vis Hercules himself. The first may be profitably considered as Hercules and the group's conscious self-presentation to adversaries in public, the second as an introduction to a client in front of spectators, and the third as an explanation to a trusted friend in private confidence. Taken together, these scenes illuminate a multifaceted new approach to the mythological strongman.

The first presentation of Hercules and his companions to the moviegoing audience occurs in the initial confrontation with the pirates. Iolaus spins his story, burnishing the name of Hercules as the prelude to his arrival. Though Hercules swiftly dispatches the first wave of attackers as Iolaus crows, "Five men with a single blow! Still think you can destroy the son of Zeus?" the pirate leader, undeterred, sends an even larger contingent of his men after Hercules with the order "Bring me his head!" At this point Hercules steps back among the beached ships to fight out of the head pirate's line of sight. As the camera spins, the audience sees Hercules look up at a hidden figure perched in a shadowy prow and say, "Seems they need more convincing, Autolycus." The figure, while throwing knives at the onrushing pirates, comments with comfortable, wry familiarity, "That's why we're here." Clearly the implication is that the reputation of Hercules depends on others and that this is *de rigueur* as far as those others are concerned. This is not to say that Hercules does not participate: he fights ferociously in his own right, but he does not fight alone. As the gang of pirates pursues him, he gives what amounts to a roll call of comrades as introduction to the audience. As he names each one, the companion appears and engages the enemy: Atalanta shoots her arrows, Amphiaraus dispatches men with his spear, and Tydeus uses his battle axes to deadly effect. The ensuing shots depict them and Hercules fighting in equal measure as a group effort. At the same time, the scene identifies Hercules as the center of the company: he defines it by naming its members and calling them to action beside him. Furthermore, the others purposefully stay out of sight among the ships and freely help construct and bolster the public image of Hercules as lone hero. Only he emerges into triumphant public view after the battle. At this point, with a bombastic musical fanfare the film displays its title "Hercules" in large gleaming letters, an effective endorsement of the titular character's primacy.

Nevertheless, the next scene complicates that primacy by showing Hercules and his comrades after the battle, carrying on with easy humor. "That was fun," Atalanta comments as Autolycus cheerfully counts dead pirates for the group's payday: "Twenty pirates at two gold pieces a head, minus the headless ones. Let's see ..." Hercules responds with satisfaction, "Not a bad night." The tone of the interactions implies comfortable familiarity and cooperation. When Iolaus chimes in with "You see how the pirates ran? My story softened their resolve!" Autolycus' reply highlights several important aspects of this Hercules: "Their resolve must be broken, Iolaus. When you spread the legend of Hercules, make it bigger, scarier! The more they believe Hercules is truly the son of Zeus, the less likely they are to fight." His words point to the group's (through Iolaus) conscious construction of an individual identity in the public sphere (the Hercules "brand," if one will) and of the importance of storytelling and fame. Furthermore, Autolycus makes the explicit connection between reputation and the response of others: this Hercules' pursuit of glory (*kleos*) is not only about fame as an end in itself but also about its practical applications for the companions' occupation as hired muscle in dangerous situations.

The second presentation of the group again occurs with Hercules naming his companions to an audience: Lord Cotys of Thrace (John Hurt) is a new client in a public official setting, a throne room surrounded by courtiers and armed guards. Cotys sees from the beginning that Hercules' fearsome reputation is a composite of him and his companions. Surprised, Cotys demurs, "But in legend you fight alone." Hercules' reply neatly epitomizes the group relationship: "My reputation would not exist without my comrades." He then formally introduces them one by one as the camera lingers on each in turn. When Cotys expresses doubts about Atalanta's fighting ability ("With respect, I fear that the task at hand might not be suitable for a woman even if she is an Amazon warrior"), she and Hercules trade a knowing look before she educates Cotys with a virtuoso display of archery. The moment is as much a defense of the composite nature of this heroic group as it is a feminist critique of Cotys' own biases: Atalanta is no weak link. Hercules' silently eloquent shared glance with her is his acknowledgment both of Cotys' error and of Atalanta's own standing in the group; the moment is not Atalanta asking permission per se of Hercules but her broadcasting her desire to teach Cotys a lesson and Hercules agreeing with her. The next scene reveals all the companions with Hercules at a large dinner table, clearly all peers as they eat and discuss their new assignment with Cotys and his general Sitacles (Peter Mullan). They end the evening joshing and joking among themselves, teasing each other and complaining about work, but they share an obvious, easy rapport.[34] In the subsequent sequence back in the public eye, Hercules is the first among equals and the public relations face of the group, but all six energetically train Thracian conscripts together. Hercules' initial motivational speech to the raw recruits refers specifically to "my companions and I" as the ones in charge of their training regimen. After the obligatory training montage, all six lead the Thracians into battle and fight alongside them. The comrades are heroic in their own right and not only by association with their famous leader.

In both scenes of introduction thus far, audiences meet the companions through Hercules. In the third scene, however, the comrades present themselves in a small, private setting to an audience of one, the Thracian princess Ergenia (Rebecca Ferguson), suspicious of their true motives and identities. When she, uninvited, crashes their camp to demand answers about the rumored murder of Hercules' family,

Iolaus attempts to fend her off by telling another fantastical story, but she will have none of it: "No myths! I want the truth." She rejects the public image and reputation of the hero, and so Hercules is absent as his companions define themselves and their relationships to him. Autolycus becomes the primary narrator, and the others add details as he relates their backstories to Ergenia, beginning with his own.[35]

According to Autolycus, Hercules as a public relations phenomenon of demigod dimensions had humble, decidedly human beginnings:

> We grew up together, both orphans trying to survive in the streets of Athens. We found a home in the army. Looked out for each other. Hercules' strength set him apart. Kings of Athens started to send him on all the most dangerous missions. And he took me with him. To fight by his side. And with each mission, our numbers grew.

The tale demythologizes Hercules and presents a competing narrative to Iolaus' many fancifully embroidered tales, but the trait of Hercules' great strength remains constant. As for growing numbers, Autolycus folds another companion into the story by noting, "Scythia, the Amazon kingdom where the royal family had been assassinated." Atalanta elaborates: "My family was gone. Everyone was gone. Hercules helped me avenge their murder. He became my brother-in-arms." A pattern swiftly emerges: wandering warriors with troubled histories and no kin who form their own family working and fighting together. Tydeus is mute, but he nevertheless expresses a pained acquiescence when Autolycus recalls, "Thebes, the city of corpses, where we found a single child still alive. Hercules took Tydeus in when everyone else saw nothing but a wild animal." This presents Hercules as a charismatic and compassionate man to whom others are drawn and whom those others admire; he is the natural core of the company, though he is no autocrat. The individuals form a group based on social ties of personal obligations and allegiances. Furthermore, in Autolycus' account Hercules' own deeds kickstarted his fame: the group took the logical next step of capitalizing on it, and the practical applications of the Hercules legend become clear:

> You know how a rumor spreads. How a legend grows. Hercules' deeds were so incredible they could not possibly have been performed by a mere mortal. So we played along. We encourage people to think Hercules is the son of Zeus. It's good. Scares the enemy.

Finally, though he has habitually teased Iolaus, Autolycus acknowledges the younger man's place in the group: "Iolaus helps. He talks nice. And that, my lady, is the truth."

The group dynamics that emerge in this third scene arise from mutual acceptance and assistance: this is a group of misfits and outcasts who have formed a closely knit social group going beyond pragmatic mercenary engagements. They are not only business partners, however loudly Autolycus might claim that his motivation is financial. The ultimate presentation of Hercules and his comrades is one of a surrogate family based on loyalty and the willingness to shoulder each other's various weaknesses and protect one's fellows. Perhaps Atalanta best encapsulates the sentiment of the group when, as the job in Thrace turns sour and Hercules urges his comrades to leave for their own safety and not to stay out of any sense of personal obligation to him, she says,

> Debt? You think we follow you because we owe you? Look around, Hercules. We're family. All we have is each other. We will fight for you. And if it's our time, we will die for you. Because you would die for us.[36]

In terms of modern cinematic adaptations of Hercules, this is an innovation that defines the hero within a complex network of multiple relationships simultaneously personal and professional. This Hercules cannot function fully without his comrades, or they without him: they are a symbiotic group.

The film's various presentations of Hercules vis-à-vis his companions present alternative narratives with differing storytellers: Iolaus, Hercules, Autolycus. Ultimately, however, the narratives are as complementary as competitive, for they highlight different aspects of group identity that, considered together, reveal a more complex corporate identity than any one alone could. Iolaus' fabulously barnstorming speech taken with the group's actual fighting highlights the link between Hercules' reputation and the group's voluntary joint construction of that fame. Hercules' formal introduction of his comrades at the Thracian court delineates further the group's active cooperation, interdependence, and division of labor. Autolycus' disarming conversation with Ergenia prioritizes the personal traumas and loyalties that bind the group together and transcend the pursuit of fame or fortune.

The film's most intriguing presentation of Hercules the individual and "Hercules" the group identity is perhaps the most overlooked. After giving the audience three different presentations of the hero and his companions, the film uses its closing credits to present one more as a final commentary and pendant to Iolaus' tale of Herculean labors that had opened the movie. Where Iolaus' story had come with video segments depicting Hercules alone, the closing sequence's stylized illustrations revisit those same labors but with a twist: the images now show the companions fighting Hydra, boar, and lion alongside Hercules. The series of drawings ends with an image of the group as a whole: Hercules stands in the center, but his companions fill the screen on either side of him. The film closes emphatically with a declaration of heroism not only for Hercules but also for each of his comrades.

## CONCLUSION

Hercules is undoubtedly an action hero in his own right thanks to his iconic strength, but he is able to accomplish much more with his company. Together he and his five friends act as force multipliers for each other and for the composite reputation of the Hercules brand as they consciously and purposefully build and employ it. By working together they dramatically increase the effectiveness of the group, and as that group they accomplish things that none of them can do in isolation. The companions themselves are all a complicated combination of ancient tradition and modern reimagining. Some of each one's major distinguishing mythological features carry through in this new narrative: Iolaus still calls Hercules uncle; Amphiaraus remains a seer, Tydeus a violent brute, Atalanta a formidable huntress, and Autolycus a man of wily intellect. Neither strictly sidekicks nor comic relief but comrades in arms, they participate in the communal construction of glory (*kleos*); they offer an alternative version of leadership and loyalty among misfits who create a surrogate family among themselves. Together they are more than the sum of their parts, and even Hercules cannot do everything alone. This is the final visual message that Ratner's film gives its audience as the evocatively drawn end credits roll: demigod or not, like other human beings this Hercules gets by with a little help from his friends.

## NOTES

1. According to one version of the myth, Eurystheus disqualified the Hydra labor because of Iolaus' help; see Apollodorus, *Library* 2.5.2.
2. The 1958 *Hercules* starring Steve Reeves generally set the genre's course; see further Solomon in this volume.
3. For instance, Disney's 1997 animated *Hercules* presents the hero accompanied by Pegasus and Phil, his satyr advisor. The TV series *Hercules: The Legendary Journeys* (1995–9) depicts Hercules (Kevin Sorbo) working consistently with Iolaus (Michael Hurst), in the show not his kinsman, though the hero has occasional adventures with recurring characters

such as Autolycus (Bruce Campbell) and Salmoneus (Robert Trebor). Depictions of Hercules as a schoolboy in *Young Hercules* (1998–9) and *Disney's Hercules the Animated Series* (1998–9), on the other hand, give him a close circle of classmates for adolescent-themed educational purposes; see Chiu (2014).

4 The exact contemporary of Ratner's film, director Renny Harlin's *The Legend of Hercules* (2014), presents Hercules (Kellan Lutz) with a single comrade-in-arms, Sotiris (Liam McIntyre), with whom he is forced into faux-Roman gladiatorial combat (!); see further Blanshard, Curley, and Stafford in this volume.

5 This chapter focuses on the theatrical version of the film, not the extended version released on DVD and Blu-ray.

6 Vamvounis (2008).

7 Vamvounis (2008).

8 Vamvounis (2008). Moore elaborates helpfully on his research: "I've never seen Edith Hamilton's book, but modern retellings have never really interested me. I have an enormous library of this sort of material, and over the years I've read virtually all the original source material in translation, such as Homer, Hesiod, Apollodorus, Apollonius and so on, including a lot of the really obscure poets ... When I wanted quick references to check things out while constructing the story, I generally used *The Oxford Classical Dictionary* for historical background and Pierre Grimal's *Dictionary of Classical Mythology* for the characters and story elements."

9 Vamvounis (2008).

10 This is an anecdote recalled by Steve Moore's friend and colleague Alan Moore in an interview with Hannah Means-Shannon (2014). Furthermore, he noted, "Steve was saying that this film sounded like it was going to be a complete abortion, that they'd dumped characters such as Hylas."

11 I am making a distinction between heroic groups and heroic pairs such as Diomedes–Odysseus, Achilles–Patroclus, Castor–Pollux, Calais–Zetes, Aeneas–Achates, Nisus–Euryalus, Theseus–Pirithous, Orestes–Pylades, Ajax–Teucer, Telemachus–Peisistratus, and the oldest known epic pair, Gilgamesh–Enkidu. The pairs form separate homosocial or fraternal bonds in mythological narratives that differ from group dynamics.

12 Aeschylus, *Seven Against Thebes*; Apollodorus, *Library* 3.6.3, Statius, *Thebaid* 4.32–344.

13 Statius, *Thebaid* 8.736–66, has not Amphiaraus but Capaneus bring the head of Melanippus to Tydeus for the cannibal feast.

14 Apollodorus, *Library* 3.9.2, states that Parthenopaeus was Atalanta's son by either Melanion or Ares.

15 *Library* 2.6.3.

16 *Library* 1.8.2.

17 *Description of Greece* 8.45.6–7. The list also includes Meleager.

18 *Metamorphoses* 8.298–328.
19 *Fables* 172–4.
20 *Argonautica* 1.122–32 for Hercules and lines 769–73 for Atalanta. Meleager appears in the roster at lines 190–201.
21 *Argonautica* 1.1187–1295.
22 *Argonautica* 1.353–4, 387. Meleager appears at 433–5.
23 *Library* 1.9.16; the passage also includes Meleager.
24 An exception is Apollodorus' account of Atalanta and Amphiaraus wounding the Calydonian boar (1.8.2). If they were not working together, they were at least working near each other with a common goal: Atalanta first shot the boar in the back, then Amphiaraus shot it in the eye, and finally Meleager delivered the killing blow.
25 *Library* 2.4.9.
26 Hesiod, *Theogony* 313–18, Apollodorus, *Bibliotheca* 2.5.2, Diodorus Siculus, *Bibliotheca* 4.11.5–6, among others.
27 *Description of Greece* 8.45.6. Similarly at 5.17.11, Iolaus voluntarily helped Hercules with multiple labors. Pausanias at 1.19.3 notes an altar to Iolaus at Cynosarges near Athens while again describing him as partner in plural Herculean labors. Diodorus Siculus, *Library* 4.29.4, describes Iolaus as accompanying Hercules on nearly all his adventures.
28 Pindar, *Pythian Ode* 9.79–83; Euripides, *Son of Heracles*, particularly 843–63.
29 As Alan Moore recalled, "he [Steve Moore] was very happy with his scholarship on that series. It was impeccably researched. There wasn't an element of it that wasn't supported by something from Greek mythology or Greek history" (Means-Shannon 2014). Steve Moore himself stated his purpose in setting his story in Thrace: "The next decision was that, to avoid the more mythological aspects, the easiest thing to do was to take Hercules and his war-band out of Greece. Since we wanted a dark, moody feel to the story, barbarian Thrace was the obvious place to set the action . . . Most of the story is set in Thrace, about which very little is known, so that gave us rather more of a free hand" (Vamvounis 2008).
30 See Wyke (2002); Clauss (2008); Rushing (2008, 2016); Shahabudin (2009); Blanshard and Shahabudin (2011: 58–76, 194–215); Cornelius (2011); Stafford (2012: 232–9); Cyrino and Safran (2015). On related issues of muscular male physique, classical ideals, and narrative in the Italian Maciste films of the 1910s and 1920s, see Bertellini (2002); O'Brien (2014); Reich (2015).
31 Cf. Pindar's description of Amphiaraus in *Olympian Ode* 6.15–17: "a man who was good both as a prophet and at fighting with the spear."
32 E.g. Ovid, *Metamorphoses* 8.380–7 and Apollodorus, *Library* 1.8.2 noting that Atalanta was first to shoot the Calydonian boar.
33 Early and Kennedy (2003); Gamel and Blondell (2005); Mainon and Ursini (2006); Nikoloutsos (2013). On Amazons and historical possibility including Scythian origins, see Mayor (2014).

34 Iolaus then tries to find a title for his next bombastic installment of Hercules' publicity/*kleos* campaign and asks the others for feedback: "Which title sounds more terrifying to our enemies: *Hercules: Savior of Thrace* or *Hercules: A Legend Is Born?*" Autolycus swiftly deflates him: "Both sound terrifyingly boring." While the film makes a theme of constructing Hercules' reputation, it also subverts and reshapes that theme. The companions help build that name in public even as in private they humorously mock both it and the process of creating it.

35 Admittedly, the mythologically savvy viewer may take this with a grain of salt, given Autolycus' traditional characterization as a liar as well as a thief and all-round scoundrel. Nevertheless, while the film version of Autolycus is sarcastic, flippant, cynical, and avaricious, he does not engage in obviously deliberate falsehoods.

36 Autolycus does leave, calling the remaining group members "mad" for staying to fight for a moral but apparently lost cause. Nevertheless, he eventually returns and takes part in the climactic final battle. He may claim to be a cynic, but his reappearance betrays a sense of personal loyalty to the group that he ultimately cannot abandon.

# 5 Sacrifice and Salvific Heroism in Supernatural (2005–)

Meredith E. Safran

## INTRODUCTION

The CW television network's long-running series *Supernatural* (2005–) follows Dean Winchester and his younger brother Sam as they drive around the continental United States enacting the series' credo: "saving people, hunting things: the family business." In its early seasons, the series balanced episodic encounters with monsters from various cultural traditions against its ongoing investigation of the brothers' formative trauma: who, or what, immolated their mother in baby Sam's nursery, over twenty years ago? As *Supernatural* became more serialized, demons emerged as the Winchesters' chief adversaries and drivers of a larger plot: to release Lucifer from his infernal prison so that he and the Four Horsemen can lead the demons of Hell into war against the angels of Heaven, who have struggled to maintain control of the universe in the absence of God. With humanity caught in the crossfire, the stakes of the Winchesters' imperative to save people, and the magnitude of the things they hunt, achieve cosmic proportions.

Given *Supernatural*'s appropriation of Christian mythology in fashioning this apocalyptic scenario, one important character is absent: Jesus. Instead, the angels have identified another mortal savior on earth: Dean Winchester. The angel Zachariah informs Dean that his destiny, as the scion of a divinely orchestrated lineage, is to serve as the earthly vessel for the archangel Michael in his single combat against a similarly embodied Lucifer. Despite admitting that Dean will experience excruciating bodily suffering and his mind will be destroyed, the angels expect that, like Jesus, Dean will consent in exchange for greater goods: universal salvation and cosmic stability. The logic of this narrative, and of the Christian worldview that suffuses the cultural matrix inhabited by the series' audience,[1] assumes that Dean will say "yes." Yet he refuses to follow in Jesus' footsteps, determined to beat the devil on his own terms. Dean thus treads the path of another ancient salvific figure: Heracles, the greatest hero of the classical tradition.

Such tension within *Supernatural*'s apocalyptic scenario, between Heaven's expectation of submission and Dean's insistence on agency, resurrects an ancient ideological conflict embodied by Jesus and Heracles, heroes with structurally similar biographical narratives representing different systems of belief. Although *Supernatural*'s plot encourages expectation of a Jesus-figure, Dean descends from Heracles in sheer number, variety, and geographic range of exploits, as well as specific aspects of his characterization and narratives. Most relevant to *Supernatural*'s grand narrative arc, the Olympians' need of Heracles' participation to win the Gigantomachy aligns with Heaven's need of Dean's participation to forestall the Christian apocalypse. Thus, given the choice of bringing salvation through agency or submission, Dean walks the Heraclean path, despite the Christian narrative context.

Dean's position at the intersecting paths of the paradigmatic classical hero and Christianity's exemplary figure highlights these traditions' divergent attitudes toward sacrifice, specifically human sacrifice, as a means of achieving salvation. Christianity's foundation story glorified a common, if extreme, form of capital punishment by transforming it into a ritual exchange of Jesus' body and life for universal salvation, which is presented as God's plan and enabled by His angels.[2] By contrast, sacrificial narratives in classical myth, including those of Heracles, are fraught with anxiety and prone to malfunction when the offering is a human. *Supernatural*, which repeatedly rejects claims that "higher powers" may use human life as they see fit, even when the designated human is willing and motivated by Christian faith, is thus far more aligned with classical myth. *Supernatural*'s commitment to the value of human life even leads it to problematize the affective power of one Winchester trading his life for another's, stigmatizing these exchanges as cowardly escapes from difficult moral responsibilities rather than simply glorifying them as loving salvific acts.

## DEAN WINCHESTER, HERACLEAN HERO

Among the characters in classical myth who defeat superhuman adversaries while accomplishing great undertakings, only Heracles was created specifically to save the world from monsters.[3] This vocation was a logical extension of aristocratic education, which trained youths to channel the brute force and tactical intelligence needed for the high-stakes contests of athletics and war, in which Heracles excelled.[4] Once he strangled Hera's serpents in his cradle, however, his fame arose primarily from killing monsters.[5] The sheer number, variety, and geographical range of these exploits proliferated throughout antiquity and encompassed every area of the Mediterranean world, including the Underworld and Olympus. After centuries of post-classical representation in literary and pictorial media, this monster-slayer's vast portfolio lent itself to the "knight errant" framework that informed scores of "sword-and-sandal" films, over a hundred episodes of the widely distributed and syndicated television series *Hercules: The Legendary Journeys* (1995–9), and Disney's 1997 animated feature film and spinoff cable television series.[6] The knight errant's episodic adventures arguably manifest in the popular American figure of the itinerant gunslinger as righteous outlaw, which informs *Supernatural*'s protagonists.

Although Dean's status as the product of angelic eugenics is not revealed until Episode 5.1, his mother's horrific death led Dean's father John, an ex-Marine, to raise his sons "like warriors," in Sam's words (Episode 1.1). Dean valued this education in combat techniques and weapons training over the succession of public schools that the brothers briefly attended during the family's nationwide quest to avenge Mary's murder (e.g. flashbacks in Episode 4.13). As an adult, Dean takes the lead in combat, frequently framed as physically dominating while delivering death blows and parting quips to his supernatural adversaries. Beyond his commanding physicality, Dean reveals his skills as a tactician against myriad monsters, e.g. vampire, werewolf, ghost, shape-shifter, lamia, wendigo, djinn, siren, kitsune, ghoul, and rakshasa.

What unifies these disparate threats is their shared hunting grounds: the continental United States. Each episode of the Winchesters' never-ending road trip takes place in a named locality within the Lower 48. These communities' shared national culture and integrated justice systems binds diverse locales together, just as a shared sense of Greek cultural identity and belief in Zeus' justice, administered by human authorities, described Heracles' main zone of action. Besides monsters, Heracles also confronted and eliminated autocrats who dealt with him unjustly.[7] Dean likewise condemns and contends with law enforcement officers who impede his supernatural investigations. In keeping with the "crime procedural" structure of many episodes,

Dean further subverts their authority by appropriating their identities to track and eliminate his supernatural prey, thereby defending communities to which he will never belong.

Heracles' itinerant lifestyle resulted from domestic disasters that drove him into exile.[8] The brute force by which the infant Heracles saved himself from Hera's persecution enabled him to kill his music teacher Linus, spurring Heracles' expulsion from Thebes. Back home as an adult, a madness sent by Hera impelled Heracles to kill his children and, in some versions, his first wife Megara. Domestic tragedy instigated by a supernatural antagonist also drove the Winchester men from home. *Supernatural* periodically reminds viewers that their hometown is Lawrence, Kansas, but only crises connected to their role in the approaching apocalypse draw the Winchesters back to the site of Mary's demonic murder (Episodes 1.9, 2.4, 4.3, 5.22). Dean's later attempt to build a home also endangers his new family: an old flame, Lisa, and her son Ben, who Dean suspects is his biological child (Episodes 3.2 and 6.1). Besides his supernatural enemies, Dean himself poses a mortal threat when a temporary supernatural infection causes him almost to kill Lisa and Ben in their home (Episode 6.5). When they are later kidnapped and tortured by demons, Dean realizes that only by severing this connection can he save his girlfriend and child. He asks a supernatural ally to wipe Lisa and Ben's memories, rendering them as lost to him as if they were dead, and permanently alienating him from his household (Episode 6.21).

As in Heracles' myths, Dean's carnal appetites counterbalance these tragic motifs with comic excess. The series uses Dean's love for two signature American foods, burgers and pie, as a recurring joke that fuels parodic sequences with his Heraclean bottomless appetite (e.g. Episode 2.15).[9] By contrast, Dean's lack of appetite during the penultimate stage of the apocalyptic narrative indicates an existential crisis (Episode 5.14). Just as Heracles' bedding the fifty daughters of King Thespius on consecutive nights exemplified his virility, a parade of nameless "hot chicks" happily engage in one-night stands with Dean, while his near-fatal sexual encounter with an Amazon (Episode 7.13) recalls the labor in which Heracles' obtained Queen Hippolyte's girdle, which instigated war with her Amazons.[10] While Dean's myriad sexual encounters, like his monster kills, play into a particular paradigm of dominating masculinity, he also admits to trying on girl's underwear and liking it (Episode 5.4): shades of Heracles' cross-dressing in Queen Omphale's court.[11] Heracles' *erastes–eromenos* relationships with Iolaus and Hylas, in which an older and higher-status man engages in a socially and sexually initiatory relationship with a younger subordinate, are refracted through Dean's long-running relationships with the angel Castiel, whose socially awkward devotion to Dean produces a gay subtext, and with the demon Crowley, who pursues his own bromance with the hero in cheekily demonic fashion.[12] These interactions mine humor from Dean's discomfort, which stems not from opinions about homosexuality per se (although the show does employ "gay panic" in banter among hunters and their non-human teammates), but rather from his reflexively self-defensive posture connected to a fear of intimacy and his lifetime of trauma.

Dean's Heraclean insistence on personal sovereignty extends to a refusal to see himself as lesser than his adversaries, which enables him to contest and sometimes overcome superhuman beings' will. When Dean is temporarily compelled to serve Crowley in Season Six, he continues to pursue his own moral ends and to challenge authority figures, as does Heracles while enslaved to King Eurystheus.[13] Dean's lifetime of vanquishing supernatural creatures trained him to face down self-proclaimed greater beings – including angels, whose indifference and even contempt toward humans leads Dean to dub them "dicks with wings" (e.g. Episode 4.2). So too Heracles did not shrink from confronting and even attacking the gods Helios, Hades, and Apollo.[14] Echoing Heracles' liberation of Prometheus from divinely mandated imprisonment, Dean "liberates" the Promethean Castiel by inspiring him to defy the heavenly hierarchy in siding with humanity during the Apocalypse, and supports the rebel angel as he suffers for betraying his heavenly brethren.[15] Dean himself does not experience lasting punishment for his acts of defiance; indeed, he repeatedly overcomes his mortality, returning to life on earth from Hell (Episode 4.1), Purgatory (Episode 8.1), and even Heaven (Episode 5.16). So did too Heracles, who returned alive from his labor in the Underworld and who achieved immortality through apotheosis, despite a lifetime of willful defiance.[16]

## HERACLES, MICHAEL, AND/OR JESUS: PLACING DEAN IN THE COSMIC STRUGGLE

Heracles' apotheosis is sometimes connected to the exploit that *Supernatural*'s apocalyptic scenario resembles: participation in the Gigantomachy, which combines monster-slaying to protect a society to which the hero does not belong with Heracles' cosmic activities, including interactions with the gods. The myth is better preserved in the visual record than in literary sources, but the basic outlines of the story are clear.[17] When earth-born Giants arrogantly attack Olympus, a prophecy reveals that even Zeus and all the Olympians together cannot defeat the chthonic spawn without the aid of the mortal Heracles. Both vase-paintings and monumental sculpture, as on temples at Athens and Pergamon, featured Heracles battling the Giants next to Zeus and Athena.[18] In antiquity, this myth was sometimes conflated with the Titanomachy, the war through which Zeus and the Olympians established supremacy over their father Cronus' faction, the Titans, whom Zeus then imprisons in Tartarus.[19] So too in Disney's *Hercules* (1997), the infernal Hades plans to depose Zeus by not only releasing the Titans from their Underworld prison, but also preventing the hero from defending the gods and Zeus' order.[20]

A cosmic war in which malevolent chthonic forces rebel against the divine order and are defeated in one decisive battle describes both the classical Gigantomachy and Christian apocalyptic eschatology in the Book of Revelation. Both consider one warrior indispensable: in classical myth, Heracles, whose subsequent apotheosis entails cult worship in the manner of a god;[21] in Christian myth, the archangel Michael, whose name means "who is like God?" Like Heracles, Michael secures salvation through combat, defeating Lucifer in a battle immortalized by Raphael, Guido Reni, and Josse Lieferinxe, the last of which is used by Zachariah in Episode 4.22 to illustrate the angels' endgame (see Figure 5.1). Yet Michael already inhabits an ontological status suitable for confronting his fallen brother, while Heracles fights as a mortal.

As in the Christian apocalyptic narrative, *Supernatural* makes combat between Michael and Lucifer the Season Five endgame. However, the prophecy that a mortal of specially engineered lineage is the key to heavenly victory resembles the classical tradition of Heracles' participation in the Gigantomachy. *Supernatural* integrates these traditions by stipulating that this mortal will participate by serving as Michael's earthly vessel for the combat, entailing a submission to divine power that will destroy the mortal as the price of cosmic salvation. *Supernatural* thus implicitly invokes the myth of Jesus' salvation of humanity through self-sacrifice as the linchpin of these classical and biblical combat myths.

By requiring that Dean, like Jesus, consent to this role in God's plan, *Supernatural* reinvents another Heraclean myth: the crossroads of Vice and Virtue becomes a choice between classical and Christian heroism.[22] This choice is not just between cultural exemplars, but between opposed modes of salvific heroism. Despite declaring that he comes with a sword, and experiencing a crisis of confidence in the garden (Matthew 10; Luke 22), Jesus finally accepts that humanity's salvation requires his submission to God's plan, as the cosmic object of exchange that redeems all humanity. Submission to divine will wins Jesus glory among humans, who acknowledge him as their savior, and transformation into a being worthy of the title "Lord." Fighting to live or inventing an alternative plan would constitute failure. By contrast, Heracles' earthly glory and apotheosis are predicated on a career defined by the imposition of his will upon beasts, humans, the landscape, even gods. He even turns periods of enslavement to his benefit: purifying himself of blood-guilt, winning fame through his labors, highlighting his greatness compared to lesser masters. Heracles' heroism is defined by his agency.

The stark opposition between these modes of heroism is underscored by the similarity between the biographical narratives of Heracles and Jesus.[23] Both were sons of the King of Heaven and a chaste virgin, whose fiancé or husband agreed to raise the god's child as his own. Both faced mortal danger from powerful enemies as infants, and manifested their divine natures early. Upon coming of age, both performed marvelous deeds away from home. As adults, both suffered persecution by political authorities that increased their fame. Each was betrayed by a close companion, leading to an excruciating public death figured as a sacrifice and culminating in apotheosis and reunion with his Heavenly Father. In their cult worship, Heracles and Jesus even shared an epithet: savior (*soter*).[24] Given this mirroring, not to mention the enormous pressure on Dean to conform to ideological imperatives understood by both characters and viewers, Heaven's attempt to divert Dean from the Heraclean path to the Christian one is not implausible.

This attempted protrepsis is interrupted when Dean, demoralized by a near-fatal confrontation with a high-ranking demon, tells Castiel to "find someone else; it's not me" (Episode 4.16). Dean's faltering confidence resembles Jesus' crisis in the garden, when he asks God to take the cup from him and an angel arrives to strengthen his resolve in accepting the events that lead to his crucifixion (Luke 22). *Supernatural* too sends an angel to reawaken Dean to his destiny. "It's a Terrible Life" (Episode 4.17) recalls not only Frank Capra's 1946 movie, but also Martin Scorsese's *The Last Temptation of Christ* (1988), in which Jesus experiences a "normal" man's life. After Jesus wishes to be released from his destiny to die on the cross, a young girl who identifies herself as an angel invites him to come down. She leads him to Mary Magdalene, whom he marries, along with other women, who give him children. But his peaceful decline into old age is interrupted by a furious Judas, who exhorts Jesus to rise from his deathbed and resume his destined path. A cut returns Jesus to the cross, where he embraces his life's true purpose.

Dean's crisis of confidence produces *Supernatural*'s own "last temptation": a parody of the American dream starring vain corporate middle manager "Dean Smith." But his safe life full of yuppie/metrosexual status symbols is interrupted by lowly customer service representative "Sam Wesson," who instinctively draws his "boss" into successfully investigating a haunting at work. When Dean's own boss offers him a hefty raise in exchange for an indefinite commitment to slowly climbing the corporate ladder, Dean offers his resignation, sensing that "there's something else I'm supposed to be doing with my life." His boss touches Dean's forehead, the vibrant lighting becomes drab, and Dean recognizes the angel Zachariah, who engineered this episode precisely to convince Dean to resume his vocation.

But Zachariah miscalculates that Dean's revived sense of purpose will entail willingness to submit to Heaven's plans. Instead, Dean immediately subverts angelic protocols in order to interrupt a prophesied sequence of events that endangers Sam (Episode 4.18). Even Lucifer's raising of the Horsemen can't elicit Dean's consent, especially upon learning that the angels are not only inducing the Apocalypse, but are indifferent to its massive human collateral damage (Episode 4.22) (Figure 5.1). Zachariah finally coerces Dean into saying "yes" by torturing Sam – but before Michael arrives, Dean kills Zachariah

Figure 5.1 Zachariah (Kurt Fuller) illustrates the angels' plan for Dean (Jensen Ackles) in *Supernatural* Episode 4.22: "Lucifer Rising." Warner Brothers.

with a divine sword and the brothers escape (Episode 5.18). No amount of pressure to accept Christ-like submission can change Dean's Heraclean nature.

## SUPERNATURAL ON SACRIFICE AND SALVATION: CLASSICAL VERSUS CHRISTIAN PERSPECTIVES

By refusing to agree that his own destruction is the necessary price of universal salvation, Dean not only derails the angels' claims about destiny within the world of *Supernatural*. He also defies viewers' expectations of what heroism entails, by challenging the hegemonic worldview that has normalized such a death as an acceptable price for salvation and glorified such a use of human life by calling it sacrifice. Dean's refusal to re-enact Jesus' choice is the culmination of *Supernatural*'s persistent and categorical rejection of the proposition that a supernatural being is entitled to appropriate human life to its own ends. While this is hardly controversial when applied to bestial monsters, such as werewolves, that feed upon humans with tooth and claw, the series also repeatedly presents sacrifice as merely an elaborate rationale for an equally morally indefensible demand. *Supernatural* thus stakes out a position closer to classical myth's anxiety about exchanging human life for salvation from a more powerful being, than to Christianity's embrace of such an exchange as the pinnacle of human moral achievement.

In the popular Western imagination, the paradigm of sacrifice has long been Jesus, who died for humanity's sins in a manner illustrated by his metaphorical rendering as the lamb led to the slaughter. This Christian paradigm has obscured the basic meaning of "making something sacred" in historical Greek and Roman rituals: setting aside an offering for a god's enjoyment by symbolically transferring it out of the human realm.[25] In exchange for such an offering, the divine recipient was expected to grant some benefit to the individual or group that dedicated the gift. Ritualized reciprocity between humans and gods was fundamental to maintaining individual and group security, and the offerings used to show reverence and secure divine benefaction ranged from vegetal products to man-made objects such as childhood toys to animals, small and large. A bloody death was not the point of sacrifice, nor was it required, but when that gift was alive, the consent of the offering was conventionally sought and at least notionally secured prior to the act of killing.[26] In rare cases, that gift was a human life.[27]

Such transgression of the notional boundary separating humans from animals was refracted through the lens of mythic narrative, wherein sacrificial rituals feature human offerings with disproportionate frequency. A human offering, generally a high-ranking member of the community, indicates a society facing an existential crisis, such as failure in war, agricultural blight, or siege by a monstrous predator – circumstances that might be interpreted as punishment for offending a god. Yet mythical corrective sacrifice often malfunctions, due to the implication of fraud or error in its prescription, or the subsequent death of the sacrificant, or the interruption of the ritual. Furthermore, special anxiety gravitates around the issue of consent. Lack of consent, as when Agamemnon sacrifices his daughter Iphigenia to ensure the Greek army's departure for Troy in Aeschylus' *Agamemnon*, intensifies the horror of her killing; consent freely given, as in Euripides' rendering in *Iphigenia at Aulis*, wins her immense glory; divine or heroic intervention saves the blameless victim when Artemis substitutes a deer for the princess in Euripides' *Iphigenia among the Taurians*. All variations save the Greek expedition from failure; all end in Agamemnon's own killing upon his homecoming to Argos.

Such sacrificial malfunctions figure in several of Heracles' myths, including two interruptions of the ritual undertaken by non-Greek peoples and his own ironic death in place of a sacrificial offering. Heracles saves the Trojan princess Hesione by killing the sea-monster sent by Poseidon to punish the city for King Laomedon's treachery, a doublet of the myth in which Perseus saves the Ethiopian princess Andromeda under similar circumstances.[28] The Egyptian king Bousiris attempts to turn Heracles into one offering in a series of traveling strangers, but is slain by the hero instead.[29] Heracles' death as a sacrificial offering, dramatized in Sophocles' *Women of Trachis*, involves a paradoxical mixture of loss and assertion of agency over his body. While performing a thanksgiving sacrifice to Zeus, Heracles is overcome by bodily suffering so intense that he complains it feminizes him (lines 1071–5). This emasculating loss of control was caused by a "love potion" that his misguided wife made from the bodily fluids of a centaur whom Heracles had killed with a poisoned arrow years ago, thus fulfilling a prophecy that he would be killed by a dead enemy (lines 1159–63). Rather than submit to this slow death by poison, Heracles asserts his agency by climbing onto the sacrificial altar and ordering his horrified son to burn him alive, as if in place of the bovine offering. Heracles continues his salvific activities upon achieving apotheosis, but only after a grotesque death.

The myth of Jesus' death, which developed in a Hellenized region under Roman rule, resembles classical mythic narratives involving human sacrifice: specifically, those that figure death as a triumph. A gruesome but common judicial punishment is transformed into a fulfillment of divine will that results in Jesus' apotheosis as a salvific deity. The latent problem of how an offering's body was used after death – a sacrificial animal would be consumed by the community, as Andromeda and Hesione were apparently to be eaten by Poseidon's sea-monster – is embraced at the "last supper," where Jesus tells his followers that the bread and wine they consume are his flesh and blood (I Corinthians 11:20–9).[30] Jesus' consent to his own killing, especially as someone blameless of the crime for which he suffers, heightens the glory that he earns for submitting to his equally undeserved destiny: to serve as the unblemished offering that placates a god angry over the original sin of humanity. Most importantly, the framing of Jesus as *exemplum* – manifested in the decade before *Supernatural*'s premiere through ubiquitous merchandising of the acronym WWJD ("What would Jesus do?") – honors his willingness to die for the benefit of others as the ultimate "good."

This interpretation of Jesus' willingness to die by divine fiat as morally unassailable and suitable for emulation is what *Supernatural* consistently rejects. In Episode 1.11, *Supernatural* expands its gallery of predatory "things" to include gods by introducing the Vanir, a Norse harvest god who ensures an Indiana town's anomalous prosperity among their failing neighbors – so long as the townspeople annually strand two passing travelers near its effigy, a scarecrow. Subsequent episodes introduce the trickster-god Loki, sating his appetite for poetic justice by brutally hoisting the arrogant on their own petards (Episode 2.15); the northern European winter solstice god Hold Nickar, exchanging a highly ritualized meal of dismembered flesh for mild winters (Episode 3.8); the Hindu Kali, the Norse Odin, the Roman Mercury, the Chinese Zhao Shen, and the Haitian Baron Samedi, trapping humans in a motel as sustenance for their summit on stopping the looming Judeo-Christian Apocalypse (Episode 5.19). While as predatory as beasts, these beings expect deferential treatment befitting their traditional status as gods. Such claims used to be validated by their devotees; Hold Nickar recalls when hundreds offered themselves willingly as the ritual meal. In this and other episodes involving gods expecting to feast on humans, the Winchesters affirm that those "good old days" are over, with deadly force.

*Supernatural* entertains the specific claim that the "greater good" merits surrendering human life to a "higher power," but always rejects it. When Dean (in Heraclean fashion) interrupts the Indiana town's annual ritual by saving the intended offerings, the townspeople offer him to the god, along with a town elder's adopted niece, who was born elsewhere. Her aunt tearfully explains, "That's what sacrifice means: giving up something you love, for the greater good. The town needs to be saved. The good of the many outweighs the good of the one." After Sam and Dean stop the sacrifice, the enraged god kills the town elders and the niece burns down the sacred tree that preserves its life-force. When Hold Nickar, who manifests as a Christmas-loving "Ozzie and Harriet"-like couple, argues that the gift of mild winter in Michigan justifies pulling a few unsuspecting townspeople up the chimney and to their deaths, Dean and Sam respond by impaling the couple on the branches of their festive evergreen tree (Episode 3.8). In Episode 3.12, a demonic ritual could exchange one "person of virtue" – a virgin marked as a devout Catholic through her crucifix pendant, rosary beads, and personal testimony about her faith – for the expulsion of demons from an entire town's-worth of people. Despite her willingness to die for her friends and neighbors, Dean insists on using combat to save them.

Divine creatures of the Abrahamic tradition are not exempted from *Supernatural*'s critique of popular sacrificial logic. In Episode 2.13, prostitutes and alcoholics in Providence, Rhode Island, believe themselves redeemed when they unquestioningly follow the instructions of an angel: to kill designated strangers, then surrender themselves to the authorities. These victims, who turn out to have been murderous sexual predators, belonged to the same Catholic congregation, but their judge was no angel; it was the ghost of a recently murdered priest acting on his flock's horrifying confessions. The series takes advantage of the popular assumption that angels, as agents of Heaven, are both benevolent guardians of humanity and entitled to use "lesser" beings to any end. Yet the episode's faithful assassins end up imprisoned as criminally insane murderers.

*Supernatural*'s introduction of genuine angels in Season Four begins on a similarly ominous note and gradually reveals their terrible methods and objectives, which differ in degree rather than kind from those of the other supernatural beings from which the Winchesters protect humanity. Castiel first manifests as an unbearably high-pitched frequency, then incinerates the eyeballs of a psychic who attempts to "see" this mysterious entity on Dean's behalf. Finally, he takes human form, as do other angels who subsequently enter the story. But angels, like demons, must possess humans in order to walk the earth; they differ only in requiring consent from the "vessel" before inhabiting it. Episode 4.20 shows in flashbacks how the incorporeal Castiel had contacted a devout Christian, Jimmy Novak, and leveraged his faith to secure this consent. Castiel did not even consider how Jimmy's family would suffer from Castiel's control of Jimmy's body and suppression of his mind, until these crises play out in the present time of the episode. Angels don't eat their human vessels, but they do effectively consume them when a human consents to such "sacrifice."

Dean, who earlier had identified himself as unencumbered by Christian belief (Episode 2.13), soon recognizes that the spectrum of supernatural adversaries includes angels, who pursue their own agenda through, but not for, humans and turn vindictive when faced with resistance. Although Dean shares their goal of defeating Lucifer, angels are indifferent to human suffering; some, such as Uriel, express as much contempt for what he calls "mud monkeys" as Lucifer himself (Episode 4.7). Zachariah's admission that his brethren had initiated the Apocalypse themselves (Episode 4.22) decisively undermines their insistence on Dean's self-sacrifice as a necessary "good." Once Zachariah discloses that his role in the apocalyptic duel is merely to serve as Michael's vessel (Episode 5.1), Dean's dismay at angelic arrogance hardens into disgusted repudiation of their claims of moral superiority and sense of entitlement to human bodies. The angel's increasingly ruthless attempts to manipulate Dean into consenting to possession result instead in Dean killing Zachariah, thus confirming angels as "things" that the Winchesters "hunt." Such elimination of an existential threat to humanity, face to face and with a manual weapon, reaffirms Dean's embrace of Heraclean agency as the appropriate salvific mode – not consent to divinely mandated death.

*Supernatural* moots one further circumstance in which the temptation to submit human life to a more powerful being's use is most acute: as the price of one Winchester man saving his son's or brother's life. This recurring scenario stems from guilt over failing to save both Mary and Sam's live-in girlfriend Jessica, a dead ringer for Mary who is killed the same way at the end of the pilot. The Winchesters' familial trauma is intensified by the hunters' warrior culture, which turns family members into brothers-in-arms and conjoins the melodramatic imperatives of "weepies," coded as feminine, with those of combat films, coded as masculine.[31] In both genres, self-sacrifice for a dear one is valorized in a manner that echoes Jesus' self-sacrifice out of love for humanity. When the Winchesters indulge in this substitution narrative, however, the series contaminates their self-sacrifice with morally ambiguous motives and a lack of gratitude from whoever is thus "saved."

From the pilot episode's present-day action, *Supernatural* exploits the pathos of one Winchester giving up something he loves for a familial "good": Sam submits to Dean's plea that he abandon the dream of a safe life as a lawyer and husband to search for their father, who has disappeared while "hunting." Their eventual reunion is tragically interrupted by a demonically engineered car crash that leaves Dean in a coma, which leads their father, John, to make a deal with the very demon who killed Mary: to immediately surrender his own life and soul in exchange for Dean's recovery (Episode 2.1). After Dean witnesses Sam being murdered before his eyes, he makes a similar deal with a crossroads demon in exchange for reviving his brother; Dean at least receives one year to live (Episode 2.22). The apocalyptic narrative climaxes with Sam consenting to possession by Lucifer in the foolish hope of being able to wrest control of his body from the archangel long enough to throw it back into its infernal prison (Episode 5.22). Sam nearly fails, but Dean's refusal to desert his brother, even as Lucifer uses Sam's body to beat Dean bloody, gives Sam the strength to work the imprisonment spell.

Although such acts of self-sacrifice are motivated partially by love, a cowardly desire to escape moral burdens contaminates the Winchesters' "gifts." *Supernatural* encourages viewers to invest emotionally in this familial self-sacrifice through these scenes' strategically intense musical scoring, but the scripting undercuts this affective manipulation by disclosing their mixed motives – nor do the "saved" accept this gift gracefully. Just before dying, John burdens Dean with deciding whether to kill his brother, whose infection with demon blood as a baby made him an unwitting demonic sleeper agent. When Dean learns how his father died, he reacts with rage, resentment, and grief. His self-loathing over later failing to prevent his brother's murder motivates Dean to revive Sam by selling his own soul: a slow-motion suicide, but "at least ... my life would mean something." When his surrogate father-figure Bobby realizes Dean's motivation, he verbalizes the series' critique: "Have you got that low an opinion of yourself? .... How is your brother gonna feel when he knows you're going to Hell? How'd you feel when you knew your dad went for you?" Indeed, Sam demands that they try to break the deal, even at the cost of his own life. Through his infernal swan dive – which saves the world, but also Dean specifically, from Lucifer – Sam also attempts to relieve his guilt over ignoring Dean's advice and accidentally releasing Lucifer by killing his original demon, Lilith. Ironically, she had died willingly to free her lord in an act of salvific heroism, for the greater good – of demonkind.

## CONCLUSION

By withholding approval even of the Winchesters' mutual self-sacrifice, *Supernatural* insists that the only morally acceptable mode of salvific heroism is living to fight another day. That is the choice the Winchesters affirm regularly, even as they acknowledge that the fatality rate for hunters is one hundred percent. Still, their choice to pursue this vocation, rather than to operate under the compulsion of a "higher" power's mandate, is framed as invaluable – especially in contrast to the totalitarian rigidity of Heaven, which allows angels no independent thought or personal emotional commitments, and punishes doubt or disobedience with death (Episode 4.10).[32] While the series never indicates that it draws intentionally upon Heracles myths specifically, its deeply humanistic ideology and steadfast rejection of Christianity's central myth leads *Supernatural* to gravitate toward classical humanism, a maneuver practiced since at least the Renaissance.[33] The Heraclean principle that valorizes personal agency against any repressive authority, no matter how "high," fuses easily with the American ideology that animates the series, including its veneration of life and liberty. In making Dean Winchester a great American hero, *Supernatural* thus modeled him, even if unwittingly, on the greatest hero of classical myth.

## NOTES

Thanks to Antony Augoustakis and Stacie Raucci for inviting me to present an earlier version of this paper at the New Heroes on Screen conference and to contribute to this volume; to Tamsin Jones and Vincent Tomasso for comments on a subsequent version; and to Matthew Lopez for assistance with the scholarship on *Supernatural*.

1. On *Supernatural* and hegemonic Christianity, see Engstrom and Valenzano (2014).
2. Many, but not all, Christian sects understand Jesus' death on the cross as salvific sacrifice.
3. On Hesiod fr. 195 MW, see Gantz (1993: 374–5).
4. Heracles as model athletic victor and founder of the Olympic Games: Stafford (2012: 160–3); as conqueror of Orchomenos, Troy, and Oichalia: Gantz (1993: 381, 400–2, 434–7).
5. Heracles as monster-slayer: Stafford (2012: 23–77).
6. Generally, Stafford (2012: 201–44); on Heracles in "sword-and-sandal": Hughes (2011); O'Brien (2014); Rushing (2016). On *Hercules: The Legendary Journeys*, see Solomon in this volume; on Disney's *Hercules*, see Ward (2002).

7 See Gantz (1993) on Erginos (379–80), Augeias (392–3), Diomedes (395–7), Bousiris (418).
8 On Heracles' exiles after killing Linus, then Megara and his children: Gantz (1993: 379–81).
9 Stafford (2012: 105–17) on Heracles' gluttony.
10 See Gantz (1993: 379) on the daughters of Thespius and (399–400) on Amazons.
11 On enslavement to Omphale, see Gantz (1993: 439–41); on Heracles' gender and cross-dressing, see Loraux (1990); Cyrino (1998); Llewellyn-Jones (2005).
12 On Heracles as *erastes*, see Mastronarde (1968); Sergent (1984); Stafford (2012: 130–6). On fraught intersections of love, sexuality, and masculinity in *Supernatural* and its fan faction, including the brother–lover theme, see Tosenberger (2008); Flegel and Roth (2010); Goguen (2013); Nicol (2014).
13 On Heracles' enslavement to Eurystheus: Gantz (1993: 381–416), Stafford (2012: 23–50).
14 See Gantz (1993: 404–10) on Helios, (413–16) on Hades, and (438–9) on Apollo.
15 On Prometheus, see Gantz (1993: 155–6).
16 On overcoming death, see Gantz (1993: 460–3); Stafford (2012: 171–5).
17 Gantz (1993: 445–57); Stafford (2012: 63–5).
18 Moore (1979, 1995); Schwab (1996); Whitaker (2005).
19 Innes (1979); Clay (2003: 113–15).
20 Gellar-Goad (2013–14).
21 Stafford (2012: 171–98).
22 On the myth in antiquity and modernity, see Kuntz (1993–4); Stafford (2005, 2012: 121–4).
23 On resemblances between Heracles and Jesus, see Aune (1990); Stafford (2012: 202–6); Safran (2015).
24 Heracles as *soter*: Stafford (2012: 189).
25 The origins and meaning of sacrifice in the classical world remain a dynamic field of inquiry; see e.g. Burkert (1983); Detienne and Vernant (1989); Bremmer (2010); Scheid (2011); Naiden (2013).
26 Naiden (2007) refutes the conceit; Bremmer (2010) distinguishes between conceit and fact. See also pictorial evidence collected by Van Straten (1995).
27 Bremmer (2007) documents the late-twentieth-century efflorescence of interest in the ancient Greek practice of human sacrifice along with his own discussion. Schultz (2010) contrasts Roman rhetoric about human sacrifice with ritual practice.
28 See Gantz (1993: 400–2) on Heracles' rescue of Hesione and (307–10) on Perseus' rescue of Andromeda.
29 See Gantz (1993: 418) on Bousiris.

30 Chilton (2002) and Lang (2002) discuss Jesus' words and actions in their original context and in subsequent developing interpretations of eucharistic practices. Tamsin Jones alerted me to medieval depictions of Jesus that figure the wound inflicted by the Roman centurion as a breast with which Jesus feeds his followers.
31 On melodrama as mode rather than genre, see Langford (2005: 29–52); on melodrama's association with the "woman's film" and family-centered film genres, see Mercer and Shingler (2005); on melodrama and gender in *Supernatural*, see Bruce (2010).
32 On *Supernatural*'s angels and their hierarchy, see Hansen (2014).
33 Many scholars note the series' humanism; for sustained commentary, see Vermeer (2014).

# PART II
*Epic Heroes*

# 6 Russell Crowe and Maximal Projections in Noah (2014)

Monica S. Cyrino

If personality is an unbroken series of successful gestures, then there was something gorgeous about him ...
(Narrator Nick Carraway, explaining the allure of Jay Gatsby, in F. Scott Fitzgerald's novel *The Great Gatsby* (1925))

## INTRODUCTION

This chapter explores how the lead actor performance of Russell Crowe in Darren Aronofsky's unconventional biblical epic *Noah* (2014) takes up Ridley Scott's blockbuster film *Gladiator* (2000) as a specific screen intertext by using what I call "maximal projections."[1] By coining the phrase "maximal projections," I mean that Crowe plays the role of the Old Testament patriarch Noah using a series of deliberately referential gestures to his character of Maximus, the general turned gladiator, in the earlier film. Further, I maintain that Crowe makes this intentional artistic choice to invite the audience of *Noah* to recognize Maximus in his performance in the biblical epic in order to captivate and appeal to them. As film historian Jim Cullen observes:

> Actors vividly display the act of choice central to the artistic process. Putting aside the fact that any acting performance includes countless renditions that are shot out of sequence or discarded on the cutting room floor, watching a movie involves witnessing an inexhaustible array of choices in language, posture, expression, and setting. A century of experience has taught us that some people make these choices so strikingly that we will watch them repeatedly not only in the same movie, but in movie after movie.[2]

## RUSSELL CROWE'S STAR TEXT

The casting of Crowe, who won the Academy Award for Best Actor for the role of Maximus in *Gladiator*, as the title patriarch in *Noah* raises the theoretical question of his celebrity "star text" that is being interpreted or "read" by the audience as they watch him on screen (Figures 6.1 and 6.2). As originally framed by Richard Dyer in his influential book *Stars*, an actor's distinct star image can both affect the production of meaning in a film and manipulate the arousal of emotions and expectations in viewers.[3] That is, when a famous actor takes on a role, they bring one or more previous roles to the new performance; thus their star text powerfully influences how an audience engages with their previous roles within the new performance. As popular culture critic Greil Marcus notes:

Figure 6.1 Russell Crowe as the Roman general Maximus in *Gladiator* (2000). DreamWorks.

# Russell Crowe and Maximal Projections in Noah

Figure 6.2 Russell Crowe as the titular biblical patriarch in *Noah* (2014). Paramount Pictures.

> When actors migrate from movie to movie, traces of their characters travel with them, until, regardless of the script, the setup, the director's instructions, it's partly the old characters speaking out of the mouths of the new ones, guiding a new character's hand into a gesture you remember from two or twenty years before.[4]

These "star-peats," as I term such repetitions – the "archaeological" layering of an actor's earlier roles one upon the other, an occurrence so ubiquitous in the epic cinematic genre[5] – have a particular impact on the later performances: that is, linking these roles together in the mind of the viewer has the power to add another level of meaning, to lend a veneer of familiarity or authenticity, and even to invite the audience to interpret the new role through the lens of the previous one.

In the film *Noah*, Crowe invites the audience to absorb, decode, and ultimately enjoy the way he plays the character of the ark-building biblical patriarch through the well-known epic cinematic figure of Maximus, the hero of *Gladiator*. This chapter demonstrates how Crowe evokes the Maximus star memory in very specific ways through physical gesture and bodily movement, interactions with other characters, and even distinctive dialogue and line readings. Moreover, I explain that these "maximal" echoes are intentionally more prominent in the first half of the film *Noah*, in order to draw the audience right from the outset into what is clearly not a conventional kind of epic movie, with its dreamy visual aesthetic and eccentric narrative structure; in particular, what could have been the very challenging task of generating audience identification with the main character – in this case, the fractious figure of Noah – which is necessary for a film's box office success, is made easier by reminding them of the attractive gladiator hero Maximus.[6] Crowe's evocation of the appealing Maximus star text allows viewers to identify with the protagonist Noah early on in the film as a compassionate father and husband, as well as a tenacious fighter for what is good and right, before the character becomes more authoritarian, ill-tempered, and seemingly implacable in the face of his family's, and indeed all of humanity's, suffering. The Maximus star text encourages the audience – both non-believers and those among the faithful who prefer their biblical heroes blemish-free – to accept Crowe–Noah as a hero who is both righteous and flawed.

## FROM ROME BACK TO THE BIBLE

To understand the artistic reasons and industry market factors that were at play around the time of Crowe's casting in the role of Noah, it is instructive to follow the trajectory of recent screen productions set in the ancient world. As students of history all know, one of the most devastating natural disasters that ever occurred in the history of humankind was the eruption of Mount Vesuvius in the Bay of Naples south of Rome on August 24, AD 79. Likewise, one of the most devastating cinematic disasters was the release on February 21, 2014, of the movie *Pompeii*, whose fiery, asteroid-spewing volcano destroyed much more than the titular city. After TriStar Pictures reported a production budget of over $100 million, *Pompeii* made only $23 million in US domestic gross; although foreign box office topped off at $94 million, eventually allowing the movie to break even, grievous damage had been done.[7] The financial and critical failure of this "chintzy *Gladiator* knockoff"[8] dealt a serious blow to the steady stream of ancient Rome-themed films and television series that audiences have been enjoying for the past fifteen years or so, ever since Maximus floated across the sand of the Colosseum on a sea of rose petals in the final scenes of the Best Picture of the year AD 2000.

After the *Pompeii* catastrophe, numerous ancient Rome-themed projects that had been announced were shelved or remain languishing in development purgatory. These include the much anticipated HBO production of a brand new series based on Robert Graves' novels *I, Claudius* (1934a) and *Claudius the God* (1934b), which the cable network announced with great fanfare they were developing in 2011; this was to have been an original adaptation of the novels, not a remake of the 1976 BBC miniseries starring Derek Jacobi, but no mention has been made of the project in a couple of years.[9] The long-gestating Sony Pictures *Cleopatra* feature, based on the bestselling Stacy Schiff biography *Cleopatra: A Life* (2010), with Angelina Jolie famously attached to star, also seems to be in limbo: no doubt the embarrassing leak of some heated emails in 2014 between producer Scott Rudin and the studio contributed to the stalling of the film. While media outlets have announced the recent addition of a new screenwriter,[10] the Sony *Cleopatra* biopic still lacks a director – though several heavyweight names have been floated – indicating an alarming lack of interest and investment in the cinematic revival of the Egyptian queen and her Roman lovers. Several attempts to launch *Cleopatra* television projects have been announced in the last few years, but none have been successful in getting off the ground: most recently, Amazon Studios have put into development a *Cleopatra* "revisionist" drama series helmed by the creative production team behind the STARZ series *Black Sails* (2014–17), but with no premiere date set.[11] Surely some of these projects may be casualties of the unwelcoming critical and financial climate for ancient Rome-themed projects in a post-*Pompeii* environment. Although Greek mythology-inspired productions remain popular – just witness the great surge of Hercules media vehicles in the last few years, as surveyed in the first part of this volume – screen projects based on ancient history, especially ancient Rome, do not currently appear to be situated in the industry forefront.

Instead, the industry trend in recent years has decisively moved to focus on biblical narratives in both feature film and television productions. Notably, the tide began with several prominent television series that boasted overt religious titles, themes, and characters. *The Bible*, which first aired on the History Channel in March 2013, was a ten-episode miniseries from Mark Burnett and Roma Downey, the husband-and-wife producing team who claim to be "publicly Christian" and to speak for the faith-based community;[12] the series delivered blockbuster ratings and was nominated for three Primetime Emmy awards, including Outstanding Miniseries or Movie.[13] The narrative of the series starts with Genesis and ends just after the crucifixion, with five hours from the Old Testament and five from the New Testament. Critical reviews of the series were mixed: not unexpectedly, religious viewers were quick to nitpick deviations from the scriptural text and complain that the series used too much creative license. Nevertheless, *The Bible* became the biggest selling miniseries in its first week of DVD release.

Burnett and Downey sought to match this success with a sensibly named sequel *AD: The Bible Continues*, which premiered as a limited series on NBC on Easter Sunday (April 5) and ran in twelve weekly one-hour episodes from April to June 2015. The drama picks up immediately after the events of *The Bible*, beginning with the crucifixion and resurrection, and continues with the first ten chapters of the Book of Acts. While the series achieved solid ratings, again reviews were mixed, and NBC canceled the series after just one season.[14] Several other religious-themed television series were produced at around this time, including Burnett and Downey's two-part CBS miniseries *The Dovekeepers* (March 2015), a critically panned adaptation of Alice Hoffman's novel about three Jewish women during the siege of Masada in AD 73; and ABC's *Of Kings and Prophets*

(March 2016), a decidedly more adult nine-episode miniseries that recounted the life of Saul, King of Israel, his family and political rivals, but was criticized by the faith-based audience for its explicit scenes of graphic sex and violence.

As for feature films, the last few years saw the release of several major movies drawn from the pages of the Bible, what one media critic cheekily called "a veritable flood by recent standards."[15] The film *Son of God*, which premiered in February 2014, was produced by Burnett and Downey as a PG-13 adaptation and expansion of their smash-hit miniseries *The Bible*, using scenes from the original telecast as well as some new footage shot specifically for the feature film: "I realized the story should be on the big screen," said Burnett.[16] As the first Jesus biopic since Mel Gibson's box office juggernaut *The Passion of the Christ* (2004), the producers aimed to use a similar strategy to market the film to Christians by lining up endorsements from religious leaders and touring United States churches to screen the film.[17] Much less gory and controversial than *The Passion*, however, *Son of God* was also less successful with theatergoers, with $60 million in domestic gross and only $8 million foreign for a total of $68 million.[18] No doubt the extreme notoriety and intense media scrutiny that accompanied contemporary extra-cinematic discussions of the Gibson film helped boost ticket sales for *The Passion* among both religious and secular viewers.

Although *Son of God* was made by and mainly for devout Christians, two other recent biblical-themed epics, Aronofsky's *Noah*, which opened in March 2014, and Ridley Scott's visually spectacular *Exodus: Gods and Kings*, starring Christian Bale as Moses, which came out in December 2014, attempted to have it both ways by appealing to mainstream audiences without offending true believers. Thus, both *Noah* and *Exodus* were primarily pitched to filmgoers as brawny, *Gladiator*-style action epics rather than as conventionally reverent Bible movies, since they hoped to avoid controversy over any supposed liberties taken with the original biblical narratives.[19] But the cinematic focus on action adventure and breathtaking special effects did not guarantee box office salvation, as religious-minded viewers tend to be exceptionally vigilant about how filmmakers deal with their sacred texts, even if the faithful themselves are often not well versed in the actual scripture: as one Christian marketing consultant puts it, "The Old Testament was a gritty, rough, violent place, but you can't take all the weight off the faith end."[20] So while both films took heat from critics all across the religious and political spectrums, vigorous marketing campaigns and diligent audience pre-screenings eventually brought positive critical support and even solid commercial success.[21] Moreover, studios learned a valuable lesson about letting faith-based moviegoers know what to expect before entering the theater.

But the feature film exception that may serve to prove the current religious rule is the big-budget *Ben-Hur* remake, directed by Timur Bekmambetov, which opened to a disappointingly weak $11.4 million its first weekend in August 2016.[22] The new film was shot at Cinecittà in Rome, just like its cinematic forerunner, the 1959 multiple Oscar-winning epic hit directed by William Wyler and starring Charlton Heston. Yet compared to that famously bold Technicolor masterpiece, the recent reboot, for all its cutting-edge CGI and fresh-faced talent, seems somehow dated, timid, and unimaginative; indeed, critics did not mince words: "A muddled, inconsequential mess... more noble, dweeby, and neutered than a Sunday-school lesson in South Dakota."[23] Produced by Burnett and Downey, seeking to replicate their recent victories with *The Bible* and *Son of God*, the new film has a much heavier emphasis on the religious aspects of the original story – Lew Wallace's 1880 novel *Ben-Hur: A Tale of the Christ* – in terms of both the overt presence of Jesus on screen and the narrative focus on righteous redemption. In addition, the studios actively targeted advertising to faith-based communities in the hopes of selling tickets to Christian filmgoers.[24] But in a media market filled with high-quality religious-themed onscreen entertainment both on television and at the movies, the new *Ben-Hur*'s blandness and lack of a clear and compelling spiritual message made it the most expensive cinematic flop of the year.

One way to explain the gigantic boom in biblical-themed onscreen entertainment in the last few years would be to look at social and cultural trends, such as the growth of political conservatism, the rise of personal religiosity, or even the widespread popularity of a new, charismatic pope. But in the movie and television business, it is often more plausible simply to *cherchez l'argent*. After the enormous success of Gibson's *Passion* astounded the industry in 2004 – the film cost only $30 million to make, grossed $612 million in worldwide ticket sales, and remains the highest-grossing R-rated film ever[25] – it might have seemed obvious that studios would fall over themselves and each other to green-light the next biblical blockbuster: as one film critic remarked with truthful candor, "Like the animals on Noah's ark, ideas in Hollywood often come in twos."[26] But keep in mind *The Passion* was made, marketed, and distributed completely outside the studio system by a devout – some would say fanatical

– believer, and many in the faith community continue to regard the film industry as their natural enemy, a moral cesspool that had produced controversial and allegedly "blasphemous" movies such as *Monty Python's Life of Brian* (1979), Martin Scorsese's *The Last Temptation of Christ* (1988), and Ron Howard's *The Da Vinci Code* (2006).[27] So, while biblical heroes regularly chewed the scenery on mid-century silver screens, Hollywood seemed to have lost the expertise to make and market entertainment for the faithful, who – to be fair to the studio executives – do often react with hypersensitivity and criticism, and sometimes boycotts and lawsuits, to any film dealing with subject matter they consider sacred.[28] Thus, although the studios dearly wanted to tap into the contemporary religious-minded audience that bought half a billion dollars' worth of tickets to see the Gibson film – and even if they had been making entertaining and profitable ancient world films and television series since *Gladiator* in 2000 – they just did not seem to know how to make credible Bible movies any more.

Following the success of *The Passion*, however, a few astute Hollywood studios during the mid-2000s launched faith-oriented divisions (including Fox Faith and Sony's Affirm Films), while others hired faith-based marketing firms and Christian-media consultants (such as Jonathan Bock of Grace Hill Media) to cultivate connections in pastoral communities that would help them turn churchgoers into ticket buyers.[29] The last decade has witnessed some successful forays into broadly religious-themed cinema, like the critically acclaimed film of the C. S. Lewis children's book, *The Chronicles of Narnia: The Lion, the Witch and the Wardrobe* (2005), and the feel-good sports savior movie, *The Blind Side* (2009), both of which attracted substantial Christian followings.[30] But the genre of the traditional biblical epic set in antiquity remained largely untested until Burnett and Downey's television miniseries *The Bible* commanded thirteen million viewers for its spring 2013 premiere. After that – and in the wake of the critical and financial devastation of Tristar's *Pompeii*, with the immediate and consequent avoidance of ancient Rome-set productions – religious-themed projects and specifically biblical productions with narratives set in the ancient world found a welcome commercial opening and took swift advantage of it. Those projects that were already in production were accelerated, and those that were languishing in development hell were suddenly resurrected; studios sought out the usual suspects among writers, directors, and stars, who were aggressively recruited for their winning industry track records.

Many of these recent Bible-themed projects clearly capitalize on and borrow from the successful production strategies set in place by the blockbuster *Gladiator* in particular and its epic cinematic and televisual descendants over the past two decades. Epic is by far the most conservative film genre – scholars of onscreen classical receptions have discussed set-piece scenes, recurring characters, narrative and thematic conventions, and common visual tropes that come up again and again in epic films and television series.[31] Whether classical, biblical, or even Western, the epic mode on screen tends to refashion, remake, and pay reverent homage to earlier movies and shows.[32] Yet Aronofsky's biblical epic *Noah* takes up the film *Gladiator* as a specific screen intertext in a way that is neither trivial nor simply conventional by casting Russell Crowe as the title patriarch, and by using "maximal projections" to refer back to Crowe's star text as Maximus the general-turned-gladiator in the earlier movie. In playing the title role, Crowe lends his considerable creative and commercial clout to the service of the contemporary religious epic film, and thereby transforms and revitalizes the character as an action hero.

## MAXIMAL PROJECTIONS IN *NOAH*

Paramount Pictures' *Noah* was the biggest Bible-based film to hit the silver screen in half a century, and the most expensive film for director Darren Aronofsky, the American *auteur* better known for edgy, artistic fare such as *The Wrestler* (2008) and *Black Swan* (2010). Aronofsky and his co-writer Ari Handel used the brief passages from Genesis (chapters 6–9) to build up the familiar biblical story of Noah, the ark, and the flood, supplementing the Old Testament text from other sacred Jewish writings (such as the Talmud, the Midrash, the Zohar, and the Book of Enoch); in addition, they used extra-biblical sources such as the flood tradition in ancient Greek myth, the Mesopotamian narrative in the Epic of Gilgamesh, and Native American sources.[33] The result was a cinematic plot with some strange, unfamiliar elements that would be quite unknown to both secular and Christian viewers: in articulating his unconventional vision, Aronofsky called it "the least biblical biblical film ever made."[34] So the studio was eager to find ways to market the controversial film – there was already some pre-release backlash from the political and religious right about the film's "extremist environmental message"[35] – to both mainstream and faith-based audiences, while soothing any discomfort they might feel about the textual authenticity of the expanded story. In the months leading up to its March 28 release, Paramount screen-tested half a dozen versions of *Noah*, some more explicitly religious than others, to predominantly Christian audiences.[36] While there were a few grumblings from faith-minded viewers that the gritty film strayed too far from their cherished "animals and rainbows" notion of the scriptural account,[37] the film was released in what is claimed to be Aronofsky's final cut together with a brief disclaimer supporting the concept of "artistic license."[38] In the end, *Noah* overcame the controversies and proved to be a robust box office success.

A major factor in Paramount's winning strategy to appeal to the widest possible audiences – and to help mitigate the inevitable controversies that come with the biblical film territory – was the recruitment of big, bankable stars with attractive, familiar faces. First and foremost was the casting of Crowe as Noah, but several other famous and likable stars were also cast in the roles of Noah's family members. The part of Noah's son Ham is played by Logan Lerman, fresh from his successes in the hugely popular *Percy Jackson* film series (2010, 2013); and Noah's adopted daughter, called Ila in the film, who later becomes his daughter-in-law when she marries his son Shem, is played by Emma Watson, perhaps one of the most recognizable female actors in the world, having embodied the marquee role of Hermione Granger in all eight *Harry Potter* films over half of her natural life (2001–11).[39] Like Crowe as Maximus, both Watson as Hermione and Lerman as Percy bring these previous celebrated star texts to their roles in *Noah* and thus invite viewers to enjoy and engage with their new performances via their famous predecessors. But the way in which Crowe reminds the *Noah* audience of the Maximus star text is distinctive and visceral: he deploys physical gestures and movements, interactions with other actors, and even spoken dialogue. These visual and verbal echoes – or "maximal projections" – are scattered throughout the film but are deliberately more ubiquitous in the first half of *Noah*, in order to encourage the audience to identify with the title patriarch as a virtuous and heroic family man before the character takes a darker, more hardhearted turn.

The film opens with a brief retelling of the beginning of Genesis in a bursting series of multicolor images and sounds, flash-cut as in a dream or hallucination. After Adam and Eve are expelled from the Garden of Eden, they had three sons: Cain, Abel, and Seth. But when Cain killed Abel, Cain was forced to take refuge under the eyes of fallen angels called the Watchers, giant, rock-encrusted creatures that "lumber across the landscape like Transformers."[40] The Watchers helped Cain and his descendants build civilization, but the wickedness of Man spread throughout the world. Only the descendants of Seth would be left to restore humankind. Soon another scene establishes the young Noah as the son of Lamech, in the line of Seth: they are shown performing a ritual on a hillside, where the just Lamech passes down the snakeskin of the serpent from the Garden, as it has been passed down through previous generations. Lamech tells Noah that everything in the land was given to them by the Creator (God). When a large crowd of Men, led by the evil king Tubal-Cain, comes toward them menacingly, Lamech tells Noah to run and hide. Tubal-Cain wants to turn the hill into a mine, but first he takes his pickax and swings it into Lamech's neck, killing him. Noah sees his father die and then runs away.

As an adult, Noah – now played by Crowe – is out foraging with his two young sons Shem and Ham. As Ham plucks a small flower from the earth, Noah tells him that they came to gather only what they need from the land, as the Creator will provide for them: the film suggests in this scene that Noah and his family are vegetarians and do not eat the flesh of animals.[41] When the boys are not looking, a drop of water falls portentously from the sky and hits the ground, and a flower instantly blooms on the spot. Then all of a sudden, Noah sees a small, scaly, deer-like creature running toward him with its side pierced. As the wounded animal falls at his feet, then closes its eyes and dies, the men who were hunting it, the villainous, meat-eating descendants of Cain, arrive and threaten Noah if he doesn't give them their prey. Crowe as Noah reaches down and stealthily pulls out the spearhead from the body of the poor animal, hiding it in the broad palm of his hand, while he buys some time to assess the situation before swiftly taking down all three of the hunters. This physical gesture is an unmistakable visual repeat of the gesture that occurs at the end of the famous battle of Carthage scene at the very heart of *Gladiator*, where Maximus and his gladiator brothers have beaten the odds to win the fixed fight and Commodus descends into the arena to address him: as he kneels in the sand before the hated emperor, Crowe as Maximus reaches behind him and grabs a buried spearpoint, broken off during the violent battle, and conceals it in the palm of his hand as he confronts Commodus.[42] Thus at a pivotal early moment in the film, Crowe uses a physical echo to invite viewers to associate the role of Noah with the warrior figure of the Roman leader at this peak moment of epic heroic performance, while at the same time establishing a sympathetic identification between the audience and the character of the biblical patriarch as protective father and hero.

In addition to the use of such physical movements, Crowe employs specific line readings and chooses certain vocal intonations to bring the character of Maximus to the mind – and ears – of the viewers of *Noah*. An actor's voice is one of the most powerful instruments they possess in their dramatic toolkits, giving them the capability to create or transform the entire ethos of a role they are playing: the sound, rhythm, and language of an important line of movie dialogue can stay with a viewer for many years after it is first heard. Crowe capitalizes on that power of aural resonance in a scene a little later in the film when Noah is just about finished building the ark and comes face to face with Tubal-Cain (now played by Ray Winstone); Noah recognizes him as the man who killed his father, and so he utters a bold "*ego* statement" that is standard in the epic genre since Homer:[43] "I am the son of Lamech," he proclaims. Compare this line, in sound, pacing, and content, to Crowe's exceptionally famous reveal of himself to Commodus in the arena after the battle of Carthage scene in *Gladiator*, one of the most recognized speeches from the well-known film: "I am Maximus Decimus Meridius." Even granting the actor's personal vocal intonations, and allowing for the conservative nature of epic film in frequently restaging these "*ego* statement" scenes, the eerily consonant "maximal" performance authorizes Noah as the heroic protagonist, while the auditor of the line, in this case the silent Tubal-Cain, is the dangerous antagonist who must be defeated. Shortly after this exchange, another verbal echo firmly establishes the contours of the conflict, when, threatened by Tubal-Cain, Noah utters a calm but determined warning: "Your time is done." Compare Maximus' words to Commodus after being taunted by the emperor with the deaths of his wife and son: "The time for honoring yourself is past."[44] Although brief, Crowe's almost incantatory recitation of the grim line of dialogue brings the audience back to the epic revenge plot of *Gladiator* and helps to justify Noah's brutal measures in the current film.

In his interactions with other characters in *Noah*, especially with actors playing family members, Crowe also evokes the Maximus star text to appeal to and generate valuable audience identification with his own character. Noah has several conversations with the character of his steadfast wife, called Naameh in the film,[45] that are nearly direct echoes of Maximus' encounters with his former beloved Lucilla, daughter of Marcus Aurelius, in *Gladiator*. Although female roles in *Noah*, as in most ancient epic films, have far less prominence and agency than male roles, the epic hero protagonist must still be sanctioned by the love of a good woman. Early in the film, Crowe as

Noah is sleepless and anxious about the state of the young world; as he is comforted by Naameh, played by Jennifer Connelly, she strokes his worried face lovingly and tells him: "Rest." After her almost magical touch and lullaby words, Noah experiences an enchanted vision of the imminent flood. Similarly, in the final dramatic arena scene of *Gladiator*, Lucilla, played by Connie Nielsen, comforts a dying Maximus by stroking his face lovingly; she urges him to leave his pain and join his family in the afterlife, saying: "Go to them." With her soothing caress and hushed command, Maximus finds himself pushing through a dreamlike stone gate to cross into the next world. While these may seem like the typical tender gestures of the devoted female to her man, in each of these two pivotal scenes the epic hero is delivered by the woman – midwifed or even reborn – into a new state of consciousness, a supernatural vision of his destiny, and the next stage of his heroic existence.[46] Crowe–Noah's capacity to expose his vulnerability with his female co-star reminds the audience of that same quality in Maximus and proves his worthy heroic masculinity in the role.

Since the epic hero expresses his worth through his relationships within the family, Crowe also substantiates Noah's protective role as a father by calling up the paternal image of Maximus. Cinematic heroic masculinity is often determined through the representation of fatherhood, whether successful or problematic: the exploration of father–son contact is a staple of epic narrative. While the biblical story of Noah emphasizes the complicated family dynamics explicit in Genesis, the film *Noah* takes pains to show the title patriarch as a gentle father first before the character assumes his more rigid stance. In a quiet scene as the ark is being filled with the numerous pairs of animals to be saved, Crowe as Noah takes time to teach his youngest son, Japheth, about the bird pairs that are nesting within the rafters to ride out the flood.[47] A similar instruction-type scene takes place in *Gladiator* when Maximus converses with young Lucius before the battle of Carthage spectacle and points out the pair of Spanish horses depicted on his breastplate. Although Maximus has lost his own son, for whose death he seeks vengeance, he is able to re-establish his heroic role as a father by protecting Lucius, the son of his ex-lover Lucilla, and by keeping their family safe. By Crowe's arousing the Maximus star memory, the audience thereby recognizes Noah as caring mentor and a fierce guardian.

But it is the hero protagonist's meeting with his own paternal figure that has the most impact within the narrative of the epic film. In a programmatic early scene in *Noah*, Crowe as Noah meets with his grandfather Methuselah, played by Anthony Hopkins in another "star-peat" that invites the audience into the familiar world of the ancient world epic: Hopkins played the role of Ptolemy in Oliver Stone's *Alexander* (2004). Noah goes to visit his proverbially aged grandfather to receive his wisdom and advice, and as Methuselah informs him of the Creator's plan to cleanse the earth of the corruption of men, he says to Noah affectionately: "Did he not send you here to drink a cup of tea with an old man." In *Gladiator*, a fundamental early scene sends Maximus to visit the imperial tent of the famously wise old emperor Marcus Aurelius, played by epic movie stalwart Richard Harris, who asks Maximus to save Rome from the corruption of the politicians, as he says to him fondly: "Give an old man another blanket." The clear verbal and visual echoes – in dialogue and *mise-en-scène* – between these two establishing scenes validate the protagonist as a man who is chosen by the paternal elders in their infinite wisdom to face dangerous challenges on the way to achieving heroic status: the hero is not only deeply loved by the father-figure but also empowered through the patriarch's approval. In addition, Crowe's allusive performances in these two scenes reveal the resonances between the Maximus star text and his role as Noah.

## CONCLUSION

To sum up, Crowe uses his earlier Oscar-winning role to imprint "maximal projections" on the biblical film *Noah*, in order to capture the valuable attention of both secular and faith-based audiences, and to invite them to appreciate this movie as a sort of God-inspired *Gladiator*, that is, both action adventure and ancient world epic. Crowe as Noah proves Maximus' claim: "What we do in life, echoes in eternity."

## NOTES

1 On *Gladiator*, see the volume edited by Winkler (2004) and Cyrino (2005: 207–56).
2 Cullen (2012); this online essay is an excerpt from Cullen (2013).
3 Dyer (1979). The analysis of stardom and celebrity image has become an important area of scholarship in film studies: see also Gledhill (1991); Fowles (1992); Mayne (1993); Dyer (2004). On how the "star text" of a lead actor in an ancient world epic can affect the success or failure of a film, see Cyrino (2010: 168–82) on Colin Farrell in Oliver Stone's *Alexander* (2004).
4 Marcus (2011: 189).

5 For example, Peter Ustinov as Nero in *Quo Vadis* (1951) and then as Batiatus in *Spartacus* (1960), or Derek Jacobi as Claudius in the BBC *I, Claudius* miniseries (1976) and as Senator Gracchus in *Gladiator* (2000). For the idea of a star's career as an "archaeological site," with different strata that can be discerned, see now Llewellyn-Jones (2018).
6 On the process of audience identification with the main character as an index of critical and commercial viability, see Cyrino (2010: 170–1). See also Woodward (2003: 45–69).
7 See boxofficemojo.com: *Pompeii*'s total worldwide box office is $117 million.
8 Gleiberman (2014).
9 The most recent mention is Whitehead (2016), who laments HBO's loss of enthusiasm for the project.
10 See Fleming (2016) for the last reference to the Sony Pictures *Cleopatra* project.
11 Andreeva (2017) reports on the new Amazon *Cleopatra* series.
12 Burnett characterizes their Christian viewers as their "community" in Rice (2014: 45).
13 Collins (2013) gives the Nielsen figures: the miniseries garnered 13.1 million total viewers.
14 See Littleton (2015) for the producers' plans to launch new religious content on a digital platform.
15 Rottenberg (2014: 43).
16 Quoted in Rice (2014).
17 See Rottenberg (2014) for the details of the "*Passion* playbook" marketing plan.
18 "Showdowns: *Passion* vs. *Son of God*" on boxofficemojo.com records the summary statistics. While *The Passion* has made over $600 million in worldwide gross, *Son of God*'s grosses are not too bad considering the film cost next to nothing to make.
19 On some of the many controversies over religion and politics in Scott's *Exodus*, see Nashawaty (2014); on the controversies surrounding *Noah*, see Vilkomerson (2014).
20 Kris Fuhr, vice-president of marketing for Christian-oriented Provident Films, quoted in Rottenberg (2014).
21 See boxofficemojo.com: on a budget of $125 million, *Noah* made $101 million domestic and $261 million foreign for a total of $362 million worldwide; on a budget of $140 million, *Exodus* made $65 million domestic and $203 million foreign for a total of $268 million worldwide.
22 See boxofficemojo.com: on a budget of $100 million, the new *Ben-Hur* made $26 million domestic and $67 million foreign for a total of $94 million worldwide.
23 McGovern (2016).

24 On the *Ben-Hur* marketing plan of co-producers Paramount and MGM, see Zacharek (2016: 44).
25 See boxofficemojo.com: domestic box office = $371 million, foreign = $241 million. On how *The Passion* stunned the Hollywood industry, see Sanburn (2014: 54).
26 Rottenberg (2014).
27 Religious controversy can both help and hurt ticket sales: *The Last Temptation of Christ* was one of the director's worst-performing movies ever with only $8 million in domestic box office, while *The Da Vinci Code* made back nearly twice its $125 million budget. See Sanburn (2014: 52); Staskiewicz (2014: 41).
28 See Reinhartz (2013) for a comprehensive social history of the use of biblical texts and themes in cinema.
29 For the expansion of Hollywood's business interests into religious markets, see Rottenberg (2014); Sanburn (2014: 52).
30 See Sanburn (2014: 54–5) for how Grace Hill Media fostered the critical and box office success of *The Blind Side*.
31 On the classical tradition in the epic cinema, see Paul (2013).
32 For the variety of epic modes, see Elley (1984); Babington and Evans (1993); Day (2016).
33 Although uncredited, *Gladiator* screenwriter John Logan reportedly rewrote Aronofsky and Handel's script, which may support the Maximus subtext: see Finke and Fleming (2012).
34 Quoted in Sanburn (2014: 55).
35 Rothman (2014: 52).
36 Some versions were screened over Aronofsky's objections: see Vilkomerson (2014).
37 In particular, test audiences were offended by the scene in which Noah gets drunk on wine, which is in Genesis (9:21) and suggests today's Christians may have a few misconceptions about the Bible, and specifically the Old Testament: see Sanburn (2014: 55).
38 The disclaimer that appears on *Noah*'s trailer, website, and marketing materials reads: "While artistic license has been taken, we believe that this film is true to the essence, values and integrity of a story that is a cornerstone of faith for millions of people worldwide. The biblical story of Noah can be found in the book of Genesis."
39 Advertising one-sheets for *Noah* that have more than one figure (Crowe) show Watson's face as large as that of Jennifer Connelly, the actress who plays Noah's wife.
40 Zoller Seitz (2014).
41 Another aspect of the film that bothered some reviewers, Noah's family's vegetarianism seems to be indicated in Genesis 9:2–4.
42 On the battle of Carthage sequence, see Cyrino (2005: 244–5).
43 Just one example is *Odyssey* 6.196, when Nausikaa tells Odysseus: "I am the daughter of great-hearted Alcinous."

44 Crowe as Noah utters a similar line to his wife later in the film, when he realizes that the human race must perish to cleanse the earth: "The time for mercy is past."
45 In the Old Testament, Naamah is the name given to the sister of Tubal-Cain in Genesis 4:22, although later Jewish rabbinical *midrashim* also name her as Noah's wife.
46 Naameh's function in *Noah* appears to be a continuation of the traditional role of the female in mid-century biblical epic films: to help the male hero find his spirituality, or more specifically his nascent Christianity, e.g. Lygia in *Quo Vadis* or Esther in the 1959 *Ben-Hur*.
47 The camera shots showing the animal pairs tucked within the woodworks of the ark sets in *Noah* are visually reminiscent of the subterranean lairs and cages of the Colosseum sets in *Gladiator*: this suggests a visual link between the ark and the arena, as the physical spaces of the epic hero's action.

# 7 The Immortality of Theseus and His Myth

Margaret M. Toscano

## INTRODUCTION

How do a hero's adventures connect with the human quest for immortality? This chapter compares two fairly recent, but very different, films that both use ancient stories about the Greek hero Theseus for their plots and characters to explore this question. The first is the 2011 fantasy and CGI action film *Immortals*, starring Henry Cavill and Mickey Rourke, and directed by Tarsem Singh.[1] The second is the philosophical art film *Ship of Theseus*, a 2013 Indian drama written and directed by Anand Gandhi, and produced by Kiran Rao, along with Sohum Shah, who is also an actor and one of the film's protagonists.[2] While on the surface these two films could not be more different in structure and purpose, both films deal with the complex connections between the desire for immortality and the struggle for personal identity and meaning, as well as the subsequent ethics of such a quest. These issues infiltrate ancient Greek myth and are still compelling today, as is evident on all levels of culture from popular media to high-brow art.

In his 2012 book *Immortality: The Quest to Live Forever and How it Drives Civilization*, Stephen Cave suggests four paths people have taken to achieve immortality. He sees the ascent to the mountain as the dominant metaphor for this quest that he argues is central to the construction of cultures in different times and places. The four paths are: (1) staying alive through either magic or science; (2) resurrection, or bringing the dead to life again; (3) the perpetuation of the self through the survival of the soul; and (4) legacy, through either progeny, fame, or monuments of art. After a long exploration of each path, Cave concludes not only that none of the paths is ultimately successful but that each can have the negative effect of sacrificing the living to save the dying, of destroying the weak to perpetuate the powerful.[3]

Taken together, the two films under analysis here examine all these mechanisms for achieving immortality, with all their inherent complications. What is most interesting in comparing the two films is the ways they overlap in exploring these questions, given their differences. The fact that the blockbuster fantasy film raises serious questions is surprising, though it does so somewhat superficially. And the Indian philosophical film, which is enmeshed in Eastern ethics and religion, connects with the West through the titular Theseus figure, as well as global financial interactions in the storyline. But neither film puts forth an unproblematized approach or answer to the questions underlying the quest for immortality. Gandhi's *Ship of Theseus* explores the tensions between secular and religious notions of the dissolution of the self within the larger universe. Singh's *Immortals* seems at first simply to idealize Theseus as a savior figure, the heroic individual who stands out among his peers; but Theseus is also the common man who fights against his divine destiny. Both films project everyday mortal life against a screen of eternal significance. Both ask how the here and now relates to the cosmic realm.

For the ancient Greeks, the contrast between "mortal" and "immortal" was a major classifying schema in a culture that tended to use binaries to describe the functioning of the cosmos.[4] While Greek myths usually show gods who desire to keep the realms separate because mixing the two brings suffering and complications, still the gods intertwine their lives with mortals as lovers, parents, mentors, and even friends.[5] Of course it is these very relationships that bring pain and problems. Mortal lovers die while their immortal partners stay alive, as seen with Aphrodite and Adonis; and the mortal offspring of such unions inevitably bring sorrow to their parents, not just with their deaths but with their human suffering, as Thetis learns with her son Achilles.[6] The fact that the great Heracles is the only hero to become fully divine in Greek myth is surprising, given these tensions.[7] Still, ancient Greek religious practice and ritual give at least semi-divine status to a number of heroes, and explorations of immortality infiltrate both Greek mythic and philosophical texts.[8] Heracles' divine fate must be juxtaposed with that of Odysseus, who rejects Calypso's offer for immortality in Homer's tale. These heroes show the Greek struggle between the longing to transcend the mortal plane and the satisfaction with – or at least resignation to – the limits of mortality.[9]

## IMMORTALS

The film *Immortals* has more action than philosophical inquiry, but still it attempts to explore the kinds of big issues raised by Cave and others about immortality. The story is set in an ancient Greek world based on fantasy more than myth. The plotline goes like this: King Hyperion is on a murderous rampage against gods and humans. To gain complete power he searches for the all-powerful Epirus bow made long ago by Ares. If Hyperion can obtain this bow, he intends to free the Titans, who were imprisoned in even more ancient times by the Olympians under Mount Tartarus, to achieve his goal. Zeus has secretly chosen the brave peasant Theseus to oppose the mad king and to save both his homeland and the Olympians from complete destruction. Some ancient law has decreed the Olympians cannot intervene before the Titans are unleashed. The gods must honor the choices of mortals, as well as the law that is above the gods. Why this must be so is not explained, though a comparison could be made to the role of fate in ancient Greek thought, which the gods themselves could not change.

In the *Immortals*, choice and the benign non-interference of the gods are crucial to encourage personal growth for Theseus and responsibility for humans. In a visually stunning scene on Mt. Olympus, the younger Olympians argue with Zeus that they must intervene before Hyperion, who has no mercy or honor, destroys everything, as he will if he is allowed to continue.[10] Zeus answers, "I obey the law! No God shall interfere in the affairs of man unless the Titans are released. If we are to expect mankind to have faith in us ... we must have faith in them. We must allow them to use their own free will." When another god protests that destruction will follow, Zeus says that for any god who intervenes, the "punishment will be death." Zeus, in fact, kills Ares later for helping mortals, though he spares Athena, who still meets the same fate later at the hands of the Titans. Obeying the law indicates Zeus' sense of justice.

The film attempts a theodicy of sorts to justify the ways of the Olympians to mortals, or at least to mortal film viewers. The questions it raises about the relationship between gods and humans reflect age-old debates about the justice, goodness, knowledge, and power of God, and how this relates to the existence of the divine. If God is all-powerful and all-good, then why doesn't God intervene to stop evil and protect the innocent? And if God exists, why doesn't he make himself known? Free will is a common answer from theologians, but many feel it is inadequate in the face of human suffering.[11]

Still, it is the answer given in *Immortals*. The fact that this and other such questions are raised in an action film shows an underlying concern with larger issues that are disguised in this film, like the gods themselves. Patricia Salzman-Mitchell and Jean Alvares connect the film *Immortals* with a large group of contemporary films (such as *Harry Potter* and *Lord of the Rings*) that picture society on "the edge of apocalypse, with chaotic evil poised to triumph" unless it is met with "an equally mysterious virtue, which can be called divine and produce the sacred hero."[12] Zeus directs Theseus behind the scenes to embrace virtue and faith in order to fight the impending doom represented by Hyperion.

The Greek gods in *Immortals* are more moral than those in most other depictions in modern cinema, where the ancient gods are either irrelevant, indifferent, cruel, morally incompetent, or corrupt.[13] Zeus' character is the most fascinating and enlightened in *Immortals*. He appears in disguise as an old man and mentor (played by the always compelling John Hurt), who does all he can to encourage responsible, humane action in Theseus without taking away his choices. Luke Evans plays the ethically tormented and powerful god Zeus in his Olympian guise, where he tries to mediate between gods and mortals. As the wise mentor, he gives Theseus Socratic-like advice about the purpose of life: "It's not living as such that is important, it's living rightly." And dying rightly is important too, for both gods and humans. Fighting for a good cause, supporting the weak and oppressed against tyranny, and sacrificing his all is what brings immortality to Theseus at the end of the film.

King Hyperion (played by Mickey Rourke) also gives Theseus advice and a choice about how to live his life and avoid obscurity. In their first encounter, he says,

> Embrace me, Theseus. They will never give you a seat at their table, but you could sit at the head of mine. Long after this war is over, my mark will be left on this world forever. This is what I offer you: immortality.

Theseus responds: "Deeds are eternal, not the flesh." He has learned from the wisdom of Zeus. In the last fight scene between Hyperion and Theseus, the question of immortality is raised again. "Die with your gods," Hyperion says to Theseus. "What does it feel like ... knowing that there will be no memory of you? I've won." Theseus responds, "My death will make me a legend. And my deeds ... will go down in history." "I'm writing your history," retorts Hyperion. But Theseus surprises the tyrant by first pinning his feet and then driving a knife into his throat until he gasps his last breath. In another part of the mountain, the Titans seem ready to destroy the Olympians, who have been killed off one by one. But Zeus gets the last word. Like Samson, he pulls down the pillars of the temple mountain to end the battle with the Titans, but the battle with evil will continue. With the dead Athena in his arms, Zeus shoots upward, as does the body or soul of Theseus, like falling stars going in the opposite direction, an apotheosis.[14] The film must redeem Zeus, as well as Theseus, to make heroism valid in heaven as well as earth.

The last scene in *Immortals* begins with a voiceover by John Hurt as Zeus:

> All men's souls are immortal, but the souls of the righteous are immortal and divine. Once a faithless man, Theseus gave his life to save mankind and earned a place amongst the gods. They rewarded his bravery with a gift, a son, Acamas.

The film breaks down the dichotomy between mortals and gods by killing off most of the Olympians at the conclusion of the film. At the same time Theseus himself is immortalized and deified in three ways at the end: he receives a place among the gods on Olympus; his story is immortalized through art and memory in the final scenes, both on earth and in heaven; and his son will continue his legacy. Theseus' son in this last scene is looking at a statue group that depicts the heroic deeds of his father, including killing the Minotaur. While he looks, Acamas sees a vision of his father still fighting in the sky along with the gods in a spiral of warriors moving upward toward eternity. Theseus' memory and work live on through his son, who is being groomed in this last scene by Zeus (in disguise again as the old mentor) to continue as a hero himself in the eternal fight against evil. Immortality in this film is not simply the reward for a life well lived, but also a sign of the ultimate, but always hard-fought, triumph of goodness. Immortality is not simply living forever but living to promote righteous causes.

## SHIP OF THESEUS

The title of the film *Ship of Theseus* references the ancient thought problem raised by Heraclitus, Plutarch, and others. According to legend, the Athenians were charged to keep Theseus' ship in good repair after he returned victorious from Crete.[15] But eventually, it began to rot, so new parts were made to replace the old ones.

> If an object's parts are all gradually replaced with new ones, is the object still the same thing as the original when all of its parts are new? And if a new ship

were to be built from the discarded parts of the old ship, which ship would be the real Ship of Theseus?

As the film begins its opening sequence, these questions are posed in a succinctly written script.

Gandhi's film is set in modern India, mostly Mumbai. Its language is a mixture of English and Hindi (and a little Arabic and Swedish) with subtitles for all. The film only makes subtle allusions to the ancient hero Theseus in its title and initial screen shots. It connects the ship analogy with the human body and human identity. Should long life and immortality be the goal of human progress? How does medical engineering of the body affect identity? And what are the larger ethical and personal costs of staving off death? *Ship of Theseus* is about three people who rely on organ transplants for their health and survival, raising many questions about fate, death, mortality, and morality. The film is divided into three distinct parts that at first seem only to be connected as stories of people whose lives are saved by organ transplants. It is only at the end that the viewer discovers that all three received body parts from the same donor, a young man who died in an accident but had previously signed a donor consent form.

The first story is about a blind photographer, a young woman named Aliya, played by the Egyptian filmmaker and activist Aida El-Kashef. In the opening of an exhibit of her black-and-white photos, she is interviewed by an art critic: "You took up photography after you lost your eyesight to a cornea infection. Why photography?" Aliya avoids the issue of her blindness and answers: "First to archive, document, and remember; then to explore, understand and see." The interviewer then asks, "So all art comes from the need to record the apparent, the need to capture the essence?" "Yes, very well put," Aliya responds. "Do you feel limitations?" the critic asks? "No!" "That's amazing!" says the interviewer. "Why is it amazing to not have limits or doubts?" asks Aliya. Of course, all art has limits, which the artist plays with and pushes against to explore both form and content. But art is also an ancient way of achieving immortality after one is dead, as the Roman poet Ovid declares at the end of his *Metamorphoses*, saying that his name will never die. And Memory is, after all, the mother of the Muses for the ancient Greeks. To be remembered is also to achieve immortality, as depicted not just in the West but in this Indian film.

But, ironically, Aliya does begin to have doubts and to feel her limits after her cornea transplants restore her sight. Will she still be acclaimed now that she is like other photographers? Who is she now as an artist? In the last scenes of this segment, Aliya goes by plane to the mountains to try and figure out what she wants to do with her art now, and who she is. As she sits on a bridge over a mountain stream in a magnificent natural setting, she drops the lens cover, which floats away, not to be recovered. Then she puts away her camera, just sits and smiles amid the beauty. She exists now between art and nature in a liminal spot ready for self-discovery. Patricia Pisters argues that as a blind photographer Aliya used touch, hearing, and smell to create her photographs that deviate from the dominant perception of the male gaze.[16] Now that her sight has returned, Aliya must reconfigure her artistic perspective, as well as herself as a woman artist.

The second story is about Maitreya, played by actor Neeraj Kabi. The character is an erudite Jain monk, who is part of an order of strict non-violence. He is a spiritual atheist (meaning non-theist) who believes in the soul and karma but not any divine power who creates or judges.[17] He has advanced cirrhosis of the liver but rejects the idea of an organ transplant because he believes such an action would support a medical system that is built on practices, such as animal testing, that perpetuate violence as much as they save lives. As his disease and pain advance, he decides to fast unto death rather than to act in a way that he believes is immoral.

This middle section about Maitreya is the longest of the three parts of the film, and it also most directly addresses issues of immortality. It reaches out to the stories before and after to create a religious and philosophical context for thinking in larger cosmic terms in all three sections about art, truth, ethics, and social engagement. Ashvin Immanuel Devasundaram argues that the film's "three sub-narratives" form a trinity that breaks open the binaries also implied in the film: "Eastern and Western philosophy, reason and nihilism, presence and absence, existence and essence, sublime and corporeal, imminence and immanence."[18] The three protagonists and tripartite structure suggest multiple parts and multiple approaches for the questions raised by the film that break away from either/or answers. But still the binaries are present and compelling for the viewer to resist and think through. The film draws viewers in and asks for moral engagement from them.

A crucial aspect of the middle section of the film is the relationship between the monk and a young man, Charvaka, who tries to persuade Maitreya through ethical arguments to receive medical help. Charvaka is a law intern who is involved in cases dealing with animal testing. Their first encounter is when the young man sees the monk rescue a centipede from being stomped on in a busy hallway in the courthouse. The viewer sees the world from the point of view of the centipede in the midst of fast moving shoes. A paper comes down to catch the centipede, and the monk puts it on a green plant in the hallway. Then we hear a voice: "And now that you've saved its life, will you also give it a proper upbringing and a good education? What if it was the worm's karma to get crushed?" the young man asks. Both the monk's action and the lawyer's joke point to the film's insistence that identity and subjectivity involve relationships that extend beyond our species.[19]

This is the first of many discussions between the monk and the younger man. They explore whether immortality comes through the soul or the body. The monk focuses on the soul, the young man on the body. He says:

> It gives me kicks to know that a part of me was part of an animal once or a flame or star. Every atom of my body will be recycled by the universe. You think you are a person but you are a colony. A microcosm that has ten times more bacteria in its body than it has human cells. How do you know where you begin and the environment ends?

There is a kind of immortality in the physical universe where particles are neither created nor destroyed, but always changed.

As the monk gets weaker and weaker, Charvaka tries one argument after another to persuade him to receive medical treatment. But finally it comes down to personal love and concern, not philosophy. "What about the violence that you are doing to yourself by not taking medicine?" Charvaka asks. "There a lot of people who love and respect you and need you, including myself." Maitreya's brother monks show their love when he can no longer care for himself as he lies on his bed close to death. Finally, when he seems beyond help, he whispers, "Call Dr. Barbhargava. Tell him I agree. I'm not ready to go yet." His brothers carry him from the room very gently. He will continue in this world; his soul has not yet entered into a new phase of eternity.

The third segment of the movie is about Navin, played by Sohum Shah. The character is a successful, young stockbroker who has just had a kidney transplant. He is close to his intellectual and socially activist grandmother, but the two of them are in an ongoing argument about materialism and social reform. When he returns to her house after his surgery, she takes a fall and has to go to the hospital herself. His grandmother thinks he is too concerned with success and does not care enough about making the world better. "I only challenge you so that you will learn," she says. "I am not interested," he replies. "Does that make me a bad person?" Navin's refusal to care about societal problems is juxtaposed with his obviously loving care for his grandmother. The film shows him changing her bedpan and doing other small acts of selfless service for her.

The same compassion Navin shows to his grandmother later comes out in his response to a relevant social issue. Navin discovers there is a man who had his kidney stolen when he had his appendix removed, and that this is a too common practice – stealing organs from poor people with no resources in order to sell the organs to rich recipients. At first Navin is worried that he may have unknowingly been the beneficiary of such an illegal practice. Even when he finds such is not the case, he is prompted to help the poor man receive a large payment for his loss from the Swedish recipient, who claims he knew nothing of the organ theft. Of course this cannot make up for the lost kidney. Navin explains his frustration to his grandmother. "After everything, nothing came of it," he says. "All that happened came because you decided to do something about it," she replies. "It's as good as it gets." Navin displays everyday heroism.

The last scene of the movie finally brings the three stories and characters together in the same room at a gathering of the many recipients of the body parts of the dead young man. They are diverse in age, color, and ethnicity. They do not interact, but sit quietly watching the movie made by the young man, a speleologist, who gave them all a chance to live longer. His amateur movie documents his visit to a cave. They see the dead donor's shadow, but not his person, since he is the one making the movie. Some of what is left of him is in the room – his organs and his film, which give the donor a type of immortality, too, through science, art, memory, and good deeds. The movie about the journey through the cave is reminiscent of Plato's Allegory of the Cave. The organ-donor filmmaker is like the prophetic figure who, having seen the sunlight, has returned from the other side to describe the shadows on the wall as only an illusion of reality, so that his viewers or the prisoners in the cave may reach enlightenment. It is significant that Plato is also indirectly invoked by the Ship of Theseus puzzle that titles the film, because many of Plato's dialogues discuss issues of identity – the relationship of the parts to the whole and between change and continuity.[20] And Plato is also recalled in *Immortals* through Socrates and the syllogism about "every soul is immortal," which is not just spoken but shown in a title card at the beginning of the film.[21]

## CONCLUSION

Juxtaposing the themes in both *Immortals* and *Ship of Theseus* highlights Stephen Cave's list of the various ways humans seek some kind of immortality: staying alive, resurrection, soul, and legacy. The characters in the Indian film all choose to benefit from modern medicine by receiving organ transplants to extend their lives. The monk Maitreya's belief in the immortality of the soul gives meaning to his life and interaction with the world around him. His ethical approach to all beings, sentient and not, leaves a legacy for good among those his life touches. While the stockbroker Navin at first only cares about success in the here and now, he finally extends himself out to his larger society for an expanded expression of self through social activism and good deeds. The photographer Aliya loses her sense of limits through her art, but ironically feels them as well. Theseus, too, achieves immortality through his deeds, his son, and the monuments of art that follow on from him (Figure 7.1). Perhaps the only missing element in the search for immortality in these particular films is resurrection, though it is unclear in what sense Theseus survives, as a soul or an embodied being of some sort. And resurrection itself is a metaphor for rebirth, which is an underlying theme in both films. All the major characters go through a death and rebirth on more than one level. Descent (*katabasis*) precedes ascent for the hero.

Figure 7.1 With the dramatic sky as backdrop, Theseus' son Acamas (Gage Munroe) gazes at the statue of his father killing the Minotaur at the end of *Immortals* (2011), visually representing various concepts of immortality. Relativity Media.

The analysis of these two movies seems to support Cave's larger thesis: that the desire for immortality drives, or, maybe more accurately, at least infiltrates civilizations. In a sense this drive could simply be restated as the underlying theory of evolution: life will find a way to survive. But what of Cave's worry that the desire for immortality is ultimately destructive? That it is at the heart of violence, greed, and tyranny?[22] While the plot of *Immortals* seems to prove this true in Hyperion, its filmmakers also assert that the sacrifice of the hero Theseus, and even the heroic Zeus, perpetuates goodness, since they are willing to give up their lives. Certainly *Ship of Theseus* more subtly examines the conundrums surrounding the question of how we can extend the power and life of the self without doing violence to the rest of creation. Though the Indian film gives no clear answer to this puzzle, it also shows that love and concern for others are at the heart of goodness, which paradoxically brings about a type of immortality that is based on the sacrifice not of others but of the self.

How does all of this relate to the new Greek heroes on screen today? They will continue to draw from the past but be transformed to meet both the artistic sensibilities and underlying human concerns of each new age. Can the old myths, here the story of Theseus, still be recognizable when most of the parts are changed? Salzman-Mitchell and Alvares call Theseus an "Ideal Hero for a Rough Age," emphasizing the way he represents both "an old- and new-fashioned view" of the classical hero at the same time.[23] Theseus in *Immortals* is indeed the old-fashioned, unproblematic hero who is morally uncompromising as he fights to protect his mother, his woman, and his people. He goes from disbelief to a close relationship with the gods, achieving godhood for himself after selflessly sacrificing his life to bring hope to others.

Viewers should not have a hard time seeing Theseus as the perfect Christ figure.[24] It is significant that many secular viewers today cannot accept discussions of soul and immortality in overtly Christian terminology or terms. While *Immortals* was not praised by the critics, it was a box office success. Obviously, the film's beautiful cinematography, action-packed scenes, and violence disguised the underlying religious themes for most; or perhaps it is refreshing for audiences to see an exciting film with a hopeful, even spiritual ending. In her discussion about the ways Greek heroes are marketed to audiences today, Stacie Raucci proposes that the new heroes must embody "a universal human nature" that "extends across time and cultures," suggesting that "heroes can be models for anyone."[25]

Theseus performs such a function since he is the underdog hero who saves his world through courage and magnificent fighting. As the trailer for the movie announced, "Even the gods will need a hero."[26]

Vincent Tomasso argues that *Immortals* offers "a radical solution" to melding the past and the present by reframing the Greek gods, remolding Christian ideas about the soul, and supporting "humanity's progress."[27] The multiple ways that Theseus achieves immortality certainly promote both progress and the hope for a better future. *Ship of Theseus* also combines the old and the new by juxtaposing a traditional religious view with modernity and science and by combining artistic, humanistic concerns with a pragmatic, business view of life. Its moral outlook is appealing to Western audiences concerned with the natural environment. Raising questions about immortality through Greek myths or environmentally conscious Eastern religions makes these issues palatable for contemporary audiences on many levels. Changing the parts of the Theseus story in each film makes the underlying myth come alive in these new contexts. Though neither *Immortals* nor *Ship of Theseus* gives a representation of the underlying Greek myth that is familiar to classicists, each film shows the relevance of taking the various parts of the Theseus story and putting them in fresh vessels for new cinematic voyages.[28]

## NOTES

1 *Immortals* received some critical praise but with mixed ratings. It was nominated for three Saturn awards, including Best Fantasy Film and Production Design. On Rotten Tomatoes, *Immortals* received two out of five stars. See Salzman-Mitchell and Alvares (2017) for a description of the film's reception. They say it is both "art house" and "sword and sandal" (2017: 159).
2 When *Ship of Theseus* premiered at the 2012 Toronto International Film festival, it received immediate critical acclaim. It has won numerous awards and praise from both Indian and international critics for its script, directing, acting, art direction, and ethical stance. For a review of the film that puts it in the context of Indian cinema, see Naidu (2013).
3 Ernest Becker's 1973 *The Denial of Death* is the seminal work that more recent studies of the quest for immortality build upon. For a philosophical exploration, see Edwards (1997); and for a psychological analysis, see Solomon, Greenberg, and Pyszczynski (2015).
4 Clay (1981–2) analyzes the immortal/mortal, ageless/aging paradigm; and Lyons (1997: 3–102) shows how this binary applies to gender.
5 The *Hymn to Aphrodite* gives the reasoning behind the Olympian desire to keep the realms apart.

6  All of the Greek myths dealing with mortals and immortals show the inherent tensions: Eos and her lovers and offspring Memnon; Aphrodite and her lovers and offspring (e.g. Anchises and Aeneas); Zeus and his lovers and offspring; even Athena's friendship with Odysseus brings her pain, as seen in Homer's *Odyssey*.
7  The half-human, half-divine hero represents this split, this tension that drives humans in both directions.
8  Farnell (1921) is still the foundational study; see also Lyons (1997).
9  For Heracles' apotheosis and immortality, see Shapiro (1983) and Griffiths (2002); for Odysseus' refusal, see Churchill (1991).
10 The mountain images (Olympus, Tartarus) in *Immortals* connect with Cave's use of the metaphor. The caves in the film suggest the *katabasis* (descent) that precedes apotheosis.
11 For a range of modern theological responses, see Blumenthal (1993); Adams (1999); Ehrman (2008).
12 Salzman-Mitchell and Alvares (2017: 178–9).
13 For a discussion of the tendency of modern cinema to condemn and even kill off the Greek gods, see Tomasso (2015b).
14 Solomon (2008) contrasts older movies about the ancients with the new ways millennial films depict the afterlife, apotheosis, eternity, immortality, and divinity, focusing on *Gladiator* (2000), *Troy* (2004), and *Alexander* (2004).
15 Plutarch gives the ancient account of Theseus' life and influence, as well as the description of the preservation of his ship. For a historical overview of the importance of Theseus, see Mills (1997).
16 Pisters (2014: 66–7) uses Laura Mulvey, as well as Rosi Braidotti, for exploring Aliya's "posthuman" and "postfeminist" subjectivity and development.
17 For an introduction to Jainism, see Dundas (2002).
18 Devasundaram also asserts that the three stories represent the Hindu ideals of "truth, ethics and aesthetics" (2014: 1).
19 Pisters (2014: 66) argues that *Ship of Theseus* is the perfect text for exploring Braidotti's notions of "posthuman subjectivity" through the lens of "contemporary scientific advances and global economic concerns."
20 Plato's dialogue *Parmenides* is especially pertinent.
21 See Plato, *Phaedrus* 245c.
22 It is Ernest Becker in his 1975 *Escape from Evil* who first posed these questions for a post-Holocaust generation.
23 Salzman-Mitchell and Alvares (2017: 157).
24 See Salzman-Mitchell and Alvares (2017: 178); Tomasso (2015b: 154).
25 Raucci (2015: 161).
26 Raucci (2015: 166).
27 Tomasso (2015: 154–5). Solomon (2008: 22) also sees a new direction for the way millennial films treat the afterlife and immortality. They

move away from "paleochristian and pagan mythological concepts" to "an ameliorating progression of eschatological and meta-human concepts."

28 In their thorough analysis of the classical elements woven throughout *Immortals*, Salzman-Mitchell and Alvares (2017) demonstrate that there are more pieces of Greek myth in this movie than first meet the eye.

# 8 The Changing Faces of Heroism in Atlantis (2013–15)

Amanda Potter

## INTRODUCTION

The short-lived BBC television series *Atlantis* presents us with a range of characters who go on their own heroic journeys. The rather bland but brave and honorable protagonist Jason (Jack Donnelly) must confront his dark side; the unheroic, greedy, drunken Hercules (Mark Addy) becomes a tragic hero; and the clumsy but likable Pythagoras (Robert Emms) uses his brains to help his friends. By the end of the second and final series female characters Ariadne (Aiyisha Hart), Medea (Amy Manson), and Medusa (Jemima Rooper) also display different aspects of heroism, moving respectively from princess to warrior, assassin to helper maiden, and victim to monster to self-sacrificing heroine. For modern readers and viewers, characters from Greek mythology can seem uninteresting and irrelevant today. Particularly Perseus, Jason, Theseus, and Bellerophon can all become interchangeable as young men who slay monsters and go on quests, with few people remembering (or caring) who did what, and there are almost no heroic women characters for female viewers to relate to (Atalanta is the notable exception). By creating male characters with their own specific peculiarities and flaws, and female characters with heroic potential, the producers of *Atlantis* present us with heroes that we can relate to, even though they are grounded in the ancient world. Modern viewers are also versed in the tradition of the bildungsroman, and are familiar with television story arcs where protagonists change and grow as individuals. By presenting us with characters who change over time and learn from their heroic journeys the *Atlantis* writers aim to sustain the interest of viewers, so that they continue to watch to the end of the series.

*Atlantis* was a family-oriented fantasy adventure series set in ancient Greece, which aired on BBC1 from 2013 to 2015 on Saturday evenings in the family drama viewing slot initially established by the return of *Doctor Who* in 2005, previously filled by *Robin Hood* (2006–9) and *Merlin* (2008–12). *Atlantis* was conceived by writing team Julian Murphy and Johnny Capps, to follow their previous popular series *Merlin*, which had concluded after five seasons. Like *Merlin*, which foregrounded the friendship between the young Arthur, played by attractive young actor Bradley James, and the young Merlin (Colin Morgan), *Atlantis* featured another good-looking actor, Jack Donnelly, as hero Jason, supported by his friends Hercules and Pythagoras. Julian Murphy says that the team play "fast and loose with history" (Series 1: "Behind the Scenes") mixing contexts that are centuries apart chronologically. For example, Atlantis is a Minoan city where convicts are trained to be bull-leapers (Episode 1.3: "A Boy of No Consequence"), as portrayed in the famous bull-leaping fresco from Knossos,[1] as well as being forced to fight in Roman-style gladiatorial games (Episode 2.11: "Kin"). *Atlantis* also makes alterations to the mythic stories, so that neither the Minotaur nor Medusa is simply a monster to be killed, as in the versions of the myths in, for example, Ovid and Apollodorus,[2] but both become sympathetic characters, the Minotaur turning out to be a man who was cursed, and Medusa choosing her own death to help others.

It was expected by the production team, and the actors, who had signed five-year contracts, that *Atlantis* would run to multiple seasons. Viewing figures were initially high at the start of season one (5.8 million viewers watched the pilot episode on BBC1), but ratings dipped for season two when the show was aired at the same time as *The X Factor*, and the series was cancelled halfway through the airing of season two because, according to the BBC, in order to "keep increasing the range of BBC One drama we have to make difficult decisions to bring new shows through."[3] Therefore only two thirteen-episode series were made, and the second series ends with Jason about to sail away to find the Golden Fleece. Sadly for viewers and fans of the series he never gets to make his heroic voyage onscreen.

## JASON: AN ANCIENT HERO FROM THE TWENTY-FIRST CENTURY

Although series co-creator Julian Murphy says that "*Atlantis* is largely about our three central guys" (Series 1: "Behind the Scenes") it is Jason who is set up as the primary hero, with two sidekicks,

Hercules and Pythagoras. Murphy says that "our Jason is a mixture of a number of Greek heroes like Perseus and Theseus and Jason himself" (Series 1: "Behind the Scenes"). This allows the production team to pick several of the best-known stories from Greek mythology, so that Jason can slay the Minotaur and Medusa, before planning to embark on a journey to find the Golden Fleece. Assigning the deeds of one mythic hero to another is nothing new in film and television, providing greater scope for a protagonist. For example, Perseus rides on Pegasus in *Clash of the Titans* (1981), when we would expect the steed to be Bellerophon, and Xena intervenes in many mythic stories in *Xena: Warrior Princess* (1995–2001).[4] Donnelly was a relatively unknown young actor when he was cast as Jason. Initially Donnelly as Jason is an attractive but rather bland matinee idol, often filmed without his shirt when other cast members go fully clothed, rather than a more complex modern or ancient Greek hero.

In the pilot episode, "The Earth Bull," a twenty-first-century Jason is at sea, looking for evidence of what happened to his father, who disappeared when his submarine went down. Jason's own submersible malfunctions, and Jason wakes on a beach, naked except for the leather necklace with a bronze bull-horn pendant that had been a gift from his father. He finds clothes on the beach, and walks up to a city, blending in well as he looks like any other inhabitant. He runs along the walls of the city as if he had been born there, and when he is struck in the shoulder by an arrow pulls it out, and dodges more arrows, again as if this were a natural occurrence for him. He can jump like a gymnast but has no idea how he learned to do this. He is clearly no ordinary twenty-first-century British young man. Harbored by Pythagoras, the resident of the house he stumbles into, Jason finds out he is in Atlantis. Sent to the temple of Poseidon by Pythagoras, Jason is told by the Oracle (Juliet Stevenson) that he was born in Atlantis, and it was his destiny to be drawn to Atlantis to help its people.

By making Jason a twenty-first-century character the production team have created a protagonist that viewers of *Atlantis* can relate to. One of my 12-year-old students wrote an assignment on *Atlantis*, and found that Jason was more "relatable" to younger viewers as he was from a "broken home," growing up without his mother and losing his father early. The "fish out of water" comedy is played out in some episodes, such as "Hunger Pangs" (Episode 1.11), where Jason eats meat from an altar to Hecate and becomes a werewolf. Jason never specifically tells his friends from Atlantis that he is from the future and Hercules exclaims "I will never cease to be amazed by your ignorance and stupidity" ("Hunger Pangs"). Jason's origins also mean that he is party to knowledge that his friends do not have, such as the fate of Medusa, but he only shares this with the Oracle.

From the beginning of the series Jason is portrayed as a man with a strong sense of honor. Donnelly finds Jason to be a character "with very good morals" and "very strict ideas on how he sees the world, but it is almost black and white in the way he sees good and bad," although "I think that changes for him as it goes on" (Series 1: "Behind the Scenes"). In "The Earth Bull" (Episode 1.1) when Pythagoras draws a black stone and so must be sacrificed to the Minotaur, Jason steals from the house to take his friend's place. This is both in recompense for Pythagoras taking Jason in and saving his life when he was running from the guards on his arrival in Atlantis, and because Jason believes he is "meant to kill the Minotaur." This show of guest-friendship to Pythagoras and belief in destiny mark Jason out as a hero in the mode of the ancient Greek heroes. However, at a screening of this episode at the Petrie Museum in Bloomsbury in 2015 some of the viewers found Jason to be a more modern hero; he was "self-sacrificing and respectful" and "did the right thing but was empathetic" unlike the "self-centred" ancient heroes. Jason's honorable actions, and his predilection for seeing the best in people, often puts him and his friends in danger, but they do not chastise him for this, as this is a key aspect of his heroic character; as Hercules says, "you see the best in people, it's your faith that makes you who you are" (Episode 2.6: "The Grey Sisters"). He picks a fight with Prince Heptarian to prevent him from hitting a "defenceless old man" (Episode 1.3: "A Boy of No Consequence") and trusts his rival for Ariadne's hand, Prince Telemon, even though Pythagoras is suspicious, and Telemon turns out to be working with Pasiphae (Episode 2.3: "Telemon"). Jason also trusts Medea, Pasiphae's niece and protégée, who becomes a temporary ally in defeating an undead army, but she then stabs Ariadne with an enchanted knife (Episode 2.5: "The Day of the Dead"). Even after this he is unable to kill Medea in cold blood, so he knocks her out to take her blood to save Ariadne's life (Episode 2.6: "The Grey Sisters").

Although Jason is initially unable to hold a sword, and is easily disarmed, he uses a sword to kill the Minotaur, and his fighting prowess grows with every episode, so that he can deflect an arrow with his sword (Episode 1.9: "Pandora's Box"), and single-handedly fights and kills a group of Scythians (Episode 1.10: "The Price of Hope"), a feat Pythagoras finds "truly amazing." Pythagoras has already remarked that Jason is "different," "special" and "runs like the wind"

(Episode 1.4: "Twist of Fate"). Pasiphae perceives that Jason is "a born bull leaper" (Episode 1.3: "A Boy of No Consequence"), satyrs will not harm him (Episode 1.2: "A Girl by Any Other Name"), and he can look at the cursed and snaky-headed Medusa without being turned to stone (Episode 1.10: "The Price of Hope"). He learns from Medea that his powers come from being "touched by the gods" (Episode 2.6: "The Grey Sisters"). As a hero with links to the gods and with special abilities, Jason is a hero in the mold of the ancient Greek heroes, such as Theseus, son of Poseidon, and Heracles, son of Zeus. Also like an ancient hero Jason believes and trusts the Oracle. He tells her that he did not feel that he belonged in his former home, and so the transition from the modern world to the ancient one takes place almost seamlessly.

The Oracle is concerned that Jason's "heart will blacken" and "he will be consumed by hatred" if he ever "learns the truth" that the evil queen Pasiphae (Sarah Parish) is his mother (Episode 2.2: "A New Dawn Part 2"). This prophecy appears to be coming true when Jason goes to kill Pasiphae in revenge for causing the murder of the Oracle, using the severed head of Medusa, and Pasiphae reveals that she, like Jason, is "immune to the Gorgon's gaze," as she is his mother (Episode 2.9: "The Gorgon's Gaze"). Jason displays his dark side, killing soldiers even if they are unarmed, so that Ariadne finds him changed from a man who would not kill in cold blood to "a cold-hearted killer," and Hercules calls him a "stark raving lunatic" who is "lost to us forever." This behavior could be compared to the murderous madness of Achilles following the death of Patroclus, or the goddess-induced madness of Heracles and Ajax. In his darkness Jason turns to Medea for comfort, temporarily preferring the witch of Colchis over Ariadne.

It is Jason's father, Aeson, who finally turns his son back "towards the light" (Episode 2.11: "Kin"), and Jason marries Ariadne in the forest, choosing her and the light over Medea and the darkness (Episode 2.12: "The Queen Must Die Part 1"). At the end of the series Jason tells Ariadne that Medea has returned to Colchis and he will never see her again, but the new Oracle, Cassandra, sees that Jason must go to Colchis and obtain the Golden Fleece with the help of Medea if Pasiphae is ever to be defeated (Episode 2.13: "The Queen Must Die Part 2"). Jason's strong bond to Medea has not really been severed, and viewers who know the stories of Ariadne and Medea will perhaps think that there is still time for Ariadne to be abandoned on Naxos, as the mythical Ariadne was abandoned by Theseus, before Medea and Jason reunite on Colchis.

## HERCULES THE UNHEROIC

Julian Murphy describes the Hercules in *Atlantis* as "unlike most Herculeses; he's a drunkard and a boaster and he's making up his own myths, he hasn't actually done anything heroic, he'd just like people to think he had" (Series 1: "Behind the Scenes").[5] Hercules is played by an established actor from Yorkshire, Mark Addy, and he is given top billing. According to Murphy the production team had wanted Addy to play Hercules, as "he fitted the sort of Falstaff that Howard (Overman, joint series creator) had written" (Series 1: "Behind the Scenes"), and unlike Donnelly and Emms he was offered the part without an audition. Addy has had a wide-ranging career as a supporting actor in film and television series, and his persona as a bluff Yorkshireman, from parts such as Dave in *The Full Monty* (1997), is translated into a comic Hercules who loves food, is often drunk, and almost lost his house through gambling debts. Addy's Hercules acts as a comic foil to Jason, and as Addy says of his character "there's a lot of fun to be had at his expense" (Series 1: "Behind the Scenes"). It is not surprising that Circe changes him into a pig, of all animals, who drinks all the wine and eats all the food (Episode 1.6: "The Song of the Sirens").[6]

From the beginning, Hercules is presented to us as an unheroic character, with all the vices of the mythical character, without the bravery, which makes him an interesting comic character. Jason describes Hercules as "a lazy no-good womanizing drunk" (Episode 1.3: "A Boy of No Consequence"), and to Hercules himself happiness is "gold in your purse, a flagon of wine in one hand and a beautiful woman in the other" (Episode 1.2: "A Girl by Any Other Name") (Figure 8.1). Hercules as a womanizer fond of wine is not dissimilar from the Heracles we meet in Greek tragedy: in Euripides' *Alcestis*, he extols the benefits of wine to combat gloominess (785–800), and in Sophocles' *Women of Trachis*, Deianeira speaks of the many women that Heracles has had (460) before he brought home his newest conquest, Iole. While Hercules' actions in the *Women of Trachis* end in tragedy, his drinking and gambling, and above all greediness, provide comic situations in *Atlantis*. Here he wakes up in a goat pen kissing a goat after a night in the tavern, bets all his money on a beetle race, and is detected trying to steal the food left in the dish of a blind man.

Wherever Hercules' legendary feats are mentioned they are immediately undercut, causing the viewer to question Hercules as a hero.[7] When he first meets Jason in "The Earth Bull" (Episode 1.1) Hercules is interested that Jason has heard of him ("The Hercules?" asks

# The Changing Faces of Heroism in Atlantis

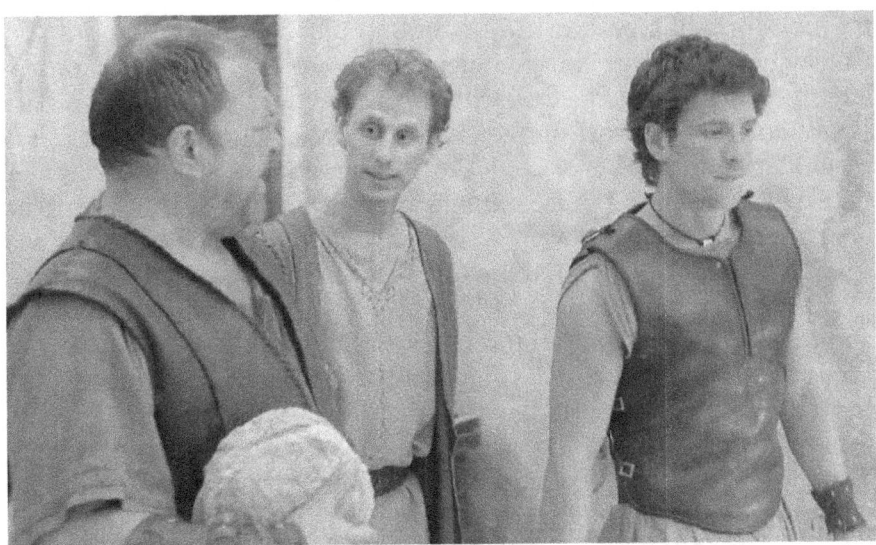

Figure 8.1 Jason (Jack Donnelly), Pythagoras (Robert Emms), and Hercules (Mark Addy) at the market in *Atlantis* Episode 1.3: "A Boy of No Consequence" (2013).

Jason), but Pythagoras immediately pokes fun, saying that Hercules is only famous for "getting fat," setting up their relationship as that of "kind of an odd couple," as Addy describes it (Series 1: "Behind the Scenes"), with a lot of banter between them. When Hercules speaks of his own feats of the past, such as "even as a baby I strangled a snake with my bare hands" (Episode 1.6: "The Song of the Sirens") and "the time when I wrestled the Nemean lion" (Episode 1.13: "Touched by the Gods Part 2"), we are not meant to believe him, as we have seen that he is more likely to take the credit for the heroic deeds of others than enact them himself. Hercules shows himself to be a coward by "running in the other direction" when Jason searches for and kills the Minotaur (Episode 1.1: "The Earth Bull"). However, Hercules is quite happy to take the glory that rightfully belongs to Jason, saying that "we" killed the Minotaur "together," and he tells his friends that their fame will allow them to grow rich and "live like hogs." Even when he does show that he has his heroic trait of strength, by bending prison bars (Episode 1.13: "Touched by the Gods Part 2"), this is undercut, as all his friends can escape through the bars without needing this; it is only the portly Hercules who cannot get through them.

Although Addy finds Hercules to be "a coward" he also says that his character has "moments of bravery and moments of bravado" (Series 1: "Behind the Scenes"). Hercules stands up for Jason when they are brought before King Minos (Episode 1.3: "A Boy of No Consequence"). Hercules, who runs from trouble, as "it's never too late to turn and flee like cowards" (Episode 2.1: "A New Dawn Part 1"), who wants to earn money wherever possible, and whose ethos is that "no good has ever come from being honest" (Episode 1.2: "A Girl by Any Other Name"), might seem to be the antithesis of the honorable Jason. However, by the end of series two, Hercules has tried to give his life for Medusa, the woman he loves, and has become Jason's trusted henchman. It is Hercules in whom the Oracle confides about Jason's parentage, entrusting Hercules to keep this secret and "protect Jason at all costs" (Episode 2.2: "A New Dawn Part 2"). It is Hercules whom Jason eventually entrusts with killing Pasiphae, something a son cannot do, and it is also Hercules who presides over Jason and Ariadne's wedding. Hercules follows Jason because he "is the real thing" (Episode 2.1: "A New Dawn Part 1"), the hero that Hercules wants to be. Hercules, then, is not just the comic buffoon that he originally appears to be, in his aspiration for heroism. Another of my young students who enjoyed the series found that the Hercules in *Atlantis* is less "stereotypical" and has more "depth" than other versions of the Hercules character that he has come across.

## HERCULES AND MEDUSA AS TRAGIC LOVERS

There is much discussion of Hercules' womanizing in *Atlantis* (conquests include Maia the baker's daughter and Sophia, a servant at the palace), but he is quickly converted to a one-woman man when he meets Medusa, and his love for her makes him a sympathetic rather than simply a comedic character. On first meeting her he describes Medusa as "a vision of beauty the like of which I have never seen" (Episode 1.2: "A Girl By Any Other Name"), for whom he immediately risks his own life, much to Pythagoras' surprise. It is only when Medusa is in peril that the greedy Hercules finds himself uncharacteristically with no appetite for food. Despite their mutual affection, Hercules and Medusa's relationship does not run smoothly, and he puts her life in jeopardy through his own self-doubt. He goes to Circe to use witchcraft to "capture the heart of the woman I love" as he does not believe that Medusa loves him (Episode 1.6: "The Song of the Sirens"). Circe's witchcraft turns Hercules into a pig and causes Medusa to fall into a sickness that medicine cannot heal. On learning of Hercules' actions Pythagoras reports that Medusa has said "a pig was too good for you," but Hercules' loyalty and belief in Medusa soon lead to their reconciliation, and they are both portrayed as being happy together. Hercules is even honest with Medusa about his past: "I have been known to drink and gamble, there were debts, there were women, many of both, it's all in the past. All the women I've known, I have never felt this way before." However, Jason, along with viewers with any knowledge of the story of Medusa from Greek mythology, know that she and Hercules are not destined to live happily ever after.

Hercules retrieves Pandora's box for Kyros, a merchant who has taken Medusa hostage. On her release, Medusa inadvertently opens the box and becomes the Gorgon with snakes for hair, whose gaze turns living creatures to stone. Hercules tries to give his life so that she can be cured, but both Jason and Medusa stop him from doing this, as Medusa "would rather stay cursed" than allow Hercules to sacrifice himself for her (Episode 1.10: "The Price of Hope"). Medusa is left alone in a cave, a blameless victim cursed for no action of her own, like Medusa in Ovid, who is cursed for being raped by Poseidon in Athena's temple (*Metamorphoses* 4.798–9). She waits for a cure to be found, but it is Pasiphae, and not Hercules, who offers this, in exchange for her causing someone's death. Medusa agrees, not knowing the victim will be the Oracle. Although Medusa is happy to be with Hercules again, she cannot live with the guilt of what she has done, so that although one curse is lifted she feels that she is still "cursed" and "damned" for killing the Oracle. Medusa conceives a plot whereby she is returned to her former state as a Gorgon using Pandora's box, so that Jason can use her severed head as a weapon to defeat Pasiphae's army. She therefore becomes a willing sacrificial heroine rather than a monster, in offering up her life to save others (Episode 2.9: "The Gorgon's Gaze").

## PYTHAGORAS, "THE TRIANGLE GUY"

On first meeting Pythagoras, Jason identifies him as "the triangle guy" (Episode 1.1: "The Earth Bull"), and his interest in triangles is a source of jokes, so that, as Hercules says, "most men dream about women, you dream about triangles" (Episode 1.10: "The Price of Hope"). Julian Murphy thinks that "our Pythagoras is perhaps quite like Pythagoras ... very clever, very honest [with a] brilliant mind" (Series 1: "Behind the Scenes"). There is very little known about Pythagoras the intellectual thinker, who lived in the sixth century BC and who is credited with discoveries in geometry, music, astronomy, and religion, best known today for the theory of triangles that still bears his name.[8] None of his writings survive, there are few contemporary accounts of his life or his work, and in the later tradition he has become a legendary character, as the son of Apollo, with a golden thigh, and the ability to perform miracles using his supernatural powers over animals and the elements.[9] It might seem a strange choice to put the historical though mysterious character of Pythagoras together with the mythical character of Hercules and with Jason, the twenty-first-century character who is an amalgamation of mythic heroes. Julian Murphy states that "In our fantasy world we can put whoever we like ... taking characters who are separated by 1000 years in real time and join them up" (Series 1: "Behind the Scenes"). In the series Emms' gawky but clever Pythagoras, as much as Addy's fat and greedy Hercules, serves as a suitable foil to Donnelly's Jason, displaying a different kind of heroism that comes from intelligence rather than speed and strength.

In *Atlantis* Pythagoras is seen from the beginning as more honorable and less cowardly than Hercules; he wants to harbor Jason while Hercules would send him away, and he accepts the black stone that means he will be sacrificed to the Minotaur, when Hercules would have left Atlantis to avoid this fate. Pythagoras is relied upon by both Hercules and Jason to come up with a logical and intelligent solution to problems. As Robert Emma states, he is the "brains of the group, problem solver, a loyal friend" (Series 1: "Behind the Scenes"). His knowledge of plants and medicine is used throughout the series to help heal wounds and illnesses and his research results in solutions to problems, such as how to cure Jason of lycanthropy (Episode 1.11: "Hunger Pangs"). He knows who should be brought in to help them, when help is needed, whether this is from the fields of religion or science, including Eunapius, leader of the cult of the Mysteries of Eleusis, who provides details of the route to be taken to Hades, or inventor Daedalus, who helps to decipher the ancient script on Pandora's box. Pythagoras is also often the first to see through people who are pretending to be something that they are not, such as Prince Telemon and the priest Melas, who are both secretly working for Pasiphae.

Pythagoras can appear dispassionate, countering Jason's optimism with probability, marveling at the invention of the brazen bull that is to be used to execute Ariadne: "a truly remarkable piece of craftsmanship" (Episode 1.12: "Touched by the Gods Part 1"); and he would have Jason kill an unarmed man when "logic" and "reason dictates it" (Episode 2.1: "A New Dawn Part 1"). He can also be relied upon to do the right thing, however difficult this might be. We learn that he killed his drunken father to protect his mother from being beaten, and it is he whom Medusa first approaches with her plan to sacrifice herself. Pythagoras confides in Hercules that the reason he follows Jason is that "You and Jason are the only real family I have. I love you, both of you. For a rational man it leaves me utterly bewildered but there it is. I do it for love" (Episode 2.1: "A New Dawn Part 1"). Pythagoras shows emotion when he sees no solution for his friends, breaking down in tears when Jason and Hercules are to be executed (Episode 2.8: "The Madness of Hercules"). As a man of science, it might seem surprising that Pythagoras is actually the emotional heart of the series, and "the kindest man" that Jason has "ever known" (Episode 1.8: "The Furies").

At the end of series two the love stories of Jason and Hercules have come to their different conclusions. Meanwhile, Pythagoras' love story with Icarus, son of Daedalus, is only just beginning. It is Hercules who first notices a change in Pythagoras, and that it is caused by his feelings for Icarus; "I remember it well the first time you feel like that about someone," Hercules says to his friend (Episode 2.12: "The Queen Must Die Part 1"). Pythagoras is devastated when he realizes that Icarus has betrayed him by working with Pasiphae's men, and finds it difficult to forgive him. However, when Icarus uses the wings created by his father to drop bombs on the soldiers loyal to Pasiphae, then falls to the ground, he is found by Pythagoras, and they kiss for the first time. Pythagoras, then, ends the series embarking on a relationship with another mythic male character. In an otherwise heteronormative series Pythagoras shows us that heroes can sometimes get the man, rather than getting the girl.

## HELPER MAIDENS AND HEROINES

Medusa is a kind character, preventing Hercules from being captured by the Maenads, and willing to lie to a dying old man about the fate of his daughter, who will not leave the cult of Dionysus, to save the man from pain. She later becomes a pawn in the game to control Atlantis, and although her final act of self-sacrifice can be interpreted as a selfless one, she is a sacrificial heroine rather than an action heroine. As a princess Ariadne inhabits the court of King Minos, and is initially confined to the world of the palace, where she also has little opportunity to be an action heroine. In "The Earth Bull" (Episode 1.1), Ariadne is drawn to the newcomer Jason, and as a helper maiden, which is her traditional role in the story of Theseus and the Minotaur, she gives him the thread that he can use to navigate his way out of the Labyrinth.[10] She helps him again by bringing the silver needed by his friends to cure his lycanthropy. At court, at first she silently watches Jason's progress with interest, but she believes that she is bound by her duty to her city to marry a prince of royal blood. After watching Jason defeat her fiancé Heptarian in the games, Ariadne finds the courage to defy the wishes of her father and stepmother, but she does this by stealth, using the disapproval of the gods as a reason for not going ahead with the marriage. She shows more courage at the end of the first series when she takes a wounded Jason into her bedroom. As she tends to his wounds she tells him "I would gladly risk my life for you" (Episode 1.12: "Touched By the Gods Part 1"). Unwilling to give up Jason as the intruder who stole into the palace to kill Pasiphae, Ariadne is condemned to die in the bronze bull for treason. She is freed by Jason and his friends, and although she is returned to the palace by Pasiphae's men she first manages to stab one of the soldiers, hinting at the change in Ariadne from helper maiden to action heroine that will occur in the second series.

Aiyisha Hart finds that in the second season, "Ariadne becomes much stronger. She turns into a woman as opposed to a teenage character who's being quite defiant. She becomes more of a mature woman fighting her corner" (Series 2: "Behind the Scenes"). The series begins with Minos dead and Ariadne the queen of an Atlantis that is facing an attack from the banished Pasiphae's army. Ariadne has become more ruthless, and gives orders to her captain that a man suspected of helping a thief who has stolen the Palladium "must be made to talk," even if this requires torture (Episode 2.1: "A New Dawn Part 1"). However, she shows that she still has compassion, returning the Colchean dead to their people for burial, and allowing the deserters to leave the city rather than having them executed, conscious that she must not become a "tyrant" like Pasiphae. Although she continues to turn to Jason for help, she is steadfast in her resolve that she cannot marry him. As queen, "I must sacrifice everything I hold dearest. We cannot be together because you are not of royal blood. If I marry you the nobles will turn against me. Everything I do must be to protect Atlantis" (Episode 2.2: "A New Dawn Part 2"). To this end she agrees to marry Prince Telemon, until it is revealed that he is working with Pasiphae, when they are ambushed on the way to their wedding. For the first time we see that Ariadne is skilled with a bow and arrow, which she uses to kill Colchean soldiers, including one who would have killed Jason (Episode 2.4: "The Marriage of True Minds"). After she is saved from the illness caused by Medea's poisoned blade, Ariadne finally decides that she can no longer "deny" her love for Jason, and asks him to marry her (Episode 2.6: "The

Grey Sisters"). She is finally convinced that she is not "weakened" by her choice to marry Jason but is rather "stronger with you at my side" (Episode 2.7: "A Fate Worse than Death"). The viewer is, however, left to wonder whether it is the appearance of a potential rival, Medea, that has caused this change of heart, and Jason hesitates before giving an answer.

When Jason is arrested erroneously for the Oracle's death Ariadne will not publicly assist him. She has learned that to maintain her position as queen she must not be seen to show favoritism. Her face is a blank mask as Jason is to be taken for execution, but secretly she has him freed. When she in turn is captured by Pasiphae she will not hand over control of Atlantis, and will not be broken even when strung up and subjected to torture. In pain, she can still say to Pasiphae "there is only one true queen of Atlantis and it is not you" (Episode 2.9: "The Gorgon's Gaze"). After she marries Jason in the forest it is a new, stronger Ariadne who ends the series. On learning that he must go to Colchis, where he will see Medea again, Ariadne tells him "I will go with you." Jason protests that "it is too dangerous, I have to go alone," but Ariadne is clear, and her words are the closing words of the series: "then who is to protect you from yourself? If Pasiphae is to be defeated we'll do it together" (Episode 2.13: "The Queen Must Die, Part 2"). Ariadne has finally grown into her role as partner to Jason rather than helper maiden. She has displayed skills in politics and combat, and is not willing to lose her husband to Medea or her throne to Pasiphae without a fight.

Up until Ariadne's transformation, Pasiphae is the most powerful, active female character in *Atlantis*, but she is the villain of the series rather than a hero (the archer Atalanta and gladiatrix Areto are both also strong women and positive characters, but each only appears for a single episode). However, the ambivalent Medea, Pasiphae's niece and protégée, is worth consideration as another potential female hero. Medea, like Jason, has special abilities, though while his are strength and speed, hers are the powers of witchcraft.[11] Amy Manson describes her character as "a Lone Ranger, a bit of a loner" with "magical powers" (Series 2: "Behind the Scenes"). She first appears at the beginning of the second series as a thief sent by Pasiphae to steal the Palladium and to cause the soldiers faithful to Ariadne to turn away from her cause. This Palladium, which in *Atlantis* is a small statue, has been borrowed from the Trojan War stories, in which Odysseus and Diomedes steal the Palladium, a wooden statue of Pallas Athena, which protected the city of Troy.[12] Medea is seen to be as ruthless as Pasiphae, but with less concern for the gods, so that when Telemon is left in the desert with a flask of water after being stabbed by Pasiphae, who will not kill a prince of royal blood, Medea throws a knife at it to ensure that Telemon does not survive (Episode 2.4: "The Marriage of True Minds").

Jason and Medea are thrown together in a cave full of undead warriors, and Medea uses her magic to save Jason from being killed, and then to mend his broken leg (Episode 2.5: "The Day of the Dead"). She tells him that she is loyal to Pasiphae because she was the only one who had ever shown kindness to the young witch, who has been "shunned" all her life. When Jason is unable to kill Medea after she betrays him by stabbing Ariadne, he tells Medea that this is because he is not as "cold-blooded" as her, but Medea suggests another reason: "You feel it as I do. We are both touched by the gods. I sense something in you, as you sense it in me. You can't deny it" (Episode 2.6: "The Grey Sisters"). When Pasiphae reveals to Medea that Jason is her (Pasiphae's) son, Medea continually tries to dissuade Pasiphae from killing him, and when Pasiphae finally tells Jason about his parentage, Medea encourages Jason to "embrace who you really are" (Episode 2.9: "The Gorgon's Gaze"). As Jason appears to be turning to his dark side he has dreams of Medea, and after he is hurt fighting Pasiphae's soldiers Medea heals him and they spend the night together in the forest (Episode 2.10: "The Dying of the Light"). When Jason is captured and forced to fight in the arena, this time it is Medea watching rather than Ariadne. Medea realizes that Pasiphae will kill Jason, and so Medea uses her magic to help him escape, choosing Jason over his mother (Episode 2.11: "Kin"). Pasiphae realizes this and forbids Medea to see Jason again, saying that otherwise she will kill her niece: "You love him. You thought you could turn him but it is he who has turned you" (Episode 2.12: "The Queen Must Die Part 1"). Medea escapes and goes to Jason, helping him to capture Pasiphae, as she "cannot" become like Pasiphae. Jason recognizes Medea for the helper maiden that she has become: "it seems you are always coming to my aid." Medea resolves to return to Colchis, and before revealing that he has married Ariadne Jason tells Medea "There's a part of me that doesn't want you to go." We do not see Medea again, but Jason is destined to meet her in Colchis, where she will resume her role as helper maiden, and perhaps even as hero. Initially an ambivalent character, Medea has displayed her heroic potential, with supernatural powers to support this.

The series ends having created lots of possibilities for the future. After losing Medusa, Hercules has turned from buffoon to tragic hero, like the Heracles who is driven mad and kills his wife and children. Jason has become a more interesting character having experienced his dark side, and Pythagoras has been given the opportunity for love, having spent the first two series helping his friends through the ups and downs of their relationships. Perhaps the most possibilities are provided for the female characters, with Medea and Ariadne both having found their skills, and also both caught in a love triangle with Jason. There is an expectation set that Atalanta will return, as one of the Argonauts, and another female hero.[13] When she appears briefly in the first series, saving Jason and his friends from the Scythians, she tells Jason that Artemis told her to protect Jason from harm as "our paths are destined to cross again in the future" (Episode 1.10: "The Price of Hope").

## CONCLUSION

Although the series was short-lived, it provides a good example of the potential for television to transform heroes and monsters from Greek mythology. Unfortunately, the storylines and the potential for heroics suggested in the first two series will not be developed, or at least not for television. Fan fiction writers have picked up where the story left off, and so the heroes from *Atlantis* are continuing to have adventures, albeit online rather than onscreen.[14]

## NOTES

1 On the bull-leaper fresco and other artifacts linked to bull sports see for example Higgins (1967: 35 and 95) and Fitton (1995: 131–2).
2 Ovid, *Metamorphoses*, 8.166–82 and 4.770–804, Apollodorus, *Library* 1.7–10 and 2.38–46.
3 Izundu (2015).
4 Examples include: "Prometheus" (Episode 1.8), where Xena and Hercules both help to free Prometheus; "Beware Greeks Bearing Gifts" (Episode 1.12), where Xena helps Helen of Troy to escape; "Ulysses" (Episode 2.19), where Xena helps Ulysses to avoid the Sirens and string his bow.
5 For a summary of the different facets of the character of Heracles/Hercules in antiquity, see Stafford (2012).
6 The character of Circe also changes sailors into pigs in the *Odyssey*, but the animal seems more apt for Hercules.
7 A questioning approach is also taken in Brett Ratner's *Hercules* (2014), where we learn that Hercules has a team to support him; see further Chiu in this volume, as well as Blanshard and Stafford.

8 For a discussion of the accounts of the life and work of Pythagoras, see Riedweg (2005).
9 Porphyry quoted in Riedweg (2005: 2–6).
10 On Ariadne as helper maiden, see Griffiths (2006: 35).
11 On Medea and witchcraft in the ancient sources, see Griffiths (2006: 41–7).
12 *Little Iliad* Fr. 1.
13 In Apollonius of Rhodes' *Argonautica*, Atalanta is refused her request to join the crew of the *Argo* as Jason is afraid her presence might cause some of the men to fall in love with her, leading to conflict (1.769–73), but she is included as one of the Argonauts in Apollodorus, *Library* 1.9.16.
14 As of April 2017, there are 360 *Atlantis* stories posted to archiveofourown.org and 225 posted to fanfiction.net, and new stories continue to be created.

# 9 Xena: Warrior, Heroine, Tramp

Anise K. Strong

## INTRODUCTION

The late 1990s television series *Xena: Warrior Princess* (1995–2001) chronicled the adventurous of a mythical ancient Greek warrior woman, Xena. She was unusual among sword-and-sandal heroes not only for her gender but also for her lack of any long-term heterosexual relationship and for her sexually active lifestyle. Xena's characterization in turn helped pave the way for more complex and proactive female characters in the modern "golden age" of televisual and cinematic historical and fantasy dramas.

The small subfield of "Xena studies" has extensively analyzed Xena's depiction as mother, as action heroine, and as half of a possible implicit same-sex relationship with her companion, Gabrielle. However, no scholarship has yet considered the precedent Xena set as a trendsetting archetype of a sexually active, polyamorous woman whose romantic decisions do not mark her as immoral or deviant.[1] Other characters within the series, such as Xena's look-alikes Meg, Diana, and Leah, each represent different sexual lifestyle and relationship choices, all of which are eventually respected by the other characters. Despite their campy origins and convoluted plot twists, these stories of Xena have helped reshape the notion of what women might do and with whom in the ancient world. They offered new and complicated models of heroism and morality that more closely paralleled those of traditional male protagonists in films and television about the ancient world.

Xena's creators, Sam Raimi, Rob Tapert, and John Schulian, as well as the actress Lucy Lawless herself, explicitly represented her as a polyamorous and desirous woman throughout the series. She was initially depicted as a "bad girl" and exhibits many of the traits of the wicked woman in classical cinema – promiscuity, greed, and lack of maternal instinct. Through Xena's encounters with her comrades Hercules and Gabrielle, she ultimately finds redemption and remakes herself as a heroine. However, she notably never embraces celibacy or settles down with any one particular romantic partner. Xena thus offers a new model of mythical heroine that rejects both the wicked seductresses and the virginal damsels or widows of earlier cinematic incarnations.

I shall first examine earlier polyamorous classical heroines in film and television, ranging from the various Cleopatras to Andromeda in the 1981 *Clash of the Titans*. Through a focus on the later genre roles of Lucy Lawless, the actress who played Xena, I analyze the ways in which this character served as a model and ancestor for later desirous female protagonists of twenty-first-century television, ranging from D'Anna Biers and Starbuck of *Battlestar Galactica* (2005–9), a science fiction series heavily influenced by classical mythology, to Lucretia and Saxa of the STARZ *Spartacus* series (2010–13).

## PROMISCUOUS WOMEN

Xena was by no means the first sexually promiscuous woman of the ancient world on screen. The reigning queen of this category is almost inevitably Cleopatra, whose films typically depict her as the lover of both Julius Caesar and Mark Antony. At the same time, juxtaposing these two relationships on screen is often awkward or results in critical judgments of Cleopatra's behavior. The 1934 *Cleopatra* starring Claudette Colbert portrays the queen as a seductress, using her charms to gain alliances with both Caesar and Antony. While she claims to love both men, she is also willing to poison Antony for political advantage. However, she engages in no other casual physical relationships. Colbert's Cleopatra is at best serially monogamous in committed relationships. In contrast, *Caesar and Cleopatra* (1945) focuses exclusively on her first relationship, which is also represented more paternally than romantically.

The most famous *Cleopatra* film, the 1963 Mankiewicz version starring Elizabeth Taylor and Richard Burton, also explores both the tropes of Cleopatra as a promiscuous seductress and as a loyal lover. Julius Caesar (Rex Harrison), before meeting her, comments:

> Her own sexual talents ... are said to be considerable. Her lovers, I am told, are listed more easily by number than by name. It is said that she chooses in the manner of a man ... rather than wait to be chosen.[2]

In this first appearance, Cleopatra was historically 20 years old and legally married to her younger brother. There are no contemporaneous allegations suggesting that she was a teenage nymphomaniac, but Caesar's description serves to color and define the audience's initial impression of the Egyptian monarch. She is prostitute-like in her level of skill, indiscriminate and excessive in her choice of partners, and inappropriately sexually aggressive. Our first story about Cleopatra in this film is that she is immoral and unwomanly precisely because of her sexual activity.

Later in the film, when Antony is first considering a relationship with Cleopatra after Caesar's death, he bitterly taunts her, demanding: "Tell me, how many have loved you since him? One? Ten? Anyone? No one? Have they kissed you with Caesar's lips? Is it his name you cry out?"[3]

Cleopatra's sexual advances to these two Roman conquerors are assumed by the male characters to be potential evidence of her general promiscuity rather than indicative of her careful political calculations about relative advantage.[4] The queen herself proclaims that Antony is her one true love; there is no direct evidence of other partners or unfaithfulness. The movie does not itself explicitly condemn her for multiple relationships, which would be especially hypocritical given the real-life scandal involving its actors. However, Taylor's Cleopatra is also presented as a dubious and flawed role-model, whose downfall is connected to the unorthodoxy of her relationships. Furthermore, the dangers of having two lovers become clear when they both accuse her of nymphomania and sexual aggressiveness. Cleopatra's independence and agency are characterized as sexual voracity and ruthlessness. The dialogue borrows from later stereotypes about Messalina and Cleopatra to attack this paradigmatic *meretrix regina* or whore-queen.[5]

In the HBO series *Rome* (2005–7, Season 1), Cleopatra is portrayed as a hypersexual drug addict, who attempts to seduce first the centurion Vorenus and then, more successfully, the legionary Pullo. However, she does not pursue these liaisons purely for pleasure but rather primarily in order to ensure the birth of a child whose fatherhood she can attribute to Caesar.[6] *Rome* implies that Cleopatra never loved Caesar, although it does depict a later romantic and highly jealous relationship with Antony.

In any case, the Egyptian queen's representation in all these versions is necessarily mediated through the historical lens of both two millennia of biography and many fictional works of reception. Most accounts of Cleopatra acknowledge her two major sexual relationships but also endow her with an aura of both desirability and scandal. Her victorious enemy Augustus' propaganda machine was effectively able to label Cleopatra as the whore-queen in explicit contrast to his virtuous, faithful, twice-married sister Octavia. Even though *Rome*'s Octavia is also unfaithful to her husband, she is still portrayed as a woman driven by romantic longings or familial pressure rather than by voracious desire or political machination. The representation of Cleopatra as promiscuous in these films and television series also significantly constructs and constrains the judgment about her by both other characters and the audience: Cleopatra is often represented more as a passionate lover than as a brilliant monarch. Her polyamory is incompatible with a narrative of a simple, virtuous heroine.

Other early representations of mythical heroines, such as Andromeda in both the original and rebooted versions of *Clash of the Titans* (1981) and (2010) and its sequel, *Wrath of the Titans* (2012), typically evoke the stereotype of the damsel in distress.[7] In Ray Harryhausen's 1981 version, Andromeda is quite literally chained to a rock during the climactic fight scene, unable to assist in her own rescue at all. While 2010's Andromeda does ultimately become a reigning queen, it is not until the critically panned sequel that she achieves the role of warrior heroine, leading her own army against the Titans. In *Wrath of the Titans*, Andromeda serves as the fulcrum of a weak love triangle, mediating between her former suitor Agenor and the hero Perseus. However, the heroes have little time for dalliance due to the urgency of their war against the Titans. Andromeda is still largely defined as a virginal maiden, ready to be eventually claimed by the widower Perseus.

## XENA'S PAST IN *HERCULES: THE LEGENDARY JOURNEYS* (1995–1999)

In contrast, Xena, the warrior princess, is always first and foremost an action heroine (or sometime villain), rather than a romantic lead. Xena first appears not in her own series but in a set of three episodes of *Hercules: The Legendary Journeys* that served as a backdoor pilot for her character. Later flashbacks within *Xena: Warrior Princess* itself also reveal more of her backstory. The young Xena was initially involved in two sequential heterosexual monogamous relationships, before she was betrayed and deserted by one particular lover, Julius Caesar.[8] Xena responded to this rejection by becoming a fierce and destructive warrior. She was so focused on violence that when she had a child by a later lover, Borias, she gave her son over to Centaurs because she would be an unfit mother. While Xena's backstory is thus tarred with traditional motifs of female immorality such as a rejection of motherhood, excessive greed, and melodramatic violence, her sexual activities are not directly associated with her villainy.

When Xena, who has become the general of a mercenary army, first meets the legendary Greek hero Hercules in his eponymous television series, she begins by ignoring Hercules and romancing his companion Iolaus instead. In the midst of lovemaking, the naïve Iolaus questions Xena about her sexual activities (*Hercules: The Legendary Journeys*, Episode 1.9: "The Warrior Princess"):

IOLAUS: Do you do this for all your warriors?
XENA: Only the special ones.
IOLAUS: Oh. I hope there aren't too many of those?
XENA: Right now, there's just you.

While Iolaus is clearly somewhat insecure about his relationship status with Xena, he does not condemn her or seem repulsed by her polyamory or lack of virginity. Furthermore, even though Xena has seduced Iolaus and lied to him about a variety of other matters, she does not deny her multiple sexual relationships. She promises him immediate primacy in her life rather than fidelity or any sort of long-term commitment. In the course of the trilogy of episodes that introduce her character, the conniving warrior princess also sends several of her other current lovers, who are also her mercenary lieutenants, to assassinate Iolaus and Hercules in pursuit of her larger agenda.

After many long debates, epic fight scenes, and some vigorous offscreen sex with Hercules (much to Iolaus' chagrin), Xena eventually repents her violent ways and resolves to help the oppressed in the future. However, there is no sense that her promiscuity is viewed as part of her immorality or evil deeds. The *Hercules* episodes never suggest that she will now be involved exclusively with Hercules, as if he had somehow tamed her. Instead, Xena's redemption revolves around her new resolve to help and protect innocent people rather than treat them as objects for her profit or amusement. Furthermore, her close relationship with her righteous and enthusiastic companion Gabrielle helps to humanize Xena. This relationship was officially platonic but had an increasingly strong romantic and queer subtext.[9]

## XENA'S "LOOK-ALIKES"

One of the recurrent tropes of later episodes of *Xena: Warrior Princess* is that Xena has multiple "look-alikes," all played by Lucy Lawless, each of whom represent a different potential career path that Xena herself might have chosen. In classic comedic form, these episodes usually feature significant role-switching and confusion among onlookers about the true identity of these identical twins. The first such look-alike is Diana, an actual princess whom Xena helps marry her one true male love and become a just and wise ruler. Diana represents the conventional path for historical or fantasy heroines – the damsel in distress whose happy ending involves a traditional heterosexual marriage and, eventually, a baby. Xena, in contrast, finds herself alternately repulsed and bored by Diana's lifestyle, although she is willing to respect and accept that these choices make the "princess" very happy.

The next and most prominent recurring twin is Meg, identified as "the Tramp," who first appears in the episode entitled "Warrior ... Princess ... Tramp" (Episode 2.6) (Figure 9.1). Meg's initial dominant

Figure 9.1 Meg (Lucy Lawless), pretending to be Xena, eagerly kisses a confused Joxer (Ted Raimi) in *Xena: Warrior Princess* Episode 2.6: "Warrior ... Princess .... Tramp" (1996). MCA Television.

character trait is her promiscuity, although that trope is later coupled with her display of both greed and gluttony; she appears to be the paradigmatic uncontrolled woman driven by her instincts rather than her brain. When Xena is taken to be Meg at the beginning of the episode, all the men in the bar are surprised that she is suddenly playing "hard to get." Gabrielle is later concerned about "Xena's" reputation, but she does not criticize or insult her for having multiple sexual partners. Xena's apparent lack of attention to their mission and the sudden disrespect she is receiving from strangers are important, rather than the issue of whether or not she was having casual sex. At the end of the episode, despite the numerous petty crimes committed by Meg, Xena and Gabrielle set her free and she says goodbye to the warriors on friendly terms. In a later episode, Meg opens a tavern after committing to a long-term, if not necessarily monogamous marriage with their male friend Joxer and bearing his children. Meg thus also represents an alternative female character trope – the "tramp" with a heart of gold who ultimately settles down into semi-respectability with her lover.

In contrast, the last look-alike that Xena meets is Leah, a virgin priestess of Hestia (Episode 3.9: "Warrior ... Priestess ... Tramp"). Leah takes the opportunity to lecture Xena and Gabrielle on their sexual mores when the pair admit to her that they are not, as she has assumed, also virgins:

LEAH, (praying to Hestia): If denying the flesh is the path to true righteousness, what lessons can I learn from these wanton strumpets?
XENA: You don't have to be a virgin to be virtuous.
LEAH: You keep telling yourself that, dear.

While Meg's character redemption arc focused on her giving up petty thievery and deception in favor of work as a cook and tavern owner, the lesson that Leah needs to learn is to abandon her prejudice toward sexually active women. She admits her error by the end of the episode, although she still offers Gabrielle a position as an "honorary" virgin. We do not see the actual Xena having casual liaisons in this episode; as usual she is too busy saving the day. However, the script's morality tale disparages narrow-minded virginity rather than critiquing Xena for her own romantic and sexual history. At the same time, Leah's choice to remain a virgin is also respected; she retains authority and success as the chief priestess of Hestia and seems to be pursuing a fulfilling career. Xena and Gabrielle never suggest that

Leah's choices are inappropriate or wrong; she simply represents yet another possible means of demonstrating sexual autonomy.

Meg the "tramp" also reappears in this episode, serving as a foil to further mock Leah's narrow-mindedness toward others while temporarily impersonating her. Meg comments to the villain, "How could I make trouble? I'm a virgin," critiquing the idea that sexual purity is necessarily associated with moral goodness. She also jokes about the difficulty of perpetual virginity as a lifestyle but does recognize the practical perks of receiving food, shelter, and respect as a priestess. Both Xena and Meg in this episode also praise masturbation as a normal and healthy part of their lives, a topic that for women only became an acceptable item for discussion on television in rare instances in the 1990s. *Xena: Warrior Princess* was one of the first non-cable television shows to joke about women engaging in masturbation.[10]

## XENA'S RELATIONSHIPS

Even within the context of mortal–immortal relationships, Xena defies traditional Greek mythological tropes by emphasizing the importance of consent and mutual desire. The war god Ares, who has a seasons-long infatuation with Xena, proclaims in a dream sequence in "Eternal Bonds" (Episode 5.13) that "I will do whatever it takes to make you trust me." In the next episode, Xena is very much the assertive, aggressive partner in her seduction of Ares, throwing him onto the couch and biting his nipples. In the farcical musical episode (Episode 5.10), "Lyre Lyre Heart on Fire," the heavily pregnant Xena rejects her mother's attempt to find her a husband who can serve as an adoptive father to her child, asserting that her chosen family of Gabrielle and Joxer can serve as co-parents instead. (This child, Eve, is the result of an immaculate conception between Xena and a version of the Hebrew God; there is thus no living father.) Xena then punches a random suitor who asks, since she doesn't want a husband, if she is in the market "for a little casual sex." Xena appears annoyed by the harassment rather than shocked at the implication.

Part of Xena's own education and maturation as a heroine, rather unlike that of comparable male heroes, involves learning to appreciate and respect the choices of other women. In a beauty pageant episode (Episode 2.11: "Here She Comes ... Miss Amphipolis"), Xena originally holds the other contestants in contempt, describing them as "bimbos" who are being exploited and degraded by men as sexual objects. Over the course of the episode, she learns that each contestant has a careful plan and a reason for their participation – saving their village from starvation, leaving home due to post-traumatic stress disorder, and other non-sexualized motivations. Eventually, the crown is given to the transgender contestant. This episode emphasizes the agency and control possible for women even in environments where they are explicitly the objects of men's desires.

Beyond Xena, the depiction of sexually active, polyamorous action heroines in media remains unfortunately rare. One of her most famous televisual contemporaneous counterparts, the eponymous *Buffy the Vampire Slayer* (1997–2003), turns her first boyfriend evil as a result of their sexual intercourse, is ignominiously dumped and publicly humiliated after a casual one-night stand, and then, upon having sex with her second serious boyfriend, causes an entire house to be possessed by sex-hating ghosts. Later sexual acts on the show result in the collapse of entire buildings.[11] In other words, unlike in *Xena*, both casual and serious sex for the action heroine of *Buffy* has almost inevitable negative consequences. Joss Whedon's other television series and films often cast similar judgments on polyamorous heroines or separate the warriors from the promiscuous characters.

## LUCY LAWLESS: *XENA* AND BEYOND

By following the career of Lucy Lawless, however, we can also trace the further evolution of sex-positive, actively desirous major female characters in genre television. The 2005–9 sci-fi series *Battlestar Galactica*, influenced strongly by Greek mythology, starred the character of Starbuck, an explicitly promiscuous, alcoholic, impulsively aggressive pilot.[12] Starbuck was played by a male actor in the original version but in the new series was incarnated by the athletic and impish Katee Sackhoff.

Another recurring character in *Battlestar Galactica*, the Cylon D'Anna Biers (Number Three), is played by Lucy Lawless. Biers initially appeared as a reporter who chronicles life aboard the Fleet. She serves as a narratorial voice for the audience as we begin to know the main characters in the course of their daily post-apocalyptic lives. In the early episode "Final Cut" (Episode 2.8), Biers openly ogles the male protagonist Lee Adama (Jamie Bamber), who is caught in his bunkroom wearing only a scanty towel, which slips ever lower over the course of the scene. "I think we've seen all we need to see," Lawless quips, and later comments to him that "I almost didn't recognize you with your clothes on." Although a minor female character moons the camera at the beginning of the interview, and Starbuck is changing clothes in the background throughout the scene, the object of the camera's focus and desire – as well as Biers' attention – is explicitly upon the chiseled abs of Lee Adama and his precariously draped towel. Biers herself turns out to be a Cylon and thus, at least temporarily, an enemy of humanity. However, her desire itself is still coded by the show as both natural and positive; it is not only the wicked Cylon females who ogle men but nearly all the female characters of the show. Starbuck, meanwhile, is involved not only in two different love triangles but also in casual flings with other men and frequent flirtatious encounters. While she is criticized within the show for committing adultery and her phobia about commitment, the rest of the crew does not seem to view her polyamory as inappropriate or immoral in any way. Starbuck is an ace pilot and a hero; she is allowed the sort of license and casual pleasures awarded to prototypical male heroes in wartime or historical dramas.

Lucy Lawless' next major television series, STARZ *Spartacus*, cast her as the provincial matron Lucretia, who was the wife of Batiatus, the master of Spartacus' gladiatorial school. In her first scene, Lucretia is depicted as a promiscuous and actively desirous woman. She orders a female slave to fluff her for sex and then herself engages in passionate intercourse with her husband Batiatus. Lucretia is another complex and morally ambiguous female villain, although she never earns the full heroic redemption shared by Xena and Biers. However, Lucretia's polyamory is also never represented as inherently shameful or immoral. Although she faces eventual deadly retribution for her rape of the slave gladiator Crixus, Lucretia's own husband Batiatus both consents and eagerly participates in her sexual affairs with other Roman matrons and her abuse of slave women.[13]

## XENA'S SUCCESSORS

Other more heroic characters in *Spartacus*, such as the freedwomen of the rebel army, are also not shamed for their sexual choices. Most of the major female characters, such as the former house slaves Naevia and Mira, choose monogamous heterosexual relationships, which are celebrated in explicit contrast to the abusive slave–master relationships that dominate the first season of *Spartacus*. Both Naevia and Mira become skilled warrior women who are supported and honored by their male gladiator lovers. However, their romantic arcs remain relatively traditional within the genre of historical drama.

In contrast, Saxa, the Germanic warrior who plays one of the major female roles in the last two seasons, is explicitly bisexual and polyamorous, engaging in sexual relationships with both the champion gladiator Gannicus and several other male and female rebels. The freed house slave Chadara explicitly uses sex as a means of gaining status and protection within the ranks of the rebel army, offering her body to numerous veteran gladiators in return for their assistance. Her behavior causes other rebels such as Mira to be concerned about whether these relationships are actually consensual, but they do not fault her for her promiscuity in general. Within the world of *Spartacus*, what determines sexual morality is not the number, gender, or legality of a character's partners but rather the degree of consensuality and mutual desire. Even loving heterosexual monogamous relationships such as that between Crassus and his slave Kore inevitably turn bitter due to the inequity of status between the couple. In contrast, more unconventional and emotionally fraught bonds, such as the tie between the two male rebels Agron and Nasir, ultimately resolve happily because the two men learn to rely upon each other as equal partners.[14]

Female action heroines and villains, especially in historical or mythical dramas, inevitably serve both as role-models and potentially as cautionary tales for their audiences. The show's treatment of their sexuality thus also sends messages about appropriate behavior for strong and powerful women; polyamory often has highly negative consequences for villainous women, as already demonstrated, and it is a rare choice for more upstanding heroines. In the influential and popular HBO *Game of Thrones* (2011–), for example, the polyamorous female characters are generally represented as villainous, prone to poor judgment, or both. For instance, Cersei Lannister's liaisons with her brother and her cousin both have highly negative long-term consequences for her and many other people. The various prostitute characters are all brutally murdered. The flirtatious and deadly Sand Sisters are eventually killed or executed by more ruthless foes. They also possess little character development beyond their fighting skills and their flirtatious behavior, lacking the nuance and complexity granted to other major characters. The only female warrior figure who does seem to engage in casual sex is the Iron Islands captain Yara Greyjoy, but her one sexual encounter to date is with a female prostitute. Yara's queerness and butch representation, while echoing some of the fandom interpretations of Xena's sexuality, still fail to offer a positive portrayal of a polyamorous bisexual or heterosexual warrior woman within the series.

In contrast, *Game of Thrones*' two most prominent female warriors, the knight Brienne of Tarth and the assassin Arya Stark, are some of the only virgins in the cast of characters after six seasons. Their role as action heroines seems to forestall an active sexual life or a positive representation as independent desirous agents. *Game of Thrones* has many complex and powerful female characters, but it continues to use female promiscuity as shorthand for immorality or poor judgment. The heroic women with whom the audience is meant to identify, such as Brienne, Arya, Sansa, Daenerys, or Catelyn, are virginal, monogamous, or rape victims. In contrast, male characters that have sex with multiple women, such as Tyrion Lannister, are still depicted as brilliant and insightful thinkers.

HBO's *Rome* features many polyamorous characters but no female warriors. Atia, Servilia, and Cleopatra do not ultimately fare well in this series, and their complex web of sexual relationships plays into their downfall in each case.[15] While Octavia and Atia do survive the final episode, they remain largely under Octavian's control, while their male relatives frequently thwart their desired sexual relationships. This show does not portray polyamory as a reasonable or safe option for heroic women in a patriarchal society, although it does delight in objectifying women engaged in many different types of sexual intercourse with many different partners. The women of *Rome* generally fall into the categories of villainess, victim, or, quite often, both, brought down by the conniving intrigues of other women.

Was Xena a strange aberration, or has her combination of sexual agency and daring combat skills influenced other series in the last twenty years? While still vastly outnumbered by male action heroes, female action heroines have begun to take a larger role in both historical television and film series. However, when sexually active at all, they are generally either widows, involved in romantic monogamous relationships, or trapped in epic love triangles full of unresolved sexual tension. Queen Boudicca of the Iceni, in the little-known *Warrior Queen* (2003), functions as a widow and grieving mother for most of the film. Her daughter Isolde, played by a young Emily Blunt, has a tragically doomed but largely asexual romance with a Roman soldier.[16] Neither of them has any time for sex while leading a rebellion against the oppressive Roman imperialists.

In the BBC television series *Robin Hood* (2006–9), Marian functions as an action heroine as well as Robin's love-interest. While she is trapped for much of the series in a love triangle between herself, Robin, and the villainous Guy de Gisbourne, she does not pursue casual or inconsequential sex with either of them. After saying her marriage vows to Robin, Marian immediately dies after being stabbed by Gisbourne; she has no chance to reframe her identity as an eponymous "Maid." Queen Gorgo in *300* (2007) and its sequel *300: Rise of an Empire* (2014) remains a faithful wife and widow to Leonidas. The warrior Mira in *The Last Legion* (2007), set in a fantastic version of late Western Roman history, pursues a devoted and monogamous relationship with the adult male Roman hero Aurelius.

The most recent prominent example of a classically inspired warrior woman is the Amazon princess Diana of Themyscira, better known as *Wonder Woman* (2017). While Diana claims to have read "the twelve volumes of Clio's treatise on pleasure," she does not evince any practical sexual experience. Her relationship with Steve Trevor appears to be both serious and monogamous, if ultimately doomed to tragedy by his death at the end of the film. However, the immortality of Wonder Woman's character may eventually allow for a narrative of serial romantic relationships, given her flirtation with Batman in the modern timeline of the DC Extended Universe.

## CONCLUSIONS

Saxa and Starbuck currently appear to be Xena's primary fictional descendants as polyamorous female action heroes. But why does the notion of a promiscuous warrior woman continue to seem so alien and challenging to modern creators and audiences? In part, it threatens the Western and classical trope that women can demonstrate virtue through their loyalty to their families and their defense of their own sexual honor. Thus, the earliest cinematic female action heroines, such as Red Sonja of the eponymous 1985 film, were rape victims seeking revenge for their own abuse and the deaths of their families. Naevia and Mira of *Spartacus* and Isolde of *Warrior Queen* become warriors in order to avenge their own rapes and the abuse of their friends and loved ones. Buffy dies in order to protect her little sister. In the Scottish eighteenth-century drama *Outlander* (2014–), the latest creation of *Battlestar Galactica* creator Ron Moore, the time-traveling heroine Claire sleeps with the king of France only in order to ensure her husband's release from prison. While she is technically polygamous, she is married only to one husband in each century and does not demonstrate any desire for casual flings.

In contrast, Xena, Saxa, and Starbuck are motivated by the same sorts of drives that lead male heroes to undertake heroic deeds – atoning for past deeds, seeking revenge, and protecting the more vulnerable. As male-like heroes, their quests define them but do not prevent them from enjoying other aspects of life, such as drinking, relaxing with friends, and having active sex lives. In each case, these women's primary relationships are their families-by-choice, such as Gabrielle and Joxer, rather than biological ties of loyalty or bonds of purely physical intimacy. For Xena, her relationships with her children lead to tragedy and devastation more than personal fulfillment. Each of these shows' creators or executive producers – Raimi and Tapert for *Xena: Warrior Princess* and *Spartacus*, as well as Ron Moore for *Battlestar Galactica* and *Outlander* – made conscious decisions to treat these women's sexual choices as precisely equivalent to the sexual decisions of male characters. These shows also featured plotlines that explicitly defended women's rights to control their sexuality and reproductive choices, as well as critiquing the idea of virginity as an inherently precious treasure.

At the same time, even these works were unwilling to completely abandon a connection between female respectability and monogamy. *Xena: Warrior Princess*'s "tramp" Meg is last shown married with three children. Starbuck dies shortly after resolving her increasingly messy love triangle in favor of a monogamous commitment to Apollo. Saxa sacrifices her own interests in favor of preserving the happiness of her most serious romantic partner, Gannicus. Only Xena rides off into the sunset at the end of each episode, allowed to have flings in new villages every week as long as she demonstrates her loyalty to her companions and her children. The *Warrior Princess* was not a complete aberration, but it may be many decades before women in classically inspired dramas are regularly represented as equally adventurous both sexually and in the pursuit of justice. Until then, the double standard regarding male and female characters will be even stronger with regard to sex than to violence. Women might be brave, reckless, or even brilliant leaders, but their sexual lives will still remain largely under both the lens of the male gaze and the control of male characters.

## NOTES

1. See Caudill (2003); Futrell (2003); Kennedy (2003); Inness (2004).
2. *Cleopatra* (1963).
3. *Cleopatra* (1963).
4. Kelly (2014: 194–6).
5. Wyke (2007: 195–321).
6. Daugherty (2008).
7. Tomasso (2015b).
8. The chronology of these legendary tales is, to put it mildly, complex and chaotic; Xena later herself impersonates Cleopatra.
9. Kennedy (2003: 40).

10 See Simmons (2004) and also *Seinfeld*, Episode 4.11: "The Contest" (1992); *Friends*, Episode 4.11: "The One With Phoebe's Uterus" (1998).
11 See Larbalestier (2004); Jowett (2005).
12 Tomasso (2015a: 243).
13 Strong (2016).
14 Augoustakis (2013).
15 Cyrino (2008).
16 Futrell (2013).

# 10 Divergent Heroism in Centurion (2010)

Hunter H. Gardner

## INTRODUCTION

The unexplained disappearance of the Ninth Roman Legion somewhere in Britannia, probably during the reign of the emperor Hadrian, has offered recent filmmakers the opportunity to explore Roman imperialism at a distance from the capital and the corruption that frequently colors the city of Rome in literary and cinematic discourses. The depiction of soldiers far from Rome, under duress, and under attack from native forces using guerilla tactics allows filmmakers to comment on the perils of modern imperialist ventures, especially Bush-era intervention in Iraq and Afghanistan. From such depictions emerges a composite portrait of the Roman legionary soldier who participates in the imperialist project, but experiences first hand the casualties of that project, and who reluctantly defers to bureaucrats who never design to get their own boots on the ground. In this chapter, I focus on one element of that composite, Centurion Quintus Dias in Neil Marshall's film *Centurion* (2010), and demonstrate how his character departs from traditional representations of Roman military virtue. I argue that this departure prompts a reassessment of the epic film genre, as well as the nationalist values the genre frequently underwrites.

In order to demonstrate just how Quintus diverges from other soldier-heroes who contribute to the composite observed above, we should initially contrast the near contemporaneous release of *The Eagle* (2011), based on Rosemary Sutcliff's novel *The Eagle of the Ninth* (1954), which covers historical ground similar to that explored in *Centurion*.[1] *The Eagle* offers viewers a vulnerable but brave Channing Tatum as Marcus Flavius Aquila, who hopes to restore the honor lost by his father, who had led the Ninth Legion on its disastrous final expedition. Marcus' resistance to and disdain for the Roman administrators hoping to secure the borders of Britain from a safe distance is duly noted, particularly in a scene where the hero criticizes the inexperienced "silk-assed politician's son" for making ill-informed pronouncements on the fate of the Ninth. Still, the film's overall endorsement of Roman military values remains largely unshaken, as Marcus successfully recovers the standard of the Ninth, and returns it to at least nominally appreciative Roman senators. Marshall's *Centurion* takes a similar soldier's-eye view of the mystery of the Ninth Legion, but ultimately disavows traditional constructions of military heroism, leaving its titular hero without an army or nation.

*Centurion* in fact articulates its disavowal by offering two models of heroism for comparative evaluation, Quintus (Michael Fassbender) and General Titus Flavius Virilus (Dominic West), both of whom initially work cooperatively within the machinery of the empire and fight against a savagely portrayed other, the Picts. Both men, moreover, demonstrate the virtues of self-sacrifice, courage, and relatively fluid social status in the field. Finally, both characters draw from a tradition of cinematic predecessors in the historical epic, men whose virtues and heroic status are developed in juxtaposition with the corrupt authority centralized in Rome: Marcus Vinicius in *Quo Vadis* (1951), Marcellus Gallio in *The Robe* (1953), Livius of *The Fall of the Roman Empire* (1964), and Maximus of *Gladiator* (2000) all offer templates for the hero-soldier whose unrewarded loyalty measures the extent of the decay at the core of Rome's imperialist projects. The film's full exposition, however, propels Quintus and Virilus along very different heroic paths: Virilus' will be cut short in terrain that refuses to recognize the value of traditional Roman military virtues; Quintus concludes his own filmic journey by adopting the very fugitive status that Rome's most illustrious hero of literary epic, *pius* ("dutiful, righteous") *Aeneas*, must labor to shed in founding an empire. Quintus enters and exits the film stripped of signifiers that would denote his national affiliation – we first glimpse him as a half-naked fugitive in an unforgiving, frozen Scottish landscape (Figure 10.1). He survives an attack on his outpost where he is second in command solely because he has learned the language of the Picts; his identity as the "son of a gladiator" (as he defines himself in an initial introduction to Virilus) registers his socially marginal status. This identity of course also functions on a meta-cinematic level, naming him cinematic heir to Crowe's gladiator, Maximus, or "the Spaniard."

Figure 10.1 Quintus Dias (Michael Fassbender) as a fugitive in Caledonia after escaping from a Pictish camp, at the opening of *Centurion* (2010). Pathé Productions.

Departing from previous constructions of cinematic gladiators, however, Fassbender's Quintus finds his own end not in sacrificial and regenerative death, as has been observed of Maximus,[2] but in a new life with a Pictish woman exiled by her own people. In the conclusion to this chapter, I will consider how Quintus' outlier status, and rejection of any national affiliation, inform the generic hybridity of the film: as critics note, *Centurion*'s meager budget and succinct exposition put it at odds with conventions of epic film.[3] At the same time, the film questions epic tropes of heroic identity in ways that undermine epic excesses as well as the ideological, often nationalistic content that such cinema frequently conveys.[4] As Robert Burgoyne notes, the epic film has traditionally been viewed as a "particularly vivid expression of the myth-making impulse at the core of national identity."[5] However, recent ventures in epic film production, as well as more recent interpretations of older productions, have shined the spotlight on more internationally collaborative aspects of the genre. Some global components of contemporary epic are the tools of production: for any given epic film, marketing and distribution, the compositing of images for CGI, casting, and shooting on location often occur in disparate nations and geographic regions.[6] *Centurion* aligns itself with these more globally invested examples of the genre, but does so not so much at the level of production as with its narrative content and upending of epic conventions.

This upending is accomplished in part through the film's heroes and their tenuous relationship to Roman history. For Quintus' and Virilus' cinematic forefathers, heroic virtues, however fictionalized, unfold as part of a frequently rehearsed historical master narrative: for example, Marcus Vinicius enduring the disastrous tyranny of Nero or Livius and Maximus challenging the spectacularly vicious Commodus. *Centurion*'s heroes, by contrast, have only a vaguely conjectured and ill-attested event in history by which viewers might evaluate the significance of their onscreen exploits. The mystery of the Ninth Legion emerges primarily from the legion's absence in an inventory of the empire's military strength in AD 165 (*CIL* 6.3492)[7] and in Cassius Dio's omission of it in his own account of legions extant after AD 197 (LV.23–4). The legion was stationed in Britain as early as the AD 80s, and we have evidence of its work on building projects in York around AD 108. But after the mid-second century, we have no further traces of the Ninth in military, archaeological, or epigraphic records.[8]

The absence of any undisputed evidence concerning the existence of the legion after its presence in York, combined with ancient sources claiming that large numbers of Roman soldiers were killed in Britain during the reign of Hadrian (AD 117–38),[9] who visited Britain around AD 120, led nineteenth-century historians such as Bartolomeo Borghesi and, soon after, Theodor Mommsen to conjecture a disaster suffered by the legion, perhaps just north of where Hadrian eventually built his wall. The legion's disappearance, in a rather mundane reality, may have been the result of a clerical error; some historians argue that the legion had been moved to fight in the east (Parthia), but the transfer failed to be recorded as such.[10] While the historical truth of the legion's loss is not my focus here, I suggest that it is in part the opacity surrounding the event, and its failure to be fully integrated into the master narratives of Roman history, that make the "loss of the Ninth" an ideal vehicle with which Marshall might detach his *Centurion* from the usual projects of foundation and destiny that have traditionally defined the epic hero.

## VIRILUS

As less generous appraisals of *Centurion* have suggested, the plot of the film is akin to that of the "chase movie":[11] after Quintus' garrison is attacked and he is taken prisoner by the Picts, the hero manages to escape – hence the opening sequence, which depicts him running nearly naked, with hands bound. Back at headquarters in Carlisle, Agricola, governor of Britannia, hears more of the losses inflicted by the Picts in the Scottish territory of Caledonia, and decides to send out the Ninth Legion to inflict a decisive blow: this legion is led by General Virilus and will be assisted by a mute Brigantian woman, Etain, enlisted as a tracker for the Romans. Early in the film, the fugitive Quintus is saved by the Ninth Legion and joins their ranks; unfortunately for the Romans, the Picts manage to wipe out nearly the entire legion in a fireball onslaught in a forest. A handful of survivors band together, initially to try to recover General Virilus, who is captured during the onslaught. After Virilus is killed in captivity, the survivors make it their mission to return home; yet all the while, the men, led by Quintus, are hunted by the Picts, guided now by Etain, who has been operating as a double agent and openly betrays the Romans. Challenges posed by both the Pictish trackers and the Scottish terrain deplete the number of survivors. While a few of the men find temporary respite in the home of an exiled Pictish woman, only Quintus survives to the film's conclusion.

As this brief exposition suggests, General Virilus does not live beyond the first thirty minutes of the film.[12] And yet his physical presence on screen and his interactions with his men convey qualities distinctly reminiscent of epic heroes in both literary and cinematic instantiations: the camera emphasizes his imposing build; he is weathered by experience and ready for a fight, but also compassionate and, above all, a beloved leader concerned for the safety of his men. When he feels pressured by Governor Agricola to choose between the honor of a possible military victory and the wellbeing of his soldiers, he assures Agricola, "my men [already] have honor enough." Yet in the same moment on screen he concedes to the authority of Rome with a nod, a half-grudging confirmation of the military's chain of command and its necessity for stability within the empire. It is this concession to an authority whose goals have become ideologically indefensible that makes Virilus' brand of heroism obsolete in the world of *Centurion*.

Our first shot of Virilus is in a tavern in York where the legion is stationed. He engages in an arm-wrestling match that will quickly turn into a bloody bar-room brawl after his defeated opponent proves to be a sore loser – an indication that the usual rules of engagement within the larger theater of the war in Britannia have already become compromised. In responding to this sore loser, the Roman soldiery encourage Virilus and fully support the general's retaliation: initial shots present him seated at the match table apart from his men, who watch with admiration; once the fighting breaks out, he is absorbed in the mayhem, engaging in the brawl along with the rest of the soldiers. This absorption continues well into the dawn, as illustrated by the quips exchanged the following morning between Virilus and one of his soldiers, Septus: to Septus' comment that "some would say it's irregular for a general to drink with men of the legion," Virilus reminds him: "I am a man of the legion."

The arrival of Agricola's soldiers at the camp of the Ninth reasserts the general's status as "one of the guys." One soldier barks at Virilus, who appears haggard after a night of carousing and is not clothed in the regalia of a general: "Take me to your commander or I'll have you flogged!" For his impertinence the soldier is duly chastened by Septus, who is quick to defend Virilus' superior status. In a late night camp scene, after the Ninth has embarked and rescues Quintus, we are offered further perspectives on the general and his leadership, focalized by Quintus and the men of the legion: after Virilus has welcomed Quintus and evaluated the junior officer's experience as a soldier, the two tour the camp and encounter a cadre of men who will later become Quintus' fellow survivors. Leaving Quintus to get acquainted with the men, Virilus departs, with the camera lingering over his figure as he comes upon a new group of soldiers and immediately engages with them in friendly (possibly ribald, judging from his gestures) revelry. The camera returns for close-up shots of Quintus and the men he has just met, who are visibly impressed by Virilus' easy camaraderie. To Quintus' comment that "I've never seen a general so beloved of his men," Bothos replies, "In training he's our scholar, in the feast he's our father, in the ranks he's our brother, in battle he's the god we pray to save our souls."

Bothos' admiration is immediately undercut by his own response to Septus' cynical questions about the origins of such eloquence ("It's written on the shithouse walls!"). The men, however, quickly resume an attitude that puts jesting aside and confirms their loyalty, epitomized in Septus' closing remark that he would die for Virilus without hesitation. The exchange demonstrates the range of roles Virilus effectively plays in leading the Ninth, as he embodies figures of higher authority (father, god) as well as those of relatively equal status (scholar, brother). Yet all roles emphasize the general's position relative to the crisis of armed conflict – whether training for, celebrating after, or experiencing the thick of it – as he demands of himself the same sacrifices he demands of his men.

This kind of leadership by example ought to be effective, harkening back to the admiration felt and expressed more succinctly by Maximus' men in the first shots of Scott's *Gladiator* and its presumptions of "strength and honor" on the battlefield. Virilus' status as the "hero of Spain," remarked upon in a deleted scene (Scene 5: "Agricola's headquarters"), also bears a faint echo of Maximus' moniker "the Spaniard," and thus confirms a brief identification between West's general and Crowe's soldier-turned-gladiator. Such remarks suggest that, while the final cut of the film more explicitly aligns Maximus and Quintus as fugitive outliers, Crowe's character informs the construction of Virilus as well. Virilus will not survive the film's exposition long enough to encounter the treachery that Maximus does within the highest ranks of imperial and military leadership, so the identification between these characters will only extend so far. Moreover, Quintus' opening voiceover initially defines the conflict in Caledonia as "a war without honor." While Maximus could identify strength and honor at the borders of Germania under the benevolent guidance of Marcus Aurelius, from the very opening frames of *Centurion* viewers are ill advised to look for traditional military virtues within this cinematic landscape.

The bravery and uniformity of purpose inspired by effective leadership such as Virilus' will be rendered ineffective, partly because the Roman *imperium* ("supreme administrative power")[13] that should authorize the honor of a military victory has been corrupted. When the general is captured during the fireball attack in the forest his body is held high, like a trophy; his elevation within the context of martial mayhem, in the absence of the proper Roman rules of engagement, paradoxically serves to humiliate him, rendering him physically impotent. His elevation is now only a symbol of Pictish victory and a visible demonstration of how Rome's centralized power, corrupted by self-serving ambitions and intent on preserving a reputation that no longer reflects reality,[14] cannot support the hierarchies it has constructed. The military titles bestowed on Virilus are rendered meaningless, failing to signify in a Pictish realm where Rome's symbolic capital has no purchasing power.

Virilus is not killed outright by the Picts and survives in the enemy camp long enough to experience a botched rescue effort by the survivors. During the effort, Virilus reminds audiences of his paternalistic love for his men and his self-sacrifice: he insists that Quintus give up the attempt to free him and instead urges him to get the survivors home. We may applaud the military virtues sympathetically embodied in the nearly prostrate figure of Virilus, but the film will graphically challenge such virtues when he is tortured the following morning and forced to do battle with Etain, who exacts surrogate vengeance against the Romans who killed her father, raped her mother, and cut out her tongue when she was a child. The engagement between Virilus and Etain visually constructs an imposing, if unsteady Roman in contrast to a non-Roman other: Etain, played by Olga Kurylenko, is a slight, mute woman in war paint, dark hair streaming over her shoulders; Virilus, with his booming, stentorian voice, remains virile to the last – rugged and unadorned, but keeping the captured Roman standards in clear sight up to his dying breath. The camera follows his final line of vision first to Etain, who has just speared him in the chest with a trident. As the general's head droops in death, however, he lifts his eyes and the camera cuts to a close-up of a golden eagle standard, initially clear, then fading out of focus.

Virilus' death illustrates the last gasp of *Romanitas* ("Romanness")[15] in the film, and confirms the meaninglessness of his heroism, since the film's diegesis ultimately leaves no *Roman* survivors to sing Virilus' praises or endorse the value of his sacrifice. Though we watch most of the general's armor burn along with the golden eagle standard, his helmet, a sign of his leadership and by extension a sign of Roman military authority, has a brief synecdochic afterlife in the film:[16] it will be recovered as a meaningful sign by the initial survivors of the forest massacre and then bestowed grudgingly by Thax (J. J. Field) on Quintus, as a concession to Quintus' authority. Yet this symbol too is stripped of any authorizing power, as Thax, who murders the young son of the Pictish leader Gorlacon in a blatant act of cowardice, turns out to be the least heroic of the survivors (in terms of a Roman code dictating courage and self-sacrifice), and Quintus in fact rejects the helmet, preferring to leave it by Virilus' burial mound.

## QUINTUS

As noted, Quintus enters the film visually absent any signifiers of social status or nationality; however, in intimate appropriation of the historical epic's traditional opening voiceover,[17] he tells us that "My name is Quintus Dias, I am a soldier of Rome and this is neither the end nor the beginning of my story." He clings to this identity while tortured during his brief captivity: "I am a soldier of Rome, I will not yield," and manages to say this in both Latin and Pictish.[18] It is this bilingualism, rather than his stalwart *Romanitas*, that saves him from slaughter during the attack on his garrison in the opening sequence, a bilingualism that anticipates how fluid movement across boundaries of language, nationality, and social status ensures his survival in Caledonia and in the film.

Quintus' personal history also enables his relatively fluid movement across the boundaries of class and nation. He is "second in command" of his garrison, thus mediating between the enlisted men and the top military authority, and makes frequent reference to the advice of his father, Scipio Dias, a gladiator. In the first conversation between Virilus and Quintus, after Quintus has been rescued and has donned his soldier's uniform, Virilus observes, "Now you look like a Roman!" Such a comment on his initial transformation anticipates the nearly Odyssean fluidity of identity that will allow Virilus to navigate the uncharted realm outside the parameters of the Roman camp. In the same exchange, the general claims to have seen Scipio Dias win his freedom in the arena, tacit recognition of how both father and son rose within the ranks of the Roman social order.

Once hostilities with the Picts are resumed, however, Quintus' actions as comrade and eventually leader of the survivors reveal how his Roman identity (and Roman heroic code) is gradually transformed into an identity unrestricted by the bonds of nationhood. During the attack in the forest, and in contrast to the physically elevated Virilus, Quintus survives the battle through anonymity, hidden under a mounting pile of Roman corpses. After Virilus has been killed and Quintus reluctantly assumes the position of leader among the ethnically diverse survivors, he solicits the personal histories of each man: one reviewer refers to the group as a "rainbow coalition;"[19] another dubbed them a "rag tag, multi-ethnic band."[20] Each character's origins (from Numidia to Greece to the streets of Rome to the mountains of the Hindu Kush) reveal the unmanageable extent of the empire, but also work to undo the presumed *Romanitas* of the very soldiers enlisted to protect Rome. Leadership of such a diverse band further distances Quintus himself from the power centralized in Rome, despite his Roman origins.

Quintus' interaction with Arianne (Imogen Poots), a banished Pict woman accused of witchcraft, who offers him a temporary haven, issues an even greater challenge to his national identity. Quintus arrives at her hut with two comrades, Brick (Liam Cunningham) and Bothos (David Morrissey), both of whom remain loyal to Quintus and cut fairly traditional figures of Roman military *virtus* ("manly spirit, valor").[21] When Arianne and Quintus first confront each other they are startled to discover a shared bilingualism: "You speak my language," Arianne notes with a pronounced Scottish brogue, to which Quintus replies in subtitled Scots-Gaelic, "And you mine." She also explicitly disavows any relationship with the Picts, claiming that "These are not my people." In contrast to his comrades, who mistrust Arianne's perceived sorcery, femininity, and presumed Pictish identity, Quintus realizes that the survival of the three Romans depends on her. As it turns out, his trust is not misplaced. Arianne feeds, hides, and heals the men before they resume their efforts to return home. In her parting conversation with Quintus, who marvels at the extent of her generosity, she explains, "I owe allegiance to no man, but whom I choose."

Time spent in her explicitly marginalized haven marks another transformation, this time for all three survivors. By the film's third act, which involves a final showdown between Bothos, Brick, and Quintus and three Pict warriors, our protagonists have long since exchanged their Roman armor for clothing that will allow them to move rapidly throughout the landscape and survive the cold. In fact, Bothos survives the showdown with the Picts only to be killed by a Roman soldier as he approaches a military outpost looking, by the end of his struggle, more native than Roman.

Unlike Bothos, Quintus lives to re-enter the Roman garrison, but Arianne's words about owing allegiance to no man except whom she chooses prove prophetic, and anticipate the condition that defines Quintus at the end of the film: as the sole survivor of a failed expedition he is quickly deemed a threat to Rome's reputation and to the personal interests of Agricola, who wishes the disaster of the Ninth Legion to be expunged from the record. After escaping an attempted assassination back at headquarters in Carlisle, Quintus' would-be assassin asks him where he plans to escape. To this he responds, "Where I belong," that is, Arianne's liminally situated non-Roman and non-Pict haven in the Highlands. With a final *mise-en-scène* capturing the two figures embracing beside the river that skirts Arianne's hut, Quintus' voiceover advises us: "My name is Quintus Dias. I am a fugitive of Rome. And this is neither the beginning nor the end of my story." The hero's final words resist narrative closure and return us to the image of a naked man struggling to survive at the film's opening.

Throughout its exposition, the film has self-consciously established the interdependence of heroism and storytelling: earlier in *Centurion*, Quintus encourages the nearly mortally wounded Bothos to press on despite his suffering and the odds against them, noting that, "Hopeless is what they sing songs about, write poems about. Hopeless is the stuff of legend, Bothos, and being a legend will get you laid." Yet, as observed earlier, for all its overtures to the epic tradition and the heroes central to that tradition, the mystery of the

Ninth Legion is defined primarily not by what the ancient record says about it – there is no legend – but by its very absence from that record. Quintus reconfigures the traditional hero's story, refusing to begin and end it properly, and does both within the context of a narrative that, from the ancient temporal perspective so crucial to the epic tradition,[22] simply does not exist. In so doing, he also forces audiences to reconfigure their own notions of heroism.

## HEROISM AND TRANSNATIONALITY

The editing of the first third of *Centurion*, which continuously alternates between Virilus embarking as leader of the Ninth, and Quintus as fugitive, encourages viewers to evaluate the qualities of these two heroes and, in the end, question what qualities allow Quintus to persevere: Virilus' death, had it proven valuable to Rome's expansionist projects, would have been written into a foundation narrative. This Rome, however, is challenged by corruption and contraction, and finds no soil on which to plant the seeds of new life.[23] As one critic noted, concerning the roughly contemporaneous release of *Centurion* and *The Eagle* with other ancient world films lending themselves to political allegory:

> The current crop of films are, in part, a study in decline and disaffection – at the edge of empire and at the end of empire. In an age of failed "civilising missions" and counterinsurgency operations ... [the legend of the Ninth Legion] resonates especially strongly.[24]

Quintus' story, unlike Virilus', can continue because it refuses to be inscribed within a foundation narrative or to promote a civilizing mission that would require an end in noble sacrifice. It is this anti-teleological movement, along with the politics of nation building such a movement challenges, that, I argue, makes the film problematically but productively epic.

Critical responses to *Centurion* have recognized the film's failure to conform to the rules of the genre. Betsy Sharkey calls the film a "fast-moving epic-on-a-shoestring tale.... All in all, an old-fashioned swords and sandals saga that may be small in scale but is a lot of bloody fun."[25] Niall Browne notes that "Marshall knows how to handle action and he doesn't skimp on battle sequences ... [but ... m]ost films detailing such events have upwards of three-hour run-times ... an extra 20 minutes to develop plot and character would have been nice."[26] Hinting at the film's uneven conformity to epic standards, Dan Jolin similarly remarks that *Centurion* is "more about swords ... than sandals, although it could have done with a lot more character meat on those bones."[27]

The film has thus been judged epic in its handling of ancient Rome and in its violent battle sequences, even in its panoramic shots of the Scottish landscape, but not so epic in its $12 million budget, meager length, and lack of the surge and splendor carefully theorized in Vivian Sobchak's well-known essay on the genre.[28] At the same time, Joanna Paul's recent work on the relationship between epic films and epic texts has observed that attempts to define the genre are simply observations about the features of texts we already consider epic; that is to say, definitions are based on reader and viewer responses.[29] Epics are not born epic – they are only judged so after the fact. As soon as we try to set boundaries on what constitutes epic, we confront literature and films that challenge those boundaries, forcing us to change them. *Centurion*'s possible failure as an epic, its challenges to scale, surge, and splendor, prompt us to rethink our boundaries and definitions of epic and to confront the question of why former rules of the genre are often broken in the contemporary world.

As one approach to answering this question, I suggest that the concept of nationalism is also crucially interrogated in Marshall's film, an interrogation that I would like to consider briefly in closing. Throughout this discussion of *Centurion*, I have recognized some of the film's resonances with Scott's *Gladiator*: even the title suggests that the story will be driven by a single hero whose identity is defined simply in relation to the Roman political and military apparatus. But where *Gladiator* ambiguously upholds the prospect of continuing the dream that is Rome (perhaps, by some accounts, the dream that is America),[30] *Centurion* overtly questions the notion of national boundaries as well as ideological extremes that fuel military defense of boundaries.

As noted at the start of this chapter, critical responses to the historical epic since the late twentieth century have demonstrated how such films frequently serve to articulate the concept of a nation, help define it and instantiate its values. Thus epic film functions as a "vehicle of national ideology and aspirations," a function especially pronounced in America's Hollywood productions (e.g. *Ben-Hur* (1959), *The Sign of the Cross* (1932)).[31] And yet, as Robert Burgoyne argues of recent receptions of the epic, and *Gladiator* in particular, there is much to be gained from reading such films "against the grain, to consider them in terms of a postnational project focusing on broad stories of affiliation and community across ethnic, religious, and geographic boundaries."[32] *Centurion* in some respects constitutes a highly nationalist project, directed by United Kingdom-born Marshall and funded mostly by Celador and the United Kingdom Film Council (though some production credits are given to Warner Brothers). The film's subject, in so far as it presumes hostilities between populations living south of Hadrian's Wall and the native populations north of it, may have contributed to the longstanding nationalist tensions governing the relationship between England and Scotland.[33]

Still, it does not take much viewing against the grain to realize that *Centurion* has somewhat violently commandeered the genre in order to dismantle its support of nationalism, by exchanging a glorious foundation narrative for one of disgrace, treachery, and lost causes. Rather than simply questioning the viability of the Roman state and its contemporary analogues,[34] *Centurion* utterly severs the hero's relationship to Rome and leaves him in a liminal, transnational state. Such positioning is not an altogether cynical pronouncement: the forsaking of a glorious foundation narrative in exchange for a final *mise-en-scène* located outside the boundaries of nation and its constructions of historical time allows Marshall to espouse a more universal, human notion of identity.

This exchange is most evident in *Centurion*'s treatment of its two heroes, one the leader of a Roman legion whose sacrifice and exemplary *Romanitas* will remain obscured, and the other a man whose story has no beginning, no ending, and no ancient authorizing voice, but whose survival is ensured by ultimately disavowing the title of centurion once bestowed upon him. The identity assumed in its place, "fugitive of Rome," is one patently at odds with the goals of empire. By naming himself at last as a fugitive, Quintus provocatively joins ranks with Rome's most famous hero, Aeneas, whose eponymous epic opens by directing readers to his desperate plight as *profugus* ("fugitive," *Aeneid* 1.2). The quintessential Roman hero's trajectory is one that charts a transformation from fugitive to founding father. Quintus, however, daringly sets out on that trajectory only to reverse it: he re-enacts his flight from the Pictish camp at the film's opening as a concluding flight from Rome itself, leaving audiences to ponder the possibilities of fugitive status as a permanent condition.

## NOTES

1 The Ninth also appears in *The Last Legion* (2007), where the emperor Romulus Augustus, recently crowned but forced to flee Rome, encounters the members of the legion hiding out in Britain after they had been forced to disband and settle as farmers.

2   On the sacrificial death of the hero as a convention of historical epic, see Burgoyne (2008: 84).
3   Browne (2010); Holden (2010); Sharkey (2010); cf. Sobchack (1990).
4   As Wyke's (1997a: 110–46) analysis of Italian productions of *Quo Vadis* demonstrates, the relationship between a film's content and the ideals of a nation is rarely transparent, not least because such ideals are regularly contested within any nation state. For more widespread interrogation of the relationship between nationalist imperatives and epic cinema, see the essays collected in Burgoyne's volume (2011), which I invoke throughout this discussion.
5   Burgoyne (2011: 83). His notion of the cinematic epic, like that of many contemporary film theorists, is partly indebted to Bakhtin's notion of the temporal distance required for epic narratives to develop their interest in "national beginnings and peak times" (1981: 15; cf. Paul 2013: 16).
6   Burgoyne (2011: 3–6).
7   CIL= *Corpus Inscriptionum Latinarum*, a comprehensive collection of Latin inscriptions.
8   Archaeological evidence has indicated its presence around the Netherlands (Wright 1978: 381), but such evidence is probably dated to the AD 80s, and may indicate the presence of a detachment, rather than the entire legion. See Russell (2011) for an archaeological perspective on the recent onscreen portrayals.
9   Cf. Fronto's comments on losses in Britain (*On the Parthian War* 2) and those in *Historiae Augustae* (*Hadrian* 5.1).
10  Campbell (2010) offers a concise overview of the history of the "mystery" and demonstrates the tendency of scholars to overlook significant evidence that counters the possibility of a military disaster suffered by the legion before the AD 120s (i.e. when Hadrian visited the area and began construction of his wall).
11  Jolin (2010).
12  One reviewer, Floyd (2010), describes his role as a cameo. This is misleading, though much of the footage that did not make it beyond the cutting room floor fleshes out Virilus' character. In footage from the deleted scenes available on the DVD/Blu-ray format, we see him rousing his men to arms ("There are only two things I believe in, my sword and my soldiers!"); we also observe his compassion and respect for the dead as he orders proper burial rites for the bodies of two Roman sentries.
13  *Oxford Latin Dictionary* s.v. *imperium* 1.
14  The personal ambitions of Agricola (Paul Freeman) concerning the deployment of the Ninth are made explicit early in the film in private conversation with Virilus at Carlisle; Rome's desire to preserve its reputation for unchallenged military strength in Britain (however at odds that reputation may be with reality) becomes clear at the end of the film; see further below.

15 A post-classical term found in Tertullian (*On the Mantle* 4). As Janan (2001: 171 n. 21) notes, however, the word concisely expresses the "powerful ideology of 'the Roman way'."
16 Monaco (1981: 187–9) discusses the meanings generated through visual synecdoche in cinema (as here, Virilus' helmet "stands for" Virilus and the Roman authority he embodies).
17 For the voiceover as a conventional feature of the historical epic, usually given by an omniscient and temporally transcendent authorizing male actor, see Sobchack (1990: 34–5).
18 The self-identification here is reminiscent of Lucilla's pronouncement over Maximus' lifeless body in the amphitheater at *Gladiator*'s conclusion: "He was a solider of Rome. Honor him."
19 Holden (2010).
20 Floyd (2010).
21 *Virtus* is difficult to translate with a single English word that captures its root (*vir*, "man") and its resonance in Roman culture. The *Oxford Latin Dictionary* offers as its primary definition: "the qualities typical of a true man, manly spirit, resolution, valour, steadfastness ... especially as displayed in war or other contests."
22 Paul (2013: 16–20).
23 To paraphrase Burgoyne's (2008: 93–7) account of Maximus' death in the arena in *Gladiator*.
24 Leith (2010).
25 Sharkey (2010).
26 Browne (2010).
27 Jolin (2010).
28 Sobchak (1990). Constraints which did not escape the notice of Marshall, who remarks in the director's commentary of the Blu-ray edition on the lack of time, budget, and extras that hindered the production of certain scenes.
29 Paul (2013: 22–3).
30 The parallels between *Gladiator*'s Rome and late twentieth-century America have been observed by film critics (e.g. Muschamp 2000) and scholars alike (esp. Cyrino 2004).
31 As observed by Deleuze (1986: 148–51, as cited in Burgoyne 2008: 75), who notes that this kind of cinema often re-enacts the birth of a nation-civilization (cf. Burgoyne 2011: 83); see also Bakhtin's (1981: 15) identification of an interest in national origins as one impulse behind the epic tradition; cf. Paul (2013: 16).
32 Burgoyne (2011: 3).
33 Cf. Russell's (2011) comments on the permanent border between Scotland and England that may have resulted from the disaster of the Ninth.
34 As, for instance, Marcus Vinicius (clad in soldier's regalia and positioned just outside Rome's walls) will do in his skeptical assessment of Galba's ability to restore Roman justice at the end of *Quo Vadis*.

# PART III
*Antiheroes*

# 11 The Hero in a Thousand Pieces: Antiheroes in Recent Epic Cinema

Dan Curley

*In memoriam* Daniel J. Curley (1934–2016), who dreamed of heroes.

## INTRODUCTION

Heroism is one of the great preoccupations of Western, if not global culture, though standards for what heroes can or should do are ever-shifting. Because they are prone to antiheroic passions such as greed, lust, and vengeance, Greek and Roman heroes often become rehabilitated in modern screen texts. The opening narration of *Hercules: The Legendary Journeys* (1995–9) exemplifies this tendency: "Hercules possessed a strength the world had never seen – a strength surpassed only by the power of his heart. . . . But wherever there was evil, wherever an innocent would suffer, there would be Hercules." His mission is not quite Superman's "truth, justice, and the American way," but the show clearly reconfigures one of antiquity's most problematic characters as a superhero of the past.

This chapter focuses on three historic and mythical figures – Alexander the Great, Perseus, and Hercules – portrayed in screen epics as both heroes and antiheroes.[1] Their antiheroic status stems not so much from gestures toward ancient authenticity as from our own ambivalence toward heroism. Furthermore, antiheroism is depicted cinematically through the dissolution or fragmentation of conventional heroic storytelling, with its familiar plot patterns and filmmaking techniques. The later, antiheroic films play quite differently from their earlier, heroic counterparts – which in turn receive the relative status of classics.

## SURROGATE CLASSICISM: FORMULATING ANTIHEROES

Antiheroes fulfill many cultural functions. Some of the more common include the following.

- *Failures.* The antihero is frequently defined in opposition to the traditionally successful hero: "A 'non-hero,' or the antithesis of a hero of the old-fashioned kind who was capable of heroic deeds, who was dashing, strong, brave and resourceful.... The antihero ... is given the vocation of failure."[2] "Vocation of failure" is provocative and suggests that antiheroes do not achieve much – or, if they do, that their achievements are feeble or unworthy.
- *Modern mirrors.* "A fragmented society – torn by war, conflicting values, cultural crisis, and different aspects of modernity – produces its own heroic model: sick, anti-social, and introspective antiheroes whose salvation is individualistic in the midst of social and cultural disarray."[3] When not failing in and of themselves, antiheroes reflect the failure of society, which is often couched in terms of fragmentation. They are broken heroes for broken times, though perhaps not without hope of transcending their limitations.
- *Disruptors.* "The negative hero, more keenly perhaps than the traditional hero, challenges our assumptions, raising anew the question of how we see, or wish to see ourselves. The antihero is often a perturber and a disturber."[4] Beyond reflecting social fragmentation, antiheroes can be fragmenters in their own right. They destabilize heroic ideals, often through unconventional attitudes and actions.
- *Hesitators.* "The hero's hesitation or inhibition reflects crises inherent in the greater world.... These cultural crises, implicit or explicit within the texts, reflect in turn the stresses that the poets sense within their own societies."[5] Hesitation is a particularly enduring mode of disruption, one with classical antecedents. Aeneas and Orestes are two paradigms of the hero prone, at a critical juncture, to indecisiveness.

The preceding notions – failing, mirroring, disrupting, and hesitating – are helpful for interrogating antiheroes not only in their social contexts, but also in their narrative contexts. We are accustomed to conceptualize heroes in terms of narratives with particular "shapes": a character arc or a journey with persistent and redeeming tropes. Such narratives are the stock in trade of the motion-picture industry, whose devotion to formula is notorious, but they are demonstrably older than cinema and established in other modes of storytelling. Because antiheroic narratives have received nowhere near the same level of formalist scrutiny, theories about heroic narratives become our starting point, just as antiheroes are defined in opposition to heroes. If antiheroes fracture or otherwise disrupt the image of traditional heroes, their narratives will do the same vis-à-vis heroic narratives. Let us briefly consider two formal theorists, whose work on heroic narrative is both pervasive in popular media and synonymous with the classicism often at odds with antiheroism.

The godfather of formalist heroic narrative is Aristotle (384–322 BC), whose *Poetics* gives precepts for constructing tragic plots. Since tragedy traffics by and large in mythical characters and situations that, according to Aristotle, require a certain magnitude (*Poetics* 7), the *Poetics* is concerned with heroes by default. From this treatise come formative concepts such as unity of action and tripartite beginning–middle–end structure (*Poetics* 7), as well as devices such as recognition (*anagnorisis*), reversal (*peripeteia*), and suffering (*pathos*), which lend intricacy to plot (*Poetics* 11). Aristotle's formulations reflect the complications inherent in Greek heroism. The ideal subjects of tragedy, neither wholly good nor evil, suffer due to their own fallibility or *hamartia* (*Poetics* 13), a concept that has become essentialized as the "tragic flaw."[6] Whether taken in its entirety or mined here and there for helpful principles, the *Poetics* has left its mark on nearly every Western genre of storytelling – including, as we will see, screenwriting.

Jump ahead twenty-three centuries to Joseph Campbell (1904–87) and *The Hero with a Thousand Faces* (first published in 1949, now in its third edition (2008)). In contrast to the literary typologies of Aristotle (or Northrop Frye, the twentieth century's *other* eminent heroic theorist),[7] Campbell's anthropological and psychological approach occupies a single construct: the *monomyth*, a cycle prescribing the universal journey of archetypal heroes in myth and legend. Here is Campbell's epoch-making summary of the monomyth, the single most-quoted passage from his work:

> A hero ventures forth from the world of common day into a region of supernatural wonder: fabulous forces are there encountered and a decisive victory is won: the hero comes back from this mysterious adventure with the power to bestow boons on his fellow man.[8]

The stages of this three-part cycle are (1) separation/departure, in which heroes receive (and often refuse) a "Call to Adventure" and enter the "Belly of the Whale," a literal or figurative underworld; (2) initiation, in which they are tested and acquire boons; and (3) return, in which they re-enter the world above and become engines of cosmic change. Along the way heroes encounter other archetypes – mentors, tricksters, allies, monsters, and villains – who either help or hinder their progress. The impact of Campbell's work on print and screen texts from the 1960s onward cannot be overstated, with *Star Wars: Episode IV – A New Hope* (1977) and its sequels the best-known examples of cinematic monomyth.[9]

Given the entertainment industry's highly competitive and comparative culture, it is not surprising that Aristotle and Campbell have become ensconced within the studio system. The *Poetics*, long considered a seminal screenwriting text, has found greater currency in summaries such as writer-director Michael Tierno's *Aristotle's Poetics for Screenwriters* (2002). Tierno, sidestepping "that translation-from-ancient-Greek issue," highlights "timeless universal truths about dramatic storytelling" in films as diverse as *Citizen Kane* (1941), *Gladiator* (2000), *Rocky* (1976), and *Pulp Fiction* (1994). Meanwhile, Christopher Vogler, a former story analyst turned independent consultant, has done for Campbell what Tierno did for Aristotle. In 1985, after recognizing the monomyth at work in the *Star Wars* trilogy, Vogler distilled *The Hero with a Thousand Faces* into a seven-page memo for Walt Disney Studios. The memo was also distributed outside Disney, and its popularity inspired Vogler to expand it into a screenwriting manual, *The Writer's Journey* (first published 1995, now in its third edition (2007)).[10]

The work of Aristotle and Campbell is classicizing in the radical sense (Latin *classicus*, "belonging to a class or rank"). Both isolate exemplars of classical myth and, by applying (neo)classical ideals of order and symmetry, bring them into system. The *Poetics* is concerned with sorting out a vast tragic corpus and, in commending some plays above others, with the formation of a dramatic canon. *The Hero with a Thousand Faces* is focused perhaps less on canon-formation, though Greco-Roman case studies are prominent, than on fitting diverse traditions into a timeless and tidy pattern. Their classicism is all the more conspicuous by way of Tierno and Vogler, whose exemplars of Aristotelian and monomythic films constitute canons unto themselves. Screen texts that partake of these systems – *as systems* – are engaged in a kind of surrogate classicism, the self-conscious creation of timeless heroic classics. If these texts are set in antiquity, the systemization becomes hyper-classicizing, imparting classically derived authenticity or authority writ large – especially where deviations from ancient sources are steep.

Antiheroic films will work to disrupt these systems. This is not to say that the outcomes are never heroic from the standpoint of achieving victories or accomplishing great tasks. Instead, the traditional heroic arcs or journeys, which are generally neat, focused, and linear, become random, diffuse, and otherwise fragmented. Our case studies begin with a pair of screen epics about Alexander the Great. The following discussion, which pits the heroic classicism of the one against the antiheroic fragmentation of the other, will inform our eventual consideration of Perseus and Hercules.

## *ALEXANDER THE GREAT* (1956) AND *ALEXANDER* (2004)

Tasked with labeling writer-producer-director Robert Rossen's *Alexander the Great*, one could do worse than "Aristotelian." The film is above all a classical tragedy in the vein of the *Poetics*,[11] a cradle-to-grave biopic in three acts: Alexander's birth and upbringing; his rise to power, first in Macedonia and then globally; his decline and death. Plutarch long before set the bar for associating Alexander with tragedy, inflecting his biography with "sustained tragic patterning and imagery."[12] And Rossen, whose background was in theater, likewise swathed his movie in thespian staginess, from his script's allusions to Euripides, Sophocles, and Shakespeare, to his principal cast of British theater veterans, who take Received Pronunciation to new heights of artifice – even by that era's already inflated standards.

In addition to these classicizing flourishes, the film presents Alexander (Richard Burton) as the Aristotelian ideal: a man not overly virtuous, whose inherent sense of superiority renders him fallible, nowhere more so than the impetuous slaying of his companion Cleitus (Gustavo Rojo). Alexander hero-worships Achilles, but the Freudian archetype of Oedipus, whose Sophoclean incarnation bulks rather large in the *Poetics*, haunts him.[13] His mistress, Barsine (Claire Bloom), pointedly summarizes his complex: "No other woman is my rival, except your mother, and your frenzied desire to outdo your father." Much earlier in the picture, at a banquet celebrating the marriage of Philip (Fredric March) to the young Eurydice (Marisa de Leza), the hero not only defends his mother's honor and nearly comes to blows with his father, but also endures a drunken Attalus (Stanley Baker) calling his legitimacy into question. In Sophocles' *Oedipus the King*, a similar incident sets Oedipus on the road to Delphi to inquire about his past: "There was a dinner" (he tells Jocasta) "and at it was a man, who was drunk; he accused me in his drink of being a bastard" (779–80). The contentious wedding is the first step in Alexander's rapid ascension. Soon he witnesses Philip's murder, is acclaimed king under the watchful eye of Olympias (Danielle Darrieux), and launches his invasion of Persia.

More Aristotelian than tropes from the *Poetics* is the presence of Aristotle himself (Barry Jones) as Alexander's tutor. Cultivating in Alexander appreciation for science, mathematics, history, and other disciplines, Aristotle makes him a paragon of Greek learning – quite unlike his so-called barbarian father. Moreover, Aristotle instills a sense of Greek nationalism, declaiming against the Persians, whose way of life (he tells a rapt Alexander and his companions) "has the seed of death and fear in it." It is the "moral duty" of Greeks to subjugate and even destroy such peoples. Aristotle envisions for his pupil a certain heroic arc, long-lived, kingly, and decidedly un-tragic, provided Alexander be kept from premature misfortune. Such concern causes conflict, not only with Alexander, but also with Philip, who offers his son command of Pella against Aristotle's advice. Alexander, however, astonishes his tutor by revealing his decision to emulate Achilles – to live a glorious life but die young – an arc antithetical to Aristotle's. Nevertheless, the philosopher's influence on Alexander, and therefore on the biopic itself, is profound. Aristotle even has the film's last words: "Wonders are many, but none is more wonderful than man himself." This sentiment, an excerpt from the famous "Ode to Man" in Sophocles' *Antigone*, was originally uttered in the gymnasium at Mieza. Here, repeated in voiceover moments after Alexander's death, it is a commentary on his life story, the eulogy of a hero who reached the summit of human achievement.

The theatrical release of Oliver Stone's *Alexander* might in turn be labeled "pseudo-Aristotelian" for its warts-and-all approach. In fact, this label applies to many of Stone's films, especially his historical biopics, which humanize or nuance "larger-than-life heroes ... by emphasizing one or more conspicuous flaws or failures."[14] *Alexander* seems founded on a scattershot reading of the *Poetics*, its engagement with the treatise less sustained than in *Alexander the Great*. Taking *hamartia* as a tragic flaw, for instance, the movie pursues a precipitous "arc of rise and fall" wherein the protagonist "pushes too far, attempts too much."[15] Moreover, this arc incorporates an Oedipus complex whose shock value, especially in the tempestuous mother–son relationship, handily outstrips anything in Rossen's film. Even Stone's singular focus on Alexander seems to contravene Aristotelian practice: "The ideal narrative of an epic or a tragedy should be constructed around a single *action*, not a single hero."[16] *Alexander the Great*, however tightly focused on its hero, nonetheless gives him the motive of revenge to unite his actions. Yet *Alexander* is hard-pressed to adduce coherent motives for its protagonist's words and deeds. Overall, the Aristotelian machinery of Stone's biopic, operating at an even further remove from the *Poetics* than its 1956 precursor, sometimes veers toward parody.

Appropriately, perhaps, Aristotle himself plays a less formative role in the 2004 release. Although the philosopher (Christopher Plummer) has a scene in which he shapes the world-view of Alexander, the task of shaping Alexander's life belongs to another old man: Ptolemy (Anthony Hopkins), whose dictated history is the film's narrative framework. This device prompts much of the fragmentation in *Alexander*, for Ptolemy is an unreliable narrator, his account subject to self-contradiction and vagaries of memory.[17] He calls Alexander "a god, or as close as anything I've seen," yet acknowledges the tendency to idolize Alexander, to "make him better than he was." After condemning Alexander's dream of unifying East and West, he orders his scribe to strike such vitriol: "Throw all that away.... It's an old fool's rubbish." Ptolemy's offscreen narration often clashes with the action on screen,[18] most notably after the battle of Gaugamela: "The Persian Empire, the greatest the world had yet known, was destroyed. And Alexander, at twenty-five, was now king of all." This victory declaration is undercut by the sight and sound of a bloodied Alexander (Colin Farrell) weeping profusely for his Macedonians, their corpses and those of the Persians littering the battlefield in the thousands (Figure 11.1). Stone's decision to present his biopic as the memoirs

Figure 11.1 Alexander (Colin Farrell) weeps antiheroically after his victory at Gaugamela in *Alexander* (2004). Warner Bros.

of Ptolemy, although proof against "accusations of anachronism and historical inaccuracy,"[19] impugns Alexander's heroism.

Even without Ptolemy, Farrell's performance is patently antiheroic. "Never hesitate," instructs Olympias (Angelina Jolie), apropos of handling serpents. Yet hesitating is what this Alexander does best, whether torn between pursuing the Persian king and aiding his own troops at Gaugamela, or earnestly asking Hephaestion (Jared Leto), "Which am I ... weak or divine?" When not beset by rage or grief, he appears tentative or diffident, his eyebrows raised in obvious concern, even fear.[20] Such emotional displays undermine Alexander's masculinity, as does his manner of dress, from the boyishly short, white tunics he wears into adulthood, to his effeminate, Orientalizing costumes (complete with long hair and eyeliner).[21] Alexander not only looks different from manly screen heroes such as Maximus (Russell Crowe) in *Gladiator* or Achilles (Brad Pitt) in *Troy* (2004),[22] he also loves differently, forging intense unions with Hephaestion and the Persian eunuch Bagoas (Francisco Bosch). In a genre that privileges heteronormative heroes, Stone's historicizing attention to Greek homoeroticism is remarkable, if not admirable.[23] However, his Alexander was too queer for straight viewers, and for gay viewers, frustrated with the tepid Hephaestion "bromance," not queer enough.[24] Nevertheless, Stone's protagonist, as embodied by Farrell, shatters the established image of Greco-Roman screen heroes as strong, straight men – the very image of Burton's Alexander, with his cool gaze, steely demeanor, and incontestable heterosexuality.[25]

*Alexander* also challenges a core construct of classicizing theory: the mythical heroic archetype. As we have seen, Rossen's hero consciously emulates Achilles, the epitome of short-lived valor, and unconsciously follows in the footsteps of Oedipus, the nadir of fraught familial relationships – two overlapping archetypes that nonetheless illuminate Alexander's epic aspirations and tragic demise. Stone, however, offers an overwhelming array of conflicting models. In a programmatic scene Philip, walking with young Alexander (Connor Paolo) through a dank underground cavern, points out legends painted on its walls: Prometheus, Oedipus, Jason (by way of Medea), and Heracles; not pictured, but mentioned at the beginning of the sequence, is Alexander's favorite, Achilles. Each in himself inspires emulation – "One day I'll be on walls like these!" cries the boy – whether for his cleverness, benevolence, great deeds, or prowess in battle. Yet in their sheer multiplicity they splinter Alexander's heroic identity and reduce him to a set of disparate influences. Furthermore, each archetype poses an equally negative exemplar liable to retribution from the gods, other mortals, or his own hand. (Even Achilles, praiseworthy for loving Patroclus and avenging his death, receives criticism from Aristotle for lacking restraint and being "a deeply selfish man.") The paintings themselves are visually fractured, shown through "flickering light, shifting camera angles, and choppy editing,"[26] and later reappearing in montage at key moments. These images, the fragments of myth, challenge viewers to piece together Alexander's complex persona.

Emerging from this discussion is a sense of how (1) antiheroism exists in synergy with cinematic strategies of fragmentation, and vice versa; and (2) a film invested in these processes colors the reception of a prior film. *Alexander* projects onto *Alexander the Great* the status of a stately, mannered classic – and the preferred classic, to judge from the reactions of audiences and critics to Stone's film.[27] Such a dynamic is to be expected between movies made in adjoining millennia. Certainly, it applies to our next case study: two Perseus films from 1981 and 2010. There, however, the dynamic intensifies, since the latter is an avowed remake of the former.

## CLASH OF THE TITANS (1981 AND 2010)

Although the Perseus legend receives minimal attention from Campbell, it is reconfigured as a full-fledged monomyth for the original *Clash of the Titans* (1981). Beverley Cross' script prioritizes the romance between Perseus (Harry Hamlin) and Andromeda (Judi Bowker); this change not only raises the stakes for Andromeda's eventual sacrifice to the Kraken (a.k.a. *ketos*), but also makes Medusa's head a boon in the noblest sense, a weapon capable of saving Perseus' betrothed. Acting as mentor to Perseus is Ammon the poet (Burgess Meredith), who sets him on the path to Medusa. What was traditionally a figurative *katabasis* (descent), with the hero scouring the corners of the earth, becomes literal when Perseus encounters the Gorgon in the Underworld by way of Charon's skiff.[28] Investing a Greek myth with classicizing structure is only part of Cross' hyper-classicizing agenda, for his entire script is rife with motifs from antiquity onward. Examples include the machinations of Thetis (Maggie Smith) on behalf of her son, Calibos (Neil McCarthy), which recall the goddess' interventions in the *Iliad*; Perseus' Oedipus-like solution to Calibos' riddle; and echoes of Shakespeare throughout.[29] Like Rossen's *Alexander the Great*, the 1981 film leverages its classical intertextuality toward authenticity of the highest order.

Louis Leterrier's remake (2010) also repeats and innovates, but to decidedly un-classical effect.[30] Due to its very nature, the movie is concerned not with classical tradition at large, but with the tradition established in the 1981 original. Within this narrow intertextual remit, the 2010 *Clash* seeks to dismantle its predecessor on every possible level and to implicate the audience, whose familiarity with the 1981 *Clash* is presumed, in the process. While the original arc remains intact – Perseus (Sam Worthington) must still retrieve Medusa's head from the Underworld to stop the Kraken and save Andromeda (Alexa Davalos) – most of the particulars have been altered: Perseus and Andromeda are no longer star-crossed lovers; Hades (Ralph Fiennes), not Thetis, is Perseus' divine antagonist; Acrisius (Jason Flemyng) is both husband of Danaë and the monstrous Calibos; the Olympian gods themselves face imminent extinction. Amid these changes are entirely new additions: Io (Gemma Arterton) as a love-interest, and the Djinn sorcerers as uncertain allies. On the one hand, these audacious inventions by writers Travis Beacham, Phil Hay, and Matt Manfredi are worthy successors to Beverley Cross' equally audacious Kraken and Calibos. On the other hand, as insertions into a closed tradition, they exacerbate the fragmentation already at work.

The 1981 *Clash* had been conceived as a showcase for Dynamation, the trademark stop-motion animation of Ray Harryhausen. If any fragments of the original film are preserved in the 2010 *Clash*, they are Harryhausen's creatures: Medusa, the Kraken, Pegasus, Calibos, and the scorpions – but not Bubo the owl, whose cameo sees him unceremoniously discarded.[31] Their presence in the remake, although intended as homage, verges on iconoclasm, due in part to their rendering as CGI. Beyond the realistic detail of the creatures' design and their fluid movements, their integration into the movie's hectic cinematography and editing is the most obvious contrast with Harryhausen's methods. Because Dynamation generally relies on a static camera with limited setups, the easier to animate models against back-projected footage or within mattes, its sequences leave a rather grounded, if not stolid impression. Leterrier's CGI sequences, with their constantly moving camera, seemingly limitless angles, and rapid cutting, are jarring and disjointed.[32] These postmodern practices both push Harryhausen's classic techniques to the breaking point and ultimately fragment the (meta-)monomyth of his career: the special effects *auteur*,[33] who typically worked alone, is supplanted by scores of digital specialists-for-hire.

Worthington's antiheroic portrayal of Perseus is well suited to the fragmented ethos of the 2010 *Clash*, right down to his character's appearance. Hamlin's Perseus "looked the part"[34] in a classical sense: a curly-haired, toned youth evoking the famous Cellini bronze. Worthington's Perseus, however, sports the closely cropped hair of both Maximus in *Gladiator*[35] and a modern soldier. His body is usually encased in dark armor, unlike the revealing tunics of the 1981 *Clash*. This Perseus even rides a black Pegasus, just as antiheroes in latter-day Westerns wear black hats. Behind his combative exterior lurks a staunch opposition to the divine, his most antiheroic quality. Whereas Hamlin's wide-eyed Perseus willingly receives assistance from the gods, as the monomyth dictates, Worthington's incarnation resists their aid at almost every turn. He denies his birthright as the son of Zeus (Liam Neeson) and refuses to utilize his father's gifts – Pegasus and a magical sword – except in times of dire need. Perseus' reticence goes well beyond the monomythic hero's refusal of the "Call to Adventure." Rather, his quest is to hasten the demise of immortal supremacy, especially that of Hades, the destroyer of his adoptive family; rescuing Andromeda is the means to this end. Nor does his story conclude heroically: having spurned both the throne of Argos and immortality, Perseus elects to live (in Zeus' words) a "mundane human existence" – albeit with a divinely resurrected Io.

The dynamic of heroic classic versus antiheroic upstart is manifest in the tension between original and remake, especially where the two are separated by technology and time. Nevertheless, this dynamic can also obtain between films conceived independently and released virtually simultaneously. Our final case study, therefore, involves a pair of movies from 2014, which proved to be a banner year for Hercules.

## THE LEGEND OF HERCULES (2014) AND HERCULES (2014)

Whatever else it is – and it tries to be many things – *The Legend of Hercules* (2014) is nothing if not a monomythic film.[36] Directed by Renny Harlin, the movie delves into Hercules' backstory and thus breaks with the cinematic norm of the fully formed and seasoned hero. The audience witnesses Hercules' divine birth and coming of age as Alcides (Kellan Lutz), a prince of Tiryns. After his mortal father, Amphitryon (Scott Adkins), and his brother, Iphicles (Liam Garrigan), exile him from the city, Alcides is captured in Egypt and endures many trials as a slave, all the while honing his heroic mettle. His eventual escape and return to Tiryns are embittered by the death of his mother, Alcmene (Roxanne McKee), and his mentor, Chiron (Rade Serbedzija). Yet Alcides eventually embraces his birthright as

Hercules and son of Zeus, defeats Iphicles and Amphitryon, and is reunited with his lost love, Hebe (Gaia Weiss). All told, the movie delivers a hero's journey of self-discovery, on a par with Disney's *Hercules* (1997) and its introspective musical numbers.

*The Legend of Hercules* is also legible within the tradition of the peplum genre: the long line of Italian B-movies exported overseas in the 1950s and 1960s, beginning with *Le fatiche di Ercole* (1958; English title: *Hercules*), which starred American bodybuilder Steve Reeves.[37] Most traditional, and conspicuous, is the display of Lutz's muscled body to gratify heterosexual and homoerotic gazes. In fact, *Legend* pays tribute to *Le fatiche* with Hercules chained between two pillars à la Reeves, his straining arms and torso exposed to view, and later wielding the same chains with deadly force.[38] Also traditional is a heteronormative love-interest, Hebe, who matches the hero in bravery and beauty, and whose body is likewise put on display. A third tradition is the understated but palpable presence of the divine. Though the Olympian gods rarely grace the screen in classic peplum,[39] they nevertheless have cosmic authority, which typically manifests itself in subtle fashion. In *Le fatiche* Reeves' Hercules asks Jupiter to rescind his immortality and receives a gentle but ominous rainstorm as affirmation. Similarly, *Legend* features Zeus' cyclone of clouds swirling above his shackled son, and Hera speaking through her oracle (Mariah Gale). Finally, the movie's uncomplicated conception of heroism locates it squarely within the realm of Hercules peplum, where monsters need slaying, tyrants expelling, and the downtrodden uplifting.

Even as *Legend* partakes of twentieth-century peplum traditions, it also pays tribute to neo-peplum cinema of the new millennium. The film opens with Amphitryon dueling a certain King Galenus (Dimiter Doichinov) for the right to rule Argos, which recalls the opening of *Troy* and the duel between Achilles and Boagrius (Nathan Jones) for supremacy of Thessaly. After being exiled from Tiryns, Hercules and company battle superior numbers of Egyptian soldiers within narrow caverns, a seeming homage to *300*, in which Leonidas and his Spartans fend off the Persians at Thermopylae. Next, Hercules is sold into slavery, forced to fight to the death in the arena, and hailed a celebrity; this, of course, is a nod to Maximus and his amphitheatrical success in *Gladiator*. Hercules also recalls something of Perseus from the 2010 *Clash*, from his short hair, to his initial denial of his immortal parentage, to his lightning-infused sword, with which he defeats Amphitryon's army. Although these tributes might seem fragmentary gestures, mere pastiche, they constitute a bid for authenticity under which the archetypal Hercules-strain of sword-and-sandal film recuperates later strains to their genre of origin. Just as Heracles was a Panhellenic hero, with labors and cult sites throughout Greece, so *Legend* posits a "Pan-peplum" Hercules, whose proving ground is the classical cinematic landscape c. 2000–14.

Released in July of the same year, a mere seven months after *Legend*, the simply titled *Hercules* (Paramount Pictures) is narratively and heroically poles apart. Directed by Brett Ratner and starring Dwayne ("The Rock") Johnson, the film depicts Hercules as an unmistakable antihero: the leader of a mercenary band; an exile from his Athenian homeland, haunted by the false memory of having murdered his wife and sons; a brooding and reticent adventurer inclined to minimize his reputation to all who would admire him; a muscular man who nevertheless confounds peplum convention by wearing armor. Like Lutz's Hercules, Johnson's antihero falls victim to political conspiracy: his cousin, Eurystheus (Joseph Fiennes), has struck a secret alliance with Lord Cotys of Thrace (John Hurt), whose troops Hercules and his companions ostensibly have been hired to train. As discussed above, Lutz's Hercules uncovers the conspiracy against him and embarks on a monomythic journey to Tiryns to set matters right, embracing his divine heritage along the way. Johnson's Hercules, conversely, remains ignorant for most of the picture, and the cause he believes he has undertaken is proven false. His redemption is earned not by restoring social order, but by overturning it – with his bare hands, as it happens.

*Hercules* inherits and fully develops two strategies of fragmentation from the 2010 *Clash of the Titans*. First is the heroic collective, which has precedent in antiquity (e.g. Jason and the Argonauts) but speaks to modern principles of collaboration and coalition. Whereas Farrell's Alexander alternately cajoles and terrorizes his Macedonian compatriots, Perseus spends much of the 2010 *Clash* working closely with a diverse team: Io, Suleiman the Djinn (Ian Whyte), two desert scavengers (Hans Matheson, Mouloud Achour), and Argive soldiers (among them Mads Mikkelsen, Liam Cunningham, and Nicholas Hoult). Though he ultimately stands alone against the Kraken, Perseus' success is predicated on a fragmentary notion of heroism, which prizes strength in numbers, multiplicity of identities, and complementary skill sets.[40]

*Hercules*, in turn, takes the heroic collective to a new level. Even if companions desert him or fall in battle, Johnson's protagonist, unlike Perseus, is never truly alone – not even when imprisoned and in chains (yet another echo of Steve Reeves in *Le fatiche*). "Team

Hercules," as it was styled for social media,[41] is also better defined than "Team Perseus," its members having distinct types, personalities, and backstories: an impious seer, Amphiaraus (Ian McShane); Atalanta, an Amazon (Ingrid Bolsø Berdal); a black-hearted rogue, Autolycus (Rufus Sewell); a clever storyteller, Iolaus (Reece Ritchie); a traumatized berserker, Tydeus (Aksel Hennie); and, by the film's end, Ergenia, daughter of Cotys (Rebecca Ferguson), and her son, Arius (Isaac Andrews). Such a roster seems almost focus-group tested to appeal to different niches of fandom. Nevertheless, within the milieu of the movie, these outsiders jointly perform and maintain the Hercules legend – or, perhaps, "brand." Outwardly, the hero's labors seem the work of a singular demigod. Behind the scenes, as revealed in the prologue's skirmish with pirates, the work is evenly and efficiently divided. From its very beginning *Hercules* fractures heroic glory, transferring it from individuals to the collective.[42]

Second, *Hercules* follows the 2010 *Clash* in displacing the "region of supernatural wonder" that underpins the monomyth. Of course, Perseus faces fantastic creatures aplenty; but the gods, though powerful, face the existential crisis of mortal disdain. *Hercules* goes further and adopts the atheistic approach of *Troy*, not only keeping divinities off screen, but also obscuring all evidence of their being. Both gods and monsters are confined to the world of mere stories, such as Iolaus relates to the pirates, and Ergenia derides as myths in the sense of falsehoods. The sequence comprising Iolaus' story provides a stark contrast with the fragmented heroism of the film proper. The storyteller relates what most moviegoers would recognize as an orthodox Hercules legend: son of Zeus and Alcmene; survivor of Hera's serpents; performer of twelve labors, including killing the Hydra, hunting the Erymanthian boar, and bringing back the skin of the Nemean lion. The visuals accompanying this summary are likewise orthodox screen heroics: a lone warrior, his semi-nude body sculpted to perfection, battling CGI beasts (rendered and choreographed with admirable restraint in comparison to the 2010 *Clash*). By revealing Iolaus' story as fiction, *Hercules* programmatically sunders itself from conventional cinematic monomyth in favor of antiheroic "reality." That said, shots of the monsters figure prominently in the trailers, perhaps to attract viewers expecting fantasy in the Harryhausen mode.

All of which brings us to the movie's climax. Hercules, with encouragement from Amphiaraus, assumes the heroic identity heretofore kept at arm's length ("I am Hercules!") and rescues his friends from certain death. The team fights its way to the steps of Hera's temple, where Hercules repels Cotys' soldiers by toppling the goddess' colossal statue, whose rolling head dispatches Cotys himself. This feat is worthy of *Le fatiche di Ercole*, at the culmination of which Reeves' Hercules tears down the palace at Iolcus to ward off the soldiers of Pelias (Ivo Garrani). While edifices of social and political power are physically demolished in each film, *Le fatiche* brings closure by installing Jason (Fabrizio Mioni) as rightful ruler, and shipping Hercules off to his next adventure via the *Argo*. Ratner's film, however, offers no such tidy resolution. As the dust settles, the surviving troops acclaim Hercules, who appears bare-chested and brandishing his club, looking his traditional peplum self. Yet his companions quickly join him to share in the soldiers' adulation. The camera, in a final shot, cranes left to right over Team Hercules and comes to rest not on Johnson, but on McShane's Amphiaraus, whose voiceover calls his own prophetic powers into question: "What the hell do I know? I'm supposed to be dead by now." Much like the film that bears his name, Hercules has proven adept at pulling down traditional structures. Whether they can be put back together is anyone's guess – or at least beyond the scope of the present film.

## CONCLUSION

Greco-Roman antiheroes, and the fragmented films in which they appear, are symptomatic of the new millennium, which has inherited and amplified the cultural and political crises of the 1960s and beyond. *Alexander*, the 2010 *Clash of the Titans*, and *Hercules* all feature volatile, recalcitrant protagonists. Their non-conformity to social mores, religious authority, and the greater good, not to mention established cinematic modes of conveying these values, reflects genuine ambivalence toward normativity in the face of turmoil. The movies that precede them, consequently, are received as models of conformity to traditional systems, whether those of the Hollywood studio, the rules of genre, or antiquated cinematic technique. *Alexander the Great*, the 1981 *Clash of the Titans*, and even *The Legend of Hercules* are classics in the sense of not only having primacy – temporal, artistic, or both – but also belonging to an era that is, or ought to be, beyond recovery. As such, these movies, promulgating outmoded strains of heroism, run the risk of becoming irrelevant, if they have not already become so.

It was not always thus. Campbell, for one, believed in heroic continuity: "The latest incarnation of Oedipus, the continued romance of Beauty and the Beast, stand this afternoon on the corner of

Forty-second Street and Fifth Avenue, waiting for the traffic light to change."[43] This sentiment, conceived in an era of Western hegemony that perhaps never existed, presupposes the persistence of classicism from antiquity to modernity. Yet Vogler, Campbell's greatest promoter, concedes that the postmodern world is ill-suited to order and symmetry:

> Young people now come to awareness in a high-intensity bombardment of random images and brief story segments torn from all the previous styles of art and literature. The bits may have an internal consistency and obey some rules of the old story world, but they assault the consciousness of the young in no apparent order.[44]

Perhaps Vogler would have us reimagine Campbell's law-abiding New Yorkers as street-level antiheroes, crossing against traffic and texting at the same time. I exaggerate, but only a little. The classicizing heroism of Campbell and Aristotle persists – not because of, but rather despite, the myriad anxieties and demands of the twenty-first century. In such an environment our work as scholars of antiquity and its reception, our marking the path between classics old and new, is more necessary than ever.

## NOTES

My thanks to the editors and to my co-presenters at the New Heroes conference in Delphi for their helpful comments and suggestions.

1. On antiheroism, see also McAuley and Tomasso in this volume.
2. Cuddon (2013: 41), with some healthy skepticism toward the "dashing, strong, brave and resourceful" type: "It is a little doubtful whether such heroes have ever existed in any quantity in fiction."
3. Neimneh (2013: 78).
4. Brombert (1999: 2).
5. Ziolkowski (2004: 4).
6. Heroic fallibility: Halliwell (1987: 127–31).
7. Frye (1957). On Frye's eminence, obsolescence, and putative renascence see Denham (2009).
8. Campbell (2008: 23). It is customary to refer to Campbell's construct as the "classical monomyth": thus Jewett and Lawrence (1977) for purposes of defining and differentiating their "American monomyth."
9. The monomyth in speculative fiction and film: Palumbo (2014); in comics: Rogers (2011). The debt of *Star Wars* to Campbell is one of the best-known facts about the series' production: see Deyneka (2012); Seastrom (2015) adds that Lucas referred to Campbell as "my Yoda." Monomythic patterning in *Star Wars* was noticed early on by Gordon (1978), a classic study.

10 Tierno (2002: xviii, xix). Vogler (2007), origin story (xxvii–xxxii). See also Hiltunen (2002), who not only traces the reception of the *Poetics* from Shakespeare to the modern entertainment industry under the rubric "proper pleasure," but also builds bridges with the theories of Vladimir Propp, Campbell (especially via Vogler), and others.
11 In the vein of the *Poetics* – and by way of the Bard: "Rossen's idea of Shakespeare's idea" of a Greek tragedy (Nisbet 2008: 93).
12 Mossman (1988: 85). See also Petrovic (2008).
13 On the film's father–son conflict and its Freudian overtones see Wieber (2008: 149–53).
14 Apostol (2016: 360–1), applying "pseudo-Aristotelian" to *Alexander* as well as *Nixon* (1995), *The Doors* (1991), and *JFK* (1991).
15 Apostol (2016: 361, both quotations).
16 Paul (2010: 28), original italics. Paul adds, "We might wonder what would have been done differently had [Stone] listened to Aristotle as carefully as his Alexander did."
17 Ptolemy as unreliable narrator: Chaniotis (2008: 185–7), Shahabudin (2010: 107–8).
18 Compare Cyrino (2010: 180): "More often than not, the heroic Alexander described by the laudatory narration is at odds with the moody, drunk, and even cruel Alexander the audience actually sees onscreen."
19 Chaniotis (2008: 186).
20 On Farrell's lack of gravitas see Cyrino (2010: 172); on his character's emasculating "emotional instability" see Pierce (2013: 138).
21 Pierce (2013: 132–3).
22 Pierce (2013: 130–2) compares Alexander with the extravagant, non-normative villains of these films: Commodus (Joaquin Phoenix) and Agamemnon (Brian Cox), as well as Xerxes (Rodrigo Santoro) from *300* (2007).
23 Skinner (2010) discusses the ways in which the sexualities of Alexander are, and are not, historically accurate.
24 Nikoloutsos (2009: 229–30, 236–43).
25 Burton's gaze and demeanor: Cyrino (2010: 172–3) notes the "rehabilitation" of Burton's performance in the wake of Farrell's. Heterosexuality in *Alexander the Great*: Nikoloutsos (2009: 224–8).
26 Platt (2010: 298), who discusses the significance of the "primitive" wall paintings and other visual archetypes in the film. See also Solomon (2010: 47–9).
27 Solomon (2010) and Cyrino (2010: 172–80) survey reactions to *Alexander*.
28 Figurative *katabasis* in the Perseus legend: Ogden (2008: 47–50). Literal *katabasis* in the 1981 *Clash*: Clauss (forthcoming).
29 Clauss (forthcoming) discusses these and other examples of intertextuality between the 1981 *Clash* and classical or classicizing models.

30 On the 2010 *Clash*, see further Tomasso in this volume.
31 Unceremoniously discarded: Curley (2015: 214–15).
32 Jarring and disjointed: a complaint among reviewers (along with derision for the theatrical release's hasty 2D to 3D transfer). See, for example, Lowry (2010): "The effects are too frequently muddied by the pace at which they flash by"; Darghis (2010): "The frenetic editing at times pitches the movie into near visual incoherence."
33 Harryhausen as *auteur*: Wells (2002: 90–4).
34 Harryhausen and Dalton (2004: 262).
35 Perseus as Maximus: Raucci (2015: 164), after Darghis (2010). Worthington sports a more lustrous coiffure in the sequel, *Wrath of the Titans* (2012).
36 On the new Hercules movies, see further Blanshard, Chiu, Solomon, and Stafford in this volume.
37 This paragraph is indebted to Blanshard and Shahabudin (2011: 58–76), a discussion of the peplum genre with *Le fatiche* as its focus; and D'Amelio (2011), who places the uncomplicated peplum heroics in their native political context. O'Brien (2014: 174) cuts to the chase: "*The Legend of Hercules* … is in essence an old-school peplum with added cut-cost digital effects." See also Solomon in this volume.
38 O'Brien (2014: 99) compares both "Hercules chained" sequences. See also Blanshard in this volume.
39 The thesis is that of Tomasso (2016). A notable exception is *Ulysses Against Hercules* (*Ulisse contro Ercole*, 1962), which initially features most of the Greco-Roman pantheon.
40 Elliott (2011: 70–1) traces the heroic fragmentation of the 2010 *Clash* back to *Gladiator*, and duly notes that Perseus in the 1981 *Clash* likewise has a band of helpers, albeit an "all but invisible" one.
41 The movie's Facebook page, still active as of this writing, highlights individual companions and offers fans opportunities to join #TeamHercules themselves.
42 For a fuller discussion of the companions in *Hercules*, see Chiu in this volume.
43 Campbell (2008: 2).
44 Vogler (2007: 268).

# 12 Trouble in the Tehran Multiplex: Xerxes, 300, and 300: Rise of an Empire in Iran

Lloyd Llewellyn-Jones

## INTRODUCTION

The bludgeoning Hollywood franchise that arose out of Frank Miller's (1998) graphic novel *300* is not alone in its fictitious use of the ancient world. The films *300* (2007) and *300: Rise of an Empire* (2014) are both contributors to a longstanding tradition of Western myth-making, which gained traction in the nineteenth century. The mythology insisted that the battles between Greek city-states and the Persian empire, the so-called "Persian Wars," were a showdown over the fate of Western civilization itself. Pre-eminent historians of the time believed that the defeat of Xerxes' forces helped preserve the lofty Greek attributes of freedom of thought and democracy.[1] The victory over Persia was a brilliant moment in the triumph of reason in the face of dark Eastern backwardness and sinister mysticism. This is a dubious view that some die-hard conservative scholars in the West continue to propagate to this day and such intransigent readings have, in fact, helped give voice to, for instance, the far-right, anti-immigrant Golden Dawn party in Greece, which holds ceremonies at Thermopylae, as *Time* reported in 2012, chanting "Greece belongs to Greeks" in front of a bronze statue of their slain hero, the Spartan king Leonidas.[2]

There can be little doubt that *300* and its sequel's vision of muscle-bound warriors chimes with the contemporary popular taste for both a particular type of gym-bodied heroism and an ever-mounting tide of intolerance of the "others" inside and outside of our communities. In the films, the Spartans and, latterly, the Athenians fight bare-chested without armor in the "heroic nude" mode so beloved in the ideology of ancient Greece, but they are so gym-pumped with bulging muscles that they easily betray their roots in the American comic-book tradition of superheroes.[3] Like superheroes, the burly Greeks are on a mission to save the world. In contrast, and as in antiquity, in the films the Persians are represented with covered bodies, clothed in trousers, tunics, and turbans; their bodies (when seen) are pale, weak, even deformed. They too have a mission: to follow their master, Xerxes, end freedom, and bring about his reign of terror.

Interestingly, King Xerxes' body is put on display, but his is a disconcerting figure. Covered in gold chains and with a face and torso lacerated with jeweled piercings, clean-shaven and bald-headed, his eyes and eyebrows defined with thick layers of black kohl, he is a huge (literally a giant at eight feet tall) figure of sexual ambiguity and Eastern malevolence (Figure 12.1).[4] The golden god-king commands the armies of the dead (the Immortals), and cavalry units of war-rhinos; his harem is composed of women whose limbs are as deformed as their sexual morals; and even, in this heightened world of Orientalist fantasy, an ibex-headed man serves as Xerxes' court-musician, scratching out a rusty tune on a Persian *kamancheh*, or bowed lute. Xerxes is described by the filmmakers as "coming out of nowhere, [a] larger-than-life, Bizarro-land character" while his ceremonial capital, Persepolis, was designed by the studio art department to be

> the very antithesis of the personal freedom and democracy then blossoming in Athens. By combining ancient Middle Eastern motifs with inspiration from modern fascist utopian visions, the result was an architecture that is overwhelmingly oppressive but with a timeless opulence – Albert Speer meets Dolce & Gabbana. That's what we went for.[5]

In Hollywood's eyes Xerxes is far from heroic. He is, in fact, a menacing despot. *300: Rise of an Empire* shows us his transformation from a good-looking (dark-haired and bearded) Persian boy into a demonic god-figure through his immersion into a pool of pure evil, a golden baptism of the unholy where every bit of his humanity is surrendered to give him the monstrous form he subsequently takes. After his immersion into the realms of darkness he returns to Persia and declares war on Greece: "For Glory's sake ... for Vengeance's sake ... WAR!"

Referred to with some frequency throughout both films as the "god-king," Xerxes' image is based on a Greek perception, which can be traced back to Aeschylus, that the Persian monarchs saw themselves as divine. In *300* Xerxes confirms that "It is not my lash [that my Persian subjects] fear, it is my divine power. But I am a generous

# Trouble in the Tehran Multiplex

Figure 12.1 Xerxes the god-king (Rodrigo Santoro); publicity images from *300* (2007) and *300: Rise of an Empire* (2014). Warner Bros.

god." Yet the Greeks were capable of more nuanced judgments too: Herodotus, no great fan of Xerxes, nevertheless wrote that "Among all these immense numbers [of Persians] there was not a man who, for stature and noble bearing, was more worthy than Xerxes to wield so vast a power" (7. 187). This was Herodotus' nod to recognizing

Xerxes as a leader of some considerable skill, the worthy successor of his father Darius the Great, a facet of his character Xerxes himself was keen to promote in his own royal propaganda:

> King Xerxes says: By the will of Ahuramazda I am of such a sort, I am a friend of the right, of wrong I am not a friend. It is not my wish that the weak should have harm done him by the strong, nor is it my wish that the strong should have harm done him by the weak ... The man who is cooperative, according to his cooperation thus I reward him. Who does harm, him according to the harm I punish. It is not my wish that a man should do harm; nor indeed is it my wish that if he does harm he should not be punished ... This indeed my capability: that my body is strong. As a fighter of battles I am a good fighter of battles. Whenever with my judgment in a place I determine whether I behold or do not behold an enemy, both with understanding and with judgment, then I think prior to panic, when I see an enemy as when I do not see one ... As a horseman, I am a good horseman. As a bowman, I am a good bowman, both on foot and on horseback. As a spearman, I am a good spearman, both on foot and on horseback. These skills that Ahuramazda set down upon me, and which I am strong enough to bear ...[6]

Based on the eponymous Frank Miller comic-book series, the Warner Bros. movies opted, then, to characterize the Achaemenid king as (in the words of his actor-creator, Rodrigo Santoro) "not human ... a creature ... an entity" lacking the nobility, piety, and probity expressed by the historical Xerxes himself.[7] His depiction in the films as a multi-pierced, bejeweled creature is greatly contrasted with his appearance immortalized on the palatial reliefs of Persepolis. In and of itself, that is not an issue for me. I am not interested in the question of *how* Hollywood gets history wrong, since lists of cinema's historical inaccuracies tell us nothing and get us nowhere. But questioning *why* Hollywood opts to recast history in a certain light is of real importance.[8] Vital too is the need to question how cinematic reworkings read among different audiences. If, as Emma Bridges puts it, Xerxes is "part drag-queen, part outlandish monster"[9] (and audiences in the West seem happy to accept that), then how does this image resonate with a non-Western audience? What happens when *300* and *300: Rise of an Empire* are viewed in Iran or by Iranians in their worldwide diaspora? This chapter focuses on the way in which *300* and *300: Rise of an Empire* have been received by an audience whose ancestral past is plundered and brutalized and, most damagingly, silenced by an American cultural creation that dominates much of the globe. What happened when *300* hit Tehran?

## LOCATING HOLLYWOOD'S WAR ON TERROR

George W. Bush began his presidency amid allegations of corrupted election results and poll-rigging and ended it in the quagmire of conflict in Iraq and Afghanistan and the collapse of America's financial world supremacy. The September 11, 2001, terrorist attacks on America were the hideous catalysts that precipitated the chaos, especially with the subsequent United States declaration of a "war on terror."[10] Who, at the time, precisely counted as the harbingers of terror was less clear. On one, official, level the Taliban and Al-Qaeda took much of the culpability, although Bush himself was less keen on exact precision: "We're at war," he said, "we're going to find who did this, and we're gonna kick their ass." For good measure, in a speech delivered from Ground Zero, Bush's bullhorn approach continued in the same vein: "I can hear you! I can hear you, the rest of the world hears you and the people who knocked these buildings down will hear all of us soon."[11] In a more moderate, officially scripted, speech of September 20, 2001, he took a more conciliatory tone, noting that, "The terrorists are traitors to their own faith, trying, in effect, to hijack Islam itself. The enemy of America is not our many Arab friends."[12]

The wording of the speech is significant. Iran, not an Arab country either linguistically or ethnically, was overlooked by the president and even though Iran had been one of the first countries to condemn the horrors of the 9/11 attacks, Bush did not exonerate Iranians by calling them "friends." Was this an oversight by the president? It is doubtful.[13] In the Clinton years, American–Iranian relations had shown signs of improving, especially so under the more liberal Western-facing presidency of the Iranian leader Khatami. But the 9/11 crisis meant that the brief honeymoon period was over, as the new Republican presidency reset the United States policy toward Iran back to its former Regan-era years of mistrust and vilification. Daniel A. Mehochko's perceptive recent analysis of American–Iranian relations at the time of the 2001 crisis notes that:

> The events of 9/11 ... provided an unprecedented opportunity for a strategic rapprochement between the United States and Iran. After 9/11, Iran not only denounced the attacks and cooperated with the United States in Afghanistan, but also offered to negotiate a comprehensive resolution of differences with no preconditions ... The Bush neoconservatives, dominating ... policy formulation process, viewed Iran through the same lens they viewed al-Qaeda, the Taliban, and Saddam Hussein. Americans have a short attention span: the administration responded to Iran through the context of [the Islamic Revolution of] 1979.[14]

Iran's response to 9/11 might have surprised many Americans, had they been given access to unbiased media coverage. There were spontaneous candlelight vigils in Tehran in mourning for the dead in America, the mayors of Tehran and Isfahan sent condolence messages to the people of New York City, and Iranians observed a moment of silence before a national soccer match. President Khatami even requested permission from the United Nations to visit Ground Zero in order to offer prayers for the victims.[15]

On January 30, 2002, Bush charged that Iran "aggressively pursues these [nuclear] weapons and exports terror, while an unelected few repress the Iranian people's hope for freedom," and he included Iran (along with Iraq and North Korea) in the so-called "axis of evil," which he said posed "a grave and growing danger." The Bush administration argued that the US should continue to pressure Iran's Islamic Republic to end its support for Islamist movements in the Middle East and give up its nuclear program, and US–Iranian tensions continued to increase. In June 2003, less than a month after sending American troops into Iraq, Bush complained that Iran was meddling in Iraq and would pay the price.

Unsurprisingly, the level of Iranophobia within the United States rocketed to levels unseen since the Islamic Revolution of 1979 and the American hostage crisis that had helped precipitate the fall of Jimmy Carter's presidency. According to the Public Affairs Alliance of Iranian Americans (PAAIA), in the period 2003–8, nearly half of Iranian Americans surveyed by Zogby International had themselves experienced, or personally knew another Iranian American who had experienced, discrimination because of their ethnicity or country of origin or appearance.

Once the American Dream's Middle East branch, following the fall of the shah and the establishment of the Islamic Republic, Iran had been transformed into a repellent and frightening external other in the American imagination. The hostage crisis of 1979–81 precipitated a wave of anti-Iranian sentiment in the United States, which was fueled by a series of popular TV and film depictions such as *John Doe* (2002), *On Wings of Eagles* (1986), and *Escape From Iran: The Canadian Caper* (1981). The 1991 film *Not Without My Daughter* told the nightmarish tale of an American woman who traveled to Tehran with her young daughter to visit the Iranian-born family of her husband, whose sojourn in his homeland sees him transform from an educated and sophisticated citizen to an abusive, backward peasant. Indeed, in Jane Campbell's analysis, the film "only serves to reinforce the media stereotype of Iranians as terrorists who, if not actively bombing public buildings or holding airline passengers hostage, are untrustworthy, irrational, cruel, and barbaric,"[16] a sentiment shared by the Islamic Republic News Agency, which claimed that "[the film made] smears ... against Iran" and "stereotyped Iranians as cruel characters and wife-beaters." Oliver Stone's blockbuster *Alexander* of 2004 brought the ancient Persians to the big screen, although few critics or moviegoers recognized the mute, inactive, and ineffectual onscreen Persians as the ancestors of America's most vilified creation.[17] That opportunity was rectified in 2006 with the release of Zack Snyder's *300*. Even in America it was criticized for its racist portrayal of combatants in the Persian army at the battle of Thermopylae. Reviewers noted the political overtones of the West-against-Iran storyline and the way Persians are depicted as decadent, sexually depraved, despotic, and animalistic in contrast to the noble and infinitely heroic Greeks.[18] Bootleg versions of the film were available in Tehran with the film's international release and news of the film's (somewhat surprising) success at the United States box office prompted widespread antagonism in Iran.

## TROUBLE IN THE TEHRAN MULTIPLEX

During the Now Ruz (New Year) celebrations of 2007, Iran, it seemed, erupted in indignation. Everyone was talking about *300*. Azadeh Moaveni, a journalist for *Time Magazine*, recalled the scene:

> All of Tehran was outraged. Everywhere I went yesterday, the talk vibrated with indignation over the film *300* – a movie no one in Iran has seen but everyone seems to know about since it became a major box office surprise in the United States. As I stood in line for a full hour to buy *ajeel*, a mixture of dried fruits and nuts traditional to the start of Persian new year festivities, I felt the entire queue, composed of housewives with pet dogs, teenagers, and clerks from a nearby ministry, shake with fury. I hadn't even heard of the film until that morning when a screed about it came on the radio, so I was able to nod darkly with the rest of the shoppers, savouring a moment of public accord so rare in Tehran. Everywhere else I went, from the dentist to the flower shop, Iranians buzzed with resentment at the film's depictions of Persians, adamant that the movie was secretly funded by the US government to prepare Americans for going to war against Iran. "Otherwise why now, if not to turn their people against us?"[19]

Several governmental newspapers in Iran featured headlines such as "Hollywood declares war on Iran" and "300 AGAINST 70 MILLION" (Iran's population) while even *Ayende-No*, a more liberal independent Iranian newspaper, said that "[t]he film depicts Iranians as demons, without culture, feeling or humanity, who think of nothing except attacking other nations and killing people." Javad Shamaqdari, the cultural advisor to President Ahmadinejad and Deputy Minister of Culture and Islamic Guidance for Cinema, accused the film of "plundering Iran's historic past and insulting this civilization ... This is psychological warfare against Tehran and its people."[20]

Four Iranian Members of Parliament called for all Muslim countries to ban the film and a group of Iranian filmmakers wrote to UNESCO highlighting the misrepresentation of Iranian history and culture. According to *The Guardian* report of March 19, 2007, Iranian critics of *300*, ranging from bloggers to government officials, described the movie "as a calculated attempt to demonise Iran at a time of intensifying US pressure over the country's nuclear programme."

For her part, Azadeh Moaveni keenly identified two factors that fueled the intensity of Iranian indignation over the film: first, its release on the eve of Now Ruz was certainly badly timed and perhaps inauspicious, but second, the box office success of *300*, compared with the relative flop of Oliver Stone's *Alexander*, was widely seen by Iranians as cause for considerable alarm, signaling perhaps more ominous American intentions. Social media within Iran and beyond its borders solicited many diverse reactions. One Facebook conversation-thread, for instance, showed a strongly polarized East–West response:[21]

> The whole "us versus THEM" theme in the movie was just very disturbing. The Persians tell the Spartans to lay down their weapons, and the Spartans shout, "Come and get them, Persian!" This constant "Spartan" and "Persian" expressions are filled with rage and hatred ... how can this material NOT be racist? [signed] JehanZeb
>
> Long live the 300! Long live the memory of Sparta! And if Iran attempts to attack us we shall prevail and we shall crush them! Sincerely, [signed] A Patriot.
>
> [Iran is] a country who probably is making nuclear weapons, doesn't barely know what the fuck is going on in the rest of the world and their president Mahmoud Ahmadinejad is a fucking psychopath ... They're just pissed cause now the entire world knows that their nation's history is full of pussys [sic], [signed] C. Robin.

While, by and large, Zack Snyder stayed clear of any political debate that touched on Iran's reaction to *300*, Frank Miller was happy to fan the flames of cultural and political polarization with some incendiary, and historically and culturally uninformed, comments:

> For some reason, nobody seems to be talking about who we're up against, and the sixth century barbarism that they [the Persians] actually represent. These people saw people's heads off. They enslave women, they genitally

mutilate their daughters; they do not behave by any cultural norms that are sensible to us. I'm speaking into a microphone that never could have been a product of their culture, and I'm living in a city where three thousand of my neighbours were killed by thieves of airplanes they never could have built.[22]

Reacting to Miller's diatribe, but unaware of what was yet to come, one vociferous Iranian social media blogger noted that "*300, the Movie* is the greatest cockamamie, Bull Shite, Hero Worship, Falsification of History, Hollywood Spoof made so far in the Twenty-First Century!"[23] And yet upon its release in 2014, *300: Rise of an Empire*, the *300* sequel, took Orientalist stereotypes to a new nadir of darkness and also triggered considerable controversy (not unlike another recent Warner Bros. movie, *Argo* (2012), a contemporary drama about the American Embassy's ordeal in revolutionary Iran). The sequel got mixed reviews and did not enjoy the wave of enthusiasm associated with its forerunner, with many critics suggesting that onscreen machismo was no compensation for the lack of a tight plot or a compelling storyline. Historical liberties abounded (most notably with the death of Darius, killed fighting at sea) and for *The Guardian* the film was the same "massive gilded embodiment of orientalism from last time round."[24] Indeed, the Persians of *300: Rise of an Empire* remain the incarnation of every Orientalist cliché imaginable: they are as decadent and oversexed as they are weak and spineless. They are also incapable of winning battles without the help of a Greek traitor: Artemisia, a woman who may be costumed like Xena, warrior princess, but whose heart is consumed by a crazed desire for power and destruction. "My heart is Persian," she declares darkly. Iranians were once again left baffled:

> Here is another Western-centric film ... which is factually flawed to the point of being downright offensive ... it screams, "Hey, look! Not only are the Middle Easterners out to get us now – they've always been after the West!"[25]

## WHOSE XERXES?
## IRANIAN CONCEPTS OF THE HEROIC

In Iran there is a highly developed sense of the "heroic." This is manifest in many ways: there are, for instance, the many tales of heroism in the Persian national epic, the *Shahnameh* (*Epic of Kings*) by Ferdowsi, a poem of over 50,000 couplets written over 1,000 years ago. It tells the largely mythical story of the kings and heroes of ancient Iran until the time of the Islamic conquest of Iran in the seventh century and is populated with commanding male figures such as Rustam, Arash, Siyâvash, Zal, Sam, and Sohrab, all strongmen of impeccable goodwill, who fight, slaughter, and kill for the good of Iran and its people.[26] Even Xerxes appears in *Shahnameh*, although in (later) disguise as the hero Esfandiyar.[27] Always loyal, always brave yet willing to shed a tear of sentimentality, Esfandiyar/Xerxes and his fellow heroes still occupy a centrality in popular Iranian thought and their deeds are as well known to school children as they are to the old men sitting in coffee houses.[28] Whether filtered through traditional storytelling performances in public squares or via internet cartoons or interactive apps, the national heroes of *Shahnameh* have molded Iran's sense of the heroic.[29]

Described as "tangled up with the soul of Iranian peoples," the epic heroes of Persian tradition found a physical embodiment in the figure of the Pahlevan, or wrestler.[30] Since antiquity the Pahlevani have practiced for sport within the special confines of the *zourkhaneh*, or "house of strength." The original purpose of these institutions was to train men as warriors and instill in them a sense of national pride in anticipation for the coming battles, but by the twentieth century some Pahlevani were reaching superstar status within Iran, and today *varzesh-e pahlavāni* (strongman rituals) is touted as the reason why Iranians are regular winners at international wrestling and weight-lifting events. The art of the Pahlevan fuses elements of pre-Islamic Persian culture (particularly Zoroastrianism, Mithraism, and Gnosticism) with the spirituality of Shi'a Islam and Sufism, and his body brings the idea of muscular development centrally into the Iranian concept of the heroic.

Finally, but of real importance, there is the heroism of martyrdom that is so central to Iranian Shi'ism (although the *Shahnameh* suggests there was a pre-Islamic origin for this national ideology). Shi'ite beliefs center on the martyrdom of the Imams Ali and Hussein, the relatives of the prophet. Their self-sacrifice is commemorated in mosques, squares, cafés, and hotels; it is in the music and performance traditions of Iran, including the *tazieh* passion-plays performed during the Shi'ite periods of mourning, Muharram and Ashura.[31] In Iran today, those who died in the 1979 Revolution and the millions of soldiers who died in the Iran–Iraq War are also considered martyrs and are treated with great respect. The Behesht-e Zahra (Fatimeh's Paradise), Tehran's main graveyard, is mostly given over to martyrs; it even has a theater that plays dramatic re-enactments of battles from the war. In Iranian cities, towns, and villages many street names and school names bear the names of martyrs, and photographic portraits of deceased soldiers still line the streets and hang from the walls in local mosques. Student activists in the 2009 so-called Green Revolution began calling those killed during protests "martyrs." When Neda Agha-Soltan, a young student, was shot and killed during a protest, her image became a symbol of resistance for the "freedom fighters" and was used to gain international political support.

All of this has implications for the way in which Iranians reacted to *300* and *300: Rise of an Empire* since Iranians are, in many ways, more in tune with how heroism and national pride are interlocked. This is not to belittle any Western regard for the heroic and the way in which, for instance, the dead of successive wars are honored in annual acts of remembrance, but in no country other than Iran is the conception of the heroic so deeply ingrained in a people's daily existence. Of course, much of the youth of Iran are feeling increasingly remote from the Revolution and the war of the 1980s, and an increasing trend in displays of nationalism among the general population can be witnessed in a spike in pre-Islamic Persian names for babies and the ever-present *farvahar* pendant, the pre-Islamic Zoroastrian symbol. As important as the *Shahnameh* is to Iranian nationalism, the tales are largely mythical and are not an accurate history of Iran, but in fact, Iran has a rich history that stretches back over 2,500 years to the Achaemenids.[32] Cyrus the Great and other Achaemenid kings were heroic figures who built an empire on (as far as the Iranians are concerned) tolerance and respect for all. This history has provided a rich foundation of heroic stories on which are built Iranian identity and national pride.[33] Leaders of Iran have used the history of Cyrus the Great, and in general the history of the Achaemenids, to great effect.[34] In the 1970s Mohammad Reza Shah compared himself to Cyrus the Great and even changed the Iranian calendar from Islamic dating to "Achaemenid dating" to make it coincide with the reign of Cyrus the Great 2,500 years ago, and in more recent times, in the wake of the disputed presidential election in 2009, Iran's President Mahmoud Ahmadinejad, hoping to regain a measure of legitimacy, began to recast himself as a nationalist leading a struggle against foreign foes. "Talking about Iran is not talking about a geographical entity or race," Ahmadinejad said at the opening ceremony of an exhibition of the Cyrus Cylinder on loan to Tehran from the British Museum, adding, "Talking about Iran is tantamount to talking about culture, human values, justice, love and sacrifice."[35]

Iranians may be relatively naive about the realities of ancient Persian empire building, but what is clear is that they are deeply proud of their pre-Islamic heritage. The Warner Bros. films were therefore regarded with bafflement by Iranians. Azadeh Moaveni, echoed the feelings of many:

I'm relatively mellow as Iranian nationalists go, and even I found myself applauding when the government spokesman described [300] as fabrication and insult. Iranians view the Achaemenid empire as a particularly noble page in their history and cannot understand why it has been singled out for such shoddy cinematic treatment, as the populace here perceives it, with the Persians in rags and its Great King practically naked. The Achaemenid kings, who built their majestic capital at Persepolis, were exceptionally munificent for their time. They wrote the world's earliest recorded human rights declaration, and were opposed to slavery.[36]

One critic of both films, Touraj Daryaee, a scholar of ancient Iran and himself a Persian immigrant to the United States, proffered a more sardonic summary of 300 upon its release, drawing clear parallels between the Spartan and Persian hostilities and American foreign policy in the Middle East, and suggesting that Xerxes and his forces were intrinsic to the film's prejudiced agenda:

> What do you get when you take all the "misfits" that inhabit the collective psyche of the white American establishment and put them together in the form of a cartoonish invading army from the East coming to take your freedom away? Then add a horde of black people, deformed humans who are the quintessential opposite of the fashion journal images, a bunch of veiled towel-heads who remind us of Iraqi insurgents, a group of black-clad Ninja-esque warriors who look like Taliban trainees, and men and women with body and facial piercings who are either angry, irrational, or sexually deviant. All this headed by a homosexual king (Xerxes) who leads his motley but vast group of "slaves" known as the Persian army against the 300 handsomely sculpted men of Sparta who appear to have been going to LA (or Montreal) gyms devotedly, who fight for freedom and their way of life, and who at times look like the Marine Corps advertisements on TV? You get the movie 300.[37]

In no other chronicle of antiquity is Xerxes a hairless, bejeweled creature of camp fetish with a violent streak. This corrupt and corrupted version of a Persian king sits uncomfortably with Iranian audiences, not just because they see the Warner Bros. movies as thinly veiled forms of Western antagonism toward their country, but because the concept of heroism that is so central to their idea of the national self is not allowed any meaningful articulation in either film. Fighting neither for freedom, country, people, nor ideology, the Persians of 300 and 300: Rise of an Empire blindly follow their demonic god-king into the brutalities of a meaningless war. Justice, faith, or mercy, the qualities of Iranian heroism, are pushed aside and the Persian troops slaughter and maim indiscriminately; their aspiration for empire is nothing more than a violently bloody land-grab.

A cartoon published in a satirical newspaper in Iran in March 2007 captures the Iranian bepuzzlement perfectly (Figure 12.2). Sitting

Figure 12.2 The Great King Xerxes looks at his Hollywood image through a distorting mirror. Iranian cartoon, March 2007. Author's copy.

on a high-backed throne, a long scepter in his hand, King Xerxes, crowned and bearded, views himself through a mirror. The ornamental mirror top is crafted in the shape of the Marvel Comic's Batman logo, and it is through the prism of the American graphic novel that a surprised Xerxes is forced to see himself. No longer the dignified Achaemenid monarch of the Persepolis reliefs, he has morphed into a thug – bald, half naked, muscly, covered in body-piercings, holding a battle mace, he is the pseudo-Xerxes of the genuine Persian past and the supervillain of the West's Persian Wars mythology.

There is something glorious in this little cartoon, though. Against all the Hollywood hype, and against all Western political rhetoric that rants against Iran, the cartoon casts a wry smile. Iran is aware of how it is (misguidedly) perceived among hostile Western (and other) forces, and while the politicians and mullahs may rant their own vitriol against the West, most of the Iranian people use a far stronger weapon: the ability to laugh.[38] They are aware of the primacy and antiquity of their culture and the depth of feeling that unites them as Persians, even though they may be scattered far and wide across the earth's surface. Ultimately the little newspaper cartoon wins out because it scoffs at the West, it laughs at the United States, and makes a laughingstock of Hollywood and of Frank Miller. That is heroism.

## NOTES

1. Bridges, Hall, and Rhodes (2007); Samiei (2014).
2. Kakissis (2012).
3. For images see DiLullo (2007).
4. DiLullo (2007: 70, 71).
5. Aperlo (2013: 40, 58).
6. Old Persian inscription of Xerxes (XPl) based on the tomb inscription of his father, Darius (my translation).
7. Cited in Bridges (2015: 194).
8. See further Llewellyn-Jones (2018).
9. Bridges (2015: 195).
10. On post-9/11 films, see further Tomasso in this volume.
11. Pavlich (2014).
12. Bush (2001).
13. None of the nineteen 9/11-terrorists were Iranian; all were Arabs – fifteen were from Saudi Arabia, two from the United Arab Emirates, and one each from Egypt and Lebanon respectively. For its part, Al-Qaeda had been increasingly singling out Iran and Shi'ites, describing the "Persians" as the enemy of Arabs and complicit in the occupation of Iraq. The powerful anti-Iranian thrust of Israeli politics played an important part in the United States' vilification of Iran; see Ram (2009).
14. Mehochko (2013: 1). See also Bill (1988) for a discussion of American–Iranian tensions post-1979.
15. See generally Mousavian (2014).
16. Campbell (1997: 180).
17. See further Curley in this volume.
18. Karimi (2007).
19. Moaveni (2007).
20. http://news.bbc.co.uk/1/hi/entertainment/6446183.stm.
21. Sadly, the Facebook conversation which was started in 2006 was deleted from the site in 2015. These transcripts come from my records.
22. Frank Miller's *Talk of the Nation* interview on NPR (January 27, 2007). In part to counteract Miller's claims, Dana Stevens (2007) stated that, "If *300*, the new battle epic based on the graphic novel by Frank Miller and Lynn Varley, had been made in Germany in the mid-1930s, it would be studied today alongside *The Eternal Jew* as a textbook example of how race-baiting fantasy and nationalist myth can serve as an incitement to total war. Since it is a product of the post-ideological, post-Xbox 21st century, *300* will instead be talked about as a technical achievement, the next blip on the increasingly blurry line between movies and video games."
23. http://iranpoliticsclub.net/history/300.
24. Von Tunzelmann (2012).
25. https://iranian.com/main/2007/xerxes-0.html.

26 Omidsalar (2011).
27 Stoneman (2015: 14–15, 95–109, 206–10).
28 Friedl (2014).
29 Omidsalar (2012).
30 Di Cintio (2007).
31 Korangy (2017); Varzi (2006).
32 Mozaffari (2014).
33 Ansari (2012).
34 Mitchell (2014).
35 https://en.trend.az/news_print.php?news_id=1749295.
36 Moaveni (2007).
37 Daryaee (2007).
38 Föllmer (2013).

# 13 Ancient (Anti)Heroes on Screen and Ancient Greece Post-9/11

Vincent Tomasso

## INTRODUCTION

Louis Leterrier's 2010 film *Clash of the Titans* features a scene that is totally absent from its predecessor, Desmond Davis' 1981 film of the same name: the destruction of a monumental statue of Zeus. The statue of the king of the Greek gods has several features that many audience members would recognize as central to popular culture's definition of the "classical": the white (CGI) marble, the smooth musculature of the chest, arms, and legs; the chiton; and the javelin-throwing stance.[1] On orders from the king and queen of Argos, soldiers break the statue's legs, causing it to topple into the sea. They cheer triumphantly at their symbolic gesture of defiance toward divinities that they believe have become arrogant and cruel toward the human world. The gods are thus the ostensible targets of humanity's anger in *Clash*, an anger mirrored by the protagonist Perseus, who is hostile toward the gods' influence and gifts and in the final scene declares his desire to live as a mortal instead of becoming one of the Olympians as his father Zeus offers.

Leterrier's *Clash* is one of several films produced in the first decade of the twenty-first century whose protagonists reject mythical thinking as it is instantiated in popular culture. "Mythical thinking" is what Darko Suvin has called the "supernaturally determined" elements that have become so central to notions of ancient Greece in modern popular culture: myths, magic, religion, and general mysticism.[2] This rejection is in part a reaction to what Jason Landrum has called the "postmillennial catastrophes" that occurred in the United States just after the turn from the twentieth to the twenty-first century, especially the terrorist attacks of September 11, 2001.[3] These episodes shook American identity to the core with concerns about the United States' "weakness and ineffectuality"[4] in the aftermath. This perceived weakness resulted in a variety of responses in popular culture, including what Susan Faludi saw as a turn toward traditional visions of gender: "an era of neofifties nuclear family 'togetherness,' redomesticated femininity, and reconstituted Cold War manhood."[5] Faludi points out how proponents of this turn frequently looked to 1950s Westerns such as *The Searchers* (1956) in their pursuit of suitable models. The three films under consideration in this chapter also respond to the post-9/11 perception of weakness by returning to films released during the Cold War whose protagonists regard mythical thinking as the core of their identity. Rather than reaffirming this, however, these films reject mythical thinking as a reaction to the radical destabilization of American identity in the wake of 9/11.

This analysis will consider three antiheroic protagonists of films set in ancient Greece: Spartan hoplites fighting the Persian empire and combating traditional elders on the home front in Zack Snyder's *300* (2007); Alexander the Great, the Macedonian leader who conquered much of the known world at that time, in Oliver Stone's *Alexander* (2004); and Leterrier's Perseus. This chapter focuses on the initial encounters in theaters that audiences had with these films. Consequently, evidence will be drawn from the theatrical cuts of the three films under consideration and not from later home video releases (such as the three subsequent cuts of Stone's *Alexander*) or deleted/alternative scenes (such as were made available on the DVD and Blu-ray releases of Leterrier's *Clash*). These films responded to previous incarnations of the same characters in American cinema: Alexander in *Alexander the Great* (1956), the Spartans in *The 300 Spartans* (1962), and Perseus in *Clash of the Titans* (1981). This phenomenon created dialogues between those two historical moments,[6] drawing attention to how protagonists of the post-9/11 films reject the mythical thinking that their cinematic predecessors had embraced.

## 9/11, THE UNITED STATES, AND CLASSICAL ANTIQUITY

The events of 9/11 had ramifications for a variety of nations beyond the terrorists' primary target, the United States, but this chapter focuses on the American response as focalized through the three films under discussion. Although Stone's *Alexander*, Snyder's *300*, and Leterrier's *Clash* had global crews and distributions – and, indeed, made much if not the majority of their box office takes from international sources – they are grounded in an American perspective, with American screenwriters, American production companies, and, in the first two cases, American directors.[7] Given the American-inflected outlook of these films, it is important to consider them along with the association between the United States and ancient Greece and Rome that had been made since the US's origins in the eighteenth century.[8] The association has become central to American notions of self through, among other things, the prominence of classical myths in education, children's literature, and popular culture,[9] and as a result Greek mythical thinking has been a central part of American consciousness.

Thomas Pollard describes how Hollywood's response to 9/11 has been an increased interest in exploring terrorism, torture, violence, the anxiety surrounding intelligence agencies, the attrition of civil liberties, and superheroes.[10] Post-9/11 films set in classical antiquity have explored similar issues, but from the perspective of places and times that are, at least on the surface, far removed from modern audiences' experiences of their own world. Such films are akin to the horror films that Kevin Wetmore describes as enabling audiences "to contain it [9/11], understand it and re-experience it under safer conditions or with a different ending."[11] Classical antiquity, in other words, offers modern audiences a safe vantage point that affords them the opportunity to explore the issues raised by 9/11 in different ways than, say, Paul Greengrass' 2006 film *United 93*, a film that straightforwardly represents terrorists' takeover of and ultimate failure to control the plane that they commandeered on 9/11 with the intention of attacking a building in Washington, DC. Alex McAuley and Hunter Gardner have looked at how films such as *Agora* (2009), *Centurion* (2010), and *The Eagle* (2011) ruminate on post-9/11 ideas about national identity, religious conflict, and war.[12] Rome has been used almost exclusively to think through such issues, in part because the United States' reception of Rome has been predominantly political in nature. The present chapter's focus on narratives from ancient Greece shines a light on a different set of issues than those about Rome do via myth. Myth, and the religion that it once supported, has been one of the most popular aspects of the West's reception of classical antiquity, and Greece, rather than Rome, is the source of most of the popular narratives about myth in American culture. More importantly, early twenty-first-century audiences tend to associate Greece with myth more than with history, conditioned by highly popular television series such as *Xena: Warrior Princess* (1995–2001)[13] and films such as Wolfgang Petersen's *Troy* (2004). Ancient Greece has allowed audiences to think through 9/11 as ancient Rome has, but from the more abstracted viewpoint of myth.[14]

## ANTIHEROES

The term "antihero" has occasioned almost as many definitions as there are antiheroic characters that have appeared in various media.[15] To some commentators, an antihero is a flawed hero – a protagonist with many of the attributes of a traditional hero along with some shortcomings. For example, in the comic books, films, and television programs based on Marvel's X-Men, Wolverine fiercely protects those in his care and at several points takes young mutants under his wing, but also will not hesitate to kill his enemies in the most feral way with his adamantium claws. To others, antiheroes are characters whose behavior endows them with stereotypical "villain" status but who are at the same time made charismatic to the audience.[16] In this definition, the "hero" part of "antihero" simply indicates that the character is the protagonist. In the television series *Dexter* (2006–13), for instance, Dexter Morgan is a serial killer whose one redeeming quality is that he has been trained by his stepfather to kill only other murderers (though by the end of the series he has also killed innocents, albeit inadvertently). These two definitions include many different character-types under the same rubric, but for the purposes of this chapter, the common feature of both definitions is that the antihero is a type of protagonist who defies or otherwise does not evince values that have been traditionally ascribed to heroic protagonists. Both types, as Victor Brombert notes, critique established heroic constructs, and thus such characters draw audience acclamation and disapprobation.[17]

Antiheroes have been identified in Western culture as early as ancient Greece in the *Iliad*'s Thersites,[18] in the Middle Ages,[19] and in the modern period in literature, in film, and on television.[20] On the whole, though, antiheroism has been seen primarily as a modern phenomenon; the term was first used in the eighteenth century, and it became popular in texts from the nineteenth century onward. This rise in popularity has been associated with feelings of the powerlessness of the individual brought on by industrial and post-industrial society.[21] Antiheroes' surges into the popular consciousness tend to coincide with historical moments of great socio-political upheaval. For instance, the resignation of United States President Richard Nixon after the Watergate scandal of 1974, coupled with the trauma of the Vietnam War, which ended in 1977, made gritty antiheroes popular in comic books, such as the Punisher (created in 1974), Frank Miller's version of Batman in *Batman: The Dark Knight Returns* (published in 1986), and Deadpool (created in 1991). These antiheroes embodied the disillusionment of many with American politics and the difficulty, if not impossibility, of determining morally correct values; heroes in the traditional mold who never killed and always did the right thing were quaint relics of a bygone era.[22]

Like the events of the 1970s, the series of post-millennial catastrophes, and 9/11 in particular, were moments of intense cultural stress and so brought on a spate of antiheroes.[23] Though post-9/11 antiheroism has often been associated with televisual texts, Wetmore makes the case for film as well: "heroic human qualities cannot and will not save the day or defeat the evil [in post-9/11 horror films]."[24] Before this point, films set in antiquity produced in the 1950s through the 1980s featured characters who fit a more traditional heroic mold: "men could be genuine heroes in the ancient past, a past where – so the reasoning went – there weren't as many ambiguities."[25] Joanna Paul qualifies this, arguing that

> [e]ven though some of the complexities may be ironed out, it is shortsighted to see cinematic heroism as concerned only with positive models of behavior; instead, heroes such as Spartacus, Ben-Hur, and Maximus are equipped with both positive qualities and failings, facing challenges as well as achieving great success.[26]

This description of ancient heroes on screen as complex and flawed human beings is an important qualification, but such characters do not dismiss mythical thinking, as the antiheroes of the three films under consideration do.

At the same time, rejecting mythical thinking is not confined to the post-9/11 media landscape; it is an intensification of a trend already apparent in many antiquity-set media products before 2001. An example relevant to this argument is Frank Miller's comic-book series *300*, published in 1998, which retold the story of the battle of Thermopylae. In it, Miller has his protagonists, King Leonidas and his 300 bodyguards, reject the "mysticism" of both the enemy Persians, who worship their king Xerxes as a god, and the Spartan elders at home, who are in the Persians' pocket and seek to prevent our heroes from marching to Thermopylae through manipulating an oracle. The depiction of the Persians as enemies has a long history in Western culture,[27] but Miller's particular provocation in the late 1990s was the 1990–1 Gulf War. That conflict resulted in his alterations to previous iterations of the Thermopylae narrative, including Rudolph

Maté's 1962 film *The 300 Spartans*, which Miller has cited as a major influence.[28] This same characterization of the Spartans' antagonists as aligned with mythical thinking appears even more prominently in Snyder's cinematic adaptation of Miller's work, also titled *300*, a subject that is treated in much further detail below. The anti-mythical stances of Stone's *Alexander*, Snyder's *300*, and Leterrier's *Clash* do not emerge *ex nihilo* but rather develop from longstanding cultural interfaces with classical antiquity. They are intensifications of earlier trends to retrofit the ancient world to the exigencies of the modern world, strengthened by the crisis of identity brought on by 9/11.[29]

## OLIVER STONE'S *ALEXANDER* (2004)

Ancient accounts of Alexander the Great's life highlight the central role that Greek myth played throughout his life, beginning from his birth with his descent from the heroes Heracles and Aeacus, and continuing through his death by drinking from "Heracles' cup."[30] In his 1956 cinematic take on the life of the late-fourth-century BC Macedonian conqueror, *Alexander the Great*, director Robert Rossen used Alexander's enmeshment in myth as an important part of his characterization. More than half a century passed before director Oliver Stone attempted his own version with the 2004 *Alexander*, in which Alexander's destructive relationship with myth exposes the problematic nature of that man's heroic identity at the same time as it destabilizes the audience.

Rossen's Alexander is imbricated in Greek myth from the opening and closing shots, which feature an image of the Macedonian conqueror as the hero Heracles wearing the Nemean lionskin.[31] This was derived from the designs on coins minted during Alexander's and his successors' reigns, which promoted his genealogical connection to Heracles. From the moment that Rossen's Alexander is born, characters discuss the possibility of his divine parentage. His mother Olympias parallels him with the Trojan War hero Achilles: "Achilles, too, was born of a god." Indeed, Achilles becomes the primary mythical reference point for Alexander throughout the film. As in Plutarch's account,[32] Rossen's Alexander sleeps with a copy of the *Iliad* under his pillow, and, after reading aloud a scene from Lang, Leaf, and Myers' 1892 translation of the *Iliad*, Alexander tells his teacher Aristotle that he, like the Trojan War hero, will have a short but glorious life. Aristotle does not respond to this declaration, but instead gives a look that may be read as sadness but also approval that Alexander has assimilated himself so thoroughly to myth.

Aristotle's silent sentiment is underscored in the next scene, in which the royal youth of Macedonia are training both physically and intellectually. Over a heroic training montage of Macedonians practicing for battle against the backdrop of famous classical statuary with trumpets braying in background, Aristotle delivers his lesson: "We Greeks are the chosen, the elect. Our culture is the best, our civilization the best, our men the best. All others are barbarians, and it's our moral duty to conquer them, enslave them, and if necessary destroy them!" This chauvinistic stance is not questioned in the film; in his conquest Alexander does desire to combine East and West, but the audience never doubts that this should happen because the Persian empire has become ripe for destruction. *Alexander the Great*'s attitude toward East and West results from the production's historical context during the Cold War, in which films about the ancient world tended to depict ancient Greeks in unambiguously positive terms as proto-Americans, and Easterners, especially Persians, in negative terms as proto-Russians.[33] Rossen's Aristotle then casts the aforementioned Greek moral superiority in terms of mythical thinking: "The gods of the Greeks are made in the image of man. Not men with birds' heads and bulls with lions' heads, but men who can be understood and felt." With these words, *Alexander the Great* aligns the Western tradition of anthropomorphism with Alexander's parallels with figures from Greek myth. In the second half of the film, Alexander calls himself "the son of God," and although this is criticized by some of his close confidants, the modern audience is meant to think that Rossen's Alexander is a Christ figure who fails in his mission to conquer the world, not because the Greek myths have deluded him, but because he "is an idealist misunderstood by his contemporaries."[34]

Stone's Alexander is similarly obsessed with Greek myth. Unlike Rossen's film, however, Stone's version plays up the darker aspects of many of the myths, which in the end consume and destroy the Macedonian conqueror. Alexander's intense early interest in figures from myth is revealed in a scene that parallels the education scene in *Alexander the Great*. When the Athenian polymath condemns Achilles for being excessive in his emotions, Alexander defends myths: "it's these myths that lead us forward to the greatest glory. Why is it wrong to act on them?" Aristotle equates these myths with "foolish passions" and the Persian empire:

> The oriental races are known for their barbarity and their slavish devotion to their senses.... Excess in all things is the undoing of men. That is why we Greeks are superior. We practice control of our senses, moderation – we hope!

Figure 13.1 In Oliver Stone's *Alexander* (2004), Alexander, dressed as Heracles, prepares to drink from the cup that will kill him. Warner Bros.

By this reckoning, all myth, including and especially Greek myth, is potentially dangerous when taken literally, as Alexander finds out to his detriment later in the film.

While Rossen's film focalizes Alexander through Achilles, *Alexander* uses Heracles as its primary mythic reference point. Ptolemy describes Alexander's foray into India as "some remorseless and crazed quest to imitate the glory of Heracles," and Alexander claims during his Asian expedition that he has surpassed the hero: "I've achieved more in my years. Traveled as far – probably farther." Alexander even goes so far as to dress like Heracles at the party where he meets his end. The party is attended by Alexander's generals costumed as figures from Greek myth: Dionysus, Apollo, Hermes, and others are in attendance.[35] As in the opening shot of *Alexander the Great*, Alexander himself is dressed as his ancestor Heracles, complete with lionskin cowl (Figure 13.1). Heracles, killing the multi-headed Hydra with his club, also appears in the silver designs embossed around the circumference of his cup. Alexander toasts the party, "To the gods!" and then glances into his cup and sees his mother Olympias on the surface of the red wine, her face framed by hissing snakes. Olympias has become Medusa, the monster of myth whose beheading at the hands of the hero Perseus might have been familiar to Stone's audience from such popular incarnations as Desmond Davis' 1981 version of *Clash of the Titans*. But whereas Perseus triumphs over Medusa, killing the monster and using her petrifying gaze to defeat antagonists, Alexander is overcome by her. He adds, "And to the myths!" downs the cup's contents, collapses, and dies soon after. The jump cut to the echoing caverns of Macedonia along with the camera's lingering gaze on one of its terrifying paintings, Medea killing her children, reassert the theme of myth in Stone's film: Alexander was inspired, consumed, and ultimately destroyed by the Greek myths.

## ZACK SNYDER'S *300* (2007)

In 480 BC the battle of Thermopylae was a tactical loss for the Greek hoplites, who were overwhelmed and slaughtered to a man by the invading Persians, but nevertheless the episode became immensely popular in Western culture afterward. The fifth-century BC historian Herodotus' rendition of the battle in the seventh book of his *Histories* is one of the best-known of the ancient accounts and contains mythical thinking, primarily concerning the important role of religious thought in Greek society and the consequences it had on the conduct of the Persian Wars. *The 300 Spartans* also includes this aspect, painting Leonidas and his fellow Spartans as respectful of religion at the same time as they are eager to defend Greece. In 2007's *300*, by contrast, the renegade Leonidas rejects the religious ideas that his predecessor had embraced, reflecting a suspicion of mythical thinking after 9/11.

Dialogue in the final scene of *300* makes clear the film's demonization of mythical thinking. As the combined Greek forces prepare to face the Persians once again in the battle of Plataea, the Spartan hoplite Dilios, who has also been the narrator of the entire film, whips up the troops' enthusiasm by describing Greece as "the world's one hope for reason and justice" that will "rescue a world from mysticism and tyranny." Dilios' rhetoric here is similar to that of Aristotle in Rossen's *Alexander the Great* and Stone's *Alexander*: reason (equated with cognitive thinking; "justice" = democracy) is cognitive and positive, while mysticism (equated with mythical thinking) is non-cognitive ("passion" according to Stone's Aristotle) and destructive.

This dichotomy plays out near the beginning of the film, when Leonidas asks the ephors, Sparta's elders, for permission to march in defense of Sparta and secure Thermopylae against the Persian invasion. As Leonidas goes to meet the ephors, Dilios depicts them as villains, "priests to the old gods" who are "inbred swine" and "remnants of a senseless tradition," a description reinforced by their dwelling, which looks like a stereotypical Greek temple isolated from the rest of Sparta atop the outcropping. Although Leonidas presents a rational plan to stop the Persian advance and urges the ephors to use their "reason," they insist on consulting an oracle, who goes into a trance and speaks in tongues. One of the ephors "translates" these utterances into mythical terms: "Pray to the winds. Sparta will fall. All Greece will fall. Trust not in men. Honor the gods. Honor the Carneia." The ephors thus forbid Leonidas from going forward with his plan, and after the Spartan king leaves in defeat, a Persian ambassador visits the ephors to give them gold in exchange for their support of Xerxes. The implication is that the ephors' mythical philosophy was a ruse, or at any rate an excuse, designed to prevent Leonidas from opposing the Persian conquest of Greece.

The ephors' corrupt mysticism is paralleled by the main antagonists of *300*, the invading Persian army. Although there are several mystical aspects to the Spartans' foes, two examples will be the focus here, neither of which appears in the comic-book source material; they emphasize the post-9/11 film's aim to heighten the equation of the Persians with mythical thinking. In a battle scene that finds the Spartans still victorious in beating back Xerxes' soldiers, Dilios characterizes the Persians as relying on mysticism instead of military might: "When muscle failed, they turned to their magic." As he says this, one of the army's contingents hurls small vases that explode upon impact, showering sparks and shrapnel. That these figures are clad in what can only be described as chainmail burkas solidifies the interpretation of an audience primed to interpret the film as a comment on post-9/11: the contingent is a barely concealed metaphor for contemporary Middle Eastern terrorists.[36] When the Greek traitor Ephialtes enters Xerxes' tent to inform him how to defeat the Greek forces at Thermopylae, he encounters an orgy of odd-looking figures in the firelight. The participants include a woman with scarred face, a multiple amputee bedecked with golden jewelry, and, most strangely of all, a goat-headed musician. This last figure recalls the hybrid creatures of Greek myth, particularly Pan, a god with goat horns, hooves, and a tail, who makes an important appearance after the earlier battle of Marathon in Herodotus' *Histories* (6.106). Given the Christian inflection of Western popular culture, perhaps the more immediate association for modern audiences is with Baphomet, familiar from the Tarot card depiction of Satan, but whether the reception is Christian or classical, the connection remains in the mythical realm.

In *300*'s cinematic predecessor and the inspiration for Miller's comic-book series, *The 300 Spartans*, the ephors similarly object to Leonidas' proposal to defend Thermopylae on the grounds that they must observe the approaching festival. The king disagrees with them, but not because he rejects mysticism as his *300* counterpart does; rather, he thinks that the larger notion of a united Greece is more important. The value he places on religion is evident in his response to the Athenian statesman Themistocles, who accuses the Spartans of using religion to justify their less-than-stellar showing at Thermopylae. "With the gods behind you, you can be far more irresponsible," he remarks wryly, to which the Spartan king replies, "Themistocles, we invoked divine help coming here. This is no time for impious remarks."

Whereas *300*'s Leonidas regards the ephors' use and manipulation of the Spartan oracle as reprehensible, the Leonidas of *The 300 Spartans* views oracular wisdom positively as a reinforcement of heroic action. The Greek seer Megistias, who appears in Herodotus' account of the battle in his *Histories* but not in *300*, gives favorable omens for the battle of Thermopylae that Leonidas receives with a smile: "As always, Megistias, your omens speak truthfully."[37] Leonidas' wife Gorgo relates that she consulted Megistias about their future and that the seer reported that he divined "wonderful good fortune for both" of them in a lamb's entrails. Leonidas smiles and embraces her happily, realizing that the prophet's words reinforce his own heroic interpretation of the Delphic oracle: that he must march in defense of Sparta and die.

## LOUIS LETERRIER'S *CLASH OF THE TITANS* (2010)

In the Louis Leterrier-helmed 2010 reboot of *Clash of the Titans*, gods and humans have an uneasy relationship. Human resistance to Olympus has apparently been going on for a while by the time the film's narrative begins; the prologue tells us that King Acrisius of Argos had led an army against the gods, and Zeus punished him for it by taking his shape and sleeping with his wife Danaë and impregnating her with Perseus. In the next generation of the conflict, King Cepheus and Queen Cassiopeia of Argos order their soldiers to dismantle the statue of Zeus on Paxos. The motives of Acrisius and the Argive monarchs seem to be rooted in arrogance more than anything, but *Clash* does not make it clear exactly why mortals desire to overthrow the gods, although their haughty disregard of Perseus' family's lives near the beginning of the film provides some rationalization for it. Leterrier's Perseus thus has all the more reason to side with mortals against the gods, especially Hades, whose Furies killed Perseus' adoptive family and who wants to destroy the city of Argos.

Throughout the film, Perseus identifies with his human half over his divine half, preferring to rely on the knowledge and help of his mortal allies rather than the gods' assistance. Draco, captain of the Argos guard, teaches him how to fight with a sword; Ozal and Kucuk, hunters who join the quest to find Medusa, give him a shield whose reflective surface Perseus uses to decapitate the Gorgon; and Io, a human made immortal by the gods, guides Perseus throughout the journey. Perseus refuses the help offered by the gods except in four instances: he uses a coin that Zeus gives him in order to summon Charon to cross the River Styx; he uses their sword in battle against the Hades-empowered Calibos; he rides the winged horse Pegasus to defeat another of Hades' minions, the Kraken; and he uses Zeus' thunderbolt to send Hades back to the Underworld. Such instances may be excused as necessary deviations from the mortal to the mythical to solve problems posed by the supernatural. Furthermore, these actions ultimately privilege "the service of humankind rather than . . . imposing hierarchy and power over it,"[38] which is a mode characteristic of modern democratic societies but not ancient Greece. The final scene has Perseus and his father-god reconcile, though the status quo has forever changed, symbolically represented by the location at the feet of the monumental Zeus statue, the only part remaining from the earlier desecration. Perseus refuses to become a god and instead wants to lead mortals, and Zeus accedes, advising, "Be good to them. Be better than we were," implying that the gods' time has passed.[39] *Clash* replaces the mythical with the human.

By contrast, in Desmond Davis' 1981 *Clash of the Titans*, of which Leterrier's version is a "more realistic" remake according to screenwriter Travis Beacham,[40] Perseus accepts the help of his divine family. Early on, Perseus gratefully receives a helmet and mechanical owl from Athena, a sword from Aphrodite, and a shield from Hera, which is more or less in line with the gifts and guidance he receives from Athena, Hera, and the Nymphs in many of the ancient Greek versions.[41] As in Leterrier's version, a divine force, this time the goddess Thetis, motivates the mortal villain Calibos, but this never occasions any retribution from the mortal sphere as it does in the 2010 *Clash*, with Perseus using a thunderbolt against Hades.

By contrast, Leterrier's Perseus accepts the divine gifts only with the encouragement of the former mortal Io. "Perseus, you're not just part man, part god; you're the best of both," she says, a comment that directs the audience to think about Perseus as a multicultural hero who spans the gap between the god and human "races."[42] This multiculturalism is also apparent in Perseus' embrace of the Djinn, a nation of sorcerers who save him and his companions from gigantic scorpions. Though they have been rescued from certain death, the soldiers from Argos are skeptical of the Djinn's intentions. Solon's description

Figure 13.2 Sheikh Suleiman's magic saves Perseus and his companions from certain death in *Clash of the Titans* (2010). Warner Bros.

dehumanizes them: "They aren't human, not anymore. Desert conjurers, cut-throats." The Djinn, whose name is an Arabic word for supernatural beings in the Quran, are swathed in layers of loose-fitting clothing and wear turbans. For Western audiences these signifiers not-so-subtly suggest an interpretation of the Djinn as Middle Easterners. But rather than reject the Djinn, as his companions from Argos would prefer, Perseus allies with them. The Djinn who chooses to help in the fight against Medusa, named "Sheikh Suleiman," turns out to be crucial to the success of the enterprise (Figure 13.2).[43] Medusa is unable to petrify Suleiman because he is not human (anymore, at least), and he activates a blue organ in his chest that detonates, killing him and severely wounding her. This, like the sorcerers in *300*, again connects the Djinn with (stereotypes of) the Middle East, with terrorist methods of attack,[44] but *Clash* advocates for alliance rather than the binary "clash of civilizations" that was so common in post-9/11 rhetoric.[45] Even though the magical nature of the Djinn conflicts with *Clash*'s desire to move away from the mythical, in the film's logic Suleiman is necessary to defeat a supernatural foe, and once that purpose is served, the Djinn are no longer part of the narrative.

## CONCLUSION

The events of 9/11 and their turbulent aftermath caused Americans to reassess their identities. A major outcome of this interrogation was a move toward traditional conceptions of gender, at least in certain arenas of popular culture. *Alexander*, *300*, and *Clash of the Titans* had a very different response: rather than return to the ideology of the 1950s, these films rejected the mythical thinking of ancient

Greek culture as instantiated in cinema of the mid-twentieth century. Post-9/11, Alexander, Leonidas, and Perseus become antiheroes who discard the behavior of their earlier counterparts and distance themselves from the supernatural in all its forms. Through their opposition to the mythical paradigm, these ancient heroes created new relationships to the legacy of ancient Greece with American identities in a post-9/11 world.

## NOTES

I would like to thank Stacie Raucci and Antony Augoustakis for editing this volume as well as for organizing the conference at Delphi in the summer of 2015 from which this chapter originated. Their comments helped improved my ideas and writing considerably. Thanks also to Michael Heyes for reading and commenting on an earlier draft.

1. On the significance of the destruction of this statue, see further Curley in this volume. He links this event to the fragmentation of the monomyth in recent screen texts; this is parallel to this chapter's analysis of how Leterrier's film deconstructs classical antiquity.
2. Suvin (1979: 7) is defining science fiction. While "myths," "magic," and "religion" are distinct phenomena in ancient Greek culture, they are often rendered as an indistinguishable mass in popular culture's depiction of them.
3. Landrum (2015: 95).
4. Faludi (2007: 9).
5. Faludi (2007: 3–4).
6. Wetmore (2012: 198) similarly suggests that the post-9/11 remakes of 1980s horror films such as *Friday the 13th* (2009) and *A Nightmare on Elm Street* (2010) mediate between the "strong" America of the Reaganite 1980s and the "weakened" post-9/11 America.
7. On the 300 movies, see further Llewellyn-Jones in this volume.
8. On the classical roots of the United States, see, for instance, Winterer (2002).
9. The back cover of Nisbet's 2006 book (2nd edn 2008) claims that the "myths and heroes [of ancient Greece] lie at the heart of our [i.e. the Western] shared sense of self." Murnaghan's 2011 article attests to the pervasiveness of Greek myth in children's literature, education, and popular culture.
10. Pollard (2009: 203–6).
11. Wetmore (2012: 24).
12. McAuley (2016a, 2016b, forthcoming); Gardner in this volume.
13. See further Strong in this volume.
14. Nisbet has argued that the ancient Greece of cinema has mirrored the Rome of cinema. The myths of ancient Greece, however "altered" in

their *mise-en-scène* and/or plotlines by "contamination by themes and motifs from Roman movies" (2006: 16), are prominent in recent media, and therefore audiences are much more likely to identify Greece as a source of myth than Rome, whose myths, such as that of Romulus and Remus, were not represented on screen in the first decade of the twenty-first century.

15 On antiheroism, see also Curley and McAuley in this volume.
16 Vaage (2016) studies the psychology of antiheroes on television.
17 Brombert (1999). Vaage (2016: xv): "I will argue that the intended response is not only to like the antihero, but also, at least ultimately, to dislike him too."
18 Papaioannou (2007: 146 n. 310).
19 See the essays in Cartlidge (2012).
20 Literature: Brombert (1999) on literary antiheroes from 1830 to 1980; film: Marshall (2003); television: Vaage (2016).
21 In his study of the antihero in American fiction, Woolf (1976: 257–8) argued that "[t]he individual was revealed as powerless, buffeted by forces too massive, too nightmarish," although he is not specific about what these forces might be.
22 Klock (2002: 80) disparages these "poorly written, violent antiheroes, who looked like, or actually used to be conceived as, villains." He links the proliferation of antiheroes in the late 1980s and early 1990s to the success of Miller's *Batman: The Dark Knight Returns* series and Alan Moore's *Watchmen* (1987) series, rather than to a larger cultural reaction.
23 Faludi's description of the perception that post-9/11 American culture was emasculated and weak intersects with the arguments made by scholars about the rise of antiheroes. Amanda Lotz (2014) traces antiheroes on television in the second decade of the twenty-first century to a crisis in masculinity. Landrum (2015: 95) similarly attributes the phenomenon to "a broken relationship between masculinity and the social bond of American culture [post-9/11]."
24 Wetmore (2012: 3). It is important to note that the reaction to 9/11 intensified the popularity of antiheroes; as noted above, there were many antiheroes on the market already, including what some consider to be the forerunner of early twenty-first-century male antiheroes, Tony Soprano in HBO's *The Sopranos* (1999–2007).
25 Trice and Holland (2001: 110).
26 Paul (2010: 27). Cf. Bundrick (2009: 92), who, using the same examples as Paul, argues that they fit into the "conventional action hero" configuration.
27 See, for instance, Tomasso (2011), with further references.
28 George (2003: 65).
29 Tomasso (2015a) argues that the television series *Battlestar Galactica* (2005–9) similarly revamps classical antiquity in response to 9/11.

30 Plutarch, *Life of Alexander* 2, 75.
31 See further discussion in Shahabudin (2010: 100–1).
32 Plutarch, *Life of Alexander* 8.
33 See, for an example, Blanshard and Shahabudin (2011: 105–7)
34 Shahabudin (2010: 112).
35 See Bundrick (2009: 90) on the gods, particularly Dionysus, at this party.
36 For post-9/11 interpretations of the film, see, for instance, Hassler-Forest (2010) and Kovacs (2013).
37 Megistias appears in Herodotus, *Histories* 7.219, 221, and 228.
38 Green (2013: 78).
39 See further Tomasso (2015b) and Gordon (2017) on deicide in popular culture.
40 http://movieweb.com/travis-beacham-penning-a-clash-of-the-titans-remake.
41 Apollodorus, *Library* 2.4.2.
42 Green (2013: 78) notes this in the context of the film's identity politics.
43 "Sheikh" is an honorific title in Arabic, but for Western audiences it evokes stereotypical Middle Eastern-ness; see e.g. Shaheen (2001: 19–22). Michael Heyes points out to me that "Suleiman" might be a variant of the Arabic transliteration of "Solomon" (Sulayman), known in both the Islamic and Hebrew traditions for his magic according to Knappert (1993: 262), and Mareike Koertner informs me that Sulayman could control djinn (Quran 34:12).
44 Although neither the film nor extra-filmic materials make the connection, a "real-world" analogy was the efforts of the Multi-National Force – Iraq, i.e. the American-led coalition force, to train the Iraqi army beginning in 2005. Thanks to Meredith Safran for making this suggestion at the conference.
45 O'Hagan (2004: 33).

# 14 Making Modern (Anti) Heroes, the Ancient Way

Alex McAuley

A noteworthy figure, be they famous or infamous, has just died. The death could have been sudden or long expected, but the same wave of public grief is channeled through various media, followed by another wave of tributes to the deceased, some opportunistic, some genuine. Mourning and uncertainty follow, as the swells of rumor and hearsay rise and fall in the days and weeks after the death. While memorials may be held in private, the public remains unsettled with the need not only for resolution of the deceased's life, but also for some clarification of the meaning of their passage through this world. A very public commemoration follows in due course, one woven by a talented writer and presented by a talented actor, heightened by clever staging and identifiable props. In the process, the life of the deceased is exhibited not just as a biography of their achievements, but also as an example to society of virtue – or vice. With this, what was once private is thrust authoritatively into the public, and the deceased's life enters the realm of common memory. A person is remembered, a lesson is learned, and in this public process, individuals are elevated into the realm of heroes – or indeed antiheroes, as their achievements merit.

What I have just described is a process with which we are intimately familiar in the celebrity culture of the twenty-first century thanks to the soaring popularity of Hollywood biopics, but this mechanism was equally visible in the traditions of mourning and public commemoration that followed the death of an elite man (and in some cases, woman) in the Roman Republic. In the Roman case, public commemoration of the death of such a noble was not given a sense of closure until the *laudatio funebris* ("the funeral oration") took place in the Roman forum for all to see.[1] This complex piece of oratory mixed moralistic instruction with an account of the deceased's career, in the process memorializing them as well as edifying the public. In the Hollywood case, the same ancient mechanism works through the decidedly modern medium of the biopic: after the death of a celebrity of any stripe, public mourning and private commemoration inevitably follow, but it has become almost a cliché that they should also be the subject of a biopic in fairly short order. These biopics, like the Roman *laudationes*, make the dead's life into a sort of morality drama, leading the audience to either praise or vilify them in different measures.[2] In both processes, societies ancient and modern create their heroes and antiheroes, both of which are equal objects of fascination.

"The relationship between a hero and an ordinary dead person," Gunnel Ekroth wrote in 2007, "lies in the relationship with the living."[3] Although this was in the context of her study on local heroes in the ancient Greek world, her observation is equally relevant to contemporary society. While the preceding contributions to this volume have examined how ancient heroes and their foils have been invented and reinvented by the modern minds that shape their projections onto the silver or small screen, it would seem salutary, by way of conclusion, to instead turn our attention in the opposite direction and consider how modern heroes are made and depicted with what I argue is a mechanism remarkably similar to the ancient one of the *laudatio funebris*. To do so, I shall examine the nuanced mixture of praise and blame inherent in this form of public eulogy in Rome, before turning to an overview of how the same process works through the modern medium of the biopic.[4] To see how, like its ancient counterpart, the biopic transforms the dead into heroes we shall use the fascinating case of the death and afterlife of Steve Jobs, founder of Apple, a figure as renowned as he was divisive. But not all subjects of biopics are heroic, and to consider the twenty-first-century fascination with antiheroism we shall examine some instances in which a film's subject is by no means praiseworthy, but nonetheless captivating. Be they contemporary heroes or antiheroes, the same mechanics of composition are at work in weaving the filmic narrative of their lives and achievements; the difference between the two, as we shall explore, lies only in our judgment of them. This chapter is not meant to be a heavy-handed direct equivalence of two media that, it can only be admitted, are vastly different, but there may be some insight to be gained from the similarities and differences in their respective politics of composition and reception. Before turning to these, however, we must first consider how lessons of virtue and vice were distilled from the life of ancient Roman notables through the elaborate public performance of their funerary tribute.

## MORE THAN A EULOGY: THE ROMAN *LAUDATIO FUNEBRIS*

In the preface to his digression on happiness and fortune in the seventh book of his *Natural History*, Pliny the Elder writes that no man can be considered truly lucky or great without a final consideration of the good and bad he experienced over the course of his lifetime, famously concluding "Alas what a vain and silly task it is, that the number of days in one's life is counted, when it is rather their weight that should be sought."[5] According to this first-century AD polymath, then, it is only with the conclusion of death that we can reflect meaningfully on one's life, and in the process of seeing the seeds of misfortune in one's fortune and vice versa, conclude whether they were lucky, virtuous, or neither. Providing this synoptic view of one's life as a whole, and glimpsing certain lessons and judgments through this wide lens, is precisely the function of the *laudatio funebris* in Roman society – and its similarities with contemporary biopics already become apparent from such a definition.

Accordingly, the *laudatio funebris* – translated literally, though somewhat minimally, as "funerary speech" – was the public commemoration of a deceased member of the Roman elite proclaimed as the climax of their funeral. The speech was a fundamentally public affair, given from the hallowed platform of the *rostra* in the Roman forum, the most important and highly visible stage of Roman politics, in front of the public audience that had assembled for the event.[6] The oration itself served to include these listeners, otherwise unrelated to the deceased, in the process of remembrance and lamentation through commemoration of the deceased individual and their – usually his – family.[7] The *laudatio* came at the climax of the *pompa funebris*, the funeral procession, in which the body of the deceased was placed on a bier and paraded through the city and into the forum, the beating heart of Roman civic life. The bier itself was only one part of a long and elaborate procession: it was preceded by hired actors who wore the funeral masks (*imagines*) of the deceased's ancestors and the insignia of the offices these illustrious forebears had held in life, as well as by their living relatives.[8] Along the way, mourners, musicians, and other members of the public would join the procession as it wound its way through the city of Rome and led to the forum. Polybius, in a detailed account of the performance of such aristocratic funerals (6.53.1–3), relates what follows next:

> Whenever any illustrious man dies, he is carried at his funeral into the forum to the so-called rostra, sometimes conspicuous in an upright posture and more rarely reclined. Here with all the people standing round, a grown-up son ... or if not some other relative mounts the rostra and discourses on the virtues and successful achievements of the dead during his lifetime. As a consequence the multitude and not only those who had a part in these achievements, but those also who had none, when the facts are recalled to their minds and brought before their eyes, are moved to such sympathy that the loss seems to be not confined to the mourners, but a public one affecting the whole people.[9]

There are two observations to be made from this account that will inform our subsequent discussion of contemporary biopics. First, it is only with the *laudatio*, this public account of the person's virtue and deeds, that the memory of the deceased and their fame are made public; the speech thrusts all of this – memory as well as mourning – into the public sphere, and thus the loss is felt by a far larger audience. The second point is all too easily overlooked: Polybius notes that the speech's visual component is of equal importance with its auditory impact. The audience sees as well as hears the accomplishments of the deceased, and the process of commemoration is fundamentally visual and performative, rather than purely oratorical and literary.

The Roman rhetorician Quintilian, writing in the late first century AD, gives us an outline of how this oration should be structured that, from our current perspective, would seem to apply equally well to biopic screenplay adaptations.[10] Accordingly, some mention of the time preceding the man's life and his family circumstances ought to be made first in order to set the stage, along with any circumstances that would have shaped his formative years.[11] Some glimpses of his future achievements should be found in his early life or career, and with all of this as preface the orator can then turn to the man's deeds as an adult; the man's later fame should be linked to this context in order to demonstrate the scale of his accomplishments.[12] But the ancients took care not to attribute all of the deceased's deeds entirely to their own agency, or indeed to their own greatness of character. Quintilian reminds these orators that the person's good fortune should be brought to the fore, along with any circumstances of which they took advantage. Cicero also elaborated this approach, writing that it demonstrated that the deceased made good use of his natural talents and gifts – health, beauty, strength, wealth, friends, and the like.[13] The source of admiration is not simply the possession of these qualities, but their gainful use. Negative experiences should not be glossed over or omitted, as both Quintilian and Cicero stress the need for the person's weaknesses to be mentioned in order to demonstrate how they were overcome. Episodes of loss or adversity should be identified and brought to the fore, and the deceased must be shown to have weathered these with patience and equanimity.

But the audience of this speech must, in the end, be entertained as well as edified. The ancient rhetoricians remind us that audiences enjoy hearing of things that the man was the first or only person to do, and some of his particularly thrilling accomplishments should be chosen as illustrative examples of his overall character.[14] If the truth must be stretched a bit in the process, so be it: Quintilian suggests that the orator should not hesitate to deviate from the literal meaning of words in order to cast the deceased in a more glowing light by means of embellishment and amplification.[15] This, of course, is how novelty is created. Ultimately, though, we must remember that all of this elaborate ornamentation served not only to commemorate the dead, but also to instruct the living – as Ralph Covino put it, "to celebrate and to teach virtue, and to couple praise with admonition in a public setting."[16] The ancients were eminently aware of this publicly didactic function, as Polybius (6.53.9) writes of these funeral speeches that "there could not easily be a more ennobling spectacle for a young man who aspires to fame in virtue."

But there is a negative side to such public embellishment, of which the ancients were equally wary. Cicero laments that funeral speeches all too often pass off praise as oratory, and Livy warns that such amplification of achievements can easily cross into outright fabrication.[17] The line between fact and fiction becomes easily blurred in such panegyric as the highly competitive realm of Roman cultural memory led orators to take ever greater creative license. Livy captures this process aptly, as he laments "I believe that our memory has been corrupted by praise at funerals and false inscriptions on statues, as each family drags the fame of achievements and honors toward itself with fallacious lies."[18] Memory and truth, then as now, did not have a requisite relationship with one another; in other words, such speeches must only be *based* on a true story.

## THE RESURGENT BIOPIC

I have elaborated on the structure and character of the *laudatio funebris* at such length because this selective emplotment, dramatization, and embellishment of one's life is precisely what the contemporary biopic does through the medium of film instead of forensic oratory. Both are formulaic, both are performative, and both use the same tricks in their arsenal to link the individual to collective history. This predictable character of biopics is one of the aspects of the genre that has drawn the most criticism – but the formula still works. This is not to say, however, that there are not differences between the two. In the twenty-first century, communal consensus as achieved in Rome is perhaps not as important as exposure, and since the advent of film and television our media have become increasingly dominated by the visual.[19] Given the ever-expanding cultural footprint of Hollywood, it comes as little surprise that film would play such an instrumental role in the composition and dissemination of what we consider to be heroic; if Hollywood can make ordinary individuals into stars, it follows logically that they could make ordinary subjects into heroes.

The genre most often associated with the creation of heroism is, of course, the biopic – a type of film caught awkwardly between fiction and history that, following a recent definition, "narrates, exhibits, and celebrates the life of a subject in order to demonstrate, investigate, or question his or her importance in the world."[20] George Custen in 2000 noted that Hollywood, perhaps not unlike the Romans, held that change occurred not because of social or economic unrest, but because of uniquely gifted individuals who must, by definition, be famous in society.[21] Hollywood biopics, he further notes, reinforce and communicate public "values" in the same way as the *laudationes*.[22] And just as in a funeral oration, the audience of a biopic knows the ending: the entire story is about the seed of the future contained in the past, and this recreation occurs in what the audience knows is a fictive, performative setting.[23] Biopics follow a similar narrative trajectory: some account of background and context is given, and the film then selectively emplots certain important episodes in the figure's life that either produce or reveal their noteworthy character traits. Defining moments of trial or triumph are brought forward, precisely as Cicero and Quintilian suggest. The turns of phrase, habits, or moments of idiosyncrasy that fascinated ancient biographers such as Plutarch are given equal importance with historical events of vast consequence, and all of this serves to narrate, exhibit, and celebrate the life of the subject in both its private and public spheres.

Dennis Bingham summed up the purpose of the genre beautifully in 2010 when he wrote:

the appeal of the biopic lies in seeing an actual person, known mostly in public, transformed into a character ... the genre's charge is to enter the biographical subject into the pantheon of cultural mythology, and to show why he or she belongs there.[24]

All of this occurs in a society that values and idealizes individual achievement as a collective virtue. Again, this is almost precisely the same function served by the *laudatio funebris* – to make a person into a hero by thrusting them into the public consciousness through an embroidered, embellished vehicle. Like the *laudationes*, though, this cinematic embellishment gives rise to controversy: John Tibbets, who himself wrote a book on composer biopics, said in an interview that the biopic "is a mendacious genre that may have little to do with historical or biographical truth."[25] Selective emplotment and amplification concealed by the impression of realism blur the line between fiction and history in the service of narrative, precisely in the way that Cicero and Livy lamented.

The fruits of this creative process have drawn audiences to the cinema long before the recent resurgence in biographical films that met with financial success. "Classical" biopics dominated the box offices of the 1930s by telling the story of heroes of science and politics: Alexander Hamilton in 1931, Louis Pasteur in 1936, and Thomas Edison in 1939 and 1940, to name only a few.[26] Different concepts of fame and heroism came to prominence in the 1950s and 1960s, though, and as the "great man" narrative went stale during the post-war years, audiences were drawn toward other cinematic avenues. After a few decades in the critical and commercial doghouse, since the mid–1990s the Hollywood biopic has been back with a vengeance. What some have termed the "neoclassical revival" of the biopic began in earnest in the early 2000s, leading to a proliferation of films that tell the purportedly historical story of some larger-than-life figure – be they already well known or not. The box office and the awards circuit have taken note of this resurgence of the biopic; for substantiation of this, one need look no further than to the dominance of the genre among the Academy Award winners and nominees for 2014 and 2015, as well as their strong financial performance.[27]

Yet there is an interesting trend in the production of biopics that has been occurring with greater frequency since roughly the mid–1990s: Hollywood tends to be closing the chronological gap between a biopic and its subject to the point that many are becoming almost immediate post-mortem tributes that seem to serve a eulogizing function. In other words, a notable person dies, and immediately production of a biopic begins while their name is still fresh in the headlines. The biopic becomes the largest, grandest reflection on the person's life, even though they have barely been dead for a year or two. The biopic makes them into a cultural hero, and communicates *why* they should be held as such. Among such films, in no particular order, we can count *Nixon* by Oliver Stone, made in 1995 shortly after the subject's death in 1994, and the film *Ray* from 2004, starring Jamie Foxx and directed by Taylor Hackford, whose production began shortly before the musician's death in the same year. Others include Joaquin Phoenix's 2005 depiction of Johnny Cash in *Walk the Line*, following the singer's death in 2004, and the hugely successful *American Sniper*, released in 2014 after the murder of Chris Kyle on February 2, 2013.

The list goes on, but the motif remains the same: the proliferation of big-budget biopics shot almost immediately after the death of their subject makes it seem as if the film is becoming an almost obligatory form of tribute to the deceased notables of contemporary society. Not all biopics fit this mold, but the sheer volume of these eulogistic biopics is certainly striking. Equally noteworthy is Hollywood's increasing penchant for producing biographical films about subjects who are not dead; nor indeed are their public careers over – Edward Snowden, Mark Zuckerberg, and Jordan Belfort are the first to come to mind.[28] Yet the biopic as a post-mortem tribute is fascinating in no small part because it is only the *culmination* of a longer process of public grief and reflection. In order to examine the dynamics behind this process more closely, we shall pass from the theoretical to the practical by considering a case study of this process: the death and heroization of Steve Jobs, the founder of Apple.

## BUSINESSMAN TO RENAISSANCE MAN: THE (AFTER)LIFE OF STEVE JOBS

At around 3 pm on October 5, 2011, Steve Jobs succumbed to a relapse of the pancreatic cancer that had been plaguing him for years. The 24-hour news cycle, for a moment, stopped, and in the days and weeks that followed his death, the founder of Apple and tech magnate was thrust into the headlines and remained there for some time. Details of his private life, his personality, his character, and his passing were thrown into the public sphere by a variety of news outlets, and as more stories were broadcast, the legend of Steve Jobs began to emerge and swell. The sheer scale of public mourning was remarkable: he was given the cover of *Time* magazine for the eighth time in his life, Bloomberg's *Business Week* magazine published a commemorative, ad-free issue about him, and *The Daily Show* eulogy ended with Jon Stewart's oddly prophetic observation that "we're not done with you yet."

This continued apace in the months that followed: Apple created a tribute page that is still live at the time of writing (September 2017), to which over a million people have sent their thoughts, memories, and feelings about Steve Jobs.[29] In the storm of media coverage the word "hero" started to be bandied about with increasing frequency: the CEO of Google and notorious Apple antagonist Eric Schmidt revealed in a touching interview with *Bloomberg* that, despite their corporate competition, Steve Jobs was his personal hero.[30] Sean Parker, one of the founders of Napster and Facebook, admitted that his own career was inspired entirely by Jobs:

> More than ever, I wanted to tell Steve Jobs that, despite whatever he may have heard about me from our mutual friends and partners at the record labels, it was his life and work alone that had put me on this entrepreneurial path to begin with. At a time when America had lost its heroes, it was not until today that I lost mine: he was and will always be Steve Jobs.[31]

The tributes continued to pour in several months after his funeral. Even four years after his death, new stories continue to appear praising his heroism from a variety of different angles: an article in the *Financial Times* from June 12, 2015, elucidated the legacy of Steve Jobs as hero of an American civil rights movement, while *The Huffington Post* wrote a nostalgic tribute to him on the fourth anniversary of his death entitled "The Last Heroic Leader."[32] Steve Jobs even became something of a pop-culture icon in Japan as the hero of his own manga series, *Steves*, in which he and his homonymous colleagues are pitted against the forces of staid corporatism.

The film adaptation, of course, could not be far off the horizon of such public attention, and in 2013 the *pompa funebris* for Steve Jobs ended with the *laudatio* that is the film *Jobs*, directed by Joshua Michael Stern and starring Ashton Kutcher in the title role. Although Kutcher's portrayal of the Apple founder was acceptable to most critics, the creative direction was largely panned as being painfully predictable and superficial to the point that it was a decidedly un-iconic treatment of an iconic figure. But it is precisely the fact that this film is so stereotypical and formulaic that makes it an ideal case study of the composition of such biopics in light of the structural principles of the *laudationes* that we have encountered above. It seems that by 2013 critics and audiences alike were so attuned to the typical trajectory of the biopic that both could easily identify a lacklustre offering, as *Jobs* garnered only a score of 44/100 on *Metacritic* and was a box office flop that placed seventh overall on its opening weekend, only going on to gross $35.9 million worldwide. While Quintilian certainly encouraged orators to bend the truth somewhat in glorifying the achievements of the deceased, *Jobs* pushed this past the breaking point in a manner that alienated some of the principal stakeholders in the narrative. Steve Wozniak, Apple Inc.'s co-founder, refused to be involved in the project after being unable to make it all the way through an early draft of the screenplay because he "felt it was crap."[33] Bill Fernandez, a user interface designer who was the first employee of Apple Computer in 1977, stated in an interview that in the midst of seemingly endless fan fiction about Apple after the death of its founder, the 121-minute film is "the biggest, flashiest piece of fan fiction that there has been to date." He went on to say "that's part of why I don't want to see it ... because the whole thing is a work of fiction."[34]

By all accounts the film took a great deal of creative license in depicting the life of Steve Jobs, perhaps too much so for the faithful realism that buttresses most biopics, but the narrative strategies it employs align perfectly with the template of the ancient *laudatio*. The film opens with the moment of Jobs' triumph: his keynote lecture releasing the iPod in 2001, which represents his return to glory after his fall from corporate grace in 1985. The usual inspirational fluff about changing people's lives is spun, and then the film immediately cuts to him in Reed College in 1974. In the next five minutes of screen time the young Jobs enrolls in a calligraphy class, lies in order to seduce a young woman, tries acid, travels to India, and then promptly emerges to change the tech industry. The subsequent vignettes chosen – his moments of triumph, such as his first computer sale, his borrowed idea to market the home computer, his expansion of the company, the revolution of Apple II, and the iMac – are then recounted in glowing praise that would likely have made Quintilian blush, and made Livy feel eminently vindicated in his pessimism.

But just as ancient orators did not shy away from mentioning failure or moments of adversity, neither does Stern hesitate to depict the less than triumphant episodes of Jobs' career. The Lisa operating system is shown to be a bust, and Jobs recovers from being forced out of the company by crying and then going home to where it all began, only to be invited back to the company and thus eventually be inspired to make the iPod with which the film began. In the process of this redemption, his vices are disguised as virtues, his rashness

Figure 14.1 Reading his own *laudatio*? Ashton Kutcher as Steve Jobs in *Jobs* (2013) recording the famous "Here's to the crazy ones" Apple commercial. Open Road Films.

becomes drive, and his ruthlessness becomes ambition. Quintilian again would be proud. The film then ends with Jobs recording the dialogue to the famous "Think Different" commercial in 1997, his tribute "to the crazy ones," which ends with him stating that "they change things, they push the human race forward. While some may see them as the crazy ones, we see genius. Because the people who are crazy enough to think they can change the world, are the ones who do" (Figure 14.1). With the societal virtue of entrepreneurism, innovation, and technology thus being reinforced and communicated to the audience through the film, it thus abruptly ends.

All that we would come to expect from the *laudatio funebris* is here, and the strands unite: scenes from the subject's life are chosen and embellished, their importance as revealing his fundamental character is driven home, the impact of his life on society as a whole is communicated. In the process, that society learns something of what it considers admirable or virtuous in the world. But none of this, interestingly, would have been of any importance to the audience had they not already essentially known his story, and where all of this was leading. Hence this, like the *laudatio*, comes at the end of the procession, not the beginning. But as Steve Jobs was led through this long *pompa funebris* in the years after his death, which brought the public into a grief that was perhaps otherwise private, his legacy was forever shaped by the process of commemoration. While in the case of Jobs this process was geared toward depicting him as a praiseworthy, virtuous figure in spite of his personal failings, such a laudatory tone does not always need to be the case in these films. By means of conclusion, then, we must turn to another process that has emerged in parallel with these post-mortem panegyric films: the creation of antiheroes through the same filmic genre.

## CONCLUSIONS: MAKING HEROES AND ANTIHEROES

Among the more intriguing characteristics of Roman art across various media is the Roman preference for what is termed by art historians as "verism." Unlike the classical Greeks, who by and large preferred to express idealized versions of their subjects in sculpture by making them youthful, strong, and vibrant, the Romans take a very different approach toward capturing the essence of those whom they wished to commemorate. Particularly in masculine portraiture of the Middle Republic onward, the Romans opted instead for what was (or rather seemed to be) extreme realism: the bust of a middle-aged man, for instance, would emphasize his baldness, his weathered features, and the craggy lines of his face that could only have been carved by long hardship. This "warts-and-all" style of the Romans did not attempt to conceal the physiognomy of a given subject; instead these marks of age, experience, and hardship were brought to the fore because they were seen as testament to the man's strenuous character, his moderation, and his constancy.[35] This penchant for verism also manifests itself in the comments of Cicero and Quintilian on the *laudatio funebris*, in which they emphasize that the flaws – physical or otherwise – of the deceased should not be swept away, but rather these and instances of failure or hardship should be brought to the fore as proof of the subject's triumph over adversity. Verism, however, need not always be in the service of virtue: Roman *laudationes* did not hesitate to mix praise with blame, and to criticize the failings of the deceased while alive. No one was a perfect exemplum in the Roman mindset, but as much could be learned from the complete absence of virtue as from its abundance. The Romans likewise did not hesitate to paint equally edifying portraits of their villains and their heroes, as we find in the character sketches of Catiline by Sallust and Caligula by Suetonius.

The same duality, in a sense, is true of Hollywood biopics since the 1960s and 1970s. While the "classical" biopics that we have encountered above are usually panegyric of a well-known and celebrated figure, the tumultuous period following the demise of the Hayes Code and the new creative freedom it gave to filmmakers gave rise to new kinds of biopics that depicted very different subjects from their predecessors. The idols of production that dominated the 1950s biopics ceded place to idols of consumption: athletes, musicians, and actors were subjects of such films rather than staid politicians, businessmen, or scientists. Conventional notions of heroism, as George Custen notes, "ha[d] been stripped bare by historical forces which undermined people's faith in individual leaders and institutions they headed."[36] Biopics came to depict subjects of fascination, but not necessarily adulation, leading to a series of "warts-and-all" films that depicted the flaws and failings of a celebrity as well as their accomplishments. Celebration of virtue was replaced by celebration of fame, however it may have been won.[37]

The neoclassical biopics that have enjoyed surging popularity since the 1990s may have larger budgets, bigger audiences, and greater exposure than some of the less successful offerings of the previous decades, but they have not lost this fascination with the less than heroic aspects of their subjects. In bringing these to the fore, in highlighting vice with equal if not greater enthusiasm than virtue, contemporary biopics have often transformed their subjects into antiheroes – figures worthy of fascination rather than imitation – by precisely the same means with which they have made other figures into heroes. Many of the post-mortem biopics listed above make their subjects into antiheroes with the same enthusiasm as Joshua Michael Stern did the opposite with *Jobs*. *American Sniper* unflinchingly shows Chris Kyle's less-than-glorious actions, however understandable, in Iraq as well as his domestic shortcomings on the home front. *Walk the Line* is a particularly fitting example of this trend, as much of the film depicts Johnny Cash's drug and alcohol abuse and the self-destructive consequences of his addictions – not least of which are his arrest and estrangement from his family and first wife Vivian. The 2009 film *Notorious* depicting the life of Christopher Wallace (a.k.a. The Notorious B.I.G.) shows his early downfall as an adolescent who is drawn into the world of drug dealing by an insatiable appetite for money and jewelry, which led to numerous arrests. The increasing rancor and violence of the East Coast–West Coast hip-hop rivalry that leads to the death of Tupac Shakur and ultimately Wallace himself comes across as pointless, wasteful conflicts whose true victims are those left behind after these murders. Interestingly, this film glorifies the musical achievements of Wallace/Biggie without glorifying the artist himself.

These are only a few examples of a very diverse trend in biographical cinema that is by no means limited to post-mortem tribute biopics, but the observation remains: the formula and mechanisms of biopics are just as well suited to creating antiheroes as they are to creating heroes. The same, of course, would be true of the Roman *laudatio funebris* if the orators had wished to denigrate as well as praise their subjects. In both cases, the mechanism remains the same: selective emplotment, embellishment, amplification, and the sage use of synecdoche elevate the individual subject above the common masses and transform the subject into a figure of fascination. This process in Rome, which was immediately post-mortem and which is becoming increasingly so in twenty-first-century Hollywood, was fundamentally public, it was competitive, and it was geared toward the entertainment of an audience whose interests were stimulated by images as much as by words. In the process, values were communicated and reinforced, broader concepts of virtue and vice elucidated by a delicate mixture of praise and blame, and the narrative of the subject's life was given a clear meaning that can only be ascertained with the finality of death. As stated earlier, I do not mean to equate two vastly different media that appealed to vastly different societies separated by over two millennia, but in the comparison of these ancient and modern social mechanisms by which people are made into heroes or antiheroes, we encounter enough similarities that make the gulf between the two seem less insurmountable than may be thought, and which enrich our understanding of both. As for the final judgment of one's life, their heroism or lack thereof is now, as it was then, as much in the eye of the artist who commemorated it as it was in the eye of the beholder.

## NOTES

My thanks, as ever, go to Antony Augoustakis and Stacie Raucci for their patience and editorial insight. This chapter greatly benefitted from the feedback of all present at the Delphi conference.

1. This chapter focuses primarily on the Middle and Late Republican *laudationes*, though the oration certainly continued into the Imperial period. Kierdorf (1980) provides the most comprehensive overview of the *laudatio*; for more recent works in English, see Kyle (1998); Ramage (2006); Rees (2010); Covino (2011).
2. Bingham (2010) provides an immensely helpful overview of the biopic genre. For specific case studies, see the edited volumes of Brown and Vidal (2013) and Epstein and Palmer (2017).
3. Ekroth (2007: 100).
4. See Covino (2011).
5. Pliny the Elder, *Natural History* 7.140. All translations of Latin and Greek are mine unless otherwise noted.
6. On the public staging of the *laudatio*, see the extensive discussion of Johanson (2008) and notes below.

7 In the Late Republic there are several attested cases of funeral orations being given in honor of women, notably by Julius Caesar for his aunt Julia and wife Cornelia, as mentioned by Suetonius, *Life of Julius* 6. Suetonius notes that these speeches were customary, so we need not presume this is exceptional. While our evidence for female *laudationes* is scant, we can presume that they would have followed the same structure as orations in honor of men, and that the same conventions still applied.
8 Polybius 6.53–4 provides the most complete extant description of a Roman funeral procession. See also the discussion of Johanson (2008: 32–81).
9 Translated by Paton, Walbank, and Habicht (2010).
10 Quintilian, *The Orator's Education* 3.7.10–16.
11 This outline is taken from Quintilian along with Johanson (2008: 101–10), who also provides a helpful compendium at Johanson (2008: 110–31). See also Rees (2010) and Covino (2011: 69–73).
12 Quintilian, *The Orator's Education* 3.7.11–12.
13 Cicero, *de oratore* 2.46; see also Tacitus, *Annals* 3.76.2 and 13.3.1.
14 Johanson (2008: 107–10), Covino (2011: 72–6).
15 Quintilian, *The Orator's Education* 3.7.6, where he states the principal function of such speeches is to embellish and amplify their subjects.
16 Covino (2011: 69).
17 Cicero, *The Making of an Orator* 2.314; Livy, *History of Rome* 8.46.
18 Livy, *History of Rome* 8.40.
19 As Custen (2000: 136) notes, "The Hollywood biopic brand of history is constructed almost exclusively around a single concept: fame." See also his discussion of the genre at Custen (2000: 134–8).
20 The definition given by Bingham (2010: 10).
21 Custen (2000: 131–2).
22 Custen (2000: 138–9).
23 This overview of the genre is taken from Bingham (2010: 3–30).
24 Bingham (2010: 10). See also Epstein (2011).
25 Quoted in Bingham (2010: 11).
26 Following the periodization of Bingham (2010: 17–18) and Custen (2000). *Alexander Hamilton* (1931); *The Story of Louis Pasteur* (1936); *Young Tom Edison* (1939); *Edison, the Man* (1940).
27 For instance, three out of five nominees for Best Actor in 2015 starred in biopics, and four out of eight Best Picture nominees were biopics. The same figures are true of the 2014 awards.
28 *Snowden* (2016); *The Social Network* (2010); *The Wolf of Wall Street* (2013).
29 http://www.apple.com/stevejobs.
30 Nieva (2014).
31 Kroll (2011).
32 Silverman (2015); Collins (2015).
33 Miller (2013).

34 Assar (2013).
35 For an overview of verism in Roman art, see Fejfer (2008: 262–75).
36 Custen (2000: 130).
37 See the discussion by Bingham (2011), and the evolution of antiheroism in relation to masculinity as analyzed by Trice and Holland (2001); see also Curley and Tomasso in this volume.

# *Filmography*

## FILMS

*300* (2007). Directed by Zack Snyder. Warner Bros.
*300: Rise of an Empire* (2014). Directed by Noam Murro. Warner Bros.
*A Nightmare on Elm Street* (2010). Directed by Samuel Bayer. New Line Cinema.
*Agora* (2009). Directed by Alejandro Amenábar. Focus Features/Newmarket Films.
*Aladdin* (1992). Directed by Ron Clements and John Musker. Walt Disney Pictures.
*Alexander* (2004). Directed by Oliver Stone. Warner Bros.
*Alexander Hamilton* (1931). Directed by John G. Adolfi. Warner Bros.
*Alexander the Great* (1956). Directed by Robert Rossen. C. B. Films S. A.
*Amazing Spider-Man* (2012). Directed by Marc Webb. Columbia Pictures.
*American Sniper* (2014). Directed by Clint Eastwood. Warner Bros.
*Amistad* (1997). Directed by Steven Spielberg. DreamWorks.
*Argo* (2012). Directed by Ben Affleck. Warner Bros.
*Ben Hur: A Tale of the Christ* (1925). Directed by Fred Niblo. Metro-Goldwyn-Mayer.
*Ben-Hur* (1959). Directed by William Wyler. Metro-Goldwyn-Mayer.
*Ben-Hur* (2016). Directed by Timur Bekmambetov. LightWorkers Media.
*Black Swan* (2010). Directed by Darren Aronofsky. Fox Searchlight Pictures.
*Cabiria* (1914). Directed by Giovanni Pastrone. Itala Film.
*Caesar and Cleopatra* (1945). Directed by Gabriel Pascal. Gabriel Pascal Productions.
*Centurion* (2010). Directed by Neil Marshall. Pathé Productions.
*Citizen Kane* (1941). Directed by Orson Welles. Mercury Productions.
*Clash of the Titans* (1981). Directed by Desmond Davis. Charles H. Schneer Productions.
*Clash of the Titans* (2010). Directed by Louis Leterrier. Warner Bros.
*Cleopatra* (1934). Directed by Cecil B. DeMille. Paramount Pictures.
*Cleopatra* (1963). Directed by Joseph L. Mankiewicz. Twentieth Century Fox.

*Conan the Barbarian* (1982). Directed by John Milius. Dino de Laurentiis Company.
*Edison, the Man* (1940). Directed by Clarence Brown. Metro-Goldwyn-Mayer.
*Escape from Iran: The Canadian Caper* (1981). Directed by Lamont Johnson. CTV Television Network.
*Exodus: Gods and Kings* (2014). Directed by Ridley Scott. Chernin Entertainment.
*Fantastic Four* (2005). Directed by Tim Story. Twentieth Century Fox Film Corporation.
*Fantastic Four* (2015). Directed by Josh Trank. Twentieth Century Fox Film Corporation.
*Fast & Furious* (2009). Directed by Justin Lin. Universal Pictures.
*Fast & Furious 6* (2013). Directed by Justin Lin. Universal Pictures.
*Fast Five* (2011). Directed by Justin Lin. Universal Pictures.
*Friday the 13th* (2009). Directed by Marcus Nispel. New Line Cinema.
*Furious 7* (2015). Directed by James Wan. Universal Pictures.
*Gladiator* (2000). Directed by Ridley Scott. DreamWorks.
*Harry Potter and the Sorcerer's Stone* (2001). Directed by Chris Columbus. Warner Bros.
*Harry Potter and the Chamber of Secrets* (2002). Directed by Chris Columbus. Warner Bros.
*Harry Potter and the Prisoner of Azkaban* (2004). Directed by Alfonso Cuarón. Warner Bros.
*Harry Potter and the Goblet of Fire* (2005). Directed by Mike Newell. Warner Bros.
*Harry Potter and the Order of the Phoenix* (2007). Directed by David Yates. Warner Bros.
*Harry Potter and the Half-Blood Prince* (2009). Directed by David Yates. Warner Bros.
*Harry Potter and the Deathly Hallows: Part 1* (2010). Directed by David Yates. Warner Bros.
*Harry Potter and the Deathly Hallows: Part 2* (2011). Directed by David Yates. Warner Bros.
*Hercules* [Italian title: *Le fatiche di Ercole*] (1958). Directed by Pietro Francisci. Galatea Film.
*Hercules* (1997). Directed by John Musker and Ron Clements. Walt Disney Pictures.
*Hercules* (2014). Directed by Brett Ratner. Paramount Pictures.
*Hercules and the Tyrants of Babylon* [Italian title: *Ercole contro i tiranni di Babilonia*] (1964). Directed by Domenico Paollella. Romana Films.
*Hercules Conquers Atlantis* (1961). Directed by Vittorio Cottafavi. Woolner Brothers Pictures.
*Hercules in New York* (1970). Directed by Arthur A. Seidelman. RAF Industries.
*Hercules Reborn* (2014). Directed by Nick Lyon. Asylum.

*Hercules Unchained* [Italian title: *Ercole e la regina di Lidia*] (1959). Directed by Pietro Francisci. Galatea Film.
*Immortals* (2011). Directed by Tarsem Singh. Relativity Media.
*It's a Wonderful Life* (1946). Directed by Frank Capra. Liberty Films.
*JFK* (1991). Directed by Oliver Stone. Warner Bros.
*Jobs* (2013). Directed by Joshua Michael Stern. Open Road Films.
*Maciste* (1915). Directed by Vincenzo Dénizot and Roman Luigi Borgnetto. Itala Film.
*Mandela* (2014). Directed by Justin Chadwick. Twentieth Century Fox.
*Monty Python's Life of Brian* (1979). Directed by Terry Jones. HandMade Films.
*Nixon* (1995). Directed by Oliver Stone. Cinergi Pictures Entertainment.
*Noah* (2014). Directed by Darren Aronofsky. Paramount Pictures.
*Not Without My Daughter* (1991). Directed by Brian Gilbert. Pathé Entertainment.
*Notorious* (2009). Directed by George Tillman Jr. Fox Searchlight Pictures.
*On Wings of Eagles* (1986). Directed by Andrew V. McLaglen. Edgar J. Scherick Associates.
*Percy Jackson & the Olympians: The Lightning Thief* (2010). Directed by Chris Columbus. Fox 2000 Pictures.
*Percy Jackson & the Olympians: Sea of Monsters* (2013). Directed by Thor Freudenthal. Fox 2000 Pictures.
*Pompeii* (2014). Directed by Paul W. S. Anderson. TriStar Pictures.
*Pulp Fiction* (1994). Directed by Quentin Tarantino. Miramax.
*Quo Vadis* (1951). Directed by Mervyn LeRoy. Metro-Goldwyn-Mayer.
*Ray* (2004). Directed by Taylor Hackford. Universal Pictures.
*Red Sonja* (1985). Directed by Richard Fleischer. Dino de Laurentiis Company.
*Rocky* (1976). Directed by John G. Avildsen. Chartoff-Winkler Productions.
*Ship of Theseus* (2013). Directed by Anand Gandhi. Recyclewala Films.
*Son of God* (2014). Directed by Christopher Spencer. Hearst Entertainment Productions.
*Snowden* (2016). Directed by Oliver Stone. Open Road Films.
*Spartacus* (1960). Directed by Stanley Kubrick. Bryna Productions.
*Spider-Man* (2002). Directed by Sam Raimi. Columbia Pictures.
*Spider-Man: Homecoming* (2017). Directed by Jon Watts. Columbia Pictures.
*Star Trek II: The Wrath of Khan* (1982). Directed by Nicholas Meyer. Paramount Pictures.
*Star Wars: Episode IV – A New Hope* (1977). Directed by George Lucas. Twentieth Century Fox.
*The 300 Spartans* (1962). Directed by Rudolph Maté. Twentieth Century Fox.
*The Blind Side* (2009). Directed by John Lee Hancock. Alcon Entertainment.

*The Chronicles of Narnia: The Lion, the Witch and the Wardrobe* (2005). Directed by Andrew Adamson. Walt Disney Pictures.
*The Da Vinci Code* (2006). Directed by Ron Howard. Columbia Pictures.
*The Doors* (1991). Directed by Oliver Stone. Bill Graham Films.
*The Eagle* (2011). Directed by Kevin MacDonald. Focus Features.
*The Fall of the Roman Empire* (1964). Directed by Anthony Mann. Paramount Pictures.
*The Fast and the Furious* (2001). Directed by Rob Cohen. Universal Pictures.
*The Fast and the Furious: Tokyo Drift* (2006). Directed by Justin Lin. Universal Pictures.
*The Fate of the Furious* (2017). Directed by F. Gary Gray. Universal Pictures.
*The Full Monty* (1997). Directed by Peter Cattaneo. Redwave Films.
*The Last Legion* (2007). Directed by Doug Lefler. Dino de Laurentiis Company.
*The Last Temptation of Christ* (1988). Directed by Martin Scorsese. Universal Pictures.
*The Legend of Hercules* (2014). Directed by Renny Harlin. Summit Entertainment.
*The Passion of the Christ* (2004). Directed by Mel Gibson. Icon Productions.
*The Robe* (1953). Directed by Henry Koster. Twentieth Century Fox.
*The Scorpion King* (2002). Directed by Chuck Russell. Universal Pictures.
*The Searchers* (1956). Directed by John Ford. C. V. Whitney Pictures.
*The Sign of the Cross* (1932). Directed by Cecil B. DeMille. Paramount Pictures.
*The Social Network* (2010). Directed by David Fincher. Columbia Pictures.
*The Story of Louis Pasteur* (1936). Directed by William Dieterle. Warner Bros.
*The Twilight Saga: Breaking Dawn – Part 1* (2011). Directed by Bill Condon. Summit Entertainment.
*The Twilight Saga: Breaking Dawn – Part 2* (2012). Directed by Bill Condon. Summit Entertainment.
*The Twilight Saga: Eclipse* (2010). Directed by David Slade. Summit Entertainment.
*The Twilight Saga: New Moon* (2009). Directed by Chris Weitz. Summit Entertainment.
*The Wolf of Wall Street* (2013). Directed by Martin Scorsese. Paramount Pictures.
*The Wrestler* (2008). Directed by Darren Aronofsky. Fox Searchlight Pictures.
*2 Fast 2 Furious* (2003). Directed by John Singleton. Universal Pictures.
*Troy* (2004). Directed by Wolfgang Petersen. Warner Bros.
*Twilight* (2008). Directed by Catherine Hardwicke. Summit Entertainment.
*Ulysses Against Hercules* [Italian title: *Ulisse contro Ercole*] (1962). Directed by Mario Caiano. Compagnia Cinematografica Mondiale.
*United 93* (2006). Directed by Paul Greengrass. Universal Pictures.

*Walk the Line* (2005). Directed by James Mangold. Twentieth Century Fox.
*Warrior Queen* (2003). Directed by Bill Anderson. Box TV.
*Wonder Woman* (2017). Directed by Patty Jenkins. Warner Bros.
*Wrath of the Titans* (2012). Directed by Jonathan Liebesman. Warner Bros.
*Young Tom Edison* (1939). Directed by Norman Taurog. Metro-Goldwyn-Mayer.

## TELEVISION SERIES

*AD: The Bible Continues* (2015). Created by Mark Burnett and Roma Downey. United Artists Media Group.
*Atlantis* (2013–15). Created by Johnny Capps, Julian Murphy, and Howard Overman. Urban Myth Films.
*Battlestar Galactica* (2005–9). Created by Glen A. Larson and Ronald D. Moore. British Sky Broadcasting.
*Black Sails* (2014–17). Created by Robert Levine and Jonathan E. Steinberg. Film Afrika Worldwide.
*Buffy the Vampire Slayer* (1997–2003). Created by Joss Whedon. Mutant Enemy.
*Cleopatra* (1999). Directed by Franc Roddam. Hallmark Entertainment.
*CNN Heroes: Everyday People Changing the World* (2007–). CNN.
*Dexter* (2006–13). Created by James Manos Jr. Showtime Networks.
*Disney's Hercules: The Animated Series* (1998–9). Directed by Phil Weinstein. Walt Disney Television.
*Doctor Who* (2005–). Created by Sydney Newman. BBC.
*Friends* (1994–2004). Created by David Crane and Marta Kauffman. Warner Bros Television.
*Game of Thrones* (2011–). Created by David Benioff and D. B. Weiss. HBO.
*Hercules* (2005). Directed by Roger Young. Hallmark Entertainment.
*Hercules: The Legendary Journeys* (1995–9). Created by Christian Williams. MCA Television.
*Heroes* (2006–10). Created by Tim Kring. Tailwind Productions/NBC Universal Television.
*Heroes Reborn* (2015–16). Created by Tim Kring. Tailwind Productions/Imperative Entertainment.
*I, Claudius* (1976). Directed by Herbert Wise. BBC.
*John Doe* (2002). Created by Brandon Camp and Mike Thompson. Camp/Thompson Pictures.
*Merlin* (2008–12). Created by Johnny Capps, Julian Jones, Jake Mitchie, and Julian Murphy. Shine.
*Odysseus* (2013). Directed by Stéphane Giusti. Making Prod/Arte France.
*Of Kings and Prophets* (2016). Created by Chris Brancato, Adam Cooper, and Bill Collage. Philotimo Factory.
*Outlander* (2014–). Created by Ronald D. Moore. Tall Ship Productions.

*Robin Hood* (2006–9). Created by Foz Allan and Dominic Minghella. Tiger Aspect Productions.
*Roman Empire: Reign of Blood* (2016). Directed by Richard Lopez. Stephen David Entertainment.
*Rome* (2005–7). Created by Bruno Heller, William J. MacDonald, and John Milius. HBO-BBC.
*Scorpion* (2014–). Created by Nick Santora. K/O Paper Products.
*Seinfeld* (1989–98). Created by Larry David and Jerry Seinfeld. Sony Pictures Television.
*Spartacus: Blood and Sand* (2010). Created by Steven S. DeKnight. STARZ.
*Spartacus: Gods of the Arena* (2011). Created by Steven S. DeKnight. STARZ.
*Spartacus: Vengeance* (2012). Created by Steven S. DeKnight. STARZ.
*Spartacus: War of the Damned* (2013). Created by Steven S. DeKnight. STARZ.
*Supernatural* (2005–). Created by Eric Kripke. Warner Bros Television.
*The Bible* (2013). Created by Mark Burnett and Roma Downey. LightWorkers Media.
*The Dovekeepers* (2015). Directed by Yves Simoneau. LightWorkers Media.
*The Odyssey* (1997). Directed by Andrei Konchalovsky. Hallmark Entertainment.
*The Sopranos* (1999–2007). Created by David Chase. Home Box Office.
*Young Hercules* (1998–9). Created by Andrew Dettmann, Rob Tapert, and Daniel Truly. MCA Television.
*Xena: Warrior Princess* (1995–2001). Created by Sam Raimi, Robert Tapert, and John Schulian. MCA Television.

# Bibliography

Adams, Marilyn McCord (1999). *Horrendous Evils and the Goodness of God*. Ithaca: Cornell University Press.
Andreeva, Nellie (2017). "*Cleopatra* TV Series in the Works at Amazon from *Black Sails* Team." *Deadline Hollywood*, May 24.
Ansari, Ali M. (2012). *The Politics of Nationalism in Iran*. Cambridge: Cambridge University Press.
Aperlo, Peter (2013). *300: Rise of an Empire. The Art of the Film*. London: Titan Books.
Apostol, Ricardo (2016). "Oliver Stone's Aristotle: Heroism, Displacement, and Aristotelian Form in *Alexander*." *Classical Receptions Journal* 8: 357–74.
Assar, Vijith (2013). "Early Apple Employees Talk Memories of Steve Jobs, New Movie." *Dice Insights*, August 16.
Augoustakis, Antony (2013). "Partnership and Love in *Spartacus: Blood and Sand* (2010)," in Monica S. Cyrino (ed.), *Screening Love and Sex in the Ancient World*. New York: Palgrave Macmillan, 157–65.
Aune, David E. (1990). "Heracles and Christ: Heracles Imagery in the Christology of Early Christianity," in David Balch, Everett Ferguson, and Wayne A. Meeks (eds.), *Greeks, Romans, and Christians: Essays in Honor of Abraham J. Malherbe*. Minneapolis Fortress, 3–19.
Aziza, Claude (ed.) (1998). *Le péplum: L'antiquité au cinema*. Condé-sur-Noireau: Corlet-Télérama.
Aziza, Claude (2009). *Le péplum, un mauvais genre*. Paris: Klincksieck.
Babington, Bruce and Evans, Peter William (1993). *Biblical Epics: Sacred Narrative in the Hollywood Cinema*. Manchester: Manchester University Press.
Bakhtin, M. M. (1981). *The Dialogic Imagination: Four Essays*. Austin: University of Texas Press.
Becker, Ernest (1973). *The Denial of Death*. New York: Free Press.
Becker, Ernest (1975). *Escape from Evil*. New York: Free Press.
Bernardi, Daniel (1998). *Star Trek and History: Race-ing Toward a White Future*. New Brunswick: Rutgers University Press.

Bertellini, Giorgio (2002). "Dubbing *L'Arte Muta*: 'Cinema Under Fascism' and the Expressive Layerings of Italian Early Sound Cinema," in Jacqueline Reich and Piero Garofalo (eds.), *Reviewing Fascism: Italian Cinema, 1922–1943*. Bloomington: Indiana University Press, 30–82.

Bill, James A. (1988). *The Eagle and the Lion: The Tragedy of American-Iranian Relations*. New Haven: Yale University Press.

Bingham, Dennis (2010). *Whose Lives Are They Anyway? The Biopic as Contemporary Film Genre*. New Brunswick: Rutgers University Press.

Bingham, Dennis (2011). "Woody Guthrie, Warts-and-All: The Biopic in the New American Cinema of the 1970s." *a/b: Auto/Biography Studies* 26.1: 68–90.

Blanshard, Alastair J. L. (2005). *Hercules: A Heroic Life*. London: Granta.

Blanshard, Alastair J. L. (2017). "High Art and Low Art Expectations: Ancient Greece in Film and Popular Culture," in Arthur J. Pomeroy (ed.), *A Companion to Ancient Greece and Rome on Screen*. Oxford: Wiley-Blackwell, 429–47.

Blanshard, Alastair J. L. and Shahabudin, Kim (2011). *Classics on Screen: Ancient Greece and Rome on Film*. London: Bristol Classical Press.

Blondell, Ruby (2005). "How to Kill an Amazon." *Helios* 32.2: 183–213.

Blondell, Ruby (2007). "Hercules Psychotherapist," in Wendy Haslem, Angela Ndalianis, and Chris Mackie (eds.), *Super/Heroes: From Hercules to Superman*. Washington, DC: New Academia, 239–49.

Blumenthal, David (1993). *Facing the Abusing God: A Theology of Protest*. Louisville: Westminster John Knox Press.

Bondanella, Peter (2009). *A History of Italian Cinema*. New York: Continuum.

Bremmer, Jan N. (2007). "Myth and Ritual in Greek Human Sacrifice: Lykaon, Polyxena, and the Case of the Rhodian Criminal," in Jan N. Bremmer (ed.), *The Strange World of Human Sacrifice*. Leuven: Peeters, 55–79.

Bremmer, Jan N. (2010). "Greek Normative Animal Sacrifice," in Daniel Odgen (ed.), *A Companion to Greek Religion*. Malden: Wiley-Blackwell, 132–44.

Bridges, Emma (2015). *Imagining Xerxes: Ancient Perspectives on a Persian King*. London: Bloomsbury.

Bridges, Emma, Hall, Edith, and Rhodes, P. J. (eds.) (2007). *Cultural Responses to the Persian Wars: From Antiquity to the Third Millennium*. Oxford: Oxford University Press.

Brombert, Victor (1999). *In Praise of Antiheroes: Figures and Themes in Modern European Literature, 1830–1980*. Chicago: University of Chicago Press.

Brown, Tom and Vidal, Belen (eds.) (2013). *The Biopic in Contemporary Film Culture*. New York: Taylor & Francis.

Browne, Niall (2010). "*Screen Rant*'s Niall Browne Reviews *Centurion*." *Screen Rant*, August 19.

Bruce, Melissa N. (2010). "The Impala as Negotiator of Melodrama and Masculinity in *Supernatural*." *Transformative Works and Cultures* 4 (http://journal.transformativeworks.org).

Brunetta, Gian Piero (2009). *The History of Italian Cinema: A Guide to Italian Film from Its Origins to the Twenty-First Century*. Princeton: Princeton University Press.

Bundrick, Sheramy B. (2009). "Dionysian Themes and Imagery in Oliver Stone's *Alexander*." *Helios* 36.1: 81–96.

Burgoyne, Robert (2008). *The Hollywood Historical Film*. Malden: Wiley-Blackwell.

Burgoyne, Robert (ed.) (2011). *The Epic Film in World Culture*. London: Routledge.

Burke, Frank (2011). "The Italian Sword-and-Sandal Film from *Fabiola* to *Hercules and the Captive Women*: Texts and Contexts," in Flavia Brizio-Skov (ed.), *Popular Italian Cinema: Culture and Politics in a Postwar Society*. London: I. B. Tauris, 17–51.

Burkert, Walter (1983). *Homo Necans: The Anthropology of Ancient Greek Sacrificial Ritual and Myth*. Berkeley: University of California Press.

Bush, George W. (2001). "George W. Bush Addresses Muslims in the Aftermath of the 9/11 Attacks." *Berkley Center for Religion, Peace & World Affairs*, September 20.

Campbell, Duncan B. (2010). "The Fate of the Ninth: The Curious Disappearance of Legio VIIII Hispana." *Ancient Warfare* 4.5: 48–53.

Campbell, Jane (1995). "Portrayals of Iranians in U.S. Motion Pictures," in Yahya R. Kamalipour (ed.), *The U.S. Media and the Middle East: Image and Perception*. Westport: Greenwood Press, 176–86.

Campbell, Joseph (2008). *The Hero with a Thousand Faces*. 3rd edn. Novato: New World Library.

Cartlidge, Neil (ed.) (2012). *Heroes and Anti-Heroes in Medieval Romance*. Cambridge: D. S. Brewer.

Caudill, Helen (2003). "Tall, Dark, and Dangerous: Xena, the Quest, and the Wielding of Sexual Violence in *Xena* On-Line Fan Fiction," in Frances H. Early and Kathleen Kennedy (eds.), *Athena's Daughters: Television's New Women Warriors*. Syracuse: Syracuse University Press, 27–40.

Cave, Stephen (2012). *Immortality: The Quest to Live Forever and How It Drives Civilization*. New York: Crown.

Chaniotis, Angelos (2008). "Making Alexander Fit for the Twenty-First Century: Oliver Stone's *Alexander*," in Irene Berti and Marta García Morcillo (eds.), *Hellas on Screen: Cinematic Receptions of Ancient History, Literature, and Myth*. Stuttgart: Franz Steiner, 185–201.

Chilton, Bruce (2002). "Eucharist: Surrogate, Metaphor, Sacrament of Sacrifice," in Albert I. Baumgarten (ed.), *Sacrifice in Religious Experience*. Leiden: Brill, 175–88.

Chiu, Angeline (2014). "Labors and Lesson Plans: Educating Young Hercules in Two 1990s Children's Television Programs." *Amphora* 11.1: 1, 6–7.

Churchill, John (1991). "Odysseus's Bed; Agamemnon's Bath." *College Literature* 18.1: 1–13.

Clauss, James J. (2008). "*Hercules Unchained*: Contaminatio, Nostos, Katabasis, and the Surreal." *Arethusa* 41: 51–66.

Clauss, James J. (forthcoming). "'Now My Charms Are All O'erthrown': Intertextuality and the Theme of Succession and Replacement in *Clash of the Titans* (1981)." *Classical World*.

Clay, Jenny Strauss (1981–2). "Immortal and Ageless Forever." *Classical Journal* 77.2: 112–17.

Clay, Jenny Strauss (2003). *Hesiod's Cosmos*. Cambridge: Cambridge University Press.

Cole, Brendan (2017). "Russian President Vladimir Putin Goes Topless in His Fishing and Hunting Holiday." *International Business Times*, August 7.

Collins, Rob (2015). "Steve Jobs: The Last Heroic Leader." *The Huffington Post*, October 1.

Collins, Scott (2013). "*The Bible, Vikings* Premieres Tell a Ratings Epic for History." *Los Angeles Times*, March 4.

Conroy, Mike (2008). "Interview with Steve Moore," in Steve Moore (ed.), *Hercules: The Thracian Wars*. Carpinteria: Radical, 124–7.

Cornelius, Michael G. (2011). "Introduction – Of Muscles and Men: The Forms and Functions of the Sword and Sandal Film," in Michael G. Cornelius (ed.), *Of Muscles and Men: Essays on the Sword and Sandal Film*. Jefferson: McFarland, 1–14.

Covino, Ralph J. (2011). "The *laudatio funebris* as a Vehicle for Praise and Admonition," in Ralph Covino and Christopher Smith (eds.), *Praise and Blame in Roman Republican Rhetoric*. Swansea: Classical Press of Wales, 69–81.

Cuddon, John A. (ed.) (2013). *A Dictionary of Literary Terms and Literary Theory*. 5th edn. Rev. M. A. R. Habib. Malden: Wiley-Blackwell.

Cullen, Jim (2012). "Actors as Historians." *History News Network*, December 17.

Cullen, Jim (2013). *Sensing the Past: Hollywood Stars as Historians*. Oxford: Oxford University Press.

Curley, Dan (2015). "Divine Animation: *Clash of the Titans* (1981)," in Monica S. Cyrino and Meredith E. Safran (eds.), *Classical Myth on Screen*. New York: Palgrave Macmillan, 207–17.

Custen, George F. (2000). "The Mechanical Life in the Age of Human Reproduction: American Biopics, 1961–1980." *Biography* 23.1: 127–59.

Cyrino, Monica S. (1998). "Heroes in D(u)ress: Transvestism and Power in the Myths of Herakles and Achilles." *Arethusa* 31.2: 207–41.

Cyrino, Monica S. (2004). "*Gladiator* and Contemporary American Society," in Martin M. Winkler (ed.), *Gladiator: Film and History*. Oxford: Blackwell, 124–49.

Cyrino, Monica S. (2005). *Big Screen Rome*. Malden: Blackwell.

Cyrino, Monica S. (2007). "Helen of Troy," in Martin M. Winkler (ed.), *Troy: From Homer's Iliad to Hollywood Epic*. Malden: Wiley-Blackwell, 131–47.

Cyrino, Monica S. (2008). "Atia and the Erotics of Authority," in Monica S. Cyrino (ed.), *Rome, Season One: History Makes Television*. Malden: Wiley-Blackwell, 130–40.

Cyrino, Monica S. (2010). "Fortune Favors the Blond: Colin Farrell in *Alexander*," in Paul Cartledge and Fiona Rose Greenland (eds.), *Responses to Oliver Stone's Alexander: Film, History and Cultural Studies*. Madison: University of Wisconsin Press, 168–82.

Cyrino, Monica S. and Safran, Meredith E. (eds.) (2015). *Classical Myth on Screen*. Basingstoke: Palgrave Macmillan.

D'Amelio, Maria Elena (2011). "Hercules, Politics, and Movies," in Michael G. Cornelius (ed.), *Of Muscles and Men: Essays on the Sword and Sandal Film*. Jefferson: McFarland, 15–27.

D'Amelio, Maria Elena (2014). *Hollywood on the Tiber and Italian Cinema: Practices of Transatlantic Stardom*. PhD diss., Stony Brook University.

Darghis, Manohla (2010). "Beware of Greeks Bearing Buzz Cuts." *New York Times*, April 1.

Daryaee, Touraj (2007). "Go Tell the Spartans / Against Hollywood War on Iran Propaganda." *Indymedia.org.uk*, March 16.

Daugherty, Gregory (2008). "Her First Roman: A Cleopatra for Rome," in Monica S. Cyrino (ed.), *Rome, Season One: History Makes Television*. Malden: Wiley-Blackwell, 141–52.

Day, Kirsten (2016). *Cowboy Classics: The Roots of the American Western in the Epic Tradition*. Edinburgh: Edinburgh University Press.

Della Casa, Steve and Giusti, Marco (2013). *Il grande libro di Ercole: Il cinema mitologico in Italia*. Rome: Edizioni Sabinae.

Denham, Robert (2009). "'Pity the Northrop Frye Scholar'? *Anatomy of Criticism* Fifty Years After," in David Rampton (ed.), *Northrop Frye: New Directions from Old*. Ottawa: University of Ottawa Press, 15–34.

Dethloff, Craig (2011). "Coming Up to Code: Ancient Divinities Revisited," in George Kovacs and C. W. Marshall (eds.), *Classics and Comics*. Oxford: Oxford University Press, 103–14.

Detienne, Marcel and Vernant, Jean-Pierre (1989). *The Cuisine of Sacrifice Among the Greeks*. Chicago: University of Chicago Press.

Devasundaram, Ashvin Immanuel (2014). "All the World's a Ship: Binary Breaking, Connectedness and Choice in the Film *Ship of Theseus*." Presentation at the Film & Philosophy Conference 2014: A World of Cinemas.

Deyneka, Leah (2012). "May the Myth Be with You, Always," in Douglas Brode and Leah Deyneka (ed.), *Myth, Media, and Culture in Star Wars: An Anthology*. Lanham: Scarecrow Press, 31–46.

Di Cintio, Marcello (2007). *Poets and Pahlevans: A Journey into the Heart of Iran*. Toronto: Vintage Canada.

DiLullo, Tara (2007). *300. The Art of the Film*. Milwaukie, OR: Dark Horse Books.
Dundas, Paul (2002). *The Jains*. 2nd edn. New York: Routledge.
Dyer, Richard (1979). *Stars*. London: BFI.
Dyer, Richard (1996). "The Peplum," in Geoffrey Nowell-Smith, James Hay, and Gianni Volpi (eds.), *The Companion to Italian Cinema*. London: Cassell, 94–5.
Dyer, Richard (1997). *White: Essays on Race and Culture*. London: Routledge.
Dyer, Richard (2004). *Heavenly Bodies: Film Stars and Society*. 2nd edn. London: Routledge.
Early, Frances H. and Kennedy, Kathleen (eds.) (2003). *Athena's Daughters: Television's New Women Warriors. Television and Popular Culture*. Syracuse: Syracuse University Press.
Edwards, Paul (ed.) (1997). *Immortality*. Amherst, NY: Prometheus Books.
Ehrman, Bart D. (2008). *God's Problem: How the Bible Fails to Answer Our Most Important Question – Why We Suffer*. New York: HarperCollins.
Ekroth, Gunnel (2007). "Heroes and Hero-Cults," in Daniel Ogden (ed.), *A Companion to Greek Religion*. Oxford: Wiley-Blackwell, 100–14.
Elley, Derek (1984). *The Epic Film: Myth and History*. London: Routledge.
Elliott, Andrew B. R. (2011). "From Maciste to Maximus and Company: The Fragmented Hero in the New Epic," in Michael G. Cornelius (ed.), *Of Muscles and Men: Essays on the Sword and Sandal Film*. Jefferson: McFarland, 58–74.
Éloy, Michel (1998). "La mythologie grecque au cinéma," in Claude Aziza (ed.), *Le péplum: L'antiquité au cinéma*. Condé-sur-Noireau: Corlet-Télérama, 28–33.
Engstrom, Erika and Valenzano, Joseph M. III (2014). *Television, Religion, and Supernatural: Hunting Monsters, Finding Gods*. Plymouth: Lexington Books.
Epstein, William H. (2011). "Introduction: Biopics and American National Identity – Invented Lives, Imagined Communities." *a/b: Auto/Biography Studies* 26.1: 1–33.
Epstein, William H. and Palmer, R. Burton (eds.) (2017). *Invented Lives, Imagined Communities: The Biopic and American National Identity*. Albany: SUNY Press.
Faludi, Susan (2007). *The Terror Dream: Fear and Fantasy in Post-9/11 America*. New York: Metropolitan Books.
Farnell, Lewis Richard (1921). *Greek Hero Cults and the Ideas of Immortality*. Oxford: Clarendon Press.
Fejfer, Jane (2008). *Roman Portraits in Context*. Berlin: Walter de Gruyter.
Finke, Nikki and Fleming, Mike Jr. (2012). "Darren Aronofsky's *Noah* Launching Finally with Russell Crowe Set for Biblical Star." *Deadline Hollywood*, March 20.

Fitton, J. Lesley (1995). *The Discovery of the Greek Bronze Age*. London: British Museum Press.

Fitzgerald, F. Scott (1925). *The Great Gatsby*. New York: Charles Scribner's Sons.

Flegel, Monica and Roth, Jenny (2010). "Annihilating Love and Heterosexuality Without Women: Romance, Generic Difference, and Queer Politics in *Supernatural* Fan Fiction." *Transformative Works and Cultures* 4 (http://journal.transformativeworks.org).

Fleming, Mike Jr. (2016). "David Scarpa to Rewrite *Cleopatra*." *Deadline Hollywood*, April 6.

Floyd, Nigel (2010). "Review: *Centurion*." *Time Out London*, April 20.

Föllmer, Katja (2013). "Satire in Iranian Media," in Annabelle Sreberny and Massoumeh Torfeh (eds.), *Cultural Revolution in Iran*. London: I. B. Tauris, 193–208.

Fourcart, Florent (2012). *Le péplum italien (1946–1966): Grandeur et decadence d'une antiquité populaire*. Paris: Éditions imho.

Fowles, Jib (1992). *Starstruck: Celebrity Performers and the American Public*. Washington, DC: Smithsonian Institution Press.

Friedl, Erika (2014). *Folktales and Storytellers of Iran*. London: I. B. Tauris.

Frye, Northrop (1957). *Anatomy of Criticism: Four Essays*. Princeton: Princeton University Press.

Futrell, Alison (2003). "The Baby, the Mother, and the Empire: Xena as Ancient Hero," in Frances H. Early and Kathleen Kennedy (eds.), *Athena's Daughters: Television's New Women Warriors*. Syracuse: Syracuse University Press, 13–26, 137–8.

Futrell, Alison (2013). "Love, Rebellion, and Cleavage," in Monica S. Cyrino (ed.), *Screening Love and Sex in the Ancient World*. New York: Palgrave Macmillan, 211–25.

Galinsky, G. Karl (1972). *The Herakles Theme: The Adaptations of the Hero in Literature from Homer to the Twentieth Century*. Totowa: Rowman and Littlefield.

Gamel, Mary-Kay and Blondell, Ruby (eds.) (2005). *Ancient Mediterranean Women in Modern Mass Media*. Helios 32.2.

Gantz, Timothy (1993). *Early Greek Myth*. Baltimore: Johns Hopkins University Press.

Garcia, Nacho (2008). "Classic Sceneries: Ancient Greece in Film Architecture," in Irene Berti and Marta García Morcillo (eds.), *Hellas on Screen*. Stuttgart: Franz Steiner, 21–38.

Gellar-Goad, Ted (2013). "Rehash of the Titans: Sequels to the Titanomachy on the American Screen (part 1)." *Society for Classical Studies*, December 15 (https://classicalstudies.org/blogs/t-h-m-gellar-goad/rehash-titans-sequels-titanomachy-american-screen-part-1).

Gellar-Goad, Ted (2014). "Rehash of the Titans: Sequels to the Titanomachy on the American Screen (part 2)." *Society for Classical*

*Studies*, January 10 (https://classicalstudies.org/scs-blog/tedgellargoad/rehash-titans-sequels-titanomachy-american-screen-part-2).

George, Milo (2003). *The Comics Journal Library, Volume 2: Frank Miller*. Seattle: Fantagraphics.

Geraghty, Lincoln (2005). "Creating and Comparing Myth in Twentieth-Century Science Fiction: *Star Trek* and *Star Wars*." *Literature/Film Quarterly* 33: 191–200.

Giordano, Michele (1998). *Giganti buoni: Da Ercole a Piedone (e oltre) il mito dell'uomo forte ne cinema italiano*. Rome: Gremese.

Gledhill, Christine (ed.) (1991). *Stardom: Industry of Desire*. London: Routledge.

Gleiberman, Owen (2014). "Reviews: *Pompeii* Movie." *Entertainment Weekly*, March 8.

Goguen, Stacey (2013). "Masculinity and Supernatural Love," in Galen A. Foresman and William Irwin (eds.), Supernatural *and Philosophy: Metaphysics and Monsters ... for Idjits*. Malden: Wiley-Blackwell, 169–78.

Gordon, Andrew (1978). "*Star Wars*: A Myth for Our Time." *Literature/Film Quarterly* 6: 314–26.

Gordon, Joel (2017). "When Superman Smote Zeus: Analysing Violent Deicide in Popular Culture." *Classical Receptions Journal* 9.2: 211–36.

Graves, Robert (1934a). *I, Claudius*. London: Arthur Barker.

Graves, Robert (1934b). *Claudius the God*. London: Arthur Barker.

Green, Stephen J. (2013). "Perseus on the Psychiatrist's Couch in Leterrier's *Clash of the Titans* (2010): Harryhausen Reloaded for 21st Century." *New Voices in Classical Reception Studies, Conference Proceedings* 1: 75–85.

Griffiths, Emma M. (2002). "Euripides' *Herakles* and the Pursuit of Immortality.' *Mnemosyne* 55.6: 641–56.

Griffiths, Emma M. (2006). *Medea*. London: Routledge.

Günsberg, Maggie (2005). *Italian Cinema: Gender and Genre*. Basingstoke: Palgrave Macmillan.

Halliwell, Stephen (1987). *The Poetics of Aristotle: Translation and Commentary*. Chapel Hill: University of North Carolina Press.

Hansen, Regina (2014). "Deconstructing the Apocalypse? *Supernatural*'s Postmodern Appropriation of Angelic Hierarchies," in Susan A. George and Regina Hansen (eds.), *Supernatural, Humanity, and the Soul*. New York: Palgrave Macmillan, 13–26.

Harryhausen, Ray and Dalton, Tony (2004). *Ray Harryhausen: An Animated Life*. New York: Billboard Books.

Hassler-Forest, Dan (2010). "The *300* Controversy. A Case Study in the Politics of Adaptation," in Joyce Goggins and Dan Hassler-Forest (eds.), *The Rise and Reason of Comics and Graphic Literature: Critical Essays on the Form*. Jefferson: McFarland, 119–27.

Hawes, Greta (2014). *Rationalizing Myth in Antiquity*. Oxford: Oxford University Press.

Higgins, Reynold (1967). *Minoan and Mycenaean Art*. London: Thames and Hudson.

Hiltunen, Ari (2002). *Aristotle in Hollywood: The Anatomy of Successful Storytelling*. Bristol: Intellect Books.

Hogg, Trevor (2014). "Herculean Tasks." *CG Society Features*, November 25.

Holden, Stephen (2010). "Two Vastly Different Enemies Share a Common Thirst for Blood." *New York Times*, August 26.

Hughes, Howard (2011). *Cinema Italiano*. London: I. B. Tauris.

Innes, D. C. (1979). "Gigantomachy and Natural Philosophy." *Classical Quarterly* 29.1: 165–71.

Inness, Sherrie A. (ed.) (2004). *Action Chicks: New Images of Tough Women in Popular Culture*. New York: Palgrave Macmillan.

Izundu, Chi Chi (2015). "*Atlantis* is Axed by the BBC After Second Series." *BBC.co.uk*, January 26.

Janan, Micaela (2001). *The Politics of Desire: Propertius IV*. Berkeley: University of California Press.

Jeffords, Susan (1993). "Can Masculinity be Terminated?" in Steven Cohan and Ina Rae Hark (eds.), *Screening the Male: Exploring Masculinities in Hollywood Cinema*. London: Routledge, 245–62.

Jewett, Robert and Lawrence, John Shelton (1977). *The American Monomyth*. Garden City: Anchor.

Johanson, Christopher (2008). *Spectacle in the Forum: Visualizing the Roman Aristocratic Funeral of the Middle Republic*. PhD diss., University of California, Los Angeles.

Johnson, Derek (2007). "Will the Real Wolverine Please Stand Up? Marvel's Mutation from Monthlies to Movies," in Ian Gordon, Mark Jancovich, and Matthew McAllister (eds.), *Film and Comic Books*. Jackson: University Press of Mississippi, 285–300.

Johnson, Derek (2012). "Cinematic Destiny: Marvel Studios and the Trade Stories of Industrial Convergence." *Cinema Journal* 52: 1–24.

Jolin, Dan (2010). "*Centurion*: Review." *Empire*, February 28.

Jowett, Lorna (2005). *Sex and the Slayer: A Gender Studies Primer for the Buffy Fan*. Middletown: Wesleyan University Press.

Kakissis, Joanna (2012). "Why the Rise of Greece's Golden Dawn Party Is Bad for Europe." *Time*, November 5.

Kann, Drew (2017). "Meet the Top CNN Heroes of 2016." *CNN.com*, April 18.

Karimi, Nasser (2007). "Iranians Outraged by *300* Movie." *The Guardian*, March 13.

Kelly, Rachael (2014). *Mark Antony and Popular Culture: Masculinity and the Construction of an Icon*. London: I. B. Tauris.

Kennedy, Kathleen (2003). "Love Is the Battlefield: The Making and the Unmaking of the Just Warrior in *Xena, Warrior Princess*," in Frances H.

Early and Kathleen Kennedy (eds.), *Athena's Daughters: Television's New Women Warriors*. Syracuse: Syracuse University Press, 40–52.

Kierdorf, Wilhelm (1980). *Laudatio Funebris: Interpretationen und Untersuchungen zur Entwicklung der römischen Leichenrede*. Meisenheim am Glan: Anton Hain.

Klock, Geoff (2002). *How to Read Superhero Comics and Why*. New York: Continuum.

Knappert, Jan (1993). *The Encyclopaedia of Middle Eastern Mythology and Religion*. Rockport: Element.

Korangy, Alireza (2017). *Martyrdom in Iran: The History of Martyrs in Classical and Modern Persian Literature*. London: I. B. Tauris.

Kovacs, George (2013). "Truth, Justice, and the Spartan Way: Freedom and Democracy in Frank Miller's *300*," in Lorna Hardwick and Stephen Harrison (eds.), *Classics in the Modern World: A Democratic Turn?* Oxford: Oxford University Press, 381–92.

Kroll, Luisa (2011). "Sean Parker's Tribute to His Hero Steve Jobs." *Forbes Online*, October 6.

Kukkonen, Karin (2013). "Navigating Infinite Earths," in C. Hatfield, J. Heer, and K. Worcester (eds.), *The Superhero Reader*. Jackson: University of Mississippi Press, 155–69.

Kuntz, Mary (1993–4). "The Prodikean 'Choice of Herakles': A Reshaping of Myth." *Classical Journal* 89.2: 163–81.

Kyle, Donald G. (1998). *Spectacles of Death in Ancient Rome*. London: Routledge.

Lagny, M. (1992). "Popular Taste: The Peplum," in Richard Dyer and G. Vincendeau (eds.), *Popular European Cinema*. London: Routledge, 163–80.

Landrum, Jason (2015). "Say My Name: The Fantasy of Liberated Masculinity," in Jacob Blevins and Dafydd Wood (eds.), *The Methods of Breaking Bad: Essays on Narrative, Character, and Ethics*. Jefferson: McFarland, 94–108

Lang, Bernhard (2002). "This Is My Body: Sacrificial Presentation and the Origins of Christian Ritual," in Albert I. Baumgarten (ed.), *Sacrifice in Religious Experience*. Leiden: Brill, 189–205.

Langford, Barry (2005). *Film Genre: Hollywood and Beyond*. Edinburgh: Edinburgh University Press.

Larbalestier, Justine (2004). "The Only Thing Better Than Killing a Slayer: Heterosexuality and Sex in *Buffy the Vampire Slayer*," in Roz Kaveney (ed.), *Reading the Vampire Slayer: An Unofficial Critical Companion to Buffy and Angel*. London: Tauris Parke, 195–219.

Leith, Sam (2010). "The Return of Swords 'n' Sandals Movies." *Financial Times*, May 14.

Littleton, Cynthia (2015). "NBC Cancels AD as Producers Plan Digital Revival for Biblical Drama." *Variety*, July 3.

Llewellyn-Jones, Lloyd (2005). "Herakles Re-Dressed: Gender, Clothing, and the Construction of a Greek Hero," in Louis Rawlings and Hugh

Bowden (eds.), *Herakles and Hercules: Exploring a Graeco-Roman Divinity*. Swansea: Classical Press of Wales, 51–69.

Llewellyn-Jones, Lloyd (2018). *Designs on the Past: How Hollywood Created the Ancient World, 1915–1965*. Edinburgh: Edinburgh University Press.

Lodge, Mary Jo (2009). "Knocked Up, Not Knocked Out: *Xena: Warrior Princess*, Pregnant Action Hero," in Lisa De Tora (ed.), *Heroes of Film, Comics and American Culture*. Jefferson: McFarland, 218–33.

Loraux, Nicole (1990). "Herakles: The Super-Male and the Feminine," in David M. Halperin, John J. Winkler, and Froma I. Zeitlin (eds.), *Before Sexuality*. Princeton: Princeton University Press, 21–52.

Lotz, Amanda D. (2014). *Cable Guys*. New York: New York University Press.

Lowry, Brian (2010). "Review: *Clash of the Titans*." *Variety*, March 28.

Lucanio, Patrick (1994). *With Fire and Sword: Italian Spectacle on American Screens, 1958–1968*. Metuchen: Scarecrow Press.

Luhn, Alec (2014). "Vladimir Putin Depicted as Hercules in Moscow Art Exhibition." *The Guardian*, October 6.

Luhn, Alec (2016). "Book Celebrates Vladimir Putin as 'Global Cultural Phenomenon'." *The Guardian*, October 7.

Lyons, Deborah (1997). *Gender and Immortality: Heroines in Ancient Greek Myth and Cult*. Princeton: Princeton University Press.

Mainon, Dominique and Ursini, James (2006). *The Modern Amazons: Warrior Women On-Screen*. Pompton Plains: Limelight Editions.

Marcus, Greil (2011). *The Doors: A Lifetime of Listening to Five Mean Years*. New York: PublicAffairs Books.

Marshall, Daniel (2003). *The Cinema Anti-Hero*. London: Athena.

Mastronarde, Donald (1968). "Theocritus' *Idyll* 13: Love and the Hero." *Transactions of the American Philological Association* 99: 273–90.

Mayne, Judith (1993). *Cinema and Spectatorship*. London: Routledge.

Mayor, Adrienne (2014). *The Amazons: Lives and Legends of Warrior Women Across the Ancient World*. Princeton: Princeton University Press.

McAuley, Alex (2016a). "Hypatia's Hijab: Visual Echoes of 9/11 in Alejandro Amenábar's *Agora*." *Mouseion* 13.1: 131–51.

McAuley, Alex (2016b). "Resurrecting the War on Terror in *Risen* (2016)." *Classical Reception Studies Network*, December 5 (http://www.open.ac.uk/blogs/CRSN/?p=351).

McAuley, Alex (forthcoming). "Broken Eagles: The Roman Soldier in Post-9/11 Film," in Meredith E. Safran (ed.), *Golden Ages on Screen*. Edinburgh: Edinburgh University Press.

McGovern, Joe (2016). "*Ben-Hur*: EW Review." *Entertainment Weekly*, August 17.

McKenna, Anthony T. (2008). *Joseph E. Levine: Showmanship, Reputation and Industrial Practice 1945–1977*. PhD diss., University of Nottingham.

Means-Shannon, Hannah (2014). "Alan Moore Calls for Boycott of 'Wretched Film' Hercules on Behalf of Friend Steve Moore." *BleedingCool*, July 17.
Mehochko, Daniel A. (2013). *Iran's Post-9/11 Grand Bargain: Missed Opportunity for Strategic Rapprochement Between Iran and the United States*. Fort Leavenworth, KS: U.S. Army Command and General Staff College, School of Advanced Military Studies.
Mercer, John and Shingler, Martin (2005). *Melodrama: Genre, Style, Sensibility*. London: Wallflower Press.
Miller, Frank (1986). *Batman: The Dark Knight Returns*. Burbank: DC Comics.
Miller, Frank (1998). *300*. Milwaukie, OR: Dark Horse Comics.
Miller, Ross (2013). "Steve Wozniak Turned Down Offer." *The Verge*, January 26.
Mills, Sophie (1997). *Theseus, Tragedy and the Athenian Empire*. Oxford: Clarendon Press.
Mitchell, Lynette (2014). "Herodotus' Cyrus and Political Freedom," in Ali M. Ansari (ed.), *Perceptions of Iran*. London: I. B. Tauris, 101–18.
Moaveni, Azadeh (2007). "*300* Sparks an Outcry in Iran." *Time Magazine*, March 13.
Monaco, James (1981). *How to Read a Film*. Oxford: Oxford University Press.
Moore, Alan (1987). *Watchmen*. Burbank: DC Comics.
Moore, Mary B. (1979). "The Central Group in the Gigantomachy of the Old Athena Temple in the Acropolis." *American Journal of Archaeology* 99.4: 633–9.
Moore, Mary B. (1995). "Lydos and the Gigantomachy." *American Journal of Archaeology* 83.1: 79–99.
Moore, Steve and Wijaya, Admira (2008). *Hercules: The Thracian Wars*. Carpinteria, CA: Radical Book.
Morton, Walt (1993). "Tracking the Sign of Tarzan: Trans-Media Representation of a Pop-Culture Icon," in Pat Kirkham and Janet Thumim (eds.), *You Tarzan: Masculinity, Movies and Men*. London: Lawrence and Wishart, 106–25.
Mossman, Judith M. (1988). "Tragedy and Epic in Plutarch's *Alexander*." *Journal of Hellenic Studies* 108: 83–93.
Mottram, James (2014). "Dwayne Johnson's Herculean Labour of Love." *Scmp.com*, July 20.
Mousavian, Seyed Hossein (2014). *Iran and the United States*. London: Bloomsbury.
Mozaffari, Ali (2014). *Forming National Identity in Iran: The Idea of Homeland Derived from Ancient Persian and Islamic Imaginations of Place*. London: I. B. Tauris.
Murnaghan, Sheila (2011). "Classics for Cool Kids: Popular and Unpopular Versions of Antiquity for Children." *Classical World* 104.3: 339–53.

Muschamp, Herbert (2000). "*Gladiator*: Throwing Our Anxieties to the Lions." *New York Times*, April 30.
Naiden, Fred S. (2007). "The Fallacy of the Willing Victim." *Journal of Hellenic Studies* 127: 61–73.
Naiden, Fred S. (2013). *Smoke Signals for the Gods*. Oxford: Oxford University Press.
Naidu, Rajesh (2013). "Ship of Theseus: An Odyssey Within." *The South Asianist* 2.3: 188–93.
Nashawaty, Chris (2014). "*Exodus: Gods and Kings*." *Entertainment Weekly*, December 19.
Nason, Richard (1959). "*Hercules* Starts Flood of Movies." *New York Times*, October 24, 13.
Neimneh, Shadi (2013). "The Anti-Hero in Modernist Fiction: From Irony to Cultural Renewal." *Mosaic* 46: 75–90.
Nicol, Rhonda (2014). "'How Is That Not Rape-y?': Dean as Anti-Bella and Feminism Without Women in *Supernatural*," in Susan A. George and Regina M. Hansen (eds.), *Supernatural, Humanity, and the Soul: On the Highway to Hell and Back*. New York: Palgrave Macmillan, 155–68.
Nieva, Richard (2014). "Eric Schmidt: Steve Jobs is My Hero." *CNet*, 2 October.
Nikoloutsos, Konstantinos P. (2009). "The *Alexander* Bromance: Male Desire and Gender Fluidity in Oliver Stone's Historical Epic." *Helios* 35: 223–51.
Nikoloutsos, Konstantinos P. (ed.) (2013). *Ancient Greek Women in Film: Classical Presences*. Oxford: Oxford University Press.
Nisbet, Gideon (2008). *Ancient Greece in Film and Popular Culture*. 2nd edn. Liverpool: Liverpool University Press. (1st edn 2006.)
O'Brien, Daniel (2011). "Hercules Diminished? Parody, Differentiation, and Emulation in *The Three Stooges Meet Hercules*," in Michael G. Cornelius (ed.), *Of Muscles and Men: Essays on the Sword and Sandal Film*. Jefferson: McFarland, 187–202.
O'Brien, Daniel (2014). *Classical Masculinity and the Spectacular Body on Film: The Mighty Sons of Hercules*. Basingstoke: Palgrave Macmillan.
Ogden, Daniel (2008). *Perseus*. London: Routledge.
O'Hagan, Jacinta (2004). "'The Power and the Passion': Civilizational Identity and Alterity in the Wake of September 11th," in Patricia M. Goff and Kevin C. Dunn (eds.), *Identity and Global Politics: Theoretical and Empirical Elaborations*. New York: Palgrave Macmillan, 27–36.
O'Kelly, Declan (2014). "The Rock's Hercules Meal-Plan." *Muscle and Fitness*, July.
Omidsalar, Mahmoud (2011). *Poetics and Politics of Iran's National Epic, The Shahnameh*. New York: Palgrave Macmillan.
Omidsalar, Mahmoud (2012). *Iran's Epic and America's Empire: A Handbook for a Generation in Limbo*. Santa Monica: Afshar.

Pallant, Chris (2011). "Developments in Peplum Filmmaking: Disney's *Hercules*," in Michael G. Cornelius (ed.), *Of Muscles and Men: Essays on the Sword and Sandal Film*. Jefferson, NC: McFarland, 175–86.

Palumbo, Donald E. (2014). *The Monomyth in American Science Fiction Films*. Jefferson: McFarland.

Papaioannou, Sophia (2007). *Redesigning Achilles*. Berlin: Walter de Gruyter.

Parsons, Louella O. (1959). "If a Movie's a 'Dog,' Joe Levine Makes It a Mint." *The Washington Post*, September 20, H7.

Paton, W. R., Walbank, F. W., and Habicht, Christian (2010). *Polybius, The Histories, Volume III: Books 5–8*. Cambridge, MA: Harvard University Press.

Paul, Joanna (2010). "Oliver Stone's *Alexander* and the Cinematic Epic Tradition," in Paul Cartledge and Fiona Rose Greenland (eds.), *Responses to Oliver Stone's Alexander: Film, History, and Cultural Studies*. Madison: University of Wisconsin Press, 15–35.

Paul, Joanna (2013). *Film and the Classical Epic Tradition*. Oxford: Oxford University Press.

Pavlich, Katie (2014). "George W. Bush on 9/11/2001: We're at War, We Will Find Who Did This and 'We're Going to Kick Their A\*\*'." *Townhall.com*, September 11.

Petrovic, Ivana (2008). "Plutarch's and Stone's *Alexander*," in Irene Berti and Marta García Morcillo (eds.), *Hellas on Screen: Cinematic Receptions of Ancient History, Literature, and Myth*. Stuttgart: Franz Steiner, 163–83.

Pierce, Jerry B. (2011). "'To Do or Die Manfully': Performing Heteronormativity in Recent Epic Films," in Michael G. Cornelius (ed.), *Of Muscles and Men: Essays on the Sword and Sandal Film*. Jefferson: McFarland, 40–57.

Pierce, Jerry B. (2013). "Oliver Stone's Unmanning of Alexander the Great in *Alexander* (2004)," in Monica S. Cyrino (ed.), *Screening Love and Sex in the Ancient World*. New York: Palgrave Macmillan, 127–41.

Pisters, Patricia (2014). "Transplanting Life: *Bios* and *Zoe* in Images with Imagination," in Bolette Blalaagaard and Iris van der Tuin (eds.), *The Subject of Rosi Braidotti: Politics and Concepts*. London: Bloomsbury, 65–71.

Platt, Verity (2010). "Viewing the Past: Cinematic Exegesis in the Caverns of Macedon," in Paul Cartledge and Fiona Rose Greenland (eds.), *Responses to Oliver Stone's Alexander: Film, History, and Cultural Studies*. Madison: University of Wisconsin Press, 285–304.

Pollard, Thomas (2009). "Hollywood 9/11: Time of Crisis," in Matthew J. Morgan (ed.), *The Impact of 9/11 on the Media, Arts, and Entertainment*. New York: Palgrave Macmillan, 195–208.

Pomeroy, Arthur J. (2008). *Then It Was Destroyed by the Volcano: The Ancient World in Film and on Television*. London: Bloomsbury.

Pomeroy, Arthur J. (2013). "The Women of Ercole," in Konstantinos P. Nikoloutsos (ed.), *Ancient Greek Women in Film*. Oxford: Oxford University Press, 189–206.

Potter, Amanda (2015). "Slashing *Rome*: Season Two Rewritten in Online Fan Fiction," in Monica S. Cyrino (ed.), *Rome, Season Two: Trial and Triumph*. Edinburgh: Edinburgh University Press, 219–30.

Potter, Amanda (2016). "Fan Reactions to Nagron as One True Pairing," in Antony Augoustakis and Monica S. Cyrino (eds.), *STARZ Spartacus: Reimagining an Icon on Screen*. Edinburgh: Edinburgh University Press, 161–72.

Ram, Haggay (2009). *Iranophobia: The Logic of an Israeli Obsession*. Stanford: Stanford University Press.

Ramage, Edwin S. (2006). "Funeral Eulogy and Propaganda in the Roman Republic." *Athenaeum* 94: 39–64.

Raucci, Stacie (2015). "Of Marketing and Men: Making the Cinematic Greek Hero, 2010–2014," in Monica S. Cyrino and Meredith E. Safran (eds.), *Classical Myth on Screen*. New York: Palgrave Macmillan, 161–71.

Rebello, Stephen and Healey, Jane (1997). *The Art of Hercules: The Chaos of Creation*. New York: Hyperion.

Rees, Roger (2010). "Panegyric," in William Dominik and Jon Hall (eds.), *A Companion to Roman Rhetoric*. Oxford: Wiley-Blackwell, 136–48.

Reich, Jacqueline (2011). "Slave to Fashion: Masculinity, Suits, and the Maciste Films of Italian Silent Cinema," in Adrienne Munich (ed.), *Fashion in Film*. Bloomington: Indiana University Press, 236–59.

Reich, Jacqueline (2013). "The Metamorphosis of Maciste in Italian Silent Cinema." *Film History* 25: 32–56.

Reich, Jacqueline (2015). *The Maciste Films of Italian Silent Cinema*. Bloomington: Indiana University Press.

Reinhartz, Adele (2013). *Bible and Cinema: An Introduction*. London: Routledge.

Rice, Lynette (2014). "*Son of God* Rises." *Entertainment Weekly*, March 7.

Riedweg, C. (2005). *Pythagoras: His Life, Teaching and Influence*. Ithaca: Cornell University Press.

Rogers, Brett M. (2011). "Heroes UnLimited: The Theory of the Hero's Journey and the Limitation of the Superhero Myth," in George Kovacs and C. W. Marshall (ed.), *Classics and Comics*. Oxford: Oxford University Press, 73–86.

Rosenburg, Steve (2014a). "In Pictures: The 12 Labours of . . . Putin." *BBC News*, October 7.

Rosenburg, Steve (2014b). "Putin Portrayed as Hercules in Art Exhibition." *BBC News*, October 7.

Roth, Lane (1987). "Death and Rebirth in *Star Trek II: The Wrath of Khan*." *Extrapolation* 28.2: 155–66.

Rothman, Lily (2014). "Nature Bites Back." *Time Magazine*, May 19.

Rottenberg, Josh (2014). "Banking on the Bible." *Entertainment Weekly*, March 7.
Rushing, Robert A. (2008). "Gentlemen Prefer Hercules: Desire, Identification, Beefcake." *Camera Obscura* 23.3: 159–91.
Rushing, Robert A. (2016). *Descended From Hercules: Biopolitics and the Muscled Male Body on Screen*. Bloomington: Indiana University Press.
Russell, Miles (2011). "The Roman Ninth Legion's Mysterious Loss." *BBC Magazine*, March 16.
Safran, Meredith E. (2015). "Re-Conceiving Hercules: Divine Paternity and Christian Anxiety in *Hercules* (2005)," in Monica S. Cyrino and Meredith E. Safran (eds.), *Classical Myth on Screen*. New York: Palgrave Macmillan, 133–45.
Salzman-Mitchell, Patricia and Alvares, Jean (2017). *Classical Myth and Film in the New Millennium*. Oxford: Oxford University Press.
Samiei, Sasab (2014). *Ancient Persia in Western History: Hellenism and the Representation of the Achaemenid Empire*. London: I. B. Tauris.
Sanburn, Josh (2014). "Films Are His Flock: Jonathan Bock Explains Christians to Hollywood." *Time*, March 31.
Scheid, John (2011). "Sacrifices for Gods and Ancestors," in Jörg Rüpke (ed.), *A Companion to Roman Religion*. Malden: Wiley-Blackwell, 263–72.
Schiff, Stacy (2010). *Cleopatra: A Life*. New York: Little, Brown.
Schultz, Celia E. (2010). "The Romans and Ritual Murder." *Journal of the American Academy of Religion* 78.2: 516–41.
Schwab, Katherine A. (1996). "Parthenon East Metope XI: Herakles and the Gigantomachy." *American Journal of Archaeology* 100.1: 81–90.
Seastrom, Lucas O. (2015). "Mythic Discovery Within the Inner Reaches of Outer Space: Joseph Campbell Meets George Lucas – Part I." *Starwars.com*, October 22.
Sergent, Bernard (1984). *L'homosexualité dans la mythologie grecque*. Paris: Payot.
Shahabudin, Kim (2009). "Ancient Mythology and Modern Myths: *Hercules Conquers Atlantis* (1961)," in Dunstan Lowe and Kim Shahabudin (eds.), *Classics for All: Reworking Antiquity in Mass Culture*. Newcastle upon Tyne: Cambridge Scholars, 196–216.
Shahabudin, Kim (2010). "The Appearance of History: Robert Rossen's *Alexander the Great*," in Paul Cartledge and Fiona Rose Greenland (eds.), *Responses to Oliver Stone's Alexander: Film, History, and Cultural Studies*. Madison: University of Wisconsin Press, 92–116.
Shaheen, Jack G. (2001). *Reel Bad Arabs: How Hollywood Vilifies a People*. Northampton: Olive Branch Press.
Shapiro, H. Alan (1983). "'Heros Theos': The Death and Apotheosis of Herakles." *The Classical World* 77.1: 7–18.
Sharkey, Betsy (2010). "Movie Review: *Centurion*." *Los Angeles Times*, August 27.

Silverman, Gary (2015). "The Legacy of Steve Jobs as a Civil Rights Hero." *Financial Times*, June 12.
Simmons, Jennifer Beth (2004). *Visions of Feminist (Porn(o)nanism): Masturbating Female Postmodern Subjectivity in American Television and Film*. PhD diss., University of Florida.
Skinner, Marilyn B. (2010). "*Alexander* and Ancient Greek Sexuality: Some Theoretical Considerations," in Paul Cartledge and Fiona Rose Greenland (eds.), *Responses to Oliver Stone's Alexander: Film, History, and Cultural Studies*. Madison: University of Wisconsin Press, 119–34.
Sobchack, Vivian (1990). "'Surge and Splendor': A Phenomenology of the Hollywood Historical Epic." *Representations* 29: 29–49.
Solomon, Jon (2001). *The Ancient World in the Cinema*. Rev. and expanded edn. New Haven: Yale University Press.
Solomon, Jon (2008). "Death, Eternity, Immortality, and Divinity in Recent Ancients." *Classical and Modern Literature* 28.1: 21–52.
Solomon, Jon (2010). "The Popular Reception of *Alexander*," in Paul Cartledge and Fiona Rose Greenland (eds.), *Responses to Oliver Stone's Alexander: Film, History, and Cultural Studies*. Madison: University of Wisconsin Press, 36–51.
Solomon, Jon (2014). "The Muscleman Peplum," in Peter Bondanella (ed.), *The Italian Cinema Book*. London: Palgrave Macmillan, 163–71.
Solomon, Sheldon, Greenberg, Jeff, and Pyszczynski, Tom (2015). *The Worm at the Core: On the Role of Death in Life*. New York: Random House.
Sorbo, Kevin (2011). *True Strength: My Journey From Hercules to Mere Mortal and How Nearly Dying Saved My Life*. Cambridge, MA: Da Capo Press.
Spicer, Andrew (2001). *Typical Men: The Representation of Masculinity in Popular British Cinema*. London: I. B. Tauris.
Stafford, Emma (2005). "Virtue or Vice? Herakles and the Art of Allegory," in Louis Rawlings and Hugh Bowden (eds.), *Herakles and Hercules: Exploring a Graeco-Roman Divinity*. Swansea: Classical Press of Wales, 71–96.
Stafford, Emma (2012). *Herakles: Gods and Heroes of the Ancient World*. London: Routledge.
Stafford, Emma J. (2017). "Hercules' Choice: Vice, Virtue and the Hero of the Modern Screen," in Eran Almagor and Lisa Maurice (eds.), *The Reception of Ancient Virtues and Vices in Modern Popular Culture: Beauty, Bravery, Blood and Glory*. Leiden: Brill, 140–66.
Staskiewicz, Keith (2014). "In the Line of Fire: A History." *Entertainment Weekly*, March 7.
Steimer, Lauren (2009). "From Wuxia to Xena: Translation and the Body Spectacle of Zoë Bell." *Discourse* 31: 359–90.
Stevens, Dana (2007). "A Movie Only a Spartan Could Love: The Battle Epic *300*." *Slate.com*, March 8.

Stoneman, Richard (2015). *Xerxes: A Persian Life*. New Haven: Yale University Press.
Strong, Anise K. (2016). "The Rape of Lucretia," in Antony Augoustakis and Monica S. Cyrino (eds.), *STARZ Spartacus: Reimaginining an Icon on Screen*. Edinburgh: Edinburgh University Press, 133–47.
Sunshine, Linda and Ratner, Brett (2014). *The Art and Making of Hercules*. New York: HarperCollins.
Sutcliff, Rosemary (1954). *The Eagle of the Ninth*. New York: H. Z. Walck.
Suvin, Darko (1979). *Metamorphoses of Science Fiction: On the Poetics and History of a Literary Genre*. New Haven: Yale University Press.
Tartaglione, Nancy (2014). "FINAL: Intl Box-Office . . . Hercules Muscles In." *Deadline Hollywood*, July 28.
Thomas, Bob (1997). *Disney's Art of Animation: From Mickey Mouse to Hercules*. 2nd edn. New York: Hyperion.
Thompson, Kristin (2007). *The Frodo Franchise: The Lord of the Rings and Modern Hollywood*. Berkeley: University of California Press.
Tierno, Michael (2002). *Aristotle's Poetics for Screenwriters: Storytelling Secrets from the Greatest Mind in Western Civilization*. New York: Hyperion.
Tolley, Kim (1999). "Xena, Warrior Princess, or Judith, Sexual Warrior? The Search for a Liberating Image of Women's Power in Popular Culture." *History of Education Quarterly* 39: 337–342.
Tomasso, Vincent (2011). "Hard-Boiled Hot Gates: Making the Classical Past Other in Frank Miller's *Sin City*," in C.W. Marshall and George Kovacs (eds.), *Classics and Comics*. Oxford: Oxford University Press, 145–58.
Tomasso, Vincent (2015a). "Classical Antiquity and Western Identity in *Battlestar Galactica*," in Brett M. Rogers and Benjamin E. Stevens (eds.), *Classical Traditions in Science Fiction*. Oxford: Oxford University Press, 243–59.
Tomasso, Vincent (2015b). "The Twilight of Olympus: Deicide and the End of the Greek Gods," in Monica S. Cyrino and Meredith E. Safran (eds.), *Classical Myth on Screen*. New York: Palgrave, 147–57.
Tomasso, Vincent (2016). "The Representation of Greek Gods in the Peplum Genre." Presentation at the Film & History Conference 2016: Gods and Heretics.
Tosenberger, Catherine (2008). "'The Epic Love Story of Sam and Dean': *Supernatural*, Queer Readings, and the Romance of Incestuous Fan Fiction." *Transformative Works and Cultures* 1 (http://journal.transformativeworks.org).
Trice, Ashton D. and Holland, Samuel A. (2001). *Heroes, Antiheroes and Dolts*. Jefferson: McFarland.
Tyron, Chuck (2009). *Reinventing Cinema: Movies in the Age of Media Convergence*. New Brunswick: Rutgers University Press.

Urbanski, Heather (2013). *The Science Fiction Reboot: Canon, Innovation and Fandom in Refashioned Franchises*. Jefferson: McFarland.

Vaage, Margrethe Bruun (2016). *The Antihero in American Television*. London: Routledge.

Vamvounis, Manolis (2008). "Moore Talks *Hercules: The Thracian Wars*." *CBR.com*, December 4.

Van Straten, Folkert T. (1995). *Hiera Kala: Images of Animal Sacrifice in Archaic and Classical Greece*. Leiden: Brill.

Varzi, Roxanne (2006). *Warring Souls: Youth, Media, and Martyrdom in Post-Revolution Iran*. Durham: Duke University Press.

Vermeer, Alicia Suzanne (2014). *Searching for God: Portrayals of Religion on Television*. MA diss., University of Iowa.

Vilkomerson, Sara (2014). "Weathering the Storm." *Entertainment Weekly*, March 7.

Vogler, Christopher (2007). *The Writer's Journey: Mythic Structure for Writers*. 3rd edn. Studio City: Michael Wiese Productions.

Von Tunzelmann, Alex (2012). "*300: Rise of an Empire* – Doesn't Know its Artemisia from its Elbow." *The Guardian*, March 12.

Wagstaff, Christopher (1998). "Italian Genre Films in the World Market," in Geoffrey Nowell-Smith and Steven Ricci (eds.), *Hollywood and Europe: Economics, Culture, National Identity, 1945–95*. London: BFI, 74–85.

Wallace, Lew (1880). *Ben-Hur: A Tale of the Christ*. New York: Harper & Brothers.

Ward, Annalee R. (2002). *Mouse Morality: The Rhetoric of Disney Animated Film*. Austin: University of Texas Press.

Weisbrot, Robert (1998). *Hercules: The Legendary Journeys. The Official Companion*. New York: Doubleday.

Wells, Paul (2002). *Animation: Genre and Authorship*. London: Wallflower Press.

Wetmore, Kevin (2012). *Post-9/11 Horror in American Cinema*. London: Bloomsbury.

Whitaker, Richard (2005). "Art and Ideology: The Case of the Pergamon Gigantomachy." *Acta Classica* 48.1: 163–74.

Whitehead, Adam (2016). "What Will HBO's Next Big Show Be?" *The Wertzone: SF&F in Print and On Screen*, April 26.

Wieber, Anja (2008). "Celluloid Alexander(s): A Hero from the Past as Role Model for the Present?" in Irene Berti and Marta García Morcillo (eds.), *Hellas on Screen: Cinematic Receptions of Ancient History, Literature, and Myth*. Stuttgart: Franz Steiner, 147–62.

Williams, Michael (2009). "The Idol Body: Stars, Statuary and the Classical Epic." *Film and History* 39.2: 39–48.

Wilson, Tim (2014). "Building the World of Hercules." *CreativeCow. net* (https://library.creativecow.net/article.php?author_folder=wilson_tim&article_folder=VFX_Hercules&page=1).

Winkler, Martin M. (ed.) (2001). *Classical Myth and Culture in the Cinema.* Oxford: Oxford University Press.

Winkler, Martin M. (ed.) (2004). *Gladiator: Film and History.* Malden: Blackwell.

Winkler, Martin M. (2007). "Greek Myth on the Screen", in Roger D. Woodard (ed.), *The Cambridge Companion to Greek Mythology.* Cambridge: Cambridge University Press, 453–79.

Winterer, Caroline (2002). *The Culture of Classicism: Ancient Greece and Rome in American Intellectual Life.* Baltimore: Johns Hopkins University Press.

Woodward, Gary C. (2003). *The Idea of Identification.* Albany: State University of New York Press.

Woolf, Michael P. (1976). "The Madman as Hero in Contemporary Fiction." *Journal of American Studies* 10.2: 257–69.

Wright, R. P. (1978). "Tile-Stamps of the Ninth Legion Found in Britain." *Britannia* 9: 379–82.

Wyke, Maria (1997a). *Projecting the Past: Ancient Rome, Cinema, and History.* London: Routledge.

Wyke, Maria (1997b). "The Classicizing Rhetoric of Bodybuilding." *Arion* 4: 51–79.

Wyke, Maria (2002). "Herculean Muscle! The Classicizing Rhetoric of Body Building," in James I. Porter (ed.), *Constructions of the Classical Body.* Ann Arbor: University of Michigan Press, 355–79.

Wyke, Maria (2007). *The Roman Mistress: Ancient and Modern Representations.* Oxford: Oxford University Press.

Zacharek, Stephanie (2016). "Movies: A *Ben-Hur* Remake Stumbles." *Time*, September 5.

Ziolkowski, Theodore (2004). *Hesitant Heroes: Private Inhibition, Cultural Crisis.* Ithaca: Cornell University Press.

Zoller Seitz, Matt (2014). "Noah Movie Review." *RogerEbert.com*, March 28.

# Index

9/11, 9, 195, 206–21
*300* (film), 8–9, 48, 53, 153, 184, 191–205, 207, 210–11, 214–16
*300: Rise of an Empire* (film), 9, 153, 191–205

Abel, 103
Acamas, 115
Achaemenid, 194, 201
Achilles, 1, 112, 129, 177–8, 180–1, 184, 213
Achour, Mouloud, 185
Acrisius, 182, 216
Acropolis, 54–5
AD: *The Bible Continues* (series), 98
Adama, Lee, 149–50
Addy, Mark, 125, 130
Adkins, Scott, 30, 183
Adonis, 23, 112
Aeschylus, 31, 83, 192
Aeson, 21, 129
Afghanistan, 156, 195
Agamemnon, 83
Agha-Soltan, Neda, 201
*Agora* (film), 208
Agricola, 160
Agron, 151
Ahmadinejad, Mahmoud, 198, 201
Aigina, 52
Ajax, 129
Al-Qaeda, 195
Alcides *see* Hercules
Alcmene, 20–1, 24, 37, 54, 65, 183, 186
*Alexander* (film), 9, 23, 107, 177–81, 197–8, 207, 211–14
Alexander the Great, 8–9, 44, 173, 177–81, 207–21
*Alexander the Great* (film), 177–81, 207, 212–14
Amazons, 43, 64, 67–8, 77, 153, 186

American monomyth, 35
*American Sniper* (film), 229, 234
Ammon, 181
Amphiaraus, 25, 49, 60–73, 186–7
Amphitryon, 24, 30, 37, 55, 183–4
*anagnorisis*, 175
Andrews, Isaac, 186
Andromeda, 83, 142, 144, 181–3
Antaeus, 20, 24, 52
Antigone, 178
antiheroism, 173–90, 206–37
Antonov, Mikhail, 44
Antony, Mark, 142–3
Aphrodite, 20, 112, 217
Apocalypse, 78, 84
Apollo, 78, 134, 154, 213
Apollodorus, 25, 61–2, 126
Apollonius, 13, 31–2, 62
Aquila, Marcus Flavius, 156–7
Arachne, 20
Arash, 199
Arcadia, 64
Ares, 20–1, 113, 148
Areto, 137
*Argo* (film), 199
Argos, 184, 206, 216–17
Ariadne, 7, 125–40
Arianne, 164–5
Aristophanes, 49
Aristotle, 175–9, 212, 214
Arius, 186
Aronofsky, Darren, 7, 93–110
Artemis, 22, 139
Artemisia, 199
Arterton, Gemma, 182
Arthur, 21
Ashura, 200
Asticus, Mt., 53
Atalanta, 25, 60–73, 125, 137, 139, 186

Athena, 54, 62, 64, 79, 113, 115, 133, 137, 217
Athens, 79, 192
Atia, 152
*Atlantis* (series), 2, 7, 24, 125–40
Atlas, 43
Augeus, 20, 43
Augustus, 144, 152
Aurelius, Marcus, 7, 105, 107
Autolycus, 20–1, 25, 60–73, 186

Bacchus, 21
Bacchylides, 52
Bale, Christian, 99
Bamber, Jamie, 149
Baron Samedi, 84
Barsine, 177
Batman, 3, 203, 210
*Battlestar Gallactica* (series), 8, 142, 149–50
*Baywatch* (series), 19–20
Beacham, Travis, 182
Behesht-e Zahra, 200
Belfort, Jordan, 229
Bellerophon, 125
*Ben-Hur* (1959 film), 38, 100, 167, 210
*Ben-Hur* (2016 film), 100
Bernardi, Daniel, 34
Biers, D'Anna, 149–50
Bloom, Claire, 177
Boagrius, 184
Bock, Jonathan, 101
Bolsø Berdal, Ingrid, 64, 186
Book of Enoch, 102
Boudicca, 152
Bousiris, 83
Bowker, Judi, 181
Brienne of Tarth, 151–2
Bubo, 182
*Buffy the Vampire Slayer* (series), 149
bulla, 54
Burke, Samson, 17
Burnett, Mark, 98–101
Burton, Richard, 142, 177
Bush, George W., 195

*Cabiria* (film), 44
Caesar, Julius, 142–4
Cain, 103–4
Caledonia, 164
Calibos, 181–2, 217
Caligula, 233
Callisto, 20
Calydonian boar, 61–2

Calypso, 112
Campbell, Joseph, 175–7, 187
Capps, Johnny, 126, 234
Carlisle, 160, 165
Carneia, 215
Carter, Earl "Jimmy" Jr., 196
Carthage, 104–6
Cash, Johnny, 229
Cassandra, 20, 129
Cassiopeia, 216
Cassius Dio, 159
Castiel (angel), 78, 80, 85–6
Catiline, 233
Cavill, Henry, 111
Centaurs, 20, 39, 145
*Centurion* (film), 2, 156–70, 208
Cepheus, 216
Cerberus, 20, 39, 43
Ceryneian hind, 43
Chadara, 151
Charon, 20, 181, 217
Chiron, 20–1, 183
Cicero, 225–8, 233
Circe, 23, 132
*Clash of the Titans* (films), 2, 9, 24, 127, 142, 144, 181–6, 206–21
Cleitus, 177
Clements, Ron, 22, 33
Cleopatra, 142–4, 152
*Cleopatra* (films), 142–4
Clinton, William "Bill" Jefferson, 195
*CNN Heroes* (series), 3
Cnossus, 54
Colbert, Claudette, 142
Colchis, 129, 137–8
Cold War, 207
Colosseum, 97
Commodus, 7, 44, 104–5, 159
Condal, Ryan, 60
Connelly, Jennifer, 106
Cotys, 31, 50, 53–5, 67, 185–7
Crassus, 151
Cretan bull, 43
Crete, 115
Crimea, 43
Cronus, 79
Cross, Beverly, 181–2
Crowe, Russell, 7, 93–110, 157, 162, 180
Crowley (demon), 78
Cunningham, Liam, 164, 185
Cupid and Psyche, 20
Cylons, 149–50
Cyrus the Great, 53, 201

Daedalus, 134–5
Danaë, 182, 216
Darius the Great, 194, 199
Darrieux, Danielle, 178
Davalos, Alexa, 182
Davis, Desmond, 206, 213, 217
de Leza, Marisa, 177
Deianeira, 20, 23–4, 130
Delphi, 177, 216
DeVito, Danny, 33
*Dexter* (series), 209
Diana, 141, 146
Dias, Quintus, 2, 8, 156–70
Dias, Scipio, 164
Dilios, 214
Diodorus Siculus, 63
Diomedes, 43, 137
Dionysus, 135, 213
*Doctor Who* (series), 23, 126
Doichinov, Dimiter, 184
Domitian, 44
Donnelly, Jack, 125–6
Downey, Roma, 98–101
Draco, 216
Dudunakis, Arius, 25, 45–6, 48–50, 55
Duval, James, 45
Dyer, Richard, 7

Echidna, 20
Edison, Thomas, 228
El-Kashef, Aida, 116–17
Eleusis, 134
Emms, Robert, 125
Ephialtes, 215
Epic of Gilgamesh, 102
Epidaurus, 54
Epirus, 113
*erastes*, 77
Ergenia, 39, 49–50, 55, 67–8, 186
*eromenos*, 77
Erymanthian boar, 38, 43, 65, 186
Eryx, 20
Esfandiyar, 200
Etain, 160, 163
Eteocles, 56
Euripides, 24, 83, 130, 177
Eurydice, 21, 177
Eurystheus, 24, 31, 63, 78, 175
Evans, Luke, 114
*Exodus: Gods and Kings* (film), 99

Farrell, Colin, 179–80
*farvahar*, 201
Fassbender, Michael, 157–8

Ferguson, Rebecca, 39, 67, 186
Fiennes, Joseph, 31, 185
Fiennes, Ralph, 182
Flemyng, Jason, 182
Forest, Mark, 29
Foxx, Jamie, 229
Francisci, Pietro, 13–15
Franzoni, David, 32
Furies, 216

Gabrielle, 21, 141–55
Galatea, 23
Gale, Mariah, 184
Galenus, 16, 184
Gallio, Marcellus, 157
*Game of Thrones* (series), 151–2
Gandhi, Anand, 111
Gannicus, 151
Garrani, Ivo, 187
Garrigan, Liam, 183
Gaugamela, 179–80
Geryon, 43
Gibson, Mel, 99–100
Gigantomachy, 75, 78
*Gladiator* (film), 1–2, 23, 32, 38, 54, 93–110, 157, 162, 167, 176, 180, 183–4
Gorgo, 153, 216
Gosling, Ryan, 21
Graves, Robert, 97
Green Revolution, 200–1
Greengrass, Paul, 208
Greyjoy, Yara, 151
Ground Zero, 195–6
Gulf War, 210

Hackford, Taylor, 229
Hades, 22, 78, 134, 182–3, 216–17
Hadrian, 156, 159, 168
Ham, 103–4
*hamartia*, 175
Hamilton, Alexander, 228
Hamlin, Harry, 181, 183
Handel, Ari, 102
Harlin, Renny, 45, 183
Harris, Richard, 107
Harrison, Rex, 142
*Harry Potter* (films), 103, 114
Harryhausen, Ray, 144, 182
Hart, Aiyisha, 125
Hay, Phil, 182
Hebe, 24, 47–8, 50, 184
Hector, 1
Helios, 78

Hennie, Aksel, 64, 186
Hennigan, John, 25, 47–57
Hephaestion, 180
Heptarian, 136
Hera, 20, 22, 24, 31, 55–6, 65, 76–7, 184, 186, 217
Heracles *see* Hercules
Heraclitus, 115
Hercules, 1–10, 28–73, 112, 125–40, 142, 144–5, 173, 180, 213
  companions of, 60–73
  cross-dressing of, 77
  representation of body of, 46–56
  survey of films on, 13–27
*Hercules* (1958 film), 13–14, 29–31, 50–1, 56, 184–5, 187
*Hercules* (1997 film), 6, 22, 32–4, 76, 79, 184
*Hercules* (2005 series), 23, 38
*Hercules* (2014 film), 4–6, 24, 28–73, 183–7
*Hercules Reborn* (film), 6, 24–5, 45–59
*Hercules: The Animated Series* (series), 23
*Hercules: The Legendary Journeys* (series), 4–5, 13, 19–23, 47, 75, 144–5, 173
*Hercules Unchained* (film), 14–15, 29–31, 52, 56
Hermes, 213
Hernandez, Laurie, 4
Herodotus, 193, 214–16
*Heroes* (series), 3
Hesiod, 61
Hesione, 83
Hestia, 147
Heston, Charlton, 32, 100
Hippolyta, 20, 77
Hold Nickar, 84–5
Homer, 61, 105, 112
Hopkins, Anthony, 107, 179
Horace, 45–6, 48–9, 55
Hoult, Nicholas, 185
Hurst, Michael, 20–2
Hurt, John, 31, 67, 114–15, 185
Hussein, Saddam, 195
Hylas, 63, 77
Hyperion, 113–15, 121

Icarus, 23, 135
Ila, 103
*imagines*, 224
Imam Ali, 200
Imam Hussein, 200

*Immortals* (film), 2, 7, 24, 30, 111–24
Inman, Jeremy, 46
Io, 182, 185, 217
Iolaus, 20, 22, 25, 38, 51, 60–73, 77, 145, 186
Iphicles, 20, 23–4, 47, 51, 55, 183–4
Iphigenia, 83
Iran, 191–205
Iranophobia, 196
Iraq, 156, 196
Islamic Revolution, 196, 200

James, Bradley, 126
Japheth, 106
Jason, 6–7, 20–1, 31, 61–3, 125–40, 180, 187
Jesus Christ, 2, 6, 74–90, 121, 212
Jobs, Steve, 222–37
Jocasta, 178
Johnson, Dwayne, 24–5, 28–42, 46–73, 185, 187
Jolie, Angelina, 97, 180
Jones, Barry, 178
Jones, Nathan, 184
Judas, 81

Kabi, Neeraj, 117
Kali, 84
*kamancheh*, 192
*katabasis*, 120, 181
Khatami, Mohammad, 195–6
*kleos*, 65, 67, 70
Knossos, 126
Kora, 21
Kore, 151
Kraken, 181–2, 185, 217
Kremlin, 44
Kurylenko, Olga, 163
Kutcher, Ashton, 230
Kyle, Chris, 229, 234

Labyrinth, 135
Lamech, 104–5
Lannister, Cersei, 151
Laomedon, 83
*laudatio funebris*, 9, 222–37
Lawless, Lucy, 21–2, 141–55
Leah, 141, 147
Leonidas, 9, 184, 191, 210, 214–16
Lerman, Logan, 103
Lernaean hydra, 37–8, 43, 60, 63, 65, 70, 186, 213
Leterrier, Louis, 182, 206–7, 211, 216–17

Leto, Jared, 180
Levine, Barry, 25
Levine, Joseph E., 13–17, 50
Lewis, C. S., 101
Lieferinxe, Josse, 79
Linus, 23, 77
Livius, 157, 159
Livy, 226, 228, 231
Loki, 84
*Lord of the Rings* (films), 114
Lucifer, 74–90
Lucilla, 105–6
Lucius, 48
Lucretia, 142
Lupus, Peter, 29
Lutz, Kellan, 24, 28–42, 47–57, 183
lycanthropy, 134
Lyon, Nick, 45

McCarthy, Neil, 181
Macedonia, 177, 179, 207, 212–13
Maciste, 44
McKee, Roxanne, 183
McShane, Ian, 64, 186–7
Maenads, 135
Maia, 132
Manfredi, Matt, 182
Manson, Amy, 125
Marathon, 215
March, Fredric, 177
Marian, 152
Marshall, Neil, 156–70
Marvel, 34–5, 209
Mary Magdalene, 80
Masada, 98
Maté, Rudolph, 211
Matheson, Hans, 185
maximal projections, 93–110
Maximus, 1–2, 93–110, 157–9, 162, 180, 183–4, 210
Medea, 7, 20, 125–40, 180, 213
Medusa, 7, 23, 125–40, 181–3, 213, 217–18
Meg, 141–55
mega-text, 28, 34–40
Megara, 23–5, 45, 50, 77
Megistias, 216
Melanippus, 62
Meleager, 61–3
Meneus, 61, 63
Mercury, 84
Meredith, Burgess, 181
Meridius, Maximus Decimus, 7
Merlin, 21

*Merlin* (series), 126
Messalina, 143
Methuselah, 107
Michael (angel), 74–90
Midrash, 102
Mikkelsen, Mads, 185
Miller, Frank, 191, 194, 198, 203, 210–11, 215
Milo, 2
Minos, 132, 135–6
Minotaur, 20, 115, 126–8, 131, 134–5
*Minotaur* (film), 24
Mioni, Fabrizio, 187
Mira, 150–1
monomyth, 175–6
Moore, Steve, 6, 25, 28, 31, 39, 46, 51, 54, 60–1, 63
Morgan, Colin, 126
Morpheus, 23
Morris, Kirk, 16
Morrissey, David, 164
Moses, 99
Muharram, 200
Mullan, Peter, 67
Mumbai, 116
Murphy, Julian, 126
Muses, 32, 116
Musker, John, 22, 33
Mussolini, 44
Mycenae, 54

Naameh, 105–6
Naevia, 150–1
Nahl, Ned, 19
Naples, 97
Nasir, 151
Naxos, 129
Neeson, Liam, 183
Nefertiti, 21
Nemea, 52
Nemean lion, 37–8, 43, 51, 65, 131, 186
Nemesis, 20
Nero, 44, 159
Nessus, 20
Nielsen, Connie, 106
Nikos, King of Enos, 25, 45, 49, 53, 56
*Nixon* (film), 229
Nixon, Richard, 209
Noah, 2, 6–7, 93–110
*Noah* (film), 93–110
North Korea, 196
*Notorious* (film), 234

O'Connor, Renee, 21–2
Octavia, 144, 152
Octavian *see* Augustus
Odin, 84
Odysseus, 1, 112, 137
*Odysseus* (series), 2
Oedipus, 20, 177, 180–1
Oliver, Christian, 45
Olympias, 178, 180
Olympic Games, 20
Olympus, 79, 113, 216
Omphale, 20, 62, 77
Oracle, 127–9, 132–3, 137
Orestes, 20
Orpheus, 21
Ovid, 116, 126, 133

Pagano, Bartolomeo, 44
Pahlevan, 200
Palladium, 136–7
Pallas *see* Athena
Pan, 215
Pandora, 23, 133–4
Paolo, Connor, 180
Parish, Sarah, 129
Park, Reg, 29, 47
Parthenopaeus, 62
Pasiphae, 128–9, 133, 136–8
Pasteur, Louis, 228
*pathos*, 175
Patroclus, 129, 181
Pausanias, 62–3
Paxos, 216
Pegasus, 127, 182–3
Pelias, 187
Pella, 178
peplum films, 13–18, 29–32, 46, 60
*Percy Jackson & the Olympians* (films), 24, 103
Pergamon, 79
*peripeteia*, 175
Persepolis, 192
Perseus, 2, 8–9, 83, 125, 127, 144, 173, 181–3, 185, 206–7, 213, 216–18
Persia, 178–9, 184, 191–205, 210, 212, 214–16
Petersen, Wolfgang, 208
Philip, 177
Philoctetes, 33
Phoenix, Joaquin, 229
Picts, 160–8
Pitt, Brad, 180
Plataea, 214
Plato, 119, 121

Pliny the Elder, 224
Plummer, Christopher, 179
Plutarch, 115, 177, 227
Polybius, 224, 226
Polyneices, 56
*pompa funebris*, 224–6, 230, 232
*Pompeii* (film), 2, 97–8, 101
Poots, Imogen, 164
Poseidon, 127, 129, 133
Prometheus, 20–1, 78, 180
Ptolemy, 107, 179
Putin, Vladimir, 6, 43–59
Pygmalion, 23
Pythagoras, 7, 125–40

Quintilian, 225–7, 231–3
*Quo Vadis* (film), 157
Quran, 218

Raimi, Sam, 141
Rao, Kiran, 111
Raphael, 79
Ratner, Brett, 6, 30, 45, 60, 62–3, 70, 185
*Ray* (film), 229
Reagan, Ronald Wilson, 195
Reeves, Steve, 13–15, 29–33, 46–7, 49–50, 184–5
Reni, Guido, 79
*retiarius*, 54
Reza, Mohammad, 201
Rhesus, 25, 53
Ridley, Scott, 93–110, 162, 167
Ritchie, Reece, 64, 186
*Robin Hood* (series), 152
Rojo, Gustavo, 177
*Roman Empire: Reign of Blood* (series), 2
*Romanitas*, 163, 168
*Rome* (series), 2, 143–4, 152
Rooper, Jemima, 125
Rossen, Robert, 177, 212
Rourke, Mickey, 111, 114
Rudin, Scott, 97
Rustam, 199

Sackhoff, Katee, 149
Sallust, 233
Salmoneus, 20
Sam, 199
Santoro, Rodrigo, 193–4
Saul, 99
Saxa, 8, 142, 150–1
Schmidt, Eric, 230

Schulian, John, 141
Schwab, Shelly, 18
Schwarzenegger, Arnold, 18, 24, 30, 44, 46
*Scorpion* (series), 3
Scythia, 64
Serbedzija, Rade, 183
Servilia, 152
Seth, 103–4
Sewell, Rufus, 64, 186
Shah, Sohum, 111, 118–19
*Shahnameh*, 199–200
Shakespeare, 177
Shakur, Tupac, 234
Shem, 103–4
Shi'ism, 200
*Ship of Theseus* (film), 7, 111–24
Shirrock, Marcus, 53
Sicily, 48
Singh, Tarsem, 111
Sirens, 131
Sitacles, 67
Siyâvash, 199
Smith, Maggie, 181
Snowden, Edward, 229
Snyder, Zack, 48, 197–8, 207, 211, 214–16
Sochi, 43
Sohrab, 199
Solon, 217
Sophia, 132
Sophocles, 31–2, 83, 130, 177–8
Sorbo, Kevin, 19–23, 47
*Spartacus* (film), 49, 210
*Spider-man* (films), 36
Spiliotopoulos, Evan, 60
*Star Trek* (series), 20, 34–5
*Star Wars* (films), 176
star-peats, 7, 93–110
Starbuck, 8, 149–50
Stark, Arya, 151–2
Stark, Catelyn, 152
Stark, Sansa, 152
*STARZ Spartacus* (series), 8, 23, 48, 53, 142, 150–1
Steele, Alan, 47
Stern, Joshua Michael, 230, 234
Stevenson, Juliet, 127
Stewart, Jon, 230
Stone, Oliver, 107, 178, 197–8, 207, 211–14, 229
Stymphalian birds, 43
Styx, 217
Suetonius, 233

Suleiman the Djinn, 185, 218
Superman, 3, 28
*Supernatural* (series), 6, 74–90
Syria, 43

Taliban, 195
Talmud, 102
Tapert, Robert, 19, 141
Targaryen, Daenerys, 152
Tartarus, 79, 113
Tarzan, 36
Tatum, Channing, 156
Taylor, Elizabeth, 142–3
Tegea, 62
Telemon, 128, 134, 138
Teti, Federico, 13
*The 300 Spartans*, 207, 211, 214–16
*The Bible* (series), 98–101
*The Eagle* (film), 156, 166, 208
*The Fall of the Roman Empire* (film), 157
*The Legend of Hercules* (film), 4, 24, 28–59, 183–7
*The Mighty Hercules* (series), 17–18
*The Odyssey* (series), 23
*The Passion of the Christ*, 99–101
*The Robe* (film), 157
Thebes, 56, 68, 77
Themistocles, 216
Theodora, 25, 45, 49
Thermopylae, 184, 191, 197, 210, 214, 215–16
Thersites, 209
Theseus, 2, 6–7, 125–7
  immortality of, 111–24
Thespius, 20, 77
Thessaly, 184
Thetis, 112, 181, 217
Thor, 3
Tiryns, 48, 53–4, 57, 183, 185
Titanomachy, 79, 113–15
Troy, 137
*Troy* (film), 1, 23, 180, 186, 208
Tubal-Cain, 104–5
Tydeus, 25, 60–73, 186
Tymek, 46
Tyron, Chuck, 35

Ukraine, 43
Ulfsparre, Christina, 45
*United 93* (film), 208
Uriel (angel), 86

Valerius Flaccus, 63
Vesuvius, Mt., 97
Vietnam War, 209
Vinicius, Marcus, 157, 159
Virilus, Titus Flavius, 8, 156–70
Vox, Dylan, 45

*Walk the Line* (film), 229, 234
Wallace, Christopher, 234
Wallace, Lew, 100
Watergate, 209
Watson, Emma, 103
Weiss, Gaia, 47, 184
West, Dominic, 157
Whedon, Joss, 149
Whyte, Ian, 185
Williams, Robin, 33
Winchester, Dean, 6, 74–90
  as Heraclean figure, 75–82
Winstone, Ray, 105
Wolverine, 209
Wonder Woman, 3, 153
Worthington, Sam, 182–3
Wozniak, Steve, 231
*Wrath of the Titans* (film), 2, 24, 144
Wyler, William, 100

X-Men, 209
Xena, 7–8, 21–3, 127, 141–55, 199, 208
Xerxes, 9, 191–205, 210, 215

York, 159–60
*Young Hercules* (series), 21–2

Zachariah (angel), 74–90
Zeus, 20–1, 24, 37, 53–5, 62, 65–6, 76, 79, 83, 113–15, 121, 129, 183–4, 186, 206, 216–17
Zhao Shen, 84
Zohar, 102
Zoroastrianism, 201
Zuckerberg, Mark, 229

EU representative:
Easy Access System Europe
Mustamäe tee 50, 10621 Tallinn, Estonia
Gpsr.requests@easproject.com

www.ingramcontent.com/pod-product-compliance
Lightning Source LLC
Chambersburg PA
CBHW061707300426
44115CB00014B/2596